Praise for *Behind The Lines*

Behind ~~the~~ Lines is an extraordinary achievement, a compendium of voices at once ~~im~~mediate and timeless, heart-breaking and entertaining. Andrew Carroll ~~b~~ears witness to cataclysm by allowing participants to speak for themsel~~ves~~, achieving an evocative power rare even in the best war literature.
— ~~Ri~~ck Atkinson, Pulitzer Prize-winning author of *An Army at Dawn:*
The War in North Africa, 1942-1943

There ~~are~~ two vastly different ways of studying war. One has to do with the great s~~to~~ry of history and of nations, the other with dying alone in a field ~~ho~~s~~~ with missing someone so much it aches; with wrestling down fear and s~~h~~~~or~~ing up courage; or enduring war's squalor and absurdity. Andrew Carro~~ll~~ studies the human side of war in this stirring, moving, and some~~tim~~es hilarious collection. *Behind the Lines* is a tribute to the human spirit

— Mark Bowden, author of *Black Hawk Down*

~~This boo~~k is more than a collection of newly-discovered war letters. There is ~~someth~~ng deeper, richer, and more intense at work here. Each letter is ~~extraord~~inary in its own right, but together they illuminate war as it is rarely ~~seen. Mo~~st importantly, *Behind the Lines* is the result of Andrew Carroll's ~~ta~~lented trip around the world to seek out these gripping, insightful, and, ~~in~~ ~~s~~o many cases, breathtaking letters. This is a book born of great pass~~ion.~~ This is a book with tremendous heart and soul.

— James Bradley, author of *Flags of Our Fathers* and *Flyboys*

From the American Revolution to Iraq, everything is here: the terror and exhilaration of bloody combat, love letters, funny letters, letters from civilians caught in the middle of war. *Behind the Lines* is worth savoring; you can dip into it at any page and find something fascinating.

— Joseph L. Gall~~oway,~~ ~~co~~author of *We Were Soldiers Once . . .and Young*
and *Tri~~umph ~~. . . ~~Persian~~ Gulf War*

This book is absolutely majestic. The letters may be about war, but taken together they are about far more than conflict. They provide an unblinking look at the best and worst that human beings can do to each other, and in so doing transcend themselves. They become the colors with which Andrew Carroll has created a kind of historical art.

– McKay Jenkins, author of *The Last Ridge: The Epic Story of America's First Mountain Soldiers and the Assault on Hitler's Europe*

In all my years of military service, I don't believe I have ever read a book that has moved me as profoundly as this one. While it is often the generals and military leaders who receive the limelight, Andrew Carroll's *Behind the Lines* reminds us that it is the individual troops in the field and their loved ones at home who most deserve our admiration and attention. *Behind the Lines* is a candid look at the fierce realities of warfare, but it is also a lasting tribute to those who have fought–and continue to fight–for freedom. I cannot recommend this book more highly.

– Lieutenant General Claudia Kennedy, US Army (retired), the highest ranking woman in the history of the Army

There is nothing more powerful then words written when life as you know it hangs in the balance. From soldiers on the front lines writing to sweethearts and family, to resistance fighters and so many others in the midst of war and its aftermath, *Behind The Lines* has letters from every conflict since the Revolution representing just about every race and many different cultures. This book is phenomenal and a must read.

– Yvonne Latty, author of *We Were There: Voices of African American Veterans from World War II to the War in Iraq*

BEHIND
THE LINES

BEHIND THE LINES

Revealing and Uncensored
Letters from Our War-torn World

EBURY PRESS

Publisher's Note
In the interests of authenticity, each letter has been printed
verbatim with its original spelling and punctuation.

This edition published in 2006
First published in Great Britain in 2005

10 9 8 7 6 5 4 3 2

First published by
Ebury Press
Random House, 20 Vauxhall Bridge Road, London SW1V 2SA

Random House Australia (Pty) Limited
20 Alfred Street, Milsons Point, Sydney, New South Wales 2061, Australia

Random House New Zealand Limited
18 Poland Road, Glenfield, Auckland 10, New Zealand

Random House (Pty) Limited
Isle of Houghton, Corner of Boundary Road & Carse O'Gowrie,
Houghton 2198, South Africa

Random House Publishers India Private Limited
301 World Trade Tower, Hotel Intercontinental Grand Complex,
Barakhamba Lane, New Delhi 110 001, India

The Random House Group Limited Reg. No. 954009

www.randomhouse.co.uk

A CIP catalogue record for this book is available from the British Library.

Cover Design by Two Associates
Text design and typesetting by Textype

ISBN 9780091903404 (From Jan 2007)
ISBN 0091903408

Papers used by Ebury Press are natural, recyclable products made from wood grown
in sustainable forests.

Copies are available at special rates for bulk order. Contact the sales development team on
020 7840 8487 or visit www.booksforpromotions.co.uk for more information.

Printed and bound in Great Britain by Cox and Wyman Ltd, Reading, Berkshire

Permissions and acknowledgements appear on page 420.

For Peter Leheny
February 14, 1970 to July 4, 2002

About the Author

ANDREW CARROLL is the editor of several *New York Times* bestsellers, including *War Letters* and *Letters of a Nation*. He is also responsible for bringing back the 'Armed Services Editions' (ASEs), which were pocket-sized editions of national bestsellers and literary classics handed out to US troops stationed abroad during World War II. Carroll revived the ASEs in 2002, and he has distributed hundreds of thousands of the books to American servicemen and women in Iraq, Afghanistan and other places around the world.

TABLE OF CONTENTS

I visited our old battlefield and was pleased to find it looked a quiet, contented area with people digging in the fields in the afternoon sun. Everything looked so peaceful and easy-going there this afternoon that I felt if this is what we are fighting to restore all over the world, it is right that we should do all we can to achieve it. Children were playing in the ditch where the German machine-gunner who shot Morgan had been lying. Nearby was Morgan's grave. It is strange that a young Irishman, living in England, should die for the freedom of Dutch children in Holland whom he never even saw and whose names he never knew. It seems to typify the tremendously generous spirit of sacrifice made by Morgan and so many others like him.

> *Irish soldier Major Charles Sweeny of the Royal Ulster Rifles, writing to his wife on February 22, 1945, during World War II, about one of his men who had been killed in the Netherlands five months earlier. Sweeny survived combat but tragically died in an accident two days before the war in Europe ended.*

INTRODUCTION

Before leaving, I had been forewarned to expect everything from indifference to outright hostility.

The purpose of the trip, which would take me to more than 30 countries across five continents, was to search for letters by soldiers and civilians from nations that had been wartime allies or adversaries of the USA throughout its history. My timing was not ideal. The Coalition invasion of Iraq in 2003 was fueling anti-American sentiment around the world. People were burning the Stars and Stripes not only in Palestine, Cairo and Tehran, but Berlin, Rome and London. And in some of the places I would be traveling to, Americans were being threatened physically, kidnapped, and, in extreme cases, executed. Due to the brief amount of time I planned to stay in the relatively more dangerous regions, the risk for me was minimal, but some degree of concern was not unwarranted. (Indeed, only days before I checked in to my hotel in Afghanistan, a bomb placed by members of the Taliban or al-Qaeda detonated behind the hotel, shattering most of the back windows. Amazingly no one was seriously hurt. The day after the explosion I called to see if the hotel was still accepting guests. The clerk assured me cheerfully, 'Oh yes, all is well! You come. Bring cash!')

The inspiration to seek out foreign letters came from an unexpected source – American veterans. In 1998, I launched an initiative called the Legacy Project that preserves wartime correspondences as a way to honor and remember those who have fought for this nation. Since then, people across the country have sent in tens of thousands

1

of previously unpublished letters from all of our major conflicts, from the American Revolution in the 18th century, to Operation Iraqi Freedom in 2003. The letters not only record extraordinary moments in time – the Battle of Shiloh, the attack on Pearl Harbor, the storming of Fallujah – they capture the more human side of warfare and reveal the thoughts and emotions of the troops who have been eyewitnesses to these events. Although I had always admired those who served in the military, I had no real concept of all that they sacrificed, on and off the battlefield, until I began reading their letters home.

For two years I traveled throughout the USA speaking with groups of veterans about the importance of saving what they had written from the front lines. During these conversations we talked about wartime correspondences in general and how essential mail was to their morale, the tricks they used to evade the censors, the letters they dreaded receiving more than any others (rejection or 'Dear John' messages from a sweetheart), and the ones that were the most gut-wrenching to write (condolence letters to the families of fallen comrades). We also discussed the changes in letter-writing from generation to generation, especially with the advent of email, and how, while the tone has become less formal over the years, the emotions have remained fundamentally the same.

One question that initially surprised me was being asked with increasing regularity: was the Legacy Project collecting letters from other countries? I responded that only a few had trickled in over the years, donated primarily by stamp collectors and bargain hunters who had discovered them at estate sales and flea markets in the USA and abroad. I was curious why these veterans were interested in foreign correspondences, and the history buffs replied that the letters would make for fascinating reading, providing a fresh perspective on familiar battles. But most of the veterans expressed the belief that these letters might contribute to our overall understanding of war and the larger impact of these conflicts on everyone involved – friend and foe alike.

An idea began to take hold. For years I had been yearning to go abroad and visit the places I had been reading about in the letters. I wanted to see the trenches of World War I that still zigzag through the French and Belgian countryside, walk along the Normandy coast where Allied forces had landed on D-Day, peer across the Demilitarized Zone marking the border between North and South Korea, explore the tunnels of Cu Chi outside Saigon, and, if possible, set foot in Baghdad, Iraq, and Kabul in Afghanistan. But instead of embarking on a mere sightseeing tour, I could give the trip a purpose and seek out war letters in every country I visited. All I had to do, I figured, was locate the main military archives and museums and dig through their collections. Ideally, I would also introduce myself to veterans and active duty personnel along the way and solicit letters from them directly.

Well-traveled friends and colleagues were more pessimistic about my plan of action. They warned me that many of the institutions I expected to visit were government-run and notorious for their unwieldy bureaucracies. Upon arrival I would have to produce a letter of introduction just to secure an appointment with the archivists, which offered no guarantee that the staff would grant me access to their holdings. There was also the larger matter of the world's political climate at the time. Acquaintances overseas prepared me for the possibility that the veterans, military personnel and other people I hoped to meet might distrust my motives or be unwilling to cooperate with an American. The very nature of the appeal was a delicate one, as I would be asking these individuals to share with me copies of their private letters. If a foreigner approached me with such a request, I'm not sure how enthusiastic my response would be.

After five months of planning, and armed with an itinerary that weighed in at 7lbs, I was – out of stubbornness, naiveté, or perhaps a bit of both – determined to go. I had secured the necessary visas, gotten my vaccinations, cancelled my magazine subscriptions, re-confirmed all reservations, said my good-byes, fibbed to my mom about having no intention of traveling to Iraq, and then headed to the airport.

Gdansk was first. A port city on the northern coast of Poland, Gdansk is celebrated as the birthplace of the Solidarity movement, where, in 1980, a 37-year-old electrician named Lech Walesa galvanized his fellow shipyard workers to demand from Poland's Communist government the right to organize trade unions. The reason I began in Gdansk, however, had more to do with what happened there on September 1, 1939, when German forces pounded the city with artillery before launching a full-scale invasion of Poland, marking the beginning of World War II. (Arguably, the clash between Chinese and Japanese troops at the Marco Polo Bridge outside Beijing, China, on July 7, 1937, which ignited a larger conflagration in the Pacific, represents the first shots fired in the war.) After Germany's assault, hostilities swept the globe like a virus, ultimately killing tens of millions of people. The Poles alone lost one-fifth of their population.

I arrived in Gdansk on September 1 curious to see where the war in Europe had erupted, but, more importantly, to find firsthand accounts written by Polish troops or civilians on that horrible day in 1939. The curators and librarians I spoke with were gracious but explained that they had nothing. They also thought it was doubtful that anyone in the city wrote about the invasion for fear of being accused by the Germans of spying. It was an inauspicious beginning to the trip.

With extra time on my hands, I briefly toured the city and wandered around Westerplatte, the site of the initial German bombardment. I watched as a steady procession of individuals, some alone, some with their families, quietly lit candles and placed flowers around the gravestones of Polish soldiers who were casualties of the attack. A group of German high school students crammed into the tiny History of Gdansk Museum and listened with rapt attention as their teacher narrated the events of that day and then described the hellish

4

occupation of Poland. One girl, apparently unfamiliar with this history, placed her hands over her mouth, aghast, and began to cry.

My next stop, Oswiecim, is better known outside Poland by its German name – Auschwitz. I arrived late in the evening and, although I needed to get up early the next morning to take a tour of the former extermination camp, I was still on USA time and couldn't sleep. The weather for the next day was forecast to be warm and perfectly clear, and I knew that, being a Saturday, the place would be crowded with tourists. Recognizing that it was an unusual request, I called for a taxi and asked the driver if he could take me over to the camp just to see the outside under relatively more peaceful circumstances. I figured I could walk around the exterior grounds for a few minutes and take a picture of the infamous – and grotesquely cynical – ARBEIT MACHT FREI (WORK BRINGS FREEDOM) greeting that adorns the top of the camp's main gate.

As soon as the taxi driver and I pulled up to the entrance, I knew we were out of luck. The actual site was well behind a large parking lot and tourist centre, and it would be impossible to see anything meaningful. The hour was getting late, and the driver had told me earlier that I was his last fare of the night. But sensing my disappointment, he seemed determined to find another entrance. Sure enough, after winding through a long, inconspicuous street off the main road, we came up to a dimly-lit wooden guardhouse. The driver stepped out of the car and approached the night watchman, who looked understandably suspicious. The two men began talking, and I overheard the guard saying, 'Nie, nie.' The driver was emphatic. Finally, the guard checked his watch, shrugged, and gestured to the entrance with a flick of his hand. The driver turned to me and said: 'OK. We go in.' He then opened his door, reached inside, and clicked the meter off. I told him I didn't think it would take us very long and that he should absolutely keep the meter running. 'No, is OK.' It was almost midnight.

All I could see until my eyes adjusted to the darkness were the tall black silhouettes of trees and the outline of what appeared to be row after row of barracks. We walked slowly and in silence. Occasionally the driver pointed to an important structure as we passed by. 'Gas chambers,' he said. 'Here, crematoria.' I would stop to look more carefully at a building or peek into a window and, every so often, blindly snap a photograph. Obviously the camp looked nothing like it did when, during the war, thousands of lives were extinguished within its walls every day. There was no sound of trains. No smell of burning flesh. No maniacal guards shrieking orders. No sense of human presence whatsoever. But the vast, shadowy emptiness of the camp worked its own kind of horror and was more haunting than any place I had ever visited before. As we drove back to the hotel, I stared out the taxi window, completely overwhelmed by what had just happened. I felt enormous gratitude toward the driver for going out of his way to make the visit possible. But mostly I remember thinking that this trip was going to be intensely more emotional than anything I had expected.

One by one the letters were starting to accumulate as well. I located some remarkable correspondences by Holocaust survivors, and a museum in Warsaw had a poignant letter by a Polish pilot telling his parents that, since they had last seen him, he had fallen in love, married a British girl, and had a son. (But other than that, not much was new.) One archivist contacted members of his own family who were veterans to see if they had any letters, and although nothing came of it, I thought it was a rather thoughtful gesture.

After Poland I went to Russia. Through an American friend living in Moscow I met my exceptional guide, Olga, who mapped out the entire schedule for St. Petersburg. Our primary stop was the State Memorial Museum of the Defense and Blockade of Leningrad, and the staff could not have been more amiable. A quick, handwritten note from me requesting access to their archives was all that was needed, and within minutes they were pulling from their files letters and other personal papers salvaged from World War II – or, as they call it, the Great Patriotic War. Leningrad, the city's name before it was changed back to St. Petersburg in 1991 after the fall of Communism, had endured one of the longest and most brutal sieges in history, lasting almost 900 days and claiming an estimated 600,000 lives.

The process of selecting letters was hardly a scientific one, but we worked out a relatively efficient system: the curator would skim through a file and summarize the contents for Olga, who then repeated it to me in English. Depending on my 'nyet' or 'da,' the item either went back into the pile or off to be copied. 'This is a long poem by a soldier describing his sorrow,' Olga said about the first document.

Me: 'Um, probably nyet. I really just want letters.'

Olga: 'Well, this next one is very moving, too, but it's a journal, so nyet?'

'Nyet,' I replied.

Olga listened to the next synopsis with growing, and then waning, interest. 'It's a letter . . . from a husband telling his wife not to forget him if they are separated . . . but it does not seem to have a lot of emotion. I think we can find better.' Nyet, she determined on her own. Sure enough, as the curator started describing a small stack of letters bound together, I could see Olga nodding her head and looking optimistic.

'These are a series of letters,' she began to explain, 'by a brother and sister orphaned during the siege who are telling their aunt all that has happened to them and begging her to come and save them.'

'Da, da, da!' I exclaimed, and within minutes I had photocopies in hand. I would not have the letters translated word for word until I returned to the USA several months later, but they were every bit as compelling as I had hoped.

The Balkans came next. My flight into Sarajevo landed late in the evening, so it wasn't until the morning that I discovered how stunningly beautiful the city is. I could easily understand why Sarajevo

Auschwitz at night; Oswiecim, Poland.

was selected as the site of the Winter Olympics in 1984. There is both a vibrant modernity and ancient patina to Sarajevo, where upscale hotels line the main avenues and cobblestone streets lead to the Old Market and its antique merchant shops. But intermingled with this beauty – and it is easy not to notice them at first, before you begin to see them everywhere – are thick clusters of luminescent white gravestones. Nestled among residential neighborhoods, in the city parks, next to schools, behind sports stadiums, and wherever it seems there should be an open space or field of grass, the cemeteries are an ever-present reminder of the terror that descended on Sarajevo beginning in the spring of 1992 when Serb forces began their assault on Bosnia. Private homes and apartment buildings are still scarred and pockmarked with bullet holes and artillery blasts. And on the streets and sidewalks, shallow impressions in the shape of splattered paint marks where mortar shells exploded during the siege. The residents now call them 'dragon's feet.'

Thirty years old when we met, Amir Telebecirovic, my guide throughout Sarajevo, was still a teenager when the war erupted. It began, in fact, on his 19th birthday. Despite having no military experience whatsoever, Amir was forced to serve in the Bosnian army, which was massively outgunned and under-trained compared to the highly-skilled Serb troops. Many of Amir's closest friends, also just teenagers out of high school, were killed in the fighting.

As we walked the city on our way to meet with archivists and historians who had letters to show us, every corner prompted a sharp memory or horrific story. We crossed the bridge now named for Suada Delbrovic, the first person to die in the war. On April 6, 1992, as Serb forces began positioning themselves in Sarajevo, Delbrovic was shot to death on the bridge during a demonstration calling for peace. Just over a year later, on the banks of the River Miljacka below, two young lovers – Admira Ismic, a Bosnian Muslim, and Bosko Brckic, a Christian Serb – died in each other's arms after they, too, were caught in the crosshairs of a Serb sniper. Amir and I went to the

Lion's Cemetery where the two are buried beneath a heart-shaped headstone. Later, when we passed the bustling open-air Markale market, Amir told me it was the site of the infamous mortar attack of August 28, 1995. Almost 40 people simply out shopping for groceries were blown to pieces. The shelling of Markale was one of several atrocities against civilians that prompted the US-led NATO airstrikes on Serb forces around Sarajevo.

Amir recounted one story that, although relatively insignificant in the larger context of the fighting, was for some reason especially unsettling to me. At the beginning of the war staff members at the local zoo were unable to move the animals to safety, and Serb snipers situated on the hills overlooking many of the cages decided, for fun, to pick off the animals one by one. The lions were on the other side of the zoo and consequently were not at risk of getting shot. Their fate, however, would be much worse, as it was impossible for the animal keepers to make their way to the lions' cages and feed them without risking their own lives. Residents who lived nearby would later recall that one of the most unnerving sounds of the war was the roar – some described it as more like a dry scream – of the trapped, emaciated lions pacing their cages as they slowly starved to death.

Just hours before leaving Sarajevo, I asked Amir about the darkest moment of the war for him personally. There were many, he responded, but the worst occurred during the first winter of the siege. With no electricity or heating fuel, residents were freezing to death in their homes. Early one evening Amir's father went outside to collect firewood, which was becoming scarce throughout the city. (By the end of the war, virtually every tree in Sarajevo had been chopped down. Some individuals went to the desperate measure of digging up graves and dismantling the coffins, simply for the wood.) A Serb soldier or, more likely, sniper caught sight of Amir's father and shot him in the back. Neighbors were able to drag him to a car and rush him to the hospital. Before the siege, the drive would have taken only a few minutes. But the direct route was cut off by barricades and some streets were too dangerous to use, so they slowly had to wind their way through Sarajevo. The hospital itself was without power and overcrowded with other critically injured patients. Amir's father bled to death before any of the doctors could even examine his wound.

After hearing this, and with all the other stories of atrocities still fresh in my mind, I blurted out: 'God you must hate the Serbs.'

'No!' Amir responded firmly. 'No, no. There's been enough hatred. I'm sick of it. My girlfriend is a Serb. Many Serbs in Sarajevo and throughout Bosnia suffered, too. Many people in Serbia didn't know what was going on because Milosevic lied to them. At some point it has to stop. There's been too much already. It has to stop.' When I asked him how he could be so forgiving, he said, 'Only people who have been through it can really understand how bad it can be.' This sentiment would become one of the most dominant themes of the trip.

The subject was first brought to my attention during my visit to Volgograd in Russia just over a week earlier. During World War II, when the city was called Stalingrad, it was the site of what is considered to be one of the bloodiest battles ever fought. Tens of thousands of civilians were killed in the first 36 hours alone of the German bombardment that began on August 23, 1942. Disease flourished as bodies decayed in the streets and dogs fed on the corpses. Troops on both sides coerced young boys and girls into serving as scouts and runners, primarily to deliver messages or fill soldiers' canteens in the Volga river. And both sides shot the children they suspected of aiding the enemy. 'For me, the philosophical question of whether violence is ever justified was once torturous,' a Russian lieutenant named Joseph Maranov wrote to his beloved, Lola, from Stalingrad on August 29. 'Now,' he continued, 'my dream, my aim is to rip apart, destroy, suffocate, and tear the enemy to pieces.' Approximately half a million Russians and half a million German and Axis soldiers died in five months of savage fighting. 'You do not understand the hatred,' one Russian said to me after noticing I was reading a book on Stalingrad. 'You have September 11 attacks in your country. How many killed? This was September 11 every day for almost two hundred days.'

A local guide took me to see the massive statue of Mother Russia, who stands majestically atop the highest hill in Volgograd and commemorates the resilience of the soldiers and civilians who defended the city. She is more than 100 feet taller than the Statue of Liberty. Her right hand holds a sword, raised in defiance, and her left is outstretched in the direction from which the Axis troops invaded. Several hundred yards away is an indoor memorial with an eternal flame that pays tribute to those who perished. When my guide and I walked in, I heard tranquil but somewhat melancholic music playing. 'Which Russian composer is that?' I asked.

My guide responded, 'Actually it's Schumann.'

I was incredulous. 'They selected a German composer for the Stalingrad Memorial? Why didn't they pick a Russian?' The guide explained that when they built the monument in the 1960s, they wanted to send a message of reconciliation to all the Germans who came to pay their respects to those who had died.

American veterans were also reaching out to former enemies. At the USS Arizona Memorial in Hawaii I met with two Pearl Harbor survivors, Dick Fiske and Everett Hyland, who, decades after the 1941 attack, befriended Japanese pilots who had flown in the raid. Fiske even put me in touch with one of these veterans, Zenji Abe, whom I met in Japan two months later. (In a terrible coincidence, the very morning I had lunch with Mr. Abe and his family in Tokyo, Dick Fiske passed away.) The two men had corresponded with each other before Fiske's death, but, regrettably, almost all of their letters have been lost.

Through a close friend named Mike Meyer who fought in Vietnam, I was introduced to Chuck Theusch, a veteran who frequently travels back to Vietnam to build libraries as a way to foster goodwill between

Memorial to the Fallen Heroes of Stalingrand. Three Russian soldiers sit at the base of the statue just under Mother Russia's left foot. They are smaller than her toes.

Photos by Andrew Carroll

our two nations. Chuck very kindly sent me copies of the letters he exchanged with a Vietnamese woman, Tran Thi Anh Thu, who worked at the My Lai Memorial. When they first met she wanted little to do with him, but they are now good friends.

Whatever concerns I had about being confronted with resistance or a lack of cooperation on my trip proved completely unfounded. In every country people were going out of their way to be helpful – and often at a significant emotional cost. Many of the stories and letters they were sharing with me brought back painful memories of losing those closest to them. An Australian woman named Olwyn Green gave me a copy of the letter she wrote to her husband Charlie in 1992, 50 years after his death in the Korean War. 'I always told you how much I loved you,' she stated in her letter, 'I probably didn't tell you: You are the finest human being I have ever known.' A Kuwaiti man named Abdul Hameed Al-Attar translated for me the last message he wrote to his son Jamal, who was unjustly imprisoned by the Iraqis during the 1990 invasion of Kuwait and then never heard from again. The uncertainty of Jamal's fate made the situation all the more unbearable for the family; '[Y]our mother is still keeping your personal belongings in your room,' Al-Attar wrote to his son, 'checking them every morning as if you will be coming soon (probably today or tomorrow) she says with tears pouring from her red eyes.' Statistics can accentuate the enormity of war but not its humanity, and these letters are stark reminders of the individual stories behind the numbers.

Many veterans generously contributed letters that were especially intimate and candid. 'I am fearing for my life for the first time,' a Dutch private first class named André Dekker in Srebrenica confided to his girlfriend before passionately declaring his love for her. 'You're everything to me,' he wrote, 'my shoulder to cry on, my love nest, and everything you give to me exceeds my expectations. I feel good when I'm with you, I can be myself and together we are invincible.' Dekker survived.

Zenji Abe in Tokyo, Japan.

Dick Fiske, who died just months after I saw him in Hawaii.

Photos by Andrew Carroll

The veterans who offered these more revealing letters hoped that they might have a cathartic value for the men and women in the armed forces now. No one can truly understand military life – the constant pressures, the separation from loved ones, both the thrill and terror of being sent into combat, the devastating shock of losing a buddy – like those who have already been through it. The older veterans empathize deeply with the current generation of troops and want them to know that there is solace in realizing that others have borne these hardships too.

A Korean War veteran named Alfred Puntasecca Jr. gave me a copy of a letter he had sent to his parents and siblings in 1953 before heading back to the USA. Nineteen years old at the time, he wanted to prepare them for the battle-hardened man he had become, and not the boy they once knew: 'I'm looking forward to seeing you again, but I'm in no hurry to see the expressions on your faces when <u>you</u> see <u>me</u>,' Puntasecca wrote. 'It is going to be hard being civilized again. What the hell ever civilized means.' He then added, 'I am going to tell you now. You'll need a lot of patience with me. Patience, and, understanding. We all will. See you soon.' Fifty-one years later, a 19-year-old soldier named Scott Curry in Iraq mailed a letter to his mom that included the following:

Mother's Day is coming so happy Mother's Day. I wish I was there for the 2nd year in a row I've miss21ed so much since I left for the Army. That's what makes coming home more scary than here. At least here we know what to do, shoot back. Home I will not know what to do, how to act, that's what worries me. Here we use violence to fix problems. I can't do that at home. So I have to re-learn how to live a normal life. I miss you so much and can't wait to see you.

What struck me about the majority of the letters that people were sharing was how graphic they were. More so, in fact, than anything I had ever read before. 'I came across one of our boys – decomposed beyond all recognition,' a Canadian chaplain named William Mayse wrote to his wife during World War I.

> [H]e lay just as he had fallen – the head was missing – but all the accoutriments was buckled on, his rifle & helmet lay close by – I cut the buckle off the belt as a momento, & we burried what remained of him – I tried to find something by which he might be identified but it was impossible – Poor boy – in some far away home in Canada someone is mourning the loss of husband – son or sweetheart – & the saddest of all is, they will never know how he died – or where he is burried, & even now they may be clinging to the hope, that he is still alive.

Both in the USA and abroad, many of the people who were contributing letters voiced a frustration with how war is often romanticized in the popular culture. As evidenced in the letters themselves, this was not a new lament. 'You say that you wish you were over here,' Major Oscar Mitchell wrote to a friend named Sylvia Helene Hairston on April 15, 1944. Mitchell was serving in the China-Burma-India theatre of World War II, and he was quick to discourage Sylvia or anyone else from idealizing life on the front lines. 'Although most people think that they are War Conscious, are they really? – so far removed from the far-flung battle fronts, can they be?' He continued:

> You are really War Conscious when you see the airplanes, information, early in the morning, flying to meet their rendezvous . . . and see this same formation returning in the evenings. But the number is not the same! Twelve went out, nine returned. You stand there, looking up, watching them fly into the distance; into and part of the horizon, then disappear. You wonder, what really did happen. Those that went down in flames . . . Do they die as you see them in the movies? I do not think so. Not with a smile on their lips and a happy gleam in their eyes, rather painfully and regretfully with the knowledge that this is it! You'd have to see the wounded streaming back from the front after a

battle . . . above all, to see the light go out of men's eyes. Young men shaking from nervous exhaustion and crying like babies. Strong men they are, or were, who did not or will not have the chance, ever, to live normal lives . . . People may think they know what War is like. Their knowledge is facts of the mind. Mine is the war-torn body, scared to soul's depth. When I was in the States, War was far away, unreal. I had read, I had seen pictures, but now I know.

Many individuals who provided letters that depict the harsh realities of war stressed to me that they do not regard themselves as pacificists. They believe that there is cruelty and brutality in the world – tyranny, genocide, slavery – and if the worst of these evils cannot be defeated through peaceful means, they must be destroyed by violent ones. The combat veterans I met, in particular, are fiercely patriotic and proud of their military service, and their letters speak with great conviction about the courage of fallen comrades and the importance of honoring the freedoms for which they gave their lives.

What they abhor is the glorification of war itself. They believe that sanitizing or concealing its ugliness only trivializes the sacrifices made by the men and women who serve. They want people to understand the toll it takes not only on combatants, but on their families – and especially those who will receive a phone call or knock on the door informing them that their loved one has been killed. The wounds they suffer are every bit as traumatic and searing as the ones sustained on fields of battle, and they will last for the rest of their lives. The emotional aftershocks of war reverberate long after the peace treaties are signed.

And while many combat veterans recognize the allure of going off to battle and can well recall the intoxicating rush that comes from being under fire, they also know the exhilaration rarely lasts. It is tempered by exhaustion and hunger and endless hours of marching and waiting. It vanishes entirely when one sees a friend get shot to pieces or blown up and later shipped home in a flag-draped coffin.

Major Oscar Mitchell

Civilians, too, often feel an initial sense of excitement when war is announced, and there is an undeniable electricity and tension in the air at the beginning of any conflict. Here again, the veterans are familiar with how easily that fervor can wane and how crippling it is to morale when troops suspect that support on the homefront has started to fade.

What they emphasize above all is that there is no greater decision a society can make than when or if it will declare war – and if it does, it must prepare itself for the consequences. What war demands of those who serve in the military, as well as the suffering it inflicts on so many who do not, is often much worse than what people who have not experienced it firsthand can imagine. This was the theme most commonly expressed, implicitly and explicitly, in the majority of the letters I found during my travels throughout the USA and around the globe, and it was the sentiment conveyed to me with the greatest urgency in the conversations I had with those who have been affected by war in some profound way. Individually, the correspondences they shared represent the private letters of troops and civilians writing to a spouse or a parent or a friend or some other loved one about what they have seen and felt and endured.

Collectively, these are their messages to the world.

FOREVER YOURS

Letters of Love, Family, and Friendship

We have just arrived here after a most fatiguing March from East Chester – I got your letter at York Island – telling me I was a saucy fellow to kiss you before all the folks – Ah My Darling – I wish the World Knew you are to marry me – The Enemy are very near us & we are only waiting for the dawn to begin our Battle – Do not be uneasy about me – Please God – I hope to come out all safe tomorrow – The thoughts of your dear promise has nerved my arm so far & will again – The officers say I bear a Charmed life – They do not Know the talisman I wear next to my heart – My loved one – I am writing this on the head of a Drum & would you believe it with a pointed Stick – Remember me all my friends Darling & tell Mother not to feel uneasy about her son. I am my Darling your very Humble Servt – & Adorer

> *Private John Eggleston, writing to his fiancée on October 27, 1776, during the American Revolution, while he and thousands of other American soldiers awaited an imminent British invasion of White Plains, New York. Eggleston would survive the battle – and the war.*

Your country needs you. Your four brothers have been killed in her defense. Unless you come, you are no longer a son of mine. I will have no coward in my family.

> *A French mother from St. Pierre, writing to her son in November 1914, during World War I.*

Dear Brother

How have you been? Here, mother and the family are all fine. Your boys are playing and doing well, so do not worry about them. It's been so long since I saw you. I worry that we might not be able to recognize each other if we passed each other on the street. I also wonder if you might not be able to find your way back home after fighting for such a long time. Even right now, I am listening to the radio announcing news about your unit, Chung-Young, in Vietnam. Last time, we heard of so many deaths in the battle. Mother becomes so anxious whenever such reports come on. Brother, please take care of yourself. Let the Vietnamese respect you for your bravery but come back safely to us. There are lots of things to say, but I will end here. Be safe. I am always praying.

> *Lee Jung Ho, writing on February 2, 1966, to his older brother, Major Lee In Ho, one of 300,000 South Korean soldiers fighting with American troops against the North Vietnamese and Viet Cong during the Vietnam War. The letter was found on Lee's body after he was killed in action.*

Thanks very much for your letter and even more for the picture you painted. It touched me more than you can possibly imagine. And not only me. My peacekeeping unit has gotten in the habit of sharing all packages and showing around any photos that come with the letters. So of course your picture, too, though not a photo

was passed around
in the semi-darkness
of our dug-out
as snow fell outside and the temperature dipped to 16 degrees below
by all of us
seated on sandbags and ammunition cases
surrounded by empty ration cans and water bottles
heavily armed
with grimy hands

and barely warm enough, and I was asked over and over again what the girl looks like who can create such a beautiful and inspiring work of art. Our thoughts drifted toward another world . . . And so it was that your painting from far away Nuremberg reminded us of home and provided us with a few hours that the members of this illustrious crew will never forget. With sincere regards from a land that has become a part of our soul.

> *Master Sergeant Michael Kaiser, writing to a female friend on February 2, 2000, while serving with peacekeeping forces in Kosovo. They represented the largest deployment of German troops abroad since World War II.*

An American officer, named James Williams, explains to his son Daniel why he is fighting in the American Revolution, and urges him to be a 'dutiful son' in his absence.

In a nation of 2.5 million inhabitants, almost one in ten served in the American Revolution. Some were highly trained soldiers, but predominantly they were common tradesmen, farmers, and merchants, who left behind family and loved ones to confront the well-equipped, professional British and Hessian forces. Although their letters home tended to be more formal in tone, especially compared to wartime correspondences today, they convey many of the same sentiments-heartfelt expressions of love, minor gripes about the hardships they are enduring, but steadfast assurances that there is no reason for concern-manifested in contemporary letters and e-mails. "We have just arrived from a rather fatiguing March from East Chester," Private John Eggleston wrote to his fiancée on October 27, 1776, as he and thousands of other American soldiers awaited an imminent British invasion of White Plains, New York. He continued:

> *I got your letter at York Island-telling me I was a saucy fellow to kiss you before all the folks. Ah My Darling-I wish the World Knew you are to marry me-The Enemy are very near us & we are only waiting for the dawn to begin our Battle-Do not be uneasy about me. Please God-I hope to come out all safe tomorrow-The thoughts of your dear promise has nerved my arm so far & will again. The officers say I bear a Charmed life-They do not Know the talisman I wear next to my heart.*

Soldiers with children began a ritual that would be repeated over time as well. Those with children began a ritual that would be repeated in almost every generation for the next 230 years – writing a first letter home to explain why they have been called away and, most importantly, to remind their sons and daughters how much they love and miss them. James Williams, a 38-year-old native of Hanover County,

Virginia, who later moved to South Carolina, was one of those quarter of a million troops called to fight. On June 12, 1779, Williams penned the following letter to his son, Daniel, gently encouraging him to be especially caring toward and supportive of his mother.

Dear Son:

This is the first chance I have had to write you. I am, by the cause of Providence, in the field in defence of my country. When I reflect on the matter, I feel myself distracted on both hands by this thought, that in my old age I should be obliged to take the field in defence of my rights and liberties, and that of my children. God only knows that it is not of choice, but of necessity, and from the consideration that I had rather suffer anything than lose my birthright, and that of my children.

When I come to lay down in the field, <u>stripped</u> of all the pleasure that my family connections afford me at home – surrounded by an affectionate wife and eight dear children, and all the blessings of life – when I reflect on my own distress, I feel for that of my family, on account of my absence from their midst; and especially for the mother, who sits like a dove that has lost its mate, having the weight of the family on her shoulders.

These thoughts make me afraid that the son we so carefully nursed in our youth may do something that would grieve his mother. Now, my son, if my favor is worth seeking, let me tell you the only step to procure it is the care of your tender mother – to please her is ten times more valuable than any other favor that you could do me in my person.

I am sorry to have to inform you of the melancholy death of Anthony Griffin, which took place on the 11th instant, while out with a scouting party. Alighting from his horse, and leaning on his gun, it accidentally went off, shooting him through the head. He never spoke after the accident. This is a fatal consequence of handling guns without proper care; they ought to be used with the greatest caution. The uncertainty of life ought to induce every man to prepare for death.

Now, my son, I must bid you farewell. I commit you to the care of Providence, begging that you will try to obtain that peculiar blessing. May

26

God bless you, my son, and give you grace to conduct yourself, in my absence, as becomes a dutiful son to a tender mother and the family. I am in reasonable good health at present, and the regiment as much so as could be expected. The death of Griffin is much lamented. I hope in God this will find you, my son, and your dear mother and the children, all well. My best compliments to you all, and all enquiring friends.

I am, dear son, with great respect, your affectionate father,

Jas. Williams

Approximately 5000 Americans lost their lives in combat during the American Revolution. (Up to 20,000 more are believed to have died from disease, accidents, and the brutal treatment suffered by POWs in the hands of the British.) Among the dead was James Williams killed in the Battle of King's Mountain in October 1780.

Hessian soldier Christian von Molitor, fighting with the British in the American Revolution, shares his first impressions of America, with a friend in Germany, regretting that 'everything will be destroyed and ruined'.

Wars, by their nature, are not only a clash of ideologies but often of cultures as well. And for many servicemen and women sent hundreds or thousands of miles from home, their deployment marks the first time they have ventured beyond their city, town or village. Suddenly they find themselves in a new land confronting mysterious customs, languages and religious practices, prompting a range of reactions from curious fascination to outright disgust. During the American Revolution, it was America – in the eyes of 30,000 German troops brought to the New World by the British to fight the colonists – that was the land of odd and unfamiliar sights and social conventions. Although the three principal German commanders, as well as many of the regiments

27

themselves, came from the Hesse-Cassel region of Germany, not all of the troops were, technically, Hessians, as they were commonly called – among other things – by the Americans. The Hessians were ferocious, well-trained warriors, and they participated in almost every major military campaign of the Revolution after they landed in 1776. But they were hardly invincible. Nearly one in six deserted, and more than 6500 succumbed to illness – many because of what they regarded as the inhospitable climate. One Hessian officer wrote in his diary: 'Since the burning wind [in the daytime] and the cold spells are coming again [at night] . . . the men die like flies and the hospitals are filled.' Captain Christian Theodore Sigmund von Molitor arrived in New York in June 1777 and was actually quite impressed with the country he and his fellow soldiers had come to conquer. While encamped in Amboy, New York, he wrote the following to a female acquaintance back in Germany on June 24.

Dear Friend,

This is the third letter that I have written to you since I have been in America. I do not know if you have received them. I wish nothing more than to know how you and your children are doing, and if you are still my gracious and good friend, and that you have not forgotten me. We are all well and it seems as if the strenuous duty makes your husband and me healthier and stronger.

We are now in camp outside Amboy, about seven and one-half miles from New York. Today five English and Hessian regiments came from Brunswick, which is about fifteen miles from here, and joined us in camp. How long we are to remain here and where we are then to march, I am unable to write. General Howe and the main army moved forward a few days ago to attack General Washington, who is not far from Brunswick. The rebels were so well entrenched that attack was impossible, even if our army were twice as strong. Our pickets were attacked twice by the rebels. Captain von Beust and I were ordered to the reserve. We had to move forward and drive the enemy, consisting of about 300 men, out of the woods. We had to withstand many bullets, before we forced them into the open, where we attacked with bayonets and drove them into flight. Only a grenadier of ours was wounded, and we killed three rebels.

I gave you a description of New York in my last letter, and also of Staten Island, where we landed. Amboy is an open city where many white people lived, who can now be locked out of beautiful houses which were well-furnished. At present there are not more than five families in all of Amboy. Most of the residents are with the rebels and have abandoned houses and property. Most of the houses are exceptionally well-built and furnished with the finest carpets. All the houses stand open and can be occupied by anyone who so wishes. We have a house near us, not twelve yards from my tent, which we took over. We cook and eat therein, and do with it as we please.

It is certainly a shame that everything will be destroyed and ruined. The land is extremely fruitful and everything grows in abundance. The very best soil in Germany does not compare to it. During peacetime it can be called a true paradise. Now however, everything lies in ruin and none of the villages with houses has a living soul. We find here in the beautiful gardens, which have now been destroyed, all possible vegetables, like we have in Germany, and, especially lots of asparagus. The wooded areas are extensive and consist primarily of nut trees, oak, and sassafras wood, of which we burn enough to supply all the pharmacists in the world. Here beer is brewed from the bark. It tastes very sweet, but is very light and healthy. Large juniper trees are plentiful, and most of the hedges and trees in the fields are almond trees. There are apple trees everywhere, often stretching out for miles and all of the best kind, but no pear trees. The fruit which hangs on the trees is still very small, and the shoots and buds are still grass green. I believe everything in Bayreuth ripens about four weeks earlier. All classes of domestic animals are here as in Germany, but the wild animals are different. The hares are small. They are a sort of rabbit. The birds are especially beautiful, some are quite red, green, blue, of various sizes. And canaries fly around as sparrows in Germany. No plum trees or fig trees are to be seen. We eat oysters daily and they are especially large. They are not considered special here. I often wish you might have some at your table.

My dear Ellrodt and I continue our close friendship. We are together the whole day and whatever one receives, he shares it with the other. During the evening we smoke tobacco and, if we are alone, talk about you and the dear children and wish you all the best a thousand times. May God keep all of you healthy. I will not allow you to suffer any need, nor that your life be shortened because of hunger.

My Ellrodt has promised me that he will send you twenty ducats with this opportunity. Therefore do not live so miserly as to ruin your health. Our daily longing and wish is to receive a letter from you. When I know that you and your dear children are healthy, I will be completely satisfied. Do not forget your true and constant friend and do not take your friendship, which I value above all others, away from me. There are few minutes when I do not think of you. How happy I would be if I were fortunate enough to see you and the dear children again. God grant us our health so that we can survive all the fatigue. The land is as wholesome as in Germany, if one can only hold on. During the day the heat is very great, and then at night again cold. You yourself know my dear friend that I was often sick while traveling. Here on land, not even a finger has caused me pain. Be so kind as to recommend me to your gracious married sister and her husband. Tell them I often think of them. I am sure that your sister and her husband will do everything possible for you. I am sending my journal to you, herewith. In it you will find of our entire trip, up to today. I know you will take time to read it. After you have read it, please be so kind as to send it to my father along with this letter. You will do me a service if you would write some lines to my father.

Do not allow any one but your brother-in-law and Lieutenant von Diskau to see this journal. It might possibly offend some people, as I am not a man of learning.

I recommend myself again to your favor, a million times, and kiss your hand. Write to me as to whether Fritz and Sophie still remember me. Whenever our recruits arrive here, I will take the opportunity to send you something from America. I have already written to you that Lieutenant von Weitershausen had the misfortune to lose his mind. A Captain von Weitershausen was also killed in America. Adieu my precious one. May God keep you in good health and bless you. Don't worry too much. God will watch over us here, also. And, regardless of what happens, I remain yours, with body and soul, as long as God and the rebels allow me to live.

Christian von Molitor

Molitor then added this postscript:

30

When we march, it may well be against Boston. When we again return to Ansbach, I will bring you a black slave. If you talk about me to good friends, you will place me in your debt, if you recommend me to them. Do not forget Major von Bose. I will bring you American feathers, pearls, and jewels. Kiss your scholars frequently for both of us. Adieu a thousand times. Write me often. I must always wear a mask before my face here so that my tender skin is not ruined and does not turn black.

Naubat Rai, the Hindu father of an Indian soldier serving in France, angrily informs his son how he will be welcomed home if he brings back a Christian wife.

During World War I, more than 1 million Hindu, Muslim, Sikh, and Christian troops from India served with the British Army in Europe. When given the opportunity to go on leave, many of these young soldiers found themselves surrounded by an abundance of temptations, and their mothers and fathers back in India worried that their sons would be corrupted by a relatively more licentious Western morality. One Muslim soldier, Mohamed Feroz Khan, received a stern warning from his father about avoiding brothels (euphemistically called 'hotels') in France. Khan adamantly replied:

> *I swear to you that although I have been in France for two and a half years, I have not even taken so much as a cup of tea in a 'hotel.' I swear also that up till this moment I have committed no evil deed in France. I am your true son, and your advice is plainly written on my heart.*

For the parents of one Hindu soldier, however, a little concern might have been warranted. Although it is not clear to whom the soldier was writing, it was obviously someone he trusted, and on November 6, 1917, he sent the following (the 250 rupees he refers to is the equivalent of several months' pay).

I am off to Paris which has been hitherto 'out of bounds' to everyone but officers. Now we can go. Paris is a city of fairyland and God will now give us an opportunity of seeing it. I will write you all about it. I am taking Rs. 250 to spend. Whatever happens do not let anyone know about this. I intend to enjoy whatever pleasures there are. Do not let anyone know that Jai Singh is spending Rs. 250 in four days. If father heard of it he would be very angry. I should like to marry in France but I am afraid the family would be ashamed. You can marry very fine girls if you like.

Another Hindu soldier considered doing just that. He wrote home asking for parental consent, and the reply from his father, Naubat Rai, was perhaps more extreme than he had anticipated. (The father's letter and the ones above were intercepted by British field censors and enabled the censors to gauge morale. The transcriptions do not include greetings or signatures.)

Consider, how could I possibly consent to your becoming a Musalman and marrying a Moslem wife, or embracing Christianity and marrying a Christian wife? Have you no shame? Do you think that I brought you up, so that you might marry a Christian wife? Could a man be so perverted as to lose his religion for the sake of a woman? You were one, who had a more promising future before you than any other man in the world, and yet you proceed to wreck your life by being a traitor to your faith!

Thousands of men have gone to France from here, but not one of them, except yourself has behaved in this unseemly fashion. There were 70 men in your own party, has anyone of them returned with a French wife? It is the greatest disgrace for a Hindu to become a Mahomedan or a Christian, do not therefore blacken your face before the whole world. I exhausted all my efforts to bring you up in culture and honour and endured all manner of trials and vicissitudes in order that your material and moral condition might be assured. Now, you proceed to disgrace yourself before the whole world!

Consider how from the commencement I strove on your behalf till in the end you became a <u>Gomestah.</u> Now I give you my last advice, viz. To put away this unprofitable idea from your mind, and never allude to a Christian wife in the future. And if you reject my advice, take care how you bring such a woman to my house, for she will be beaten on the head with a shoe a thousand times, and take steps also to provide for your mother and for your present wife. Why do you deal thus with me in my old age when I am past further work? Return home and take your present wife to you. If there is any fault in her, we can arrange another marriage for you here, four marriages if you like; but cease to think of disgracing yourself by taking a Christian wife.

Whether or not the soldier married the girl or dared to introduce any other young woman, for that matter, to his shoe-wielding father is not known. Nor is it clear exactly how his 'present wife' – more likely, a fiancée – felt about the whole matter, although an awkward homecoming could certainly be imagined.

British soldier Edward Hassall writes to a young girl, Joan Burbidge, in England after he discovers a small gift she had sent to British troops fighting on the Western Front during World War I — & — Hassall responds to a letter by Mr. Burbidge telling him that Joan now wants to marry her 'chocolate soldier'.

Regardless of the conflict, combatants often cling to any vestige of civilization they can find during the maelstrom of battle – letters and photographs, books, music, delicacies, anything that will distract them from the filth and turmoil of war, and remind them of calmer, more pleasant times. In the spring of 1916, a British soldier named Edward Hassall found a small package of chocolate with five words inscribed on the outside of the carton: 'From little Joan, Whiterock, Wadebridge.' Hassall was deeply moved by the gesture, and he sent the following letter from France in late June 1916:

Dear Miss Joan,
During a bombardment of our position some time ago, I was taking cover in

33

the trenches recently captured from the enemy, when I idly picked up the enclosed empty chocolate packet. I dont know whether I am getting sentimental but I can assure you that in the midst of the turmoil of the bombardment the inscription on the packet came as a message from home, a message from the children of England in whose defence we are fighting. A few moments earlier a gallant Officer & our Wheeler Gunner had both been killed & several others wounded, which had a naturally depressing effect on all, but your little message cheered me. How your packet came there, by whom or when it was dropped I have not the least idea, but I sincerely hope that for it holds no tragic memories. Many gallant British officers & men cheerfully met their death in the capture of that trench, and the toll has since been paid by our Battery in the vicinity, but I sincerely hope that your friend came safely through.

I have carried the packet about with me, off duty and on, for probably a fortnight, & have at last found time to send it to you. Please forgive me for writing. I thought that you would be interested to know that your name had reached the German line in the hottest contended battle of the War.

With best wishes to your parents & yourself

I am

Yrs sincerely

E Hassall   Bombardier

49 Siege Battery   RGA

<u>B E F</u>

PS/ I enclose a German coin picked up in some trench. I forgot to say that I have passed your message to the Germans, inscribed on a 6'' shell. I hope it also landed in their new trenches.

EH

Six-year-old Joan Burbidge received the letter, and her father asked Joan if she wished to respond. 'Oh yes, Daddy,' she said, 'tell him I'll marry him when I grow up.' Mr. Burbidge dutifully obliged and forwarded Joan's message. On August 13, 1916, her father received a letter directly from Joan's new admirer.

34

Dear Mr. Burbidge,

Many thanks for your letter. I am now more than delighted to think that I had the good sense to return the chocolate packet. Had I not done so I should not have received the beautiful photograph of Her ladyship & should still have been on the shelf. Whereas I am now as proud as a newly engaged man should be.

Being thirty three years of age, 6 feet long, decidedly plain & as clumsy as the clumsiest long fellow living, I had abandoned hope long ago, but as Joan has honoured me with a promise (or is it a threat) of marriage, I bow with the most humble grace.

Perhaps if she saw me in my 'tin hat' she would not think me the Prince Charming she had so fondly imagined, but 'Love laughs at tin smiths', & I really don't look too bad <u>when</u> I get a wash & a shave. Newly brushed I look something like a Chinese Mandarin or a super in San Toy or the Geisha, but these tin hats were not intended to catch the eye. I am afraid you will have to get me out of hot water for a start, as I find that I am only possessed of half a franc & am unable to purchase the necessary diamonds & rubies. Kindly prevail on Her Ladyship to accept the enclosed as a temporary substitute. It is really a splendid example of the jewellers art, & made by my own humble fingers from a piece of German time fuze, & engraved with the Battery identification stamp applied with a sledge hammer. We used to have ample time in which to turn out these wonderful works of art but now all our skill is applied to turning out the Germans.

I also send, with my sincere love, a small card which our Ration Carrier got for me at C———, a few miles behind the line, which I think should be sufficient to clinch the matter. Of course, it has rather caught me on the hop, as it were, but I take it that I shall have ample time in which to pull my socks up. I have balanced my pay book & find that I am 7.12.0 in credit, & if I have the good fortune to reach the other side of the Rhine I hope to make another eighteen pence out of the Germans, if all the ready cash has not been absorbed in War Loans, so altogether, Sir, I hope that my lady's future is secure.

You ask for news regarding myself, & under the circumstances I think some recital of my career is due from me, although I am afraid you will not find it at all interesting. On the outbreak of War I was employed as a clerk in the Counting House of Messrs Brough Nicholson & Hall, Leek Staffordshire, my native town. Having served eight years in the Cape Police

I felt it my duty, as a trained man, to enlist forthwith, which I did, & being too heavy for the Cavalry, was posted to the RGA. I walked out of the office at 10 am on the 29th August & returned in half an hours time a duly sworn & attested Artilleryman, when I handed over, said goodbye to all & sundry, including the typists, & left at noon with the blessings of the Cashier & a 1 note in recognition of my patriotism. After being vaccinated, inoculated, subjected to dental treatment & fitted with false dentures, I was considered fit to take up arms against this mighty sea of trouble & here I am & there's Joan's chocolate packet.

Rather commonplace, is'nt it, except for the chocolate packet & the fact that I am engaged to a lady I have never seen & am addressing this to a friend who is really a stranger.

We have been in some decidedly warm positions, but the one I will call Joan's trench was the warmest of the lot, & cost us rather dearly. We have since moved to pastures new & I am more than thankful to the Almighty that I came though safely, although our present place of abode is far from healthy I can assure you. Still I suppose everything is judged by comparison, & compared to the Infantry our lot is a happy one. People at home may be rather impatient with the slowness of the advance, but if they only knew what our men have to endure they would marvel at the progress they have already made. It is one thing to rush a position in the excitement & enthusiasm of an advance, but it is a totally different thing to hang on in the face of the fury of hundreds of guns concentrated on the spot. Yet they have hung on, in face of all, & men who a few short months ago had no knowledge of War or even of discipline have proved themselves the greatest heroes in British History.

The Battle still goes on & the resistance becomes daily stronger, but they will fight on & on until they got through, & you need have no fear for the future.

Needless to say my own branch of the service is having an exceptionally busy time, & we have almost worked ourselves to a standstill. How we have managed to keep up the pressure is a matter for wonder, but we all know how much really depends on us & we continue to do our best.

I am afraid I have not time to write more just now. I shall be pleased to hear from you again & will write when I get a favourable opportunity.

I am extremely sorry to hear you are in such poor health, & hope the cure will be beneficial.

Once more thanking you for the photo, & with regards to yourself & Mrs Burbidge & love to Joan

> I remain
>> Yrs very sincerely
>>> E Hassall

Although Hassall survived combat, he became terribly ill after returning to England and died in February 1922. 'He was never the same after the War,' his mother wrote to Mr. Burbidge, informing him of her son's death. 'Before then he was always so full of fun and joy of life but afterwards] he was much more serious and grave which was not to be wondered at considering what he had been through. All through he carried with him the photo of Joan you sent out to him which he regarded as his mascot.' Unfortunately Joan Burbidge and Edward Hassall never had the opportunity to meet before he died.

British soldier John Bateman Beer's sweetheart, Ivy, shares with him some unexpected news about their relationship during World War I — & — Charlie, an American soldier stationed in England during World War II, assures his girlfriend back home he always liked her a lot, but . . .

In September 1917, a British soldier named John Bateman Beer, serving in the 2/22nd London Regiment, received a long-awaited letter from his girlfriend. It was not, suffice it to say, the letter he was expecting.

My Dear Jack,

For the last month I have been endeavouring to pluck up sufficient courage to write and tell you that everything must be over between us. No doubt you will think me awfully unkind and perhaps fickle to write like this while you are away, but this matter has worried me a great deal, and I have been halting between two opinions, as to whether it would be kinder to let you know now, and let myself be called unfaithful, or to wait until you come home, although knowing all the time in my heart that I was untrue. When you went away, and I told you that I loved you best, I really meant it Jack, but such a lot seems to have happened since then. I really thought that I had forgotten Charlie in my love for you, and during the past nine months have been fighting against his love for me, wishing and longing for your return, but it is no use Jack, I cannot help loving Charlie best. I suppose it is because he was first. At first I made up my mind to fight it down <u>and be true to you, and if you still wish to keep me to my promise under the circumstances, I will do so.</u>

Don't take this too much to heart Jack. I am not worth it but don't think me altogether heartless. I would not hurt you dear unless I could help it, but unfortunately we cannot control our own feelings. Will you believe me when I say that I am very sorry, for I am, more so than perhaps you think. Anyway, forgive me if you can, and <u>I trust that you will still let us be friends,</u> whatever happens. Have not had the courage to tell your Mother yet, perhaps you will do so. Write back as soon as you can do say you forgive me Jack, shall wait impatiently for your answer.

One word about Charlie before I finish. He would have waited in honour bound until you came home.

All at home send their love to you.

Trusting this will find you in the best of health.

I remain,

Yours Very Sincerely

Ivy

Although the term originated in World War II, 'Dear John' letters date back for centuries (and with the advancement of electronic communication, troops can now receive 'Dear John' e-mails). Usually the message is from a girlfriend, fiancée, or, in the worst case, a wife who has fallen for someone else. As much as servicemen joke about the letters or try to make light of them, the effect of receiving one of these rejections in the mail can be devastating. 'On the fifteenth of this month a German man in the 52nd Regt. P V committed suicide by shooting himself through the head,' Civil War soldier Ephraim Sheuy wrote to his sister in March 1864. 'The cause of it was he got a letter that his wife got married and that troubled him so much.' John Bateman Beer was markedly less troubled by his Dear John letter and – more defiant than hurt – wrote the following to his father on October 12, 1917.

> Last week, I had a letter from Ivy, and I was surprised to know that everything between us was at an end. It seems as though a fellow named C. Hall, has been attending on her & of course in my absence, she has allowed herself to be talked over & change her mind. This is certainly a big surprise & of course I did not know what to do, so after thinking it over I have at present decided not to write to her at all, & let the affair finish up. I should like your advice on the subject. It is no good playing about on the matter, & I am not going to play second fiddle to anybody.

Women, too, can find themselves on the wrong end of a rejection letter. During World War II, British troops repeatedly complained that American servicemen courted all the most attractive ladies in England. Women back in the USA who had been dating those American soldiers discovered that the grievance was not entirely a rumor. Gertrude 'Trudel' Geschwill, a young nurse in Clifton, New Jersey, received the following from her American beau stationed across the pond in the fall of 1944.

England, 19 September

Dear Trudel:

The letter you wrote from the shore on the 25th of August arrived the day after the one you wrote on the 10th, and I was very glad to hear from you. Apparently you had a good time there, and I am glad it was a pleasant break in your routine, which seems rather strenuous. It was quite an idea to write your letter on a map – I have been around that vicinity, and it brought back some very pleasant memories. Several times I went out on fishing trips through that inlet, starting from the Manasquan side. One time, three days after the hurricane we had in 1938, I steered a forty foot cruiser for a half hour or so when we were about fifteen miles offshore and the skipper wanted to take a look at the engines, with all the other passengers seasick. I did not handle the boat as smoothly as an experienced helmsman would, and the seasick ones were loud in their suggestions that the captain should take over again. The sea was quite rough, but I did a fair job of steering toward a water tower somewhere south of the inlet, probably in Point Pleasant.

That picture of the ocean in the moonlight was really very beautiful; there have been times in England when I could see a similar scene, but the moon was setting across the ocean, rather than rising from it, and the point of view makes quite a difference.

I had a date with my Wren Sunday; it meant being away from camp over twenty hours to be with her five hours, as she is now stationed some distance away, but quite a lot happened in those few hours. We discussed those differences I mentioned in my last letter to you, and I discovered that Barbara was willing to make the concessions necessary to get around them; she has agreed to follow the rules set by the Catholic Church in such situations, and to come to the States with me. She probably thought, as you did, that I could be broken of the idea of being a confirmed bachelor, and she has been right. If the war had not started so soon after you and I met, and had not kept me here so long, things would have been different. I would have probably asked you the same question, although I always felt that you regarded your religion as highly as I did mine, and could not change or make any concessions any more than I could.

Writing to you, I can remember very well the night before Pearl Harbor, when we met, driving over the winter roads during the next two months between Jersey City and Clifton, and our most enjoyable dates together. War changes everyone, I guess, and I realize now that it has changed me more than I knew. I guess I'll never know now the method I once asked you about, but I suspect, that if we could have eliminated the obstacle in the way, it probably would have worked. I've always liked you a lot, and found you very attractive, which is a good start in any language.

Things are different now than I thought they would be when I last saw you and as a matter of fact look different than they did even one year ago. I made a decision in a situation full of unknown factors; in fairness to Barbara I cannot say I am sorry, but I can honestly say that if I had not come to England, and stayed so long, things might have been quite different.

Perhaps we shall see each other again, if this war ever ends; I hope things go well with you, and I hope you will write to me, if you don't mind.

Your friend,
Charlie

Geschwill was stung by the rejection, but not for long; almost a week later she met a handsome, twenty-four-year-old army technical sergeant named Henry Kempe, who asked her out. After four months of dating, Kempe proposed, and they married a year later. They had two children and stayed happily married until Henry Kempe's death in 1991.

Zbigniew Janicki, a Polish pilot serving with the Royal Air Force, writes to his mother and father about the effect that being alone in a new country has had on him.

Marriages between civilians and military personnel in both allied and enemy nations are common in times of conflict, and during World War II, well over 1 million servicemen proposed (oftentimes after only a brief courtship) to women they had met while stationed overseas. Zbigniew Janicki – a Polish airman flying with the famed Royal Air Force (RAF) and defending England from waves of Luftwaffe attacks – was one of these lovestruck men. (The Kosciuszko Squadron, comprised of Polish pilots and air crews, was responsible for shooting down more German aircraft than any other RAF squadron.) Yet despite the heroics and the confidence that airmen like Janicki exuded, they had been separated from their parents and siblings and were not immune to feelings of loneliness and homesickness. In the following letter to his parents, Janicki offers some insight into his emotions about the accelerated nature of a wartime romance.

November, 1941

Dear Mother and Father!

Following my departure from Poland, I wrote letters to you for a period of time, and then stopped, knowing that the chances were slim that you would receive them.

I am writing this letter for the sole reason of sharing my feelings with you. Years have passed since I have last seen you, and trust me, when I recall my last 'invasion' of our home on the seventh day of the war, that moment is still vivid in my memory. Now, the third year has begun and time is passing very quickly. My last letter to you was written in Eastchurch in England, but of course, never sent. I decided to overcome what we call 'sentimentalism,' or maybe I didn't want you to get in trouble with the Gestapo. Anyway the letter you sent through the Red Cross in the spring of 1940 reached me in May and comforted me a little.

Since my arrival in England, I have changed a lot and so has my life. I must admit that not everything has happened the way it should have. After arriving in England we had to wait nearly eight months to fly and do real work. That period was difficult for me and my comrades, especially after our sojourn in France, and it had a depressing influence on my friends and me (weak consolation that I wasn't the only one). The English acknowledge our military ranks from Poland and this is why, as a young officer, especially during war in a foreign country, I let loose and lived the life without thinking about tomorrow, afraid that tomorrow would be too late. My longstanding interest in the English language and living among the English helped me quickly improve my vocabulary and enabled me to live an easy and pleasant lifestyle. But also I have to say that nothing demoralizes people as much as boredom, which I began to experience myself. Our urge to fly was restrained to the point that we had nothing more to do than wait and 'learn' about England and its customs. Finally at the end of the summer, our group was sent to flight training. Believe me, after such a long period of inactivity, it was an incredible experience to climb back into a fighter plane. I felt like a person who had re-discovered his purpose and passion.

During the time in between training, a big change happened in my personal life. I met a girl by the name of Violet. As it turned out, she embodied everything I dreamed about in a woman. Being quite inexperienced in

42

dealing with the other half of humanity, I was overwhelmed by this Irish-Englishwoman. Her personal charm and beauty caused me to fall for her in just a few days, like I had never before. Because of our mutual feelings (the best proof of which was her voluntary break up with a good and wealthy fiancé), after one month I was ready to marry her, but was still fighting a battle within me. I was afraid I might be confusing my affection for her with my loneliness here, along with my normal youthful feelings (I have Marysia on my mind).

This spiritual conflict between my desire for this English girl, in thoughts and in deeds, and my old principles, lasted for some time. Being as sentimental as I am, in the end I couldn't resist having somebody to fill the emptiness of separation from family and home, and having someone intimately close to my heart and body: a woman – a companion. I am sure that I could be a bachelor for a long time and resist all romantic ideas, but Violet was someone I couldn't lose. One month was sufficient to realize that there was no life for us without each other. Her breaking off of the engagement with her fiancé proved that my feelings were being reciprocated, and convinced me to propose and get married right away. This happened a few weeks later at a little Catholic church, without fanfare, but with a deep sense of mutual affection.

At that time I was stationed near New Castle in northern England, attached to an English fighter squadron. After training on Hurricanes, we were assigned to various English squadrons, before our own was formed. Overall I served in English squadrons for almost eight months (until May 1941), and after that I was assigned to Polish Squadron 302. Because military units often have to change locations, I have been all over England and Scotland, mostly with convoy patrols, or, as it happened last month, fighting Messerschmits over England and France. I have to confess that I have had very few opportunities to catch a Kraut in my sights, but my time will come . . . My recent success is of a very different nature. Most of all I would like you to know that you are . . .the grandparents and I am the father of a healthy son!!!

That is my greatest joy and, at the same time, my biggest worry because of the responsibility I am now facing. I hope you will be able to see my son (his name is Piotr) in the future, bless him, and watch him become a brave and honest man, as I do from the bottom of my heart. I want him to grow up to be a Polish gentleman, and have the best Polish and English qualities about him.

I would like him to appear in front of you and say what I am telling you now: I have the best and most loving parents a man could hope to have. In loving memory of you and my son, I would like to live honorably and never shame my family. This war is affecting thousands of people's lives, including my own. Life is precious to me as never before, but I know my duty, and I will avenge all the suffering Poland is going through and with God's help will kill more than one Kraut.

It is difficult for me to imagine what your life is like these days. I console myself thinking that all of you are carrying on with the hope for a better future. If you are suffering – sooner or later justice will come. Dad's hair has probably grayed, and Mom's is likely not as dark as it used to be. Dasia is probably married by now. She would be happy to know that we planned to give her name to our daughter. Even though I have my own so-called house, you are my family and my home forever. I dream of coming back one day with Violet and Piotr to see you all in a good health and receive your blessing.

Your loving son

Zbigniew Janicki would never have the opportunity to introduce his parents to their new grandson; Janicki was shot down and killed in June 1944.

Through a series of increasingly impassioned love letters, Captain Harry Kipp, an American marine fighting in the Pacific during World War II, attempts to court a young woman named Norma Clinton back in the USA.

The two had never met. Norma Clinton was an exceptionally intelligent, attractive young honors student living in rural Georgia. Harry Kipp was a US Marine Corps captain from Minnesota who had survived the attack on Pearl Harbor and was shipped off to the Solomon Islands to fight in the Pacific. In early 1944, at the request of her Aunt Jean (who had once dated Kipp), Norma sent him a letter and a photograph to raise his morale and simply let him know that

44

people back in the USA were thinking of him and all the troops in harm's way. Upon seeing her picture and reading her thoughtful and engaging letter, Harry was smitten. 'Although Jean had told me that you might drop me a line I was nevertheless quite surprised and very pleased to receive your letter,' he began his first missive to her, dated February 12, 1944. He continued:

When you said, 'If you answer this letter I will send you another,' did you mean another picture or another letter? I hope you meant both for I would enjoy looking at my pin-up girl in two different moods.

Your wish to become a nurse is a worthy goal to shoot at and I wish you success in realizing your aspirations. Might I hope to enjoy the priviledge of your services in the event I should ever need them? – or even though I didn't really need them? But since you are so proficient in chemistry you will probably be a labratory technician who does not personally attend patients. I knew there was a reason for my dislike of chemistry other than that I was too slow on the uptake to understand the elusive movements of the molecule.

It <u>has</u> been a long time since you saw Jean. You must have been a cute little tyke at that time. I haven't seen her either since nearly four years ago. Little wonder she married some one else. Would you wait that long for just an ordinary marine?

Your hobbies are very akin to mine. I too enjoy movies and like to write letters. In that we are on common ground but I must admit that sewing holds very little fascination for me, that is if I am the one doing it but I do find pleasure in watching a good housewife sew.

Perhaps you believe that I deliberately delayed answering your ~~lettlr~~ (sorry) letter but that isn't the case. You see I am in a very remote corner of the world and mail reaches us much more slowly than it takes to reach the States from here. Your letter arrived just yesterday. I hope that soon there shall be another (with a picture in it) and more to follow.

Goodnight sweets, won't you write again soon.

Yours,
Harry.

Capt. H.E. Kipp, U.S.M.C.
'A' Btry., 9th 55 MM Gun Bn.,
3rd Corps Arty., 3rd Phib Corps,

By summer, and after exchanging several more letters (most of which were lost or destroyed during the war), Harry had not just fallen, but plunged deliriously in love with Norma. Unable to contain his adoration, he expressed the depth of his emotions and addressed the question of how he would inform Aunt Jean that he was in love with Norma. Although – from his standpoint – there was no longer anything between them, it was still an awkward matter. (Aunt Jean's marriage had ended in divorce, and there was speculation that she was interested in Harry again.)

27 June, 1944

Dearest Norma;

Today your letters of 19 March and 1 May arrived, which makes four that I have gotten from you, and still leaves two unaccounted for. I am eagerly looking forward to their arrival.

Your pictures (I mean <u>you</u>) are heavenly. Now I do want to be two persons. Not so I could love you and someone else too, but so that both of me could love you. Looking at you lends meaning to the story of Mark Twain who when he first saw the picture of Veli? gazed at it long and earnestly, then said, 'This girl shall be my wife' I said those same words of you to your picture, Norma, and I pray that my words shall come to pass as his did. Heaven knows I meant them.

In my last letter I tried to explain my feeling for Jean, and why. I hope you will understand and forgive me, and realize that even though I had never known of you or never been thrilled by your loveliness it would still have been the same. It will be difficult, but tomorrow I shall tell her.

You cause me to believe that you exercise great care and much thought in writing to me. Norma, please don't compose letters to me. Just record your thoughts as they occur to you. Talk to me. Just as if you were here (How I wish you were!)

Must close. I can't write tonight. Your picture distracts me. I gaze at it continuously, marveling, hoping, imagining, fascinated – wondering if I can possibly ever be happy without you. Will write again when I recover a bit. In the meantime I'll be dreaming of you.

Love, Harry.

The photograph Norma Clinton sent to Captain Harry Kipp
that prompted their correspondence – and eventual love affair.

The comment about marriage was not an offhand remark. Harry truly believed that Norma Clinton was the woman with whom he wanted to spend the rest of his life. But while he had seen a photograph of her, she had virtually no idea what he looked like. He was afraid she might not be attracted to him, and, not having a photo to hand, offered instead a candid written description – along with an official declaration of his intentions in the following letter on July 16, 1944.

Am sorry I can't send you a picture now, but you did ask me to describe myself, and threatened me with your anger should I fail to comply. Remembering what you told me of your terrible temper, I hasten to tell you (and this hurts) that I am not at all handsome, am only five feet seven inches tall, have straight blond hair, blue eyes, weigh 170 pounds, and worst of all, have a childishly affectionate disposition. Now you tell me your reaction. As for your reserve in the letters you write to me, of course I understand. How could you write in any other way? You haven't even seen a picture of me, have never heard my voice, and know so little about me. There is something I do want you to know. Perhaps you will think me very naive and impulsive but I am sincere in the protestation of my love for you. I do love you. Norma, I want you to be my wife just as soon as I can possibly come for you ... Won't you tell me frankly, honestly, if you would marry me when I come home, should you find that you could care for me? ... Considering everything I've already said more than you expected to hear, so 'Goodnight', sweets. Will you answer just as soon as you recover from the shock?

Shocked she was. It was only his eighth letter to her. She had not told her parents of the relationship, and she knew they would vehemently disapprove of the whole affair and accuse her of being impetuous and gullible for believing this faraway stranger honestly wanted to marry her. And if he did, based on a few photographs and letters, he was perhaps even more suspect. At the time, Norma still did not have an image of him. (She would later receive, forwarded by his uncle, a studio portrait of Harry in uniform. 'He looked like a Roman God,' she would say of his picture. '[F]rom deep blue eyes came a mixture of appraisal and curiosity, a man who viewed the world with interest and without reservation.') Norma entertained a number of doubts and reservations about his motivations, but after considerable thought, she penned her reply:

My Dearest Harry,
Yes, yes, yes, I will marry you! Just as soon as you can come for me. I want more than anything in the world to be your wife, forever! I love you with all my heart!
Your Norma

Norma did not tell her family; she would wait until Harry returned to the USA. There was no point in worrying them now, and there was a far graver matter both she and Harry faced than her parents' reaction. It was not addressed directly, but broached only occasionally and somewhat obscurely. 'One other thing, sweets,' he wrote in a letter dated November 28, 1944,

> *please don't worry about my safety. I am as safe as you are and I will be for at least a couple of months. After that, if you must worry you may, but just a little bit, because I have a charmed life. If it were intended that anything unpleasant should happen to me, it would have happened long ago. We are not supposed to tell anyone when we go into actual combat until after we are aboard ship and on the way to make a landing on Jap territory and that letter doesn't get in the mail until several days or possibly weeks after we leave our base. To let you know that there will be no letters for a long time I'll end my last letter before leaving by saying, 'Goodbye for a little while'. Will you remember that?*

Norma would remember, and she could not refrain from sharing her anxiety. On March 4, 1945, as the war in the Pacific was becoming increasingly ferocious, Kipp responded to her concerns:

> *Norma darling, you mustn't feel badly when I say, 'Goodbye for a little while.' Even though it may be soon, I feel happy, and confident that*

everything will be all right. At other times in the past I used to wonder a little and my thoughts were not too cheerful but this time it's different because I know your spirit is with me and I'll always sense your presence. It will seem as if I can always reach back and touch your hand, and feel your reassuring answering pressure. Don't you see dear, that God didn't bring us together just to be torn apart? One day soon we'll be sitting hand in hand before our fireplace, silently dreaming as we gaze into the dancing flames while some little body near us in a little white crib stares in uncomprehending wonder at the new toe he has just discovered. Believe in that Norma dear, and it will come true.

Less than three weeks later, after nonchalantly commenting about how beautiful Georgia must be at this time of year and his wish to be with her, Harry concluded his March 23 letter with the words Norma was dreading. *'I must say "Good-bye for a little while" . . . Don't worry, dear. I'm not afraid because I am taking you along and everything I do will be right because you are with me. Harry.'* Just over one week later, Clinton was listening to the radio when a news report broke into regular programming and announced that *'United States Marines have invaded Okinawa, largest of the Ryukyu Islands on Japan's southern doorstep.'* Kipp was there, Clinton had no doubt, and she froze after hearing the bulletin. If he were killed, she might not know for months. She was not his wife, and only spouses and family members received official notification. The wait was unbearable. If Okinawa was anything like the battle for Iwo Jima, which had begun almost six weeks before and cost nearly 7000 American lives, it would be a bloodbath. An estimated 100,000 heavily entrenched Japanese troops defended the island, which was ten times the size of Iwo Jima. Days passed, and then weeks, and still no word from – or about – Harry Kipp. And then, almost a month after his last letter, while literally waiting by the mailbox, she saw the postman driving down the road and heard him excitedly honk the horn. His beaming face told her everything she wanted to know, and after skidding to a stop,

Captain Harry Kipp, USMC

he waved the airmail letter with Harry's name listed in the return address. 'My Beautiful Darling!', his letter began,

> *Turn your back to the mirror and look over your shoulder. Do you see wings? You must, because you are an angel. Today I received nineteen heavenly letters from you. Norma Mine, I hope I shall be deserving of your wonderful devotion. You've done so much to make me happy, and I love you more and more as time goes on and our wedding day draws nearer. I can't possibly answer all of your questions or reply to your suggestions in this one letter, but I'll try to catch up, sweets, in the near future. I'll write a few lines every time I have a moment to spare and perhaps I shall be able to send a letter at least once or twice a week. I think that from now on our mail deliveries will be quite frequent and regular...*

Their correspondence resumed, and along with their exclamations of love and longing, they wrote with growing enthusiasm about the day they would be married. Finally, in August 1945 the war came to an end, and Harry was heading home. On September 22, he landed in California, and, after he and Norma were able to speak by telephone – which represented the first time they had heard each other's voice – Harry sent the following letter.

8:30 Sunday evening

Darling,

I don't remember a word you said, but I still hear the sound of your sweet voice echoing in my heart. How can I wait seven whole days to hear you talk to me again? But this is the end of our long time of waiting. Will you marry me soon? Monday? Tuesday? I've never loved you more than at this very moment.

We didn't say much in our conversation, did we, honey? You were simply breathless and I was nearly the same, and we could hear each other so very faintly, but I wouldn't have missed it for worlds. The sound of your voice went straight to my heart.

If my present plans carry through I will leave here Tuesday evening and should reach Chattanooga sometime Sunday, and unless I let you know otherwise, I'll call you at eight that evening. Do you suppose we'll be as excited then as we were tonight? Well, why shouldn't we be excited? Nothing as important as this has ever happened to us before. I can hardly realize that so very soon the dearest, sweetest, loveliest little darling in all the world will be my wife. We've waited nearly two years now, and if we do find ourselves a bit embarrassed when we meet, it will be no more than it is natural to expect and the awkwardness will disappear in a moment, because deep in our hearts we understand each other, and we know that our two individual lives are bound to each other inseparably and nothing under the sun can ever change that.

Oh, Honeychild! Monday! Monday! Monday! I'm so happy I could turn handsprings in the middle of Market Street. And Monday morning I am going to give you the greatest, biggest hug you have ever hear[d] about 'cause I love you, I love you, Norma, I love you and that's for sure!!

Harry.

One week later, Harry Kipp and Norma Clinton exchanged vows. Harry retired from the Marine Corps in 1953 after eight years of active duty in the USA, primarily recruiting and training marines. Norma finished college and became an elementary school teacher. The couple raised two children and remained together until May 1965, when Harry died from cancer.

A Swiss national named Werner Walti carries with him an affectionate letter from a woman in California – or so it would seem ...

The letter was like any other expression of love and yearning from a distant sweetheart, and Werner Walti, a Swiss national visiting Scotland, kept the missive with him at all times. Written by a woman named Marion (last name unknown) from Palo Alto, California, the brief but intimate letter fondly recalled wonderful days together between two people who were meant to be united once again. It is dated June 1, 1939 – exactly three months before the outbreak of war in Europe.

Goodmorning, silent one! I have been wondering where you were, and have been afraid you would leave without saying goodbye. You may have gone already, but you can't be farther than my wishes for your happiness can travel.

Easter has come and gone without a word exchanged between us! I thought of you on Easter.

Will you forgive me for something? Do you remember the time I gave you the new penny? I was in very bad discipline that night. I was foolish as in the summer on Ridge Road and you brought me to my senses again. You are the strong wise one. And your help and affection have meant more to me than you can know.

Your Christmas letter – and the beautiful El Greco and Cathedral Sculptures are my treasures. Never will I forget that perfect Christmas day and your wonderful surprise.

Do you remember the little cow we had on Ridge Road and the little wooden Virgin and how you objected to their standing together? It was a funny little thing, or so I thought, that you should object. But since then it has showed me something deep in you that I was slow to appreciate. . . I love you for all that is fine in you, and for all your encouragement. I want to be worthy of your friendship.

> My love goes with you –
> Affectionately,
> Marion

Not a word of the letter was true. It is not that Marion did not harbor these feelings, but that Marion did not exist, and Werner Walti was, in fact, a German spy named Robert Petter. The letter was believed to be part of Petter's cover in Scotland, where he had just arrived to investigate the strength of Royal Air Force units in the region. Caught in Edinburgh's Waverly train station with a fake passport and other incriminating evidence, Petter was later sentenced to die under the Treachery Act, and, along with another spy named Karl Drugge, was executed in August 1941. The Germans were not alone in manu-

facturing love letters for secret missions. In one of the most creative counter-intelligence schemes in World War II, an anonymous corpse was dressed as a British major from the Combined Operations Headquarters, given the name William Martin, and, on April 30, 1943, dumped in the ocean off the coast of Huelva, Spain, where German agents were believed to be working. (Although Spain was officially neutral in the war, its fascist leader, General Ferdinand Franco, was pro-German.) Chained to 'Major Martin''s wrist was a briefcase containing what appeared to be highly sensitive documents indicating that the Allies were planning to invade Greece and the island of Sardinia, not Sicily as they actually intended. To substantiate that Martin was a real person, several love letters by a fiancée, 'Pam,' were included with the official papers. One expressed with persuasive anguish how much he would be missed after departing for his latest mission.

> I do think dearest that seeing people like you off at railway stations is one of the poorer forms of sport. A train going out can leave a howling great gap in one's life & one has to try madly – & quite in vain – to fill it with all the things one used to enjoy a whole five weeks ago. That lovely golden day we spent together – oh! I know it has been said before, but if _only_ time could sometimes stand still just for a _minute_ – But that line of thought is too pointless... Bill darling, do let me know as soon as you get fixed & can make some more plans, & dont please let them send you off into the blue the horrible way they do nowadays – now that we've found each other out of the whole world, I dont think I could bear it – All my love, PAM.

After Martin's body washed ashore, the contents of the briefcase made their way to Berlin and convinced the Germans to concentrate their forces closer to Greece and Sardinia. In July 1943 the Allies launched their successful assault on Sicily. The ploy, code-named Operation Mincemeat, was an extraordinary achievement. Decades after the war, the true identity of the corpse was revealed to be that of a thirty-four-year-old homeless Welshman named Glyndwr Michael who had committed suicide in a

London warehouse. Michael's body remains buried in Huelva under a gravestone that now bears his name, as well as a dedication to 'Major William Martin'.

Frrom 1942 to 1945, Kenelm Clifton Johnson-Hill, an English lieutenant captured by the Japanese, writes a series of 'letters' that he plans to give to his wife if he survives the war.

Taken prisoner by the Japanese after the fall of the Philippines in 1942, Major Horace Greeley was able to smuggle out an uncensored letter to his wife, Jeanne, in late November 1944, succinctly chronicling more than two excruciating years as a POW. American troops led by General Douglas MacArthur were swarming into the southern islands of the Philippines, and liberation seemed close at hand. Greeley, however, would not be rescued, as he was among the POWs whom the Japanese considered 'healthy' enough to be exploited as slave laborers. Forced onto a transport ship and sent to Japan, Greeley would not survive the journey. In the final paragraph of his November letter, Greeley wanted to prepare his wife for whatever idiosyncratic traits or habits he might display when he returned. His appeal poignantly reflected the concerns of many long-term POWs who worried about the emotional aftershocks of their confinement and how they would be received by loved ones back home. 'I realize that when you write it is like addressing a void – you don't know if I will receive your letters or not,' he remarked.

> *You have kept up with the world and its change while I am thinking and living in terms of 1941 – here it is three years later. You say that nothing has changed, but when I come back, I'll show you the changes. Be patient with me – let me eat my fill – ride in elevators – walk the streets – have a cup of coffee, candy, ice cream – clean clothes – take a*

turkish bath to get really clean – read three year old issues of Time Life,
etc . . and other fool things, like cooking at one or two in the morning.
I'll have some peculiar ideas – will ask you if so and so took place and so
and so said thus and so. Don't laugh too much. We have lived on rumor
for years and some people have terrific imaginations. Yes, Honey, you
have a difficult task ahead – to keep me educated and up to date. Time
here seems like an eternity, but I never lose hope that it will soon be
over and we'll be together again. Every day I thank a kind Fate that
gave me you. I love you now and forever, with all my heart and soul,
honey, so very, very much.

Kenelm Clifton Johnson-Hill was also imprisoned by the Japanese in
1942 and became one of tens of thousands of Allied POWs – along
with hundreds of thousands of Burmese, Chinese, Javanese, and Tamil
enslaved workers – forced to build the Burma-Siam Railroad that
would extend for hundreds of miles through dense jungle and over
large rivers. (The railway is the subject of the Oscar-winning 1957
film classic The Bridge on the River Kwai.) English by birth, Johnson-
Hill was living in Singapore with his pregnant wife Joyce, who was
known by the nickname 'Pooh,' and their two-year-old son Brian. Six
weeks before the Japanese invaded on December 8, 1941, Pooh and
Brian left their home for Australia. Before the war, Johnson-Hill had
enlisted as a second lieutenant in the Straits Settlements Volunteer
Forces, which was attached to the 16th Defence Regiment RA. When
the Japanese attacked Singapore, Johnson-Hill was immediately called
up and ordered to man a gunnery position. Singapore fell on February
15, 1942, and Johnson-Hill was captured a week later with a piece of
shrapnel embedded in his leg. In defiance of Japanese prohibitions
against keeping journals (the penalty being torture and even death if
they were discovered), Johnson-Hill began writing a series of short
'letters' to his wife in a small notebook, knowing she might never read
them. His first message, which was more of a general statement about
his purposes, was dated April 23, 1942.

It is difficult even to begin to put on paper one's thoughts, impressions, fears and hopes, and the hundred and one little events that make up the daily life of a POW. As for trying to finish this treatise, that is of course, beyond the bound of conjecture, no human being can foresee the horizon of events, or anywhere near the end of this little bit of world's history into which one has been flung as indiscriminately as bombs are dropped on civilian women and children. However, let us attempt a start anyway – and add a resolution to try and keep it up to date at least once a week.

That same day, he added another entry that acknowledged the gravity of the crisis but also emphasized his determination to ensure that the experience – 'a bad dream lived only by half a man with his other half in Australia' – would fortify their love and strengthen their family in the end.

We have lost EVERYTHING and as far as I am able to ascertain, stand little or no hope of recovering an iota of the wreck. At the age of 36, and with a wife and (I pray) two children, we have got exactly nothing, that is in the material sense of the word. Spiritually on the other hand, we have each other and our children, and being a prisoner of war has most emphatically taught me to appreciate, and to love my wife and children more deeply and more wholeheartedly than I ever thought conceivable.

Johnson-Hill was intensely aware that they were not alone in their ordeal, and he frequently wrote of all those who were going through the same agonizing separation:

Another pink letter day darling in that we were allowed to send off another p.c. not that we were allowed to say very much or even hint or put a date on it. Whenever you do receive it sweetheart mine at least you will know that I am still alive. Several hundred who have died in the meanwhile will only be able to leave their loved ones to guess by the absence of a card that they are dead. What a terrible tragedy, it may take years for the truth to come out definitively.

When Pooh left for Australia in November 1941, she was halfway through her pregnancy. Ten months into his imprisonment, Johnson-Hill still did not know whether Pooh had delivered a baby boy or girl, and he referred to the child as 'Blank'. One year after his wife's evacuation from Singapore, he wrote the following from a prison camp called Tonchan, which he spelled 'Tong Sha,' in Thailand (known then as Siam).

26th November 1942

Tong Sha. Even in the middle of the Siamese jungle I can not help thinking deeper than ever of my sweet Pooh, my darling Brian and Blank. This time a year ago, a whole year – more like a whole lifetime – we said goodnight and goodbye on the steps of the 'Boysie Vain' How little did we know or realise what fickle fate had in store for us. Hell, hell and more hell. Wonder if we shall all 4 be together for the next anniversary and even when I shall know what poor sweet blank is? Great excitement this morning when large two engined planes flew over the Camp. Rangoon is only 250 miles away by air and wonder if they were British and if they are likely to bomb us thinking we are Japanese Troop Concentration.

Although there is not, unsurprisingly, much humor within the pages of Johnson-Hill's notebook, an occasional spark of levity comes to light. In one entry, he wrote simply:

Big discovery, sleeping partners say I am now cured of snoring. Won't my Pooh be pleased. Darlingest One.

Johnson-Hill and his comrades lived on rancid vegetables and paltry handfuls of rice. All of the delicacies in which he planned to indulge when freed were inventoried throughout the journal and with almost the same emphasis as seemingly more important matters. On December 10, 1942, he wrote:

Tong Sha. Another death, another Last Post, another grim reminder. Note – after war must try Golden Bells Preserving Victoria; most marvelous marmalade.

A year after the birth of his second child, Johnson-Hill still had not received one word about the baby's gender – or, more importantly, its health and well-being. On May 22, 1943, he wrote the following.

Received letter from Beryl in which she says 'Glad Pooh, Brian and question mark are in Australia' so I have received congratulations today on our baby but am still in the dark with poor blank. Hello little blank. What happened to your letters darling there are lovely ones that count for me and any time. Her letter is dated 5th July 1942, nearly a year ago. However it was sweet of her to write and I ought to be and am grateful.

The much-anticipated news finally arrived.

10th June 1943, Thursday

Well, well here is a BIG date and a curious story. I will start at the very beginning. Major Watson Hyatt, you may remember him as a schoolmaster in Singapore, we went to their house, as he called in here the other day, I asked him to take Beryl and Cyril's letters up to Gerald as I knew they would interest him especially the bit about Pam. He duly went away with them. Two days later, today McGrath went south to Ta Sao where he met Watson Wyatt and handed him the letters back. He arrived back here soon after lunch and of course I opened the letter straight away inside was a chit from Gerald saying 'Congratulations on your second son, Alan.' Information gleaned from Eric Griffiths Jones letters!! Such are the ways of the world. Well, darlingest one I can't possible tell what a relief it was to know our child was born alive and that you must have recovered from it sufficiently to have him christened Alan, a name I like immensely and an initial which will not only not confuse him with any other Johnson-Hill but will put him first on O.R. lists. I wonder what other names you have chosen and if you had an easy time with him. What weight he was and whether he looked like our sweet Brian or whether there is a big difference like the Andre children. I am simply dying to get your first letter to hear all the details. As you can imagine what a hell it is to be a Prisoner of War under

Japanese hands, not even allowed to know the sex on one's child until he is over 14 months old. Poor Boving does not know about his yet. I wonder on what date he made his appearance? Oh for your letter Beloved.

Holidays and anniversaries remained, emotionally, often the most agonizing time for the prisoners. On Brian's birthday, he wrote the following:

It is quite unbelievable that our sweet child is 5 years old today, this making his 3rd birthday without his father while he is a POW. It is really rather tragic that he should be going through this interesting period without any paternal influence. I know darling that you will see that he does not forget me altogether. I am just literarily living for the day when we can all be together again and I can be introduced to Alan, sweet thing. I do hope he had as happy a birthday as possible in the circumstances and that lots of kind uncles and aunts remembered him.

On September 25, 1943, Johnson-Hill asked: 'Further mail rumours have arrived in camp but nothing I hear from Australia. Wonder when I shall ever hear from my beloved Pooh again. Your last letter received was dated 2nd January 1942. Long before Alan was born and here he is nearly 18 months old and probably walking. Sweet thing!' Two weeks later he wrote ecstatically:

6th October, 1943 Wednesday

Darling, Darling at last after nearly two whole years – a letter from you, my sweet dated 4th September 1942. Such a great day today will not write more until I have thoroughly digested your marvelous letter. Am far too excited and tired to write more tonight. Bless you all dear ones.

Mail was everything to the prisoners, and while on 'rubbish duty' (i.e., cleaning up trash around the camp), Johnson-Hill discovered piles of letters sent to the POWs by their loved ones that the Japanese never forwarded but ripped up and threw in the garbage instead. Much to his own astonishment, he even found a torn-up photo of Pooh, Brian, and Alan. The mail that did get through was delayed by up to two years.

8th March, Wednesday, 1944

Another week over, another week nearer freedom. I have another go of malaria, my seventeenth in just over a year and as so often happens my ulcers on my heel and ankle have gone back on me and are far worse . . . Short letters – one in every 100 men have been allowed to be sent home. They convey no idea of the awful conditions in which we exist and no accounts of the hundreds of deaths. We are all rather depressed and tired after two years of it. A letter from my mother dated 24th June 1942 turned up yesterday, nearly two years old. She says let me know what you want though, through the Red Cross! I must start making out a list at once! Alan nearly two – how sad, they grow so quickly.

Throughout the entire journal, there is only one instance where Johnson-Hill expresses even the slightest frustration with his wife, and it came during a time when he was physically worn down, which understandably worsened his mood. (The malnourished and overworked men suffered from a host of illnesses, including cholera, fever, malaria, tropical ulcers, and dysentery.) Johnson-Hill had sent one of his allotted mailcards to his wife via England ('home'), thinking it would be faster. In fact, it only delayed the card's delivery, and Pooh made reference to this in one of the few letters of hers he ever received. He could not contain his irritation.

Denghi fever has left me thank heavens, but I am feeling rather weak and am suffering from lack of sleep, chiefly due to your letters darling. I hate rows and recriminations but let me quote from your letters first. 'Did you imagine that I had gone home? I don't quite know when you thought I had been able to go, because you may remember that there was a little matter of having a baby which complicates traveling a bit', well darling I think that is hardly fair. I know I am only the father, but few fathers go through the torments of

14 months waiting to know if their wife is even alive or whether their baby is male or female. Enough jokes go on in peace time about fathers having to pace up and down the room for three or four hours, but how does that compare with 14 whole months under terrible conditions?
He then added pointedly:

When you complain darling of a rather dreary life of domestic duties with few parties etc you certainly make me laugh which is a good thing! Here we have all the fun that you miss my darling, work, work, work with 14,000 deaths of British troops and over 30,000 deaths amongst the conscripted groups of Tamils, Chinese and Malays.

All was forgotten by the time of the next entry, however, and Johnson-Hill focused on a much happier subject.

Yet another wedding anniversary darling with us not 'we' at all. It seems quite impossible to believe that we have been married 6 whole years. It seems much more like six months to me, so little have we seen of each other darling one. Have fever again, so will not add more to this now, but quietly think of you, Brian and Alan bless you.

Johnson-Hill could not know, of course, that the war would continue for almost another full year, but the ensuing months brought signs of hope. Allied warplanes were closing in on Japanese positions. Bombs could be heard in the distance like approaching thunder. As the Japanese tried to retreat further away from the air raids, they hurried the prisoners along from camp to camp, and it was harder for Johnson-Hill to keep up with his writing. The messages became increasingly sporadic, and entire months were skipped or summarized in hastily jotted sentence fragments. And then, after the atomic bombs were dropped on Hiroshima and Nagasaki, the word came that the POWs were finally free. In his last entry, Johnson-Hill's impatience to get home was palpable:

Wonder if there is any chance of us being together again this month ...
I suppose one shouldn't grumble about 30 days but Oh My God how I
long to see you again my darlingest one ... 1,100 officers left camp this
morning and some expected to leave today. Not me however.

Two months later, Johnson-Hill sailed on the USS Orduna into Liverpool, England, where his family was waiting for him, and he was personally able to give his wife the three small notebooks of letters he had been saving for almost four years. At the same time that Johnson-Hill was a prisoner of war secretly writing messages he could not mail, 10,000 miles away in San Antonio, Texas, a woman named Katherine Netting was addressing letters to her husband, a fighter pilot in Europe, not knowing if he would ever see them. 'Dearest Conrad: You may never read this, my darling, but I'm writing it because I want in some way to tell you all of the things that have happened since I got word of your being missing,' Katherine began her first letter to her husband. Conrad J. Netting III was a 26-year-old lieutenant in the 8th Air Force, US Army Air Corps who disappeared over France in June 1944, only days after the Normandy invasion. His wife went on to describe to him how she learned the awful news. 'I heard those fateful steps on the porch,' she wrote,

I couldn't get to the door at all, it seemed. And when the man asked me
'Mrs. Katherine H. Netting?', I knew for sure what I was about to
read. I took the book and very carefully signed Mrs. K.H. Netting
someplace. I'm sure I don't know where, but he handed the wire to me.
I turned away from the door and tore open the envelope very carefully.
And I didn't read it. I just looked to see Conrad J. Netting 'Missing'
'France' '10 June'. I think I sat in the large chair then, but I'm not sure.
I wandered around the room aimlessly for a few minutes then. I walked
back to Grannie's room and I noticed, as though I weren't myself, but a
third person watching myself in a dream, that I was shaking
terribly ... I can't think of you as any way but alive. And if they ever
do finally tell me that you aren't I shall never be able to accept it. I shall
never be able to remember you as anything but the most vivid, alive

person I've ever known. They could even show me pictures to prove it, and I will never believe it. It will be my cross, my curse, and my joy forever, that in my mind, you shall always be vibrantly alive as you were when I had you with me. I'm tired now, my darling, so I shall stop for this night.

Like Pooh Johnson-Hill, Katherine Netting was pregnant when she and her husband were separated by the war. Confident that it would be a boy, she and Conrad had already picked out the child's name before her husband left for Europe – Conrad John Netting IV. Lieutenant Netting even had his son's nickname, ConJon, painted on the side of his P-51 Mustang. On July 16, Katherine wrote to her husband about the birth of their first child.

Dearest Conrad –

Yes, my darling, Conjon came this morning at 5:50 ayem – O, Conrad, he is so much your son. His little nose is an exact duplicate of the one you arrived with according to your baby pictures. His hairline is the same and he has BIG feet and hands. They say at the hospital that he is the largest baby delivered that the night nurse ever saw – NINE POUNDS 4 OZ. I don't know how long he is but for comparison Butch weighed 6 lb, 12 oz and Barbara weighed 6 lb, and after a remarkable gaining tipped the scales a day or two ago at 9 lb, 2 oz. The nurses say he is going to be a very big man.

Just after I wrote a bit yesterday, the water broke. I called the hospital and they said I could wait until the pains (which hadn't started) were 10 min. apart. So the pains came and at about 6:45 I got Fanny and Mom and Dad and I went to the hospital. Fanny was expecting Tennille so she was to return. They got me all fixed and said the baby should be here about 12. About 10:30 the pains got a bit rough so I got some shot in the leg. That made me groggy and I barely remember seeing Tennille. About 11:30 they gave me the caudal and I immediately became numb from the waist down and sure enough, Conjon liked it that way so much he just stopped. I'm glad you weren't here for I'm afraid I wasn't nearly as brave as I planned to be. So they let the caudal wear off and I proceeded to urge him along the old-fashioned way. And it hurt! No kidding. Finally, it looked as though Conjon was going to be difficult so they gave me more caudal about 5. They waited for that to take effect good and then we went into the delivery room. As it is air conditioned, they had to wrap me in blankets. Major Seivers cussed and hollered and had to use emergency instruments. I asked him if the baby would be scarred. He nearly fainted. I got to hold him this morning, and he is the spitting image of you. If only I knew you were safe. How happy I would be. Thank you my darling for your son. I love you.

For almost seven months, Katherine waited for any word, any information whatsoever about her husband – whether he had been captured, critically injured, or killed, and, if so, whether or not his body had been recovered. The answer finally came on January 7, 1945, and one week later, Katherine wrote the following.

Dearest Conrad

Well, this shall probably be the last time I shall ever write these beloved words – Dearest Conrad – except perhaps to your son. Yes, I went to Corpus on the 7th and the next day Frances had word to call Charlotte. When she came out of the drug store, I could see she was upset. I immediately thought her father was worse. I was driving and I didn't say anything for a block or two. Then I asked if she wanted to stop for some bread. Then she sort of dropped her head and I reached over and patted her shoulder. She said, 'but it's not about me.' And I knew at once what it was. I drove on for a block or two – shocked and stunned and overcome – then I had a desire to be home with your son. I turned a corner and pulled over to the side and just caved in for a moment. It wasn't too long, darling, for uppermost in my mind was – and always will be – Conrad can see me now and I must make him proud of me. Fanny suggested I wait and talk to Tennille and so I stayed on and came home with them Saturday.

I feel so strange. I believe all the anguish – wild anguish – was spent when I first knew you were missing and might never return. Now I feel sad – empty – immeasurably lonely – and sick at the waste of so marvelous a life,

Katherine and Conrad J. Netting III

the waste of both our lives together. I know you are dead. First the wire – then the letter – now a condolence card from General Marshall, Chief of Staff – each throws another spadefull on your grave. But above all, I am resigned. I haven't 'cried' it out. I've shed tears, but not in abundance. And, although it is not what I prayed, dreamed, hoped for, I am making plans for my life – our lives without you.

I have talked to Charlotte regarding a ½ day job in her adv. agency. I will go to work as soon as she will take me on. I won't make much, but it will be something. But above all, I will be laying a firm foundation for a career. I could return to the govt but I want to take from my work more than money alone. I want security, a sense of accomplishment, a future, an interesting job, a pleasant one. As I learn, I can build something on my own hard work and I will. For I want Conrad to be proud of me and through me, of you. I also want him to have everything I can buy for him. I want to fill your shoes as I know you would have, if God had heard and answered my prayer that if one of us had to die, it would be me. So I shall work hard and long for our son, and I'll make him proud of all he has received from you. Before too long, I hope to put aside all your insurance and my pension and I will. On Tennille's advice, I will invest all the lump sum I receive over a $1,000 back in war bonds. I am going to write concerning that Socony Vacuum Policy, also. You left your family extremely well provided considering you were only 26 years and 3 days old.

I intend to see Sam in a week about a memorial service. Also, I will give something to the church in memory of the finest husband a girl ever had.

I intend to see about insurance on my own life for Conrad.

Darling, you know, I'm sure, how deeply I love you. I say love because I still do. I haven't stopped and I won't. Always, I love you as much as I did July 17, 1943, and all the days before and all the days since. I just can't stop. But, can you know the need I feel to marry again? When I look forward to emptiness after such happiness, I can't bear it. I hope God will let me be happy, not wildly, consumingly happy as I was with you, for I know I was amongst the chosen for having had you for a while. But quietly happy, the physical side is not so important, tho I will miss you so much – your hands, your kiss, your body. It is having no one interested in my life to the least detail that I miss tremendously. I want companionship – I don't want to live out my life – God knows, how beastly long I shall live – all alone for I'm afraid lest I be twisted, abnormally interested in Conrad or my work. I want a normal life, with a husband who knows my life was you. I believe if I ever should remarry, it will be long from now and to some older man who, too, has already known the greatest love. For me to marry a young boy – say Bob or Carl or anyone of that type – would be selfish. I believe all men are entitled to having a love such as I gave you. And I cannot give such love twice.

Well, my darling, from October 17, 1942 to June 10, 1944 or to January 8, 1945, really is a terrible, pathetically short time. Yet the love you gave me, the happiness, the joy, the magnificent son – could be copied in no one in a full lifetime. My dear, I am saying goodbye to you now – until we meet again. Please help me through the hard years to come, help me to do my best for your son and mine, help me keep alive your spirit by never being bitter. I need your help so – you may be dead to others, but you will live forever in my heart. I hate to stop writing for this is my last letter to you. O, my darling, how I love you.

Forever,
Your ~~wife~~
widow

In an extraordinary postscript to the story, 58 years after his father was shot down over France, Conrad J. Netting IV received an envelope in the mail with a French postmark. 'Dear Sir,' a woman named Sylvie Grandin wrote, 'My father is looking for more information about a brave soldier called Conrad J. Netting, killed in action, during the second world war in Normandy and buried in France.' Grandin was trying to find anyone related to Lieutenant Netting because her grandfather had witnessed the crash and raced to the site in hopes of aiding the fallen pilot. Netting was dead when he arrived, so the grandfather, who happened to be a cabinetmaker, made the casket that was used to bury him. He then tended to Netting's resting place until he himself passed away. His son (Sylvie Grandin's father) was also profoundly affected by Netting's death and proposed that a memorial be created in his honor in Saint Michel des Andaines, the town nearest to where his plane had crashed. On June 8, 2002, Lieutenant Netting's son, Conrad IV, and his family (including Conrad V), stood with the Grandins in Saint Michel and unveiled the plaque dedicated to the American pilot whose sacrifice had touched the lives of so many people.

—— FEATURED SERIES ——
'Letters to Mom'

Thakur Singh, a Sikh soldier fighting in World War I, assures his anxious mother that he will return to her — & — American Private First Class William Smith, serving in World War II, tells his mother that, with four sons in the war, she is the 'Best Soldier' and most courageous person he knows — & — Lieutenant Junior Grade Joseph Ball Crallé II, serving in the Solomon Islands during World War II, writes an emotional letter to his mom on Mother's Day, 1944 – the year after her death — & — An Italian soldier named Fiorigi A. Contro describes for his mother in graphic detail his terrifying escape from El Alamein, during World War II — & — A guilt-stricken Iraqi soldier, later killed during Operation Desert Storm, confesses to his mother that he believes he is destined for hell.

The two-paragraph letter by Lieutenant E.C. Victorsen, informing Mrs. Eula Owen on April 22, 1944, that her son had earned a commendation for valor, was written with only the best intentions at heart. 'I, as

Commanding Officer of the Guard Detachment,' the letter stated, 'together with each and every man belonging to it wish to convey our deepest appreciation for that honor instilled in it by such action as taken by your son.' The result could hardly have been more calamitous.

My dear Lt. Victorsen: Just a few hours ago I received your most gratifying letter concerning the commendations accorded my fine old boy – Richard Owen. I am at a perfect loss, though, in knowing what happened. I have not heard from him since a letter written 3/12/44 and received on 3/19/44. He isn't usually negligent in writing, but I was growing quite uneasy about not hearing from him when your letter came, and now I am frantic. Naturally, I have conceived the idea that he was in some manner injured and unable to write. You see, Lt. he is all I have. He is my life; my heart; my <u>all</u>. All my people have been taken from me except him and my mother, who will soon be 93 years and is failing fast. I have not told her of this yet, until I can know definitely his safety. Is it asking too much of you to let me know if he is safe and sound, also the details of his action. I can stand to know <u>bare facts</u>, but I cannot stand <u>silence</u> and <u>suspense</u> . . . I shall always treasure your letter. I expect to add below your message, an outline of the episode which sponsered it, frame it and hang it over the mantle. It came from your heart, your expressions held just the shade of meaning to show you were sincere in your appreciation and from the bottom of my heart, I thank you. But <u>please</u>, oh <u>please</u>, let me know about my boy.

In fact, Robert Owen was alive and well, and Lieutenant Victorsen would later express his regret for putting Owen's mother into such a state of alarm. Troops on the front lines are generally sensitive to the anxiety their own parents are experiencing and try to reassure them that they are not in danger – even if they are – and that there is no reason for concern. A Sikh soldier named Thakur Singh (whose fate is not known) sent the following message to his mother in Punjab, India, on June 7, 1916, while fighting with the British against German forces in Europe. ('Sirdar' is another term for an Indian officer; 'ghi' is a variation of 'ghee,' a form of clarified butter; and 'Khalsa' is the community of Sikh warriors into which males are initiated at puberty.)

71

Mother, the news is that once only in five months I have not received a letter from you. My thoughts are always with you.

Mother, put your ear down and listen to me, do not fret and I will soon be with you again. Put your trust in God, and imagine that I have merely gone to Lyallpur, think that I have been delayed there by the Sirdar or that I am not yet ready to return home. Mother, think of me always as though I were sitting near by, just as I imagine you always as being beside me.

Be of good cheer Mother, because there is nothing that I have done which is hidden from you. I tell you truly Mother, I will salute you again. Do not grieve, for I tell you confidently, that I shall bow before you again in salutation. I will come in the dead of night and knock at your door, and I will call loudly so that you may wake and come and open the door to me. With great delight you will open the door and fold me to your breast in a loving embrace. I will then sit beside you and narrate all that has happened to me of good and evil. Then, having rested the night in comfort, I will go out after daylight has come. Those brethren of the Khalsa whom I meet, I will salute. Returning home, I will eat my bread with pleasure and happiness. You, mother, will say to me 'Shall I give you some ghi?' I will shake my head in refusal and say 'Mother, I do not want any.' You will press me to have some, and I will gently push my plate towards you. You will fill the plate with ghi, and I shall eat it with much delight. Believe Mother that this homecoming will take place, just as I have described it. I see you constantly before me. It seems to me as if it were but yesterday that I bent to your feet in salutation, while you placed your hand lovingly on my head. I am indeed a very fortunate man to see you again so, in imagination.

Some mothers have not one, but two, or even several, boys to worry about. Allie Smith had four; Floyd and Charles in the Marines, Fred in the Air Force, and William in the Army, all fighting overseas during World War II. Three of them would come home. On January 4, 1945, William was killed during Hitler's last major offensive of the war, the Battle of the Bulge, which came just months before Germany ultimately surrendered. Less than four weeks before he died, William sent a letter to his mother simply to express his gratitude for her strength and love over the years.

December 5, 1944

Dear Mother,

I hope this will find everyone well.

I wrote to you on the third of December but as I am thinking so much about home to-night, I might as well write again. I would like to be there very much. I miss everything that goes along when I am there. Such as; talking about the old days, the good cooking, and all the love and little things that goes with a home. I miss all that very much.

I know you miss having all your children around too. Maybe it won't be long until we can all be together again. We can only keep praying for that.

I read in the papers about good soldiers but seldom read about the best soldiers. Those that are Mothers and Fathers of sons in the service. For my part, you are the best soldier I know. You fight a bigger problem than we do. You fight it with better courage too. With that courage in mind I will be able to fight my battles a lot easier.

I hope you won't worry too much about me. I am getting along just fine.

I must close before I get too homesick.

Tell everyone Hello for me.

Love & best wishes,

Your Son,

William

Either of their own volition or at the urging of their commanding officers, American servicemembers overseas customarily put pen to paper and send a special message home to mom on Mother's Day. (The special day itself was promoted tirelessly by Ann Maria Jarvis, who established Mother's Day Work Clubs in the late 1800s to foster unity between grieving Northern and Southern women who had lost their sons in the Civil War.) What is unusual about the letter that Lieutenant Junior Grade Joseph Ball Crallé II, a 27-year-old Virginian serving in the Solomon Islands, wrote on Mother's Day in 1944 is that his mother had passed away the year before. The pain of her death was still raw, and he felt compelled to write the following:

My darling Mother,

Wherever you are, I have a feeling you are watching me on this day, the first Mother's Day I can ever remember us being apart.

And I want to tell you on this, your day, that I stand as I am a tribute to your moulding. You guided me through many crises, you steered me clean of many pitfalls, you formed my habits and my personality. My very life is a monument to your untiring efforts, your never-ending thoughtfulness, your tender love.

I shall always be thankful that you were spared the agony and uncertainty of this period, of weeks without news of my safety and whereabouts.

But today I want you to know that I face the future with confidence and without fear, knowing that we have a job to do, that our cause is just, and that we shall be victorious.

And so I send my love, wherever you are, and know that we shall meet again somewhere, someday!

Your devoted son

Joe

Fathers are often the ones in whom troops are most likely to confide about the graphic violence of war or the severity of their own situation, and they will often do so with the admonition, 'Don't tell Mom.' But in times of great emotional distress, when perhaps sons fear showing weakness to their fathers or have perhaps reverted to an almost childlike state of vulnerability, they often appeal instead to their mothers for comfort and solace pouring out their feelings on paper. Fatally wounded soldiers on the field of battle are known to scream out for their mothers as they slip in and out of consciousness. It is a sound many veterans recall as one of their most searing auditory memories of warfare. During World War II, an Italian soldier named Fiorigi A. Contro escaped the crushing defeat of German and Italian troops at El Alamein, Egypt, by General Bernard Montgomery's British Eighth Army. Of the almost 70,000 casualties overall at the pivotal 1942 battle, more than 50,000 were Germans and Italians, and Contro came within inches of being one of them. After he was far removed from danger, he wrote the following to his mother describing the harrowing retreat.

To my mother,

You do not know how many difficulties I have encountered in my life; I won't tell you the ones you don't know, so as not to make you any sadder, but one memory among many remains stronger than the others.

It was a gloomy April evening, Palm Sunday. After a sudden, brief alarm caused by a group of approaching enemy fighter planes, we tried to take off from a makeshift airport. We made it out, but ten minutes later, a whole squadron of Junkers came flying in formation just above the surface of the water to prevent being detected by radar. We were attacked head-on by the planes, which were more nimble and better armed than we were, and in an instant we were completely overwhelmed and began to drop helplessly into the gulf one by one.

I felt bullets graze my back four times. Our plane was struck several times: in the engine, now on fire, in the nose, and in the tail.

A soldier in front of me became my shield and I got drenched in his blood. The pilot who gave the orders to jump had his intestines hanging out of his body.

The plane with its eighteen dead and wounded men on board was now on fire and losing altitude, and the only choice we had was to jump out as we had no parachute, just a life-jacket.

I was the first to get to the hatch and while I was hesitating about what to do I felt a strong push against my back, which knocked me out into the air and I fell into the water near Cape Bon.

I was terrified by the enormous danger I faced and still under the fire of machine-guns, I desperately struggled to reach the shore, which didn't seem too far away.

But when I got the water out of my mouth and caught my breath, I called out two names: 'God!' and 'Mamma!' I had never before been in such a situation.

By now I was exhausted and had no strength left. At that moment another plane was struck and crashed nose down with a deafening hiss right near me. . . I closed my eyes and thought I was going to die. I gave myself up to whatever God had destined for me.

But it wasn't my time yet, and the fiery mass fell so close to me that the giant surge of the wave pushed me to land like a cork. I sought shelter in a sort of cave, and stayed there nearly dead and exhausted, listening to the horrible sound of never-ending machine-gun fire from the airplanes.

I was found by the coast guard in very bad physical condition. Later I came to and woke up as though from a nightmare with my eyes full of tears. I described my long odyssey to the curious bystanders standing in a circle around me, who were stunned by what had happened.

But I really just wanted to be left alone so that I could replay in my mind a memory in which you, my dear, good mother, were the main figure.

You remember when I was little there was that big tank behind the country house, which we used for watering the neighborhood cattle? I was still in diapers, it was a beautiful spring day, and I went up to the tank to pick some little yellow flowers. I got close and stretched all the way out . . . and lost my balance and fell into the water. I screamed and you came running, my watchful and kind mother, and you carried me into the house and dried me off by the fire. You changed my little outfit and promised that you would stay close.

But your words and my promises were useless, because as soon as you turned around I ran out to the tank and fell in again. And you came running again and, gently, explained to me why I needed to be more careful and reproached me a little, and then told me to watch the chickens. One of them ran towards the tank, and I saw those little flowers that I had found so attractive, so, holding on to a reed, I stretched out my hand, but the reed broke, and I fell in the water again.

You collected me again with so much patience, and decided to carry me to bed where I fell into a deep sleep, dreaming of those flowers.

When I woke up, my little bed was heaped with yellow flowers; who had gone to pick them? 'Daddy,' you said.

Life takes such strange turns.

When I woke up in that unknown land after falling into the sea, I did not have the sweet comfort of flowers, only sad reality.

When I was a little boy I had no fear, and when I was hesitating in the fuselage hatch, when only a push from a friend gave me the courage to confront the danger, I couldn't count on your help because you weren't physically there to reassure me. But I know it was your hand that saved me from the wreckage. Your prayers every day and your faithful spiritual presence are always with me, reaching out to me wherever I am. Souls communicate! The force of a mother's care extends very, very far.

So this memory, which I will never forget, is for you. To you I give all my affection and love, and all my care, above everything else.

Fiorigi A. Contro

At Capua, near Naples 7 May 1943

It is not known what the Iraqi soldier did to prompt such an outpouring of shame in the following letter-poem to his mother (though considering the atrocities committed against Kuwaitis in 1990 and 1991, there are numerous possibilities), but he clearly felt the need to confess that he had betrayed his faith and would be punished for it. His letter, however, would never be sent; it was found on his body during Operation Desert Storm, the American-led multinational campaign to liberate Kuwait from Iraqi forces. (The last two quotations are from the Holy Qur'an. There is no signature to the letter, which, clearly written in a state of great mental turmoil, is incoherent in parts.)

Mother

What a lovely name!

Mother

How enchanting to hear your beautiful, calm voice. Will I hear your voice calling me once more?

Mother

I've never forgotten your face and your voice calls me each day in my sleep.

Mother

When am I to see your smiling face? Have mercy on me.

Mother

How I long to be embraced to your tender chest.

Mother

How much have you suffered and are still suffering for ten years.

Oh, Mother Mother Mother

Tell me about our home. How are my brothers? My longing and craving are increasing. Are they safe? Or have they gone to no return? to the day of my longing?

Oh, Mother

Please tell me because I know you are crying every now and then.

Mother

Please tell me. I hear crying, unable to sleep, longing so much for you.

Mother

Please tell me mother

Please pray to God to protect them.

I don't want him to protect me.

It satisfies me if he kept them safe for me.

Mother

Please have mercy on me. I know there is nothing you can do. Had it been in your hands you would have taken me out of hell.

Mother

Please ask God the Gracious, the Merciful to protect them. I don't want Him to protect me.

Mother

How is my poor father? I know he was burdened since the time we were born until this shameful black day. Any father would close a window that allows the wind to enter.

Mother

Tell me, is my father still waiting for me on the street corner, calling my name?

Give my regards to them until I see you once again, and if I don't, then it's sure I'll be in Hell. You will never see me. Our roads are different and God has no mercy on arrogant people.

If you don't see me, then this is God's promise Who has mercy on those who pray one day for them, another for me and to later on.

Mother

By God don't ask Him to have mercy on me. Don't ask Him to forgive my sins, because by doing that you'd hurt me. My God, since the day I was born until today, You denied me mercy and enrichment!

Mother

By God have mercy on me.

'In the Name of God, Most Gracious, Most Merciful. The sun and moon follow courses exactly computed . . . Then which of the favors of your Lord will you deny?' God, Most High, has spoken the Truth.

In the Name of God, Most Gracious. Most Merciful. 'They don't forbid what God and His Apostle forbid.'

American Corporal William D. Taylor, writing from the front in World War II, asks his newborn daughter, Edith Ann, to love her mom as much as possible while he is away – and to be especially good to her if he does not come back — & — Japanese officer Yanagida Eiichi confides to his wife that he becomes distraught when he thinks of the innocent children who might lose their fathers under his command during World War II — & — Heather Ashline, the wife of a US soldier fighting in Afghanistan, tells her husband that their two young boys miss him terribly and are always thinking of him.

For military parents serving abroad for extended periods, the separation from their children becomes all the more difficult when they cannot be there for special family moments and their child's significant 'firsts' – first steps, words, birthdays, etc. To nurture, as best they can, a presence in their children's lives, those far from home regularly send messages offering their affection, encouragement, and words of advice, even if their children are too young to understand or fully appreciate them. Corporal William D. Taylor, fighting in Europe during World War II, wrote frequently to his newborn daughter, Edith Ann, to express his love for her and to impart words of fatherly wisdom, all with the realization that any one of his letters could be his last. Taylor had never held or even seen his daughter, however, as he was overseas when she was born. Edith Ann was still an infant when her father sent the following on January 14, 1944:

My darling daughter,
This letter is coming many miles away from you dear, but even tho miles do separate us I'm always thinking about you as I do your Mother. Now, your to young to understand this, but someday you'll be able to read it and understand what I mean. Your Dad was called away dear to do a job and which at present is being done very well. When I left home I left a million dreams behind me. The most important your mother and secondly even tho at the time you wasn't born yet, I left you. Its not easy for a fellow to leave things like that behind, take your father's word for it. What I'm trying to say is right now and forever your Mother is the swellest Mom alive. Chances are you may never see your Pop, so here's what I ask. Never leave your Mother.

Always respect her and love her, she was made for it dear. I love Mom more than anyone or anything this world can offer. When I do come back your Mom, you, and myself are going away where we can be by ourselves. All the happy hours Mom and I use to spend will now be enjoyed by you also. For this reason alone your Mom and I fought. I'll sign off now dear, and before I do, ask Mom to set this letter aside for you. Be a good girl and give my love to Mom.   Love and kisses,

> Daddy

William Taylor returned home to Jersey City, New Jersey, after nearly four years abroad, but he would never speak of his war experiences and he kept his letters hidden. Edith Ann did not read the letter her father wrote to her in January 1944 until after his death in 1999 at the age of 76. Edith Ann was 55 years old. For many troops away from their families, the mere sight of other children is enough to induce a powerful surge of emotions. 'Tasya, if only you knew how overjoyed I am when I see children the same age as Maya,' wrote a Russian lieutenant named Sergei Galkin to his wife before he died in World War II.

> I think about how I have a daughter just like them who hasn't seen her papa for 10 months already, and he hasn't see her. The children in liberated areas jump into the arms of the fathers who have liberated them from Hitler's cannibals. I guess Maya does the same – jumps into the arms of other soldiers and wonders where her papa is. That's why I write about Maya so much. My soul lights up when I meet a child here and he hangs from my neck asking where is our papa and when is he coming home.

For a Japanese lieutenant who was also fighting in World War II, the responsibility he bore for the lives of his men, and the recognition that each death would inevitably traumatize a young son or daughter, weighed heavily on him. Thirty-three years old at the time, Yanagida Eiichi sent the following message, which is not dated and does not have a salutation, to his wife before he and his men embarked. (Eiichi himself was later killed in battle.)

80

Thank you for writing so often, and forgive me for not responding sooner. Mobilization and organization have kept me busy every day, from 5:00 in the morning until midnight.

Yesterday, most of the work was completed. Today was visiting day, and confusion reigned. Some of the soldiers were holding babies in their arms. Others were leading small children by the hand as they headed out, perhaps for a brief excursion. Will my men be separated from their families for only a short time, or forever? When I see the innocent children, I get a lump in my throat. The knowledge that I am responsible for the fates of several dozen subordinates weighs heavily on my shoulders.

Is Kyoko feeling any better? I may be asking the impossible, but please do all you can to ensure that her illness is cured promptly, no matter how much it costs. I worry about her all the time. Whatever the case, please take good care of her until I return.

Take care of yourself, too, and don't ruin your health by working too hard. Please take care of Kyoko.

Also, please write to my mother in the country once in a while (about twice a month). I've caused her a lot of worry. At least while I'm away, look after her on my behalf. Please be sure to take care of Kyoko.

Please convey my best wishes to your mother, brother and sister.

Spouses on the home front see firsthand the emotional impact the absence of a father or other family member has on the children, and they frequently emphasize to their loved ones how dearly they are missed. Writing from Saigon in 1962–3, the wife of a South Vietnamese officer, serving with the Americans, reminded her husband that she and their children, Tram and Hao, were thinking of him always. (Her full name and parts of the letter have been cut for reasons of privacy. The letter was found in 2004 at an antiques store in what is now Ho Chi Minh City, and the officer's fate is unknown.)

My love, I miss you so much, I miss you so much my love . . . Tram speaks of you all day, making my soul feel lonelier. She misses you so much that she refuses to let anybody sit in your dinner chair and says, 'Dad's chair is saved for him, so that when he returns he can sit there.' If anyone made fun of her, she just replies 'I'll tell my Dad, just you see.' At night, she tosses and turns. Hao is no less than her, every evening he makes a fuss, asking to be taken out like Dad used to do for him. If I knew things were going to be so desolate without you, I would have never let you leave, even if your trip brings us many glories and benefits. . . I had wanted not to write to you, I had wanted not to miss you, yet I still write and miss you. . . Just a few lines to you, since I have not received my letters, so I know not what else to write. The children and I give you many kisses.

In December 2001, Heather Ashline sent a remarkably similar letter to her husband, Jason, a private first class with the 10th Mountain Division fighting in the mountains of Afghanistan against al-Qaeda and Taliban forces. Their eldest son, Jason II, was two-and-a-half, and their youngest, Alec, was only three months old.

Hey Babe,

Jason is constantly thinking about you. He talks to you on the phone (pretending) and makes your mother and I do it too, he plays with you (pretend again) and he will ask about you. When we went home, he asked if we were going to go pick you up. When I said no, he said he wanted to. I don't think there's a minute when he isn't thinking about you. He's even trying to teach Alec to say 'Dada.' It's a little early, but we still try.

Tonight, Alec was staring at a picture of you on your mother's fridge. He was just fixated on it. Don't you worry about him knowing you, he'll remember. Now, let's talk about me. I love you, and nothing will ever change that. You have brought so much happiness into my life, and I'm not just talking about the two beautiful boys you gave me. I know in the past we've had some hard times, and there were moments when we almost let each other go, but our love was still there holding us together. That will stand true while we're apart and always. When we got married, I vowed to love you forever, and I plan to. We still have plenty of time to make our life together; we just have to wait a little while. Everyday I think about you coming home and how much I want to be able to hold you, touch you, see you come through the door after work. I miss cooking you your meals, dragging you out of bed in the morning, and kissing you goodnight at the end of every day. I need you in my life. Without you I would be lost, I wouldn't know how to carry on. If I ever lost you for any reason, my world would shatter. I'm going to go now; I'm exhausted. I love you.

Love Always,
Heather

During a major clash with enemy combatants, Private First Class Jason Ashline was shot in the chest. Fortunately, his Kevlar vest prevented him from being killed, and he returned to the USA alive and well.

Lawrence Hoppner, an Australian private fighting in the Vietnam War, exchanges a series of letters with his sweetheart, Lorraine Woodward, who is anxiously awaiting his return to Melbourne.

Over a 12-year period beginning in 1961, when President John F. Kennedy ordered 2000 military advisors to the region, the USA sent approximately 3 million troops to fight against North Vietnamese and Viet Cong forces in Southeast Asia. The Americans did not go it alone, however. Along with the native South Vietnamese and Montagnards (mountain people from the Central Highlands), hundreds of thousands of soldiers from South Korea, Thailand, the Philippines, New Zealand, and several other countries also participated in the war. (Thousands of Canadians joined up with US military units, although Canada itself was not an official ally. Some of the troops joked that they were filling in for the Americans who went to Canada to escape the draft.) More than 50,000 Australian soldiers served as well, and one out of every hundred of them died. The conflict remains the longest war, to date, in Australia's history. In February 1966, a 20-year-old private named Lawrence (nicknamed 'Laurie' and then later 'Hoppy') Howard Hoppner from the state of Victoria was called up for national service. While on leave during recruitment training, Laurie began dating a 19-year-old girl named Lorraine Woodward whom he had met in a café in Melbourne. (Actually, Laurie had struck up a conversation with both Lorraine and a friend of hers named Anne, and he decided to pursue Anne first. While literally in the process of writing her a letter, he received a birthday card from Lorraine and spontaneously decided to cross out Anne's name and scribble in Lorraine's instead. The relationship blossomed from there.) Laurie and Lorraine wrote regularly to each other after he left for Vietnam in April 1967 as a forward scout with the 7th Battalion, Royal Australian Regiment, A Company, and their correspondence is unique in that many of her letters ultimately survived the war. Frontline troops are rarely able to save even their most cherished letters from home, but Lorraine's letters endured despite the humidity and filth of jungle combat. A letter by Laurie of May 8, 1967 offers a vivid reminder of how treacherous the conditions truly were. (VC refers to the Viet Cong.)

> Hi love. Well I have just come back from a 7 day exercise & have finaly realized just how dirty war can be. Our company came back all in one piece but don't know about the others. We killed 3 VC & wounded several others . . . Our first night we were in an ambush on the edge of a river & we slept in the middle of a swamp. There were millions of mosquitoes & on top of that it poured rain all night. We walked through swamp for 5 days & were we cheesed off; we were covered in mud & wet through the whole time still not to worry. One thing is for sure we are far superior than they & as well we have them on the run. Any how darling never worry as we are never in any real danger as we have support of artillery & fighters which are available ~~wh~~ within a couple of minutes. . .

Lorraine took him to task for the comments about his safety. 'You say not to worry,' she wrote incredulously. '<u>Not to worry!</u> You have to be kidding. I worry all the time, whether I know you are on an Op[eration] or not.' Her anxiety was growing with every report on the radio and television or mention in the newspapers about Aussie troops *in Vietnam. On July 14, Lorraine sent the following. (Her expression 'going to the pack' is another way of saying 'going crazy.')*

My dearest darling,

Hi darling. Have just read in tonight's herald about 2RAR 7RAR & the Yanks are all out on the biggest operation the Australians have been on yet. According to the paper it states you have been out 5 days.

I was beginning to worry why I haven't heard from you for so very long (over a week). I was starting to think that perhaps you were still in Saigon on leave and wouldn't hear from you again, or perhaps you had found yourself a nice little Viet. girl and had gone off. Terrible thoughts of mine don't you think?

Nothing much has happened around this place. All very boring really.

Tomorrow night, Sue & I are going to a Cabaret with Bluey & Jack for the Mordialloc Football Club. I suppose it should be quite good. Quite a lot of grog, probably too much. As for the rest of the weekend I probably won't be doing anything or going anywhere, so actually I will be having a very quiet weekend, and I will be able to lay around & dream & think of you.

I had a dream last night. It was about when you came home. It was really a beautiful dream. I can remember you kissing me for the first time since you went away & was I in heaven. The trouble was that the dream ended with a bump. Mum woke me up to tell me it was time to get up for work. I'm always having dreams like this. Hardly a night goes by without me dreaming something nice about you. It proves that I go to sleep thinking of you each night. And what better way than to go to sleep thinking of you.

I worried, really worried darling. More than ever, of you, if you're out on this big operation. I'm scared of how this rotten so called War will leave you. I don't mean physically, but more so mentally. If you get what I mean. You might come home too mature & think of things in different ways to what you thought of them when you left Me. You might change your mind about me too. If you haven't already.

Maybe, these are silly female thoughts of mine, but they are still worrying me. But more than ever, I worry about your health. I couldn't bear to have anything happen to you, so please darls look after & take care of yourself always. No matter where you are, please oh please, look after yourself.

I still haven't written to your Mum yet. She must think me terrible. I've really grown idle when I'm at home. I can't be bothered doing anything at all, except sit & watch T.V. I have two frocks cut out, waiting for me to finish, but I just can't be bothered. All I want to do is write letters to you and I'm even slipping there abit. I'm going to the pack I think. A real wreck. Not that I wasn't before you left, but more so now, & the trouble is I don't really care.

I've had a long black evening frock made up. It has black beading all down the front, a low neck line, a low back. I really think it's lovely, as I simply adore black.

Have you received the fruit cake yet? If not you should have. It's been gone over three weeks now.

Well darling. This is it again. Please look after & take care of yourself always, as I will take care of myself. Only the good go young & I'm far from being good, as you know.

I love you so very, very, much & miss you just as much.

Will write again over the weekend. So until then, I close for now.

> I remain,
> Yours forever &
> All my life
> Lots, lots of love & kisses
> Lorraine

xxxxxxxxxxxxxxxxxxxxxxxxx

Laurie responded soon after to put to rest any doubts concerning his love for her, but the remainder of the letter would certainly do little to assuage her fears about the hazards he was facing.

My dearest darling

Hi love, received another wonderful letter from you last night so are taking the opportunity to answer it today. When you are not getting any mail from me darls you can be rest assured it is because I am out on an Opp, ambush or patrol I nor any one else is allowed to write to say what we are doing as sometime if mail gets into the wrong hands it can cause a lot of trouble.

That is why my letter may stop all of a sudden. So I have said before darls I will write every chance I get I hope your Cabaret at the Mordialloc football

Private Lawrence Hoppner

club went off O.K. Another thing darls I will would never go off as you say over any Viet girl or any one else for that matter you should know that darls I quite often or actually nearly am always dreaming of you & me. of all the times we have spent together & of the times we will spend together.

I was on that big opp & there were over 200 confirmed VC. killed but we didn't do very much it was a real easy opp. As for me coming home more mature well I am sure I will but it will be for the best that I can assure you darls.

Now for the not so good part. You say I might change my mind about you if I hadn't done so all ready.

I am very disappointed in you for saying that love You should know by now ~~the~~ that you are the only person for me now & forever. Those thoughts ~~nevr~~ never even enter my head I know they never will I fully realize it is difficult me being over here & so much distance between us but bear for a little while longer darls. its only another 18–20 weeks before I am with you again.

Well darling thats about all there is for now so until my next letter.

All my Love
All my life
Yours Forever
Laurie

xxxxxxxxxx

On August 7, less than three weeks later, Lorraine received a phone call from Laurie's mother. Laurie had been hit by shrapnel and shot during a firefight. He had already been evacuated to a US military base hospital in Vung Tao, and despite the severity of the wounds, the medical staff indicated that there was every reason to believe he would pull through. Not knowing for certain his condition, Lorraine wrote him the following letter. (Jan and Bern are Laurie's sisters, and 'Flinders St.' refers to a railway station in central Melbourne.)

My dearest, dearest, darling,
Your Mum rang early this morning to tell me the bad news, but alas, I had left for work and so Mum had to talk to her and didn't catch everything your Mum said. So Mum rang me at work at 9:00 am but I hadn't arrived by then, & when I did get to work I got the message to ring Mum back. I knew

straight away that something was wrong either with you or Dad. I rang her back straight away, and when she told me she had a phone call from your Mum about you I just broke down.

Have just heard on the wireless that five boys were killed & later one died of wounds and fifteen others wounded, but no names have been ~~real~~ released.

Oh darling, why did it have to be you to be one of the injured. Why. I just can't understand it. How I hate the Army, the government & anyone whom has anything to do with it.

I love you so very very much. I don't know what to do. I feel so sick and upset, even worse since I've heard the news bulletin.

I met your Mum in Flinders St. and after we got her to 'Traveller's' Aid we rang up the Army where you can get news. He told me there was no more news, but will ring either one of us, when he gets more news. But I intend to ring him quite alot each day. He also said that there is a good chance you will be sent home. I hope so, I really hope so. They have got to send you home. We couldn't stand anymore of this. I want to be with you darling & I cant be, when you are over there.

I feel so confused & sick, I can't think what to write. My stomachs all tied up in knots. I don't think your mother or I will be getting much sleep tonight, or any other night, until we know for sure, that you aren't too badly injured. Also Bern & Jan.

Please get well soon Darling, please. I want & need you so very, very much. Please get well. I love you so much & want you so much. They just have to send you home. They've got to. Just have to.

Get well please darling. I can't think straight anymore. You just have to get better. I've got to see you soon or I'll go mad.

The rotten, stinken' government & Army. I hate the bloody lot.

I am waiting for the news to come on the radio again to see if there's any more news. Also will watch the late news at 10 10 pm or Channel 2 as they might know more.

Sue has just rang me to see if I found out any more & she told me she has sent a telegram over to Ron to let him know that you were injured, so by the time you get this you should have had a visit from him. Have you seen Paul?

Don't worry about answering this letter darling as I know how things will be with you.

Please get well darling. I love you so very, very much & want you. I'll pray and hope with all my heart that you weren't ~~hert~~ hurt too badly and that they send you home soon.

I'll close for now, my love and only love. Hope to see you soon. My love, thoughts and wishes are with you always darling.

Please get well darls. I love you and am thinking of you always

All my love

All my life

I remain

Yours forever & ever

Lorraine

xxxxxxxxxxxxxxxxxxxxxxxxx

<u>PS</u> Please get well. I love and miss you very, very much.

A week after his injury, Laurie was finally able to attempt a letter home. (Lynn is Lorraine's younger sister.)

VIET NAM

13/8/67

My dearest darling Lorraine,

Hi darls this is my first ~~thr~~ try at writting. By now you will have received my tape, I know it sounded shocking. I received your tape & cake yesterday.

I can not put into words how I felt when I heard you voice again

My right hand has been stitched up. There is 8 stitches on the back of my thumb is a bit of a mess I may not be able to bend it for some time a bullet went through a knuckle. I had 24 stitches on my right side of my head. 2 stitches in my cheek. 4–6 on my right shoulder.

I don't know what my back is like but I know there is quite a hole in it but don't worry darling I will be as fit as a fiddle in a few weeks.

They have just brought 3 letters & a card to me so will stop the letter & read them. Back again there was a card & letter from you & a letter from Lynn.

I will be very surprised if you can read this as it's hard to write. I was very lucky darling & have never come so close to death befor. We were pinned down for nearly 1 1/2 hrs it is one experience I will never forget.

Any how darling one good thing is I am coming home. I am due to leave here on the 28th of August so I should arrive back in Australia by the 1st Sept.

It will take up to a week before I am sent down to Melb. There I will stay until I am completely cured. You should see some of the Yanks here some are shot up real bad. There are about 50 patients in this ward I am the only Australian

The other Aussies are in different wards. 3 are being sent home today & rest of us are going in a fortnight, wont it be wonderful to be home again

We will be able to get engaged a lot earlier & married as soon as I get out of the Army. I saw Paul yesterday he was the one who brought your parcel in He is quite well & also looking forward to when he goes home.

Well my darling that about does it for now I doubt if you could read this. I love you darling & miss you so very much, hoping this finds you in the best of health & spirit.

> All My Love
> All My Life
> Your Forever & ever
> Laurie
> xxxxxxx
> xxxxxxx

Lawrence Hoppner was home in Australia within three weeks, and he and Lorraine married the following March. For his service in the military, Hoppner received one Australian Vietnam medal, one Vietnam Campaign medal, one Australian Active Service medal, and one Australian National Service medal.

In a letter to his brother E. J., British Captain Denis W. Boyd lauds the courage of his crew on the *HMS Illustrious* during World War II — & — Stunned by the death of a close friend during the Iraqi War, American Specialist Christopher Hurd confides to his mother how profoundly he has been hurt by the loss — & — American Sergeant Justin Merhoff, fighting in the Iraqi War, tells his grandfather about the assignment he has volunteered for and how it has affected his perception of the military and those who serve.

Despite the longstanding rivalries between the different service branches within the armed forces and the intensity with which troops can bicker and fight among themselves (not unlike real siblings), active duty personnel can develop a loyalty to one another that transcends family relations. When they go into combat, they put their lives into the hands of their fellow soldiers, marines, airmen, and sailors, and this dependency creates a closeness unlike any other. And, notwithstanding the stoicism and reserved demeanor they tend to project in public, no individuals write with greater emotion about the sacrifices made by those who serve in the military than their comrades-in-arms. During World War II, a US Army sergeant named Bernard Paul Lyons remarked to his wife, Agnes, on the perserverance of the young soldiers he had witnessed battling entrenched German forces in Europe. '[The fighting] gets plenty tough up there at times,' he wrote,

> *[and] calls for plenty of what it takes and costs heavily in precious life and limb. But soldiers of the line see it through. Guys who used to put gas in your car or clerk in the stores you bought your meats and groceries, who worked in the offices and factories, or who used to plough the good earth of our farms. . . I'm talking about soldiers now – soldiers of the line – officers and men of the infantry regiments and those units attached to them as combat teams. All those men up there in the fox holes facing the enemy only a few score yards away. Say a little extra special prayer for those guys every time you can, too, will you?*

Men of the sea enjoy their own sense of solidarity, particularly when they – like British Captain Denis W. Boyd and his ship the HMS Illustrious – *have narrowly averted catastrophe. On January 10, 1941, Boyd and his crew suffered a withering air raid that almost sent the* Illustrious *and everyone on board to the bottom of the ocean. Three weeks after the attack, Boyd sent the following short letter to his brother.*

31 Jan 1941

My dear old E.J.

Just a line to tell you that your Godchild HMS Illustrious who has never done anything by halves has come through 14 days of the biggest hell that could be imagined and with flying colours too. We are not quite what we were and we lost 136 dead and 146 wounded but we lived through a straffing greater than that ever given to a ship in history. Tell Ormston that we are still more proud of our ship now. We are not out of the wood yet but are better off than we were and hope to be able to tell you all about it as soon as we are allowed.

Of your friends all came out safely and not only safely but heroicly. Bill was supreme and although shocked and blasted nearly out of his senses we kept our terrific gunfire going through ten bald headed attacks on us alone. Baker too was grand and Russell & Tosswill & Ducks. Our little Joyce Keevil steeped in blood from head to foot kept going through ten ghastly hours and with the other doctors who were equally good succeeded in saving many otherwise certain deaths. Young Peter Gregory Elizabeths favourite was killed. He was helping the wounded when we were hit again and a splinter hit his spine. He knew at once he was dead and just asked for morphia. His last words to me were when he came to the bridge after our first blitz and said oh thank God you are safe sir. He was worried because a bloody great bomb went off twenty ~~flee~~ feet from me and he expected us all to be dead. How any of us escaped is a miracle. I must say we have seen life since we came out here and even if we were sunk we would still be quids in on the enemy as we have made a fearful nuisance of ourselves. I have had letters and signals of congratulations from everyone out here on the show we put up this time. The C in C himself said that the most wonderful sight was this ship burning from bow to stern helm jambed steering in circles but still firing every gun at yet another attack. I took her in steering by the engines and we then had a series of terrific attacks in harbour. I tell you it was just frantic. But by God's good grace we have survived and please God we shall be back on the job before long.

Give Marion my love and Jolette. I saw Les at Suda and he took back about a hundred weight of stores. Saw chisels plates nails knives forks spoons I was facing having to pay for the latter but now they have been conveniently lost in the battle. Les looked grand & very happy. All send their respects God bless you.

Your D W

That sense of camaraderie is not limited to bygone eras; active duty personnel continue to express heartfelt sentiments about their fellow troops in their correspondences home. In the spring of 2003, a US Army specialist named Christopher Hurd wrote to his mom from Kuwait about the death of Captain Christopher Scott Seifert, who, like Hurd, was with the 101st Airborne. Seifert's death was a stark example that relations between servicemembers are by no means immune to tension and outright hostility; on March 23, 2003, as American troops prepared for the ground campaign into Iraq, a US Army sergeant named Hasan Akbar, who had purportedly been overheard voicing anti-American statements before the invasion, tossed several grenades into the tents of other soldiers at Camp Pennsylvania in Kuwait and fired off numerous shots from his rifle. More than a dozen troops were seriously wounded, and, along with Chris Seifert, a US Air Force major named Gregory Stone was killed in the late-night assault. Seifert and Hurd had been close friends, and in his letter home, Hurd revealed both the depth of his pain and his attempt to forge something positive out of the loss.

Hey mom,

The loss of Cpt. Seifert has left a void, not only in our little group, but within our hearts as well. As soldiers and men we seldom if ever let our peers know how much they mean to us, until it is too late. I loved Cpt Seifert, as a soldier, as a man and as a friend. I remember the first day I met Chris, for some reason or another I was the only one running that morning when he first showed up. We ran together chatting and getting to know one another, right away I took a shine to him. Seldom in my travels or my life for that matter does one meet someone as special as Chris; needless to say I liked him from the first day.

I wept a great deal when I found out we had lost Chris. I was working late when it happened, I remember saying good-night to Cpt Seifert, and making some off handed joke, just to get one of those Chris Seifert smiles (anyone who knew him knows the smile I'm talking about); never once thinking that would be the last time I would ever see him. The events of that night will live with me forever, as well as the good friend that was lost to me . . . to us.

However if one flower sprung from the ashes of that night, it is for me this: never let the love you hold for someone go unappreciated, for life is too damn precious and short. Do not shelter that love until it is too late, for what good is a candle if you shield the light, instead let the light out feel the warmth and let it illuminate your way. Chris will live with me in my heart for the rest of my life, and so will the lesson of these events.

Love,
Chris

The bond between those in the armed forces extends intergenerationally as well. While serving in the Middle East during Operation Desert Storm, United States Marine Corps (USMC) Private First Class Raymond Ortiz received some words of support from a family friend named Edward J. Moore, a 66-year-old veteran who had fought at Guadalcanal, Tarawa, and Okinawa during World War II. 'Ray Sr. informed me of your being sent where you are and I wasn't surprised of that movement,' Moore began his letter.

As I may have told you more Marines on a percentage basis go overseas than any other branch. Of course you remember the words from our Marine hymn 'We have fought in every clime and place – that we could take a gun . . .' Your deployment bears that out very well. Needless to say I am proud of you and all your comrades-in-arms. I tried to be there but the 'old man' told me to sit this one out. Damn it!! You carry on for me as I know you and all the other Marines will do an A-One job out there. As far as being scared and/or apprehensive, I understand very well ... Don't you and your buddies worry about your feelings. Those before you and me, that made Marine Corps tradition what it is, also went through their moments of doubt. Keep your butt below ground during an incoming attack and you'll be O.K. Take care dear friend and let me hear from you from time to time. Semper Fidelis.

Conversely, younger generations of men and women who join the military often develop a greater appreciation for older veterans, particularly within their own families. In November 2004, a 24-year-old US Army sergeant named Justin Merhoff, serving in Iraq, handwrote the following letter to his grandfather, Hugh Merhoff, a World War II veteran. Justin had been designated the Non-Commissioned Officer in Charge (NCOIC) of an assignment that deepened his understanding of the sacrifices made by his contemporaries, as well as by those, like his grandfather, who had served before them. (Kari is Merhoff's wife, and Brandon is their newborn son.)

Dear Gramps,

I want to write you and let you know what I am doing these days. I found out that my unit was responsible for manning five of the twenty-two funeral honors teams that represent the 10th Mountain Division. I know this might sound a little morbid, but I really wanted to be on one of those teams so I volunteered myself, something you do not normally do in the Army, as you know from your own experiences in the military.

Since I've never been to a funeral before, I did not know what to expect. There were times that I had to try not to cry after seeing the family go through the turmoil that death brings. These emotions were new to me and were hard to take at first. All of the funerals are sad in their own way, but one in particular was for a Polish-born soldier who only had his sister there. A few times we were told that we were requested to perform honors and then told that the family members had changed their minds. I guess that it is either too hard for them to handle or they do not like the fact that the person who died fought in a war they don't agree with.

Every time I have performed honors for these fallen soldiers, I have gotten different degrees of response, from a handshake and a thank you to an invitation to eat with the family. These people thanked us for being there, and I thanked them for enabling me to honor their family member. I think that is why we are there – to help the families come to peace with the passing of these great men and women. What really got me was that there were guys who were not U.S. citizens but were fighting for our country. I might never have met these soldiers, but they are all my brothers and sisters in arms. We will forever, even in death, be bound to each other by our service to our country.

I know that not everyone agrees about war and the military, but my personal belief is that every man and woman who has fought for this country should be honored, both in death and in life. Before 9-11, there were people who did not respect those who serve. I did not even feel comfortable going off post in my uniform. Now I think the country as a whole has changed and most people I talk to respect us. Some questioned why I was serving with all that is going on over in Iraq, but most of the time the response is supportive.

During my time as the NCOIC of my funeral team, I have met a lot of people with great stories about their years in the service and the soldiers we are there to honor. I do not know which unit he served under, but I was also intrigued when I found out that one older veteran we buried was African American and had served during World War II. He fought for a country that at the time would only recognize him as a second-class citizen due to the color of his skin. In my eyes, if you are willing to fight for our great country, you should be treated as a hero, no matter your race, sex, or religious beliefs. I wished I were able to thank him in person, but I hope that by being there to represent the Army he fought in will be enough for the great sacrifice he made as a young man.

A lot of the funerals were for married men, and their wives were there mourning their death. With what is going on in Iraq and Afghanistan and with the chances of me going over there soon being high, I thought of what Kari might feel if something happened to me. Brandon would be too young to understand. At another funeral for a Jewish veteran a man had to bury his father. Regardless of when I die, I hope Brandon will have kind words for me such as this man had for his father.

This whole experience has helped me better understand what happened during World War II, Korea, and Vietnam, and the sacrifices made by those who served honorably – and by their families. I know that you say you do not consider yourself a veteran because you were drafted and did not see action. You used the time you served to your advantage and became a doctor. You saved countless lives. Maybe you were not meant to fight. You are the reason I am in the Army today. You instilled in me the values that you learned during your service, and it has made me a better soldier. Most important, it has made me a better person.

Love,
Justin

LINES OF FIRE

Letters of Combat

No doubt you must have thought that I have forgotten you altogether. If such thoughts have entered your head I hope you will forgive me, for I have been very bad even now my hand is all in a tremble. I have had some marvellous escapes.I got wounded in my leg with pierces of shell but only flesh wounds. I have had my hat shot off a couple of times and felt for the blood, but the nearest was when I got hit on my cheek with a bullet cutting it with the blood all over my tunic, and another bullet took all the hairs of my eye brow just leaving a little scratch, very strange it was just then when we see blood your own blood when you get right in the thick of it, of course I got into some scrapes and thank God that I am alive to tell the tale. It was simply dreadful at times. Fancy living amongst shell and bullet nights and days with out sleep. It use to turn me sick at times to see the dreadful pieces of human bodys lying about, with a head rolling without a body legs and arms all over the place, often I have taken cover behind our own dead, as the Turk was having a shot at you, the bullet would plunk in the body in front of you; Oh Gill this was Hell on Earth for if Hell can be worse, but I really think it can't be worse.

> *Frederick C. Trenne, a soldier from New Zealand, writing on January 12, 1916, to his friend G. Harry Gillespie about the fighting at Gallipoli during World War I.*

Eleven o'clock had just struck, when my attention was attracted by repeated bursts of machine-gun fire. I soon saw three planes right above my head: one French, two German. The fight was going on for about half an hour when suddenly I saw the French plane turn all over, a black body came out of the plane and descended slowly. It was the airman falling, but I thought at first it was like a bird, so slowly was he coming down. Later on I understood my mistake: his coat had opened, acting somewhat like a parachute. He had his arms stretched out and hit the ground feet first. He had fallen in a small pond, not deep and frozen. The ice was broken but his body was not in the water. The Germans arrived soon, and with some hooks took him to the bank. Tuesday morning he was put in a coffin. On his grave they put a cross, made from a propeller. More than once I brought flowers, but the Germans forbade it, and always took them away. I don't know why.

> *Jean Thuiller, a French woman, writing on August 26, 1928, to the parents of Flight Lieutenant Harry R. Wambolt, describing the fate of their son during World War I.*

As the lone farmhouse was the only possible place for any Krauts to be, the Lieutenant sent out just one squad to clear it should it need clearing. Five of the six of us who went had never even seen a live German soldier. We ran into three Jerries in the farmyard one of whom tried to hide in a half-filled rain barrel, of all places. I'll never forget the neat triangle of holes Joe's tommy gun put in that barrel! I was almost hypnotized as I watched the water change gradually pink and then red as it spouted out the oaken bullet holes. As we started off across the fields I glanced back at the rain barrel. A dog sniffed warily at marshy ground around it. A large rooster, which had disappeared in a flurry of feathers such a short time ago, now crowed defiantly at the world.

> *Maitland Livsey, an American corporal writing from France on February 25, 1945, during World War II, to his father back in Portland, Oregon.*

Hello All! I'm sure your thoughts and concern are for us in Saudi, but we are fine. Keep watching the news and you'll see more action than myself. I'm sorry for not being able to call you but the first chance I get I will call. Please take care and don't worry. You don't realize that our unit is well out of danger. John

> *Twenty-six-year-old Sergeant John Madden, US Marine Corps Reserve, with the Eighth Tank Battalion, TOW Company, writing to his parents and relatives in Florida from Saudi Arabia on February 16, 1991 during the Gulf War.*

Dear Mike & Minnie! I've received a total of 3 letters from Ron & Louis from Canton, also I've received a letter from that lady who roomed with Sheila. I'm amazed at their concern. So far it is going fine. All is cool, and we train daily for our mission. I'll be honest in respect as to your concern. The flies are huge! Tell Mary K and Greg I said Hi! I should be home soon. See ya later, John This goes no further! Seriously.

> *Madden, writing on the same day of the Iraqi War to both his brother and sister-in-law. 'The flies are huge!' was a pre-arranged code Madden had given only to his brother – as he did not want to worry their parents – to indicate that a land battle against Iraqi forces was imminent. 'Tell Mary K and Gregg. I said Hi!' was code for the fact that Madden would, in fact, be near the front of the invasion and very much in danger. (He survived the war.)*

Writing to his father after the first shots of the American Revolution were fired, Samuel Bard articulates his fears about the bloodshed to come. Expecting a swift victory, a British officer expresses how much he will enjoy crushing these 'vile' American enemies during the American Revolution.

'My Dearest Father, I am most sincerely sorry to confirm the afflicting reports, which, before this, I suppose you have heard,' wrote a New York physician named Samuel Bard just days after the April 19, 1775, clash outside of Boston between British troops and Massachusetts militiamen. 'It is but too true, that the sword of civil discord is at length unsheathed, and the horrors of that worst of wars begun among us.' It is unlikely that Bard knew just how prescient his words would be. The Revolution was not America's first major conflict, but it would claim tens of thousands of lives, and would be a conflict of astonishingly brutal hand-to-hand combat. Bard continued with his letter:

Mr. Seagrove writes from Boston, that on Tuesday a body of eight hundred troops marched suddenly from Boston, in the night, with intention to seize a magazine which had been prepared at Concord, or, perhaps, the delegates, who were there met. On their way they encountered a company of minutemen exercising, and ordered them to disperse, who refusing to do so, the troops fired twice over their heads, and, as they still stood their ground, a third time, among them, and killed eight; upon which the country was immediately alarmed by the firing of cannon, and the troops intercepted on their return. General Gage sent out a thousand men, under the command of Lord Percy, to their assistance; these two bodies united, and made a kind of retreating battle into Boston. Many officers were wounded; and between two and three hundred private men killed. Seagrove adds, that preparations were making, on both sides, as if it was to be very soon renewed. What number of the inhabitants was killed is not known; but all agree their loss must have been considerable. Other letters make the number of the troops killed to be near five hundred; but I suppose the truth is not exactly known;

enough, however, is known, to fill every humane breast with the deepest affliction. We have had some commotion among us on the occasion, though, on the whole, we are remarkable quiet; and I am not without hopes, shall remain so, through the interposition of those who have interest among the common people.

I have ever preserved a moderate and temperate course, and you may be assured, shall, on this occasion, rather increase my caution than lessen it. God, and God only, knows where these unhappy disputes will end; it can hardly, however, be hoped they will subside before we have felt heavily the inconveniences of them.

Yet it is not impossible but that the resolution and spirit which have now been shown by our neighbors, may convince the British ministry that they have not much to expect from America by force; and in that way, will never get a revenue out of us which will pay the expense of collecting. God send that it may be so, and that we may again see our former happy days of peace and quiet.

Your affectionate son,
S. B.

Passions flared on both sides. British troops mocked the ragtag militia that the American Colonists had assembled and warned them that, as traitors to the motherland, they could expect no pity. Many American soldiers, in time, would reciprocate that merciless spirit as well. The sheer animus the British felt toward their enemy was evident in the following letter, written by an English officer (whose name was not recorded) just after General Washington and his men were forced to retreat from Long Island. The sentiments were shared by many in the British forces.

September 3, 1776

Rejoice, my friend, that we have given the rebels a d – – 'd crush. We landed on Long-Island the 22d ult. without opposition. On the 27th we had a very warm action, in which the Scots regiments behaved with the greatest bravery, and carried the day after an obstinate resistance on the rebel side.

But we flanked, and overpowered them with numbers. The Hessians and our brave Highlanders gave no quarters; and it was a fine sight to see with what alacrity they dispatched the rebels with their bayonets after we had surrounded them, so that they could not resist.

Multitudes were drowned and suffocated in morasses, a proper punishment for all rebels. Our battalion out-marched all the rest; and was always first up with the rebel fugitives. A fellow they call Lord Sterling, one of their Generals, with two others, is prisoner, and a great many of their officers, men, artillery, and stores.

It was a glorious achievement, my friend, and will immortalize us, and crush the rebel colonies. Our loss was nothing. We took care to tell the Hessians, that the rebels had resolved to give no quarters to them in particular, which made them fight desperately, and put all to death that fell into their hands. You know all stratagems are lawful in war especially against such vile enemies to their kind and country.

The island is all ours and we shall soon take New-York, for the rebels dare not look us in the face. I expect the affair will be over [with] this campaign, and we shall all return covered with American laurels, and have the cream of American lands alloted us for our services.

A Continental soldier named Henry Johnson, working with the British in the American Revolution, sends a short but poignant letter to his parents assuring them he is well — & — In a series of letters appealing to the Government for a Military Pension, William Hutchinson, William Johnson and Moses Hall describe the violence and atrocities they saw firsthand during the American Revolution.

While there are countless letters from the Revolutionary era, many of them stirring and eloquent, by the nation's commanding officers, letters by common soldiers are harder to come by. The reasons are manifold. There were, compared to other major conflicts, fewer soldiers writing letters and, therefore, fewer letters to be passed down from one generation to the next. Paper was hard to come by for the average soldiers in the field, and there was virtually no reliable postal service to ensure that their mail would be received. Correspondents primarily depended on acquaintances or an informal delivery network to drop off their personal letters at a public place, such as a tavern, to be collected later. And while officers were for the most part highly literate, many enlisted men were tradesmen whose reading and writing skills were modest. The letters of Henry Johnson (which he even misspelled as 'Henery Jonson'), a young Continental soldier from New Jersey, are representative of what many young men wrote home from the front lines when they were able.

Feb[r]uary 25 1778

Onered perents

I am in Good helth Att present And I hope these will find you All the Same

The Situation of our Armey Is so that I dont Expect to Com home Very Soon You must Not look for mee till you See mee But if you Could Send me a Letter to Lett me no how you All Are It Would gave me grate Satsfaction to See the Same. But our ofisers have Left us without Money & Cloth and hear we are forsed to Stay Exposed to All Wether Let it Come As It will

Remember me to All my friends that Ask after me

So No More Att Present But I Remain your Dear and Loving Scion

Henery Jonson

On June 7, 1780, during the Battle of Connecticut Farms, Johnson was shot in the head, but the injury was not a mortal one; one week later, Johnson himself reported to his parents from the 'Ospitreal' (hospital):

I have taken this opertunyty to let you know what misfortu[n]e I met with. A party of the Enemy Came to Elisebeth town [and] ma[r]ched to the Conecticut Farms We lay at Newark Mountain A Bout twelve oclock at Night we was Alarmed and Marched to the farms and about Sun Rise We [attacked] them . . . there was a Bout five thousand of them   we kept up a a hot fire about fore hours and in the atack was wounded Col Ogden of the forth Regt and a number of Soldiers kild and wounded and I got a Wound in the head very Bad But I am in hopes With the Assistance of god that I Shall git wel again

Henry Johnson returned home after his recuperation and eventually became a shoemaker. While letters like Johnson's, which describe combat on a firsthand basis, are scarce, there are numerous correspondences written after the war by veterans petitioning the government, both state and local, for a pension. Within their appeals are often dramatic stories that reveal the true brutality of the violence these veterans and their comrades faced during the Revolution. (Applicants who could not write often related their accounts to a third party, such as a lawyer or court clerk, who made a transcript of the narrative.) A native of Pennsylvania, William Hutchinson, was in his early 20s when he fought with the Chester County militia and, later, the Second Delaware Regiment at Trenton, Brandywine, and Germantown. Hutchinson recalled the abuse that one man, who had been brought to their camp caked in blood and barely alive, suffered when British troops attacked – some used the word slaughtered – American soldiers at Paoli, Pennsylvania. (The selections below are from the letters of Hutchinson and other applicants, sometimes called declarants or deponents, and the originals do not include salutations.)

A Quaker, a stranger, came to our quarters & brought with him a man which he said he had found lying in the woods whose clothes coat, vest & trousers were stiff with gore & declarant believes they would have stood alone when taken off him. he was a virginian and had shared in the consequences of the massacre; had been singled out at the close thereof as a special subject for the exercise of the savage cruelty of the British soldiers. he told us that more than a dozen soldiers had with fixed bayonets formed a cordon round him & that every one of them in sport had indulged their brutal ferocity by stabbing him in different parts of his body & limbs, & that by a last & desperate effort, he got without their circle & fled. & as he rushed out, one of the soldiers struck at him to knock him down as the finis to the catastrophe in which only the front of the bayonet reached his head & laid it open with a gash as if it had been cut with a knife – he made, however, his escape & when brought to our captain, he had laid in the woods twenty-four hours. he had neither hat shoes nor stockings, and his legs & feet were covered with mud and sand which had been fastened to his skin by mixing with his own blood as it ran down his limbs.

Our Captain immediately dispatched his Lieutenant for a Physician who when he returned was so fortunate as to bring two with him. we then procured the means of washing & cleansing the wounded man & upon examining him there was found as our captain afterwards announced to the men forty six distinct bayonet wounds in different parts of his body, either of which were deep & sufficiently large to have been fatal if they had been in vital parts. but they were mostly flesh wounds & every one of them had bled profusely & many of them commenced bleeding again upon being washed. his wounds were dressed his bloody garments were burned and by orders of our captain he was waited upon with strict attention until he was able to walk & then was by Lieut Corry (our Lieut) taken somewhere not distant to an hospital.

William Johnson was a teenager who volunteered for the New Jersey militia and fought, off and on, for almost the entire Revolution. One of his most vivid memories concerned a brief encounter between an Irish soldier serving with the Colonists and a fallen, though still living, redcoat.

The first marching service which this, and the other militia companies stationed at Newark, rendered was to cross over from Elizabethtown Point to Staten Island to attack the British troops who were stationed at different places on that Island, On our approach, the enemy retreated to their principal fortifications at the Narrows, and our troops then returned to Newark – Gen Wines commanded the American troops on duty on this occasion, who in all numbered about 1500 men, this must have occurred more than a year after deponent was first attached to the militia. In this skirmish some British were killed, one in particular he remembers, was lying on the ground mortally wounded, he had a green coat on, which one of our company (an Irishman) espied, and said, 'Your coat is better than mine, I'll have it.' he immediately took the coat off the wounded soldier and put it on his own back, and immediately run his bayonet in the body of the wounded soldier, who on his march back lay quite dead.

Moses Hall, who was only 15 when the war began, also witnessed an atrocity committed by American troops, but he was not unsympathetic to the rage behind it. The troops had seized half a dozen British soldiers and were debating what to do with them when someone evoked the memory of Buford's Massacre. The fate of the prisoners was sealed at that moment. In May 1780, a British lieutenant colonel named Banastre Tarleton, already reviled by the Americans, purportedly disregarded a white flag of surrender offered by Colonel Abraham Buford and ordered his men to kill Buford's entire regiment, which they proceeded to do. A doctor familiar with the incident later wrote that the 'demand for quarters, seldom refused to a vanquished foe, was at once found to be in vain.' He continued:

> [N]ot a man was spared – and it was the concurrent testimony of all the survivors, that for fifteen minutes after every man was prostrate [Tarleton's troops] went over the ground plunging their bayonets into every one that exhibited any signs of life, and in some instances, where several had fallen one over the other, these monsters were seen to throw off on the point of the bayonet the uppermost, to come at those beneath.

In his pension appeal letter, Moses Hall related what happened to the British prisoners they had caught, as well as the chain of thoughts and emotions he experienced afterwards.

The evening after our battle with the Tories we having a considerable number of prisoners I recollect a scene which made a lasting impression upon my mind. I was invited by some of my comrades to go and see some of the prisoners. We went to where six were standing. Some discussion taking place, I heard some of our men cry out, 'Remember Buford,' and the prisoners were immediately hewed to pieces with broadswords.

109

At first I bore the scene without any emotion, but upon a moment's reflection, I felt such horror as I never did before nor have since. And returning to my quarters and throwing myself upon my blanket I contemplated the cruelties of war untill overcome and unmanned by a distressing gloom from which I was not relieved untill commencing our march next morning before day by moon light.

I came to Tarleton's camp which he had just abandoned leaving lively rail fires. Being on the left of the road as we marched along I discovered lying upon the ground something with appearance of a man. Upon approaching him he proved to be a youth about sixteen who having come out to view the British through curiosity for fear he might give information to our troops they had run him through with a bayonet and left him for dead. Though able to speak he was mortally wounded. The sight of this unoffending boy, butchered rather than be encumbered on the march, I assume, relieved me of my distressful feelings for the slaughter of the Tories and I desired nothing so much as the opportunity of participating in their destruction.

Such incidents would continue throughout the Revolution, with each side justifying its actions as fair reprisals for the 'inhumanity' of the other. It was a vicious cycle that had occurred in previous conflicts, and one that would be repeated in wars to come.

Private Benny Hobson, serving with the Mesopotamia Expeditionary Force, details for his Cousin Norman how Norman's brother died in battle.

For most servicemen and women – officers and enlisted personnel alike – few tasks are more emotionally demanding than writing to a fallen comrade's next of kin. Every word will be read and reread by grieving relatives and will affect how the lost soldier, marine, airman, or sailor will be remembered forever. Those called upon to perform the somber duty of writing condolence letters are often dealing with their own

emotions over the loss as well, and their grief is all the more
pronounced when the deceased is a family member. During the 1917
invasion of Mesopotamia (present-day Iraq), British forces lost an
estimated 30,000 soldiers before ultimately defeating the Turks, who
ruled over Mesopotamia. On the day after British troops seized
Baghdad, Private Benny Hobson wrote to his cousin about the death
of a fellow soldier and beloved member of their family. (Coy is short
for company, and Batt for battalion.)

March 12, 1917

Dear Cousin Norman,

I hardly know how to write to you yet I suppose I must come to the point
and although it seems terribly hard tell you the worse and that is of your
Dear brother's death in action on the the night of the 9th. I was not with him
at this time but not far away but from information gathered from the
comrades of his platoon it seems he was at this time on sentry and met his
death at the hands of a sniper who got him in the head. His end Dear Cousin
I believe was quite short and painless as he fell to the ground without
murmering. I did not hear of this till the day following and then my coy or
what remained of it, where given orders to get back across the river. Now I
will give you an idea of what we had to face and the glorious deeds which
some day sooner or later will come to light.

Our division have has you will already know been on the heels of the
retreating turks since the fall of Kut when our marching days begun and we
had got within 12 miles of Bagdad when our way was suddenly stopped by a
canal which had to be bridged by some means or other and so material for a
Pontoon was soon at hand but Johnnies artillary fire soon put an end to this
idea so it was discided upon that our Batt should proceed across in boats 10
men to each but this was cancelled after half of us had got over and then the
band began to play. just try to imagine a weak force like us trying to hold a
very much larger force, yet God only knows we held on like grim death
every hour brought depletion in our ranks men fell wounded and killed, our
rifles fairly blazed and became to hot to handle and ammunition began to
run out and to save as much as possible we had to only fire in case of extreme
neccessity, once the turks began to bomb us and we were obliged to retire to

111

put it in words as deep as I can it was Hell, but some day Dear Cousin if God spares me I will tell you it all, I do not know how I escaped Death as pals around me fell and I had my helmet knocked off by a piece of Turkish shell, help came just as day broke on the 10th and under the devasting fire of our own artillary the turks began to retire many coming in to our lines and giving themselves up.

These two nights I shall never forget this trying ordeal and now I mourn the lost of one who could not have been more to me if he had been my brother. You must excuse this letter Dear Cousin if it be by any means to[o] sudden or in any sense too cruel for I did not know how to break this sad news to you and yet I thought you ought to know, I dare not write to my Dear Aunt as I know she will be in a way so Dear Norman I leave it to you to break this news to her in a way you will think best with the one consolation for thought it is in comparison to the loss of one so dear that he died with his face to the enemy in one of the pluckiest engagements ever known ~~evry~~ every inch a soldier and a man. I have made enquiries about his personal belongings but find out that his sargent got them all but was himself wounded as I intended could I have got them posting them to you at my first oppurtunity but perhaps he may have the kindness to return them to you I hope you will take my deepest sympathy in this sad time and trust with me that your dear departed Brother my good old Chum has joined the favoured throng and now dwells in Heaven with our love-ones only gone before. Now I will close as I do not feel as I can write any more at present. . .

I Remain

Your Sad and Lonely Cousin

<u>Benny</u>

PS. Will you kindly break the news to Gertee.

An Indian soldier fighting with the British on the Western Front during World War I writes with sadness and amazement about the terrible assortment of weapons being used in the war — & — British soldier Ian H. Macdonnell writes to his mother after surviving a gas attack during the Battle of Passchendaele, during World War I.

Few of the weapons were new to warfare. The Flammenwerfer (flamethrower) was first proposed to the German army in 1901, but a crude version had existed in the fifth century BC. There are allusions to hand grenades in the 15th century, and references to landmines dating back to the 18th. In September 1776, the Turtle became the first submarine to attack, albeit unsuccessfully, an enemy vessel. Machine guns were tested in the American Civil War (1861–5) and later proved their efficacy at the Battle for San Juan Hill in Cuba in 1868. During the Turko-Italian War (1911–1912), the Italians used airplanes for reconnaissance and bombing missions – just eight years after Orville and Wilbur Wright's first flight in December 1903. But from the outset of World War I in the summer of 1914, all these instruments came together to form an efficient killing machine that would decimate a generation of young men on a scale never before witnessed in history. Bullets, bombs, and bayonets would still account for most of World War I's fatalities, but the technologically 'improved' weapons were particularly fearsome to the vast number of soldiers who had never heard of or seen such things before. 'This war is very terrible,' a Gurkha soldier named Shed Karn Das wrote home to India. 'There is no safety for a man on the earth, or under the earth, in the air, or on the sea. Is this true warfare? ... From all this it would seem that God is displeased with the peoples of the world.' Of the estimated 1 million Indian troops – also known as sepoys – who fought with the British against the Germans on the Western Front during World War I, approximately 10 per cent of them were killed or wounded. An Indian soldier from Gujarat named Maganlal (last name unknown) wrote the following letter articulating the sentiments of many combatants, regardless of their country of origin. (A maund, which Maganlal refers to, is a unit of weight. There is no salutation or signature to the letter.)

What a dreadful thing is this time of battle and strife, in which the most devilish weapons for the destruction of mankind, are being used by civilized and cultured nations of the Christian faith. Poisonous gases, bombs, machine guns which fire 700 bullets per minute, large and small cannon throwing cannon balls 30 Bengali maunds in weight, Zepplins, large and small flying machines which throw bombs from the air, land mining and the blowing up of sepoys located in the trenches, liquid fire that causes the clothes on the body to ignite, the firing of torpedoes under water without warning or giving any time to lower boats, and the using of star shells which turn the nights into day. Such are the modern and scientific processes by which nations seek to destroy one another. Every effort is being made to win over neutral countries. Alas! there is no God-like man who tries to stop this deadly war, but it seems that such must be the will of God for the punishment of sinners. That our benign Government may be victorious and that, once more, there may be peace on earth, such is my prayer.

One weapon, unleashed on a wide scale for the first time during World War I, caused particular alarm. In the late afternoon of April 22, 1915, after a ground-shaking bombardment by German artillery earlier that morning, a second barrage thundered throughout the farmlands of western Belgium. French and Algerian sentries on the Ypres salient watched with curiosity and then growing apprehension as a strange, smoky green vapor floated gently across the fields and into their lines. As it enveloped the men, some of whom had already started to flee, they clutched their throats and began gasping for air. It was chlorine gas. French and other Allied troops had used tear-gas grenades in the first month of the war, but this was the first time poison gas had been used by either side. Over the course of the war more potent gases were developed, and it is estimated that they caused almost 100,000 deaths – every one of which was excruciating. In addition, more than 1 million troops were

114

injured by gas, including a British soldier named Ian H. Macdonnell who survived an attack in 1917 at, it is assumed, the third battle of Ypres, also known as Passchendaele (named after the little village captured at the end of the campaign by British and Canadian forces). Macdonnell feared that his mother might hear that he had been gassed and wanted to assure her that he was fine and there was no cause for alarm – despite the obvious scare he and his men had just endured. (The 'smoke' reference at the end of the letter was Macdonnell's not-so-subtle hint to his mother that, gassed or not, he wanted her to send him cigarettes.)

Dearest Mother,

I write this in bed from 15th Corps Dressing Station – I hope to heaven this will catch you before the war office list. I am all right no danger at all, but it will reach you as 'gas poisoning.' The Huns shelled our camp – which is about 2 miles between the lines – our 13th – most are pleasant – a lot of men were hit – we had most of our men out on working parties at night – up in the line – thank goodness they were.

We at the camp went to sleep & at 12.15 there was a yell, & I woke with my mouth full of a choking stench, to the tune of screaming shell – Gas!

We got masks on in the dark. Shells hitting everything. The Col. & I in our masks tried to get to the Brigade. We were lost in the dark & the shell holes. & came back to the hut under the sand bank. The rest is a night mare – an 8 inch gas shell hit the edge of the hut smashed it in & knocked us all endways broken glass, darkness, – & men, vomiting, & raving for air. Two had legs blown off. We wore our masks from 12:15 till 4. & the shell fell like rain. Ones' eyes were blinded even through the mask. However the net result is nothing to speak of – All the food in the camp was poisoned of course. & the beautiful cake you sent had of course to be buried!

I was all right at about 10 o clock in the morning – barring dizziness, & runny eyes – but the doctor stethescoped me & said I had to go down. I didnt want to but they put me in bed when I got here. Mother dear I shall be out of hospital & going back in perhaps 4 day – thats all dont be anxious. All I have now is a filthy taste in my mouth & a little discomfort in chest & throat.

Already my eyes are better & I can read – & smoke! (please note) – so if you get a notice saying I am <u>gassed</u> you will know it is nothing & I shall probably be back to duty by the time you get it. I am not bad.

Your loving son
Ian

After a visit to the Western Front during World War I, British artist Paul Nash vows to his wife that he will express the 'bitter truth' of the war in his paintings — & — A Canadian Army clergyman named William Mayse writes to his wife about a battlefield death that profoundly affected him during World War I.

The Passchendaele offensive fought at Ypres in 1917, commanded by Sir Douglas Haig, was a prolonged bloodbath fought in knee-deep mud by exhausted troops that, in the end, achieved little. The Allied forces gained several miles of strategically insignificant land at a cost of 310,000 casualties. (For the Germans, the count was about 260,000.) A 28-year-old artist named Paul Nash was at Passchendaele, but not to fight; Nash had enlisted in 1914 but returned to England due to an accident unrelated to combat. He became an official war artist and, after recuperating and making numerous appeals to get back into the action as soon as possible, was sent to the Western Front. 'My beloved,' Nash began a letter to his wife from Ypres soon after his arrival, 'This afternoon I go up the line to stay at a Brigade H[ead] Q[uarters] for a night or two from where I shall see wonderful things.' Nash was filled with anticipation that he would be able to watch a battle in all its dramatic fury, but what he discovered was a spectacle of despair and annihilation beyond his imagination. Government officials had encouraged Nash and his colleagues to create uplifting and patriotic art, but, overwhelmed by the almost apocalyptic vision he had seen, Nash was emphatic that his work would be a testament to the war's barbarity, regardless of what the bureaucrats wanted or instructed. He wrote to his wife:

116

I have just returned, last night, from a visit to Bde HQ up the line, & I shall not forget it as long as I live. I have seen the most frightful nightmare of a country more conceived by Dante or Poe, unspeakable, utterly indescribable. In the fifteen drawings I have made I may give you some vague idea of its horror, but only being in it and of it can ever make you sensible of its dreadful nature & what men in France have to face.

We all have a vague notion of the terrors of a battle, & can ~~imagine~~ conjure up with the aid of some of the more inspired war correspondents and the pictures in the Daily Mirror some vision of a battlefield, but no pen or drawing can convey this country – the normal setting of the battles taking place day & night, month after month. Evil and the incarnate fiend alone can be master of the ceremonies in this war; no glimmer of God's hand is seen. Sunset & sunrise are blasphemous, mockeries to man; only the black rain out of the bruised & swollen clouds on thro' the bitter black of night is fit atmosphere in such a land. The rain drives on; the stinking mud becomes more evilly yellow, the shell holes fill up with green white water, the roads & tracks are covered in inches of slime, the ~~blacken~~ black dying trees ooze & sweat and the shells never cease.

They whine & plunge over head, tearing away the rotting tree stumps, breaking the plank roads, striking down horses & mules; annihilating, maiming, maddening; they plunge into the grave which is this land; one huge grave, and cast up the poor dead. O it is unspeakable, Godless, hopeless. I am no longer an artist interested & curious, I am a messenger who will bring back word from men fighting to those who want the war to last for ever. Feeble, inarticulate will be my message, but it will have a bitter truth, and may it burn their lousy souls.

No letters at all yet, I wish they would send them on. Be kind to your love & chide him not for writing so little, he had written to no one else yet. In a day or two he will have more to say & not so gloomy. I am longing to hear all about my darling. Tell me if you have sent John his Danae & my news of pictures generally.

For a little time, adieu, my sweet little baby
With a long long kiss the kind only we can give
    From
Your most loving idolatrous lover
    Paul

Despite the almost 600,000 casualties, Passchendaele was by no means the worst battle of the war. More than 1.2 million soldiers were killed and wounded at the Somme, and just under a million at Verdun. Soldiers in the field found it especially difficult to grapple with the enormity of the bloodshed, and they reacted in different ways. Some were emotionally cauterized by it all. 'We all lay with our nerves strung up, waiting for the attack for which we supposed the artillery fire had been preparing,' a German soldier named August Hopp wrote home. 'But it didn't come. In spite of it all they would have found us at our posts, although they were still firing on our flank and killing and wounding many. But one gets by degrees so callous about death that one hardly looks round when anybody falls.' Others could be shaken by a single death. William Mayse served with the Canadian Army as a clergyman, and in a graphic letter to his wife, Betty, he related a sight that emphasized to him the human cost of the war behind the incomprehensibly large statistics.

My Dear Betty:

I received you letter No 5 last eve in which you tell of Smalley's invitation – I guess I have already answered it, after reading your letter Pryor & I went for a ramble over another part of the battlefield, & we saw still more awfull sights than hithertoo – I would not be exaggerating if I said that we saw scores of unburried Germans in battered trenches & arround shell-holes, here & there what had been a French soldier & sometimes we would come across one of our own Canadian boys – when we found any remains that looked like a Canadian, we would bury them as well as we could – for there are all kinds of picks & shovels etc, lying around – I came across one of our boys – decomposed beyond all recognition but he lay just as he had fallen – the head was missing – but all the accoutriments was buckled on, his rifle & helmet lay close by – I cut the buckle off the belt as a momento, & we burried what remained of him – I tried to find something by which he might be identified but it was impossible – Poor boy – in some far away home in Canada some-one is mourning the loss of husband – son or sweetheart – & the saddest of all is, they will never know how he died – or where he is burried, & even now they may be clinging to the hope, that he is still alive, a prisoner, for he would be listed among the missing.

Talk about the 'glory of war' there is no glory, it is hellish devilish. We saw places too where the trenches & ground arround was literally bloodsoaked & here & there shell holes with blood & water still standing in them. I must close this letter now, will write as often as possible. I have written to Rose & also the Bank about that money. Love & kisses.

Will

Harold 'Pompey' Elliott, Commander of the 7th Australian Battalion, describes to his friend J.C. Richardson the bloody Battle of Lone Pine during the Gallipoli Campaign of World War I — & — In a letter found on the body of a Turk who fell at Gallipoli in World War I, his wife bemoans their separation and wishes for his safe return.

In no other conflict has trench warfare been as integral to the fighting as it was during World War I. And while most of it occurred on the Western Front, which stretched for more than 400 miles, primarily through Belgium and France, Allied forces in Turkey faced enemy troops that were, in spots, entrenched a mere 20 feet away. On April 25, 1915, the first wave of approximately 16,000 mostly untested soldiers in the Australian and New Zealand Army Corps, or 'Anzacs,' landed at Gallipoli in western Turkey as part of a larger Allied operation to take over the peninsula. Their objective was to secure the region, allowing the British fleet unimpeded passage to Constantinople through the Dardanelles Straits, with the ultimate aim of knocking Turkey – a German ally – out of the war. Due to poor planning, particularly on the part of the British First Lord of the Admiralty, Winston Churchill, and the unexpected resolve of the Turkish soldiers, the Anzacs made little headway. Thousands died

119

during the initial invasion at what would become known as Anzac Cove and the struggle to take the heights above it. A protracted stalemate ensued – not unlike the deadlock on the Western Front that the Gallipoli landings were intended to circumvent – and the Anzacs ended up perched in a cramped area that, at its farthest inland point, was only three-quarters of a mile from the sea. In August the Anzacs launched an ambitious, multipronged offensive, with the largest battle occurring at Lone Pine. Prominent in the action was the commander of the 7th Australian Battalion, Harold 'Pompey' Elliott, a 37-year-old lawyer from Victoria. In January 1916, just over a month after he and his men had evacuated the Gallipoli coast, Elliott wrote to a friend and colleague, J. C. Richardson, about the historic confrontation at Lone Pine between the Anzacs and the Turks.

TEL EL KEBIR, EGYPT
25th Jan. 1916

My Dear J.C.,

Your letter of the 22nd Oct. reached me this day having been apparently delayed in transit. I was very interested indeed to hear that your brother was with the 7th. They are out on parade at present, but I will see him when they return. With reference to my last letter to you and my expectation of going out, I owe my deliverance to one thing, At the time I wrote I had orders to attempt the capture of a position with a totally inadequate force in my opinion. We were saved from meeting the fate of the 8th and 10th Light Horse, who were practically exterminated attempting a similarly hopeless task by the fact that we were urgently needed for another task, namely, to hold the position known as the 'Lone Pine' which had been captured by our first Brigade. All these attacks were ordered with one object, viz., the distraction of the Turks' attention from the landing at Suvla Bay then in contemplation. My task was (with a Battalion counting cooks and all details, signallers, it did not amount to quite 700 men) to attack a formidable enemy's work known as 'Johnston Jolly' We knew it was held by a large number of men with machine guns giving three tiers of fire. We have since ascertained that it was held by three complete battalions. You can guess

120

whether my doubts were justified. However, just as we were making preparation for the attack by making blanket pathways attached to wooden poles to throw over the enemy's wire entanglements as we rushed forward; I was sent for hurriedly, ordered to cease all preparations for the attack and move at once to the support of the 1st Brigade whose remnants were being hard pressed in Lone Pine. Owing to the haste and to some of the men being engaged on fatigue carrying food and water from the beach to the firing line and to our machine guns being already engaged with the enemy, I had to move off with only 511 men and 16 officers. Our task here was comparatively simple compared to the previous attack which we were preparing for. Merely to hold a position already won, although only partially prepared for defence. Here we sustained the attack of some 3,000 Turks for about 20 hours practically without food and no rest.

The worst attack was made at dawn about 4.30 and kept up till nearly 8 o'clock. During this attack 344 rank and file and 12 officers fell, killed and wounded. I myself, my signalling officer and two other officers being the only unwounded officers and 167 men unwounded survived. My Adjutant had had his arm shattered by a bullet after a hand to hand fight with a Turk who jumped into the trench and tried to bayonet him but whom he shot with his revolver in the stomach. As he fell his friends threw a bomb over which burst and blew his head to pieces and so saved further trouble. Four of my boys got the 'V.C.' in this fight which is a record for one Regiment in one fight. I account for it by the fact that the Divisional Commander himself came down about 2 o'clock. He judged by the number of wounded streaming by his Head Quarters that we were getting a warm time and came down personally to tell me that we must hold the position to the very last man, and if necessary he and his staff would come and personally weld rifles and bayonets with the men if it became necessary.

He saw with his own eyes the trenches choked with the dead and dying trodden on by their comrades because they could not be removed from the narrow trenches, and torn to pieces by the bombs and shells the enemy were hurling over. Three times I, myself, thought it was all over and drew my revolver to do my little bit but each time the living never faltered as they reached the trench and it was only a very few, not more than six, who were brave enough to jump into the trenches on to the bayonets and in practically every case they were dead before their feet touched the bottom. In one place a line of dead men with their bayonets still over the parapet held about 20 or 30 yards of trench. In the early morning a machine gun swept that part of the line and killed every man at that spot – the trench sloped forward and as they died each man so suddenly that he simply leaned forward on the parapet and in many cases their hats and bayonets could be seen standing steadily behind the parapet and curiously enough that part of the line was avoided by the enemy.

I had supports in the rear ready to rush anyone who came in there but I did not replace the men owing to the fact that the trench was shallow and exposed to fire from the left rear of the position while the Turks still had a position with machine guns and these men were all shot through the back of the head but apparently the Turks in front of them did not know this nor that they were dead. After a few hours sleep we were again sent back and again lost men from bombs but no sustained attack was again made.

But these partial attacks were sufficient to prevent us attending properly to the wounded and from removing the dead. The weather was hot and the flies pestilential. When anyone speaks to you of the glory of war, picture to yourself a narrow line of trenches two and sometimes three deep with bodies (and think too of your best friends, for that is what these boys become by long association with you) mangled and torn beyond description by the bombs and bloated and blackened by decay and crawling with maggots. Live amongst this for days in spite of taking advantage of every night to work with respirators endeavouring to remove them this is war and such is glory – whatever the novelists may say.

The trouble was that the space of 100 yards over which we charged to take these trenches was after the first surprise swept continually with shrapnel and machine gun fire and it was impossible in the daytime to get across without enormous risk. By working night and day a narrow tunnel was put through underground connecting the new position, but it was often choked by parties bringing food and water and ammunition and bombs and the men were so fatigued that the labor of carrying out a few dead utterly prostrated them in the heat. Eventually we buried hundreds by the simple method of digging the fire trench a few feet deeper and covering them over but the smell still persisted. In one place we found a sort of underground cellar used by the

Turks for disciplinary purposes. When I examined it, I found its occupant was a dead Turk chained to a stout post. In the first attack evidently some of our men had entered and in the semi-darkness had spotted an enemy and run him through with his bayonet without enquiry. I had over 30 corpses friends and foes alike fitted into this chamber, covered with chloride of lime and the entrance sealed with sand bags. Still the corpses did not diminish appreciably and we dug a huge tunnel back towards our own lines underground and packed in corpses in hundreds until it was full, then strewed lime over them and blocked them up. For over three weeks we labored night and day feverishly strengthening that position, erecting barbed wire entanglements and pushing them out in front night and day engaged in bombing and sniping at the enemy who had dug a new line a few yards from us burying corpses living and eating in a slaughter house. We were not allowed to have blankets or even overcoats lest we should be more likely to sleep sound and be hard to arouse in the event of an attack, but a few men at a time by reliefs were sent back to rest and then relieve others.

I got a chill from this developed a sort of fever and subsequently pleurisy, after three weeks of this sort of thing, was sent to Malta and subsequently to England. I managed to get back by the 9th Dec. and took part in the final retirement from Gallipoli and the fact that we were not simply decimated during the evacuation will always seem to me due to a special interposition of providence in our favor.

Looking back now I still cannot understand how, unless, their eyes were blinded, we could have eluded their vigilance for in many places the trenches were only a few yards apart.

All the Reserves and Supports were sent off gradually a few thousands each night for a week beforehand until there was only the firing line and supports we cleared and a few guns. Finally the last night they were gradually thinned out until all got away. One of my N.C.Os. suggested a plan (which was adopted by for deceiving the Turks) was very successful; by means of two bully beaf tins so placed that water in the higher one would drop into a lower one and by its weight pull the trigger and fire the rifle. By adjusting the size of the hole in the upper one we found that we could fire a rifle at any interval up to an hour.

The plan was adopted and we gained a full hour by this dance before the

Turks could suspect our departure from its trenches by the sudden cessation of fire along the line and it cost us only some 10 damaged rifles.

Your brother has just seen me. I have arranged for him to attend an N.C.Os' class. He will be useful as an officer later if he survives. I am only too glad to get hold of anyone who will likely make an officer for we use them up very quickly. I have had over 70 in my own regimental list since I left Australia and I am several under strength still.

We have orders to move from here very shortly, our destination is secret, don't know if there will be any fighting but I suspect plenty of sand and digging in.

Kindest regards to

Yours very sincerely,
Pompey

Anzac fatalities by the end of the entire eight-month Gallipoli campaign numbered more than 10,000. (In total, approximately 40,000 Allied soldiers were killed. The Turks lost twice that many.) Although defeated, the Anzac troops had displayed, in the eyes of their countrymen in Australia and New Zealand, such valor and resourcefulness throughout their ordeal that April 25 was named a national holiday – 'Anzac Day' – in both nations. (Within a month of writing his letter, Pompey Elliott was promoted to Brigadier General, and after the war he was elected to the Australian parliament. Elliott was afflicted, however, with what would later be considered 'post-traumatic stress disorder,' and in 1931 he committed suicide.) Correspondences from Gallipoli by Turkish troops are rare, but a fragment of one letter by a soldier conveys the sense of determination that made the Turks such formidable opponents. Writing to his mother, he recalled a moment of faith:

I opened my hands, looked up to the heavens and said: 'God of Turks, Master of the Birds, the sheep, the leaves, the mountains. You have given all this to the Turks. Please leave it to the Turks. God, all this soldier wants is to keep this land from the British and the French. Grant me this wish.'

And just as the parents and spouses of Allied soldiers fretted about the well-being of their sons and husbands at the front, so did the loved ones of Turkish troops. The following letter was taken off the body of one Turkish soldier.

To my dear Husband:

I humbly beg to enquire after your blessed health. Your daughter sends her special salaams, and kisses your hands. Since you left I have seen no one. Since your departure I have had no peace. Your mother has not ceased to weep since you left. We are all in a bad way. Your wife says to herself 'While my husband was here we had some means' since your departure we have received nothing at all. Please write quickly and send what you can. All your friends kiss your hands and your feet.

May God keep you and save us from the disasters of this war.

Your wife,

Fatima

There were an estimated 200,000 French, British, Indian, and Canadian casualties overall during the Allied operation in Turkey (in which the Anzacs played an essential part). The Turks sustained 250,000 casualties.

Alfred Dougan Chater shares with his mother an incredible story of humanity and camaraderie from the front lines of World War I.

'What would happen, I wonder,' First Lord of the Admiralty, Winston Churchill, remarked in a November 1914 letter, 'if the armies suddenly and spontaneously went on strike and said some other method must be found of settling the dispute!' For a fleeting moment one month later, this seemingly fanciful notion became a reality. On December 25, 1914, a British soldier named Alfred Dougan Chater,

125

serving with the 2nd Battalion, Gordon Highlanders, sent the following letter home reporting on the momentous occasion.

<u>Christmas Day.</u>

Dearest Mother,

I am writing this in the trenches in my 'dug out' – with a wood fire going and plenty of straw it is rather cosy although it is freezing here and real Christmas weather –

I think I have seen one of the most extraordinary sights today that anyone has ever seen – About 10 o'clock this morning I was peeping over the parapet when I saw a German waving his arms, and presently two of them got out their trenches and came towards ours – we were first going to fire on them when we saw they had no rifles. So one of our men went out to meet them and in about two minutes the ground between the two lines of trenches was swarming with men and officers of both sides, shaking hands and wishing each other a happy Christmas – This continued for about half an hour when most of the men were ordered back to the trenches.

For the rest of the day nobody has fired a shot and the men have been wandering about at will on the top of the parapet and carrying straw and fire wood about in the open – we have also had joint burial parties with a service from some dead – some German and some ours – who were lying out between the lines. Some of our officers were taking groups of English and German soldiers – This extraordinary truce has been quite impromptu – there was no previous arrangement and of course it had been decided that there was not to be any cessation of hostilities.

I went out myself and shook hands with several of their officers and men – from what I gathered most of them would be as glad to get home again as we should – we have had our pipes playing all day and everyone has been wandering about in the open unmolested but not of course as far as the enemies lines – The truce will probably go on until someone is foolish enough to let off his rifle – we nearly messed it up this afternoon, by one of our fellows letting off his rifle skywards by mistake but they did not seem to notice it so it did not matter – I have been taking advantage of the truce to improve my 'dug-out' which I share with D. McBain the Scotch fellow – we put on a proper roof this morning and now we have got a tiled fire place and brushwood and straw on the floor – we leave the trenches tomorrow and I shant be sorry as it is much too cold to be pleasant at nights.

27th I am writing this back in billets – the same business continues yesterday and we had another parley with the Germans in the middle we exchanged cigarettes and autographs and some more people took photos – I dont know how long it will go on for – I believe it was supposed to stop yesterday but we can hear no firing going on along the front today except a little distant shelling. We are, at any rate having another truce on New Years Day as the Germans want to see how the photos come out! Yesterday was lovely in the morning and I went for several quite long walks about the lines – It is difficult to realise what that means but of course in the ordinary way there is not a sign of life above ground and everyone who puts his head up gets shot at.

With heaps of love and wishes to you and everyone for a happy new year.

Your loving son

<u>Dougan</u>

I'm so sorry I forgot to wish Father many happy returns – I do so now though somewhat late –

It was the first and last time such a Christmas truce would take place, both because the enmity between the British and Germans would intensify as time went on and because the senior officers ordered an end to unofficial cease-fires. 'Divisional Commanders [must] impress on all subordinate commanders the absolute necessity of encouraging the offensive spirit of the troops,' Sir Horace Smith-Dorrien, the British commander of II Corps, sternly instructed after the unsanctioned truce. 'Friendly intercourse with the enemy, unofficial armistices (e.g., "we won't fire if you don't" etc.) and the exchange of tobacco and other comforts, however tempting and occasionally amusing they may be, are absolutely prohibited.' But the memory could not be easily discarded by those on either side of the Western Front. 'Christmas 1914 will remain unforgettable to me,' a German soldier named Josef Wenzl wrote to his parents. 'The British burst into song with a carol, to which we replied with "Stille Nacht, heilige Nacht." It was a very moving moment – hated and embittered enemies were singing carols around the Christmas tree. All my life I will never forget that sight.'

After the Armistice is announced in 1918, a chaplain named Melville Montgomery tells his family that, despite having been in combat for less than a day, he has 'Seen Enough' of war to last a lifetime.

With the infusion of fresh US troops in the final year of World War I and the climactic 47-day Meuse-Argonne offensive, the Allies were finally able to force the Germans into surrendering. Using an old typewriter and 'liberated' German paper, a 28-year-old US army chaplain named Melville Montgomery wrote to his family in Kansas two days after the cease-fire on November 11, 1918. 'At the present sitting I am burning the last little piece of candle that I have,' Montgomery noted in the beginning of his letter. Like many American troops, and despite the relatively brief amount of time he spent under fire, he was acutely aware of the incalculable toll the war had inflicted on so many nations. He had seen the detritus of battle scattered across the fields of France, and, as his letter indicated, the images had been burned into his memory. He continued:

At about six o'clock on the morning of the 11th two batallions of the 129th went into the front trenches. There was to be a 'hop over.' Five thirty is usually the zero hour. There was a delay in getting ready this time. At 9:10 the order was given. The men climbed over the trenches and started on a run out into a fog on no man's land. Soon Jerrie opened fire and the battle was on. At 9:15 the Adjutant of the Third batallion climbed over the top and shouted for the men to come back, but they were gone. He called a bugler and ordered him to blow recall. He blew recall three times and then blew assembly. The men came back. As far as we were concerned the war was over. It ended with our men going over the top.

One man was killed and several wounded. If the order had reached the line five minutes sooner they would have been saved. The order came to headquarters at 8:30 to stop all hostilities. Runners were sent to each batallion. The one to the third lost his way. Because of the delay they went over the top after peace was declared.

The Germans did not stop firing but increased their barrage. They sent a large amount of shells into our line and into the village headquarters. They sent over gas shells and we all had to don our masks. Exactly on the dot of 11 o'clock Fritz stopped firing. The whole front was as quiet as a country field. I went out and gathered together some of the dead of the 130th in preparation for burial. Jerry came over into our lines and we went over into his village. I talked about the reasons for the war with a German Captain out in no man's land. He said he was glad it was over and he was going back to his family.

The armistice is on. We are now praying that it may be a permanent peace. We are all tired of it no matter how long or how short a time we have been here, whether it is three weeks or four years. The eleventh hour of the eleventh day of the eleventh month of the year 1918 was one of the most important that the world has ever known. A great weight has been removed from the hearts of people all over the world.

Since then I have been seeing the gruesome results of war. I buried a man today who was killed in a swamp many days ago. He was a man hidden with a machine gun in the tall grass and killed at his post. No one knew he was there until some one happened to run across him today.

I have seen a German air plane crushed on the ground with the blood of the driver sprinkled over it. I have seen graves torn open with the remains of decaying men scattered about. I have seen wounded men and dying. I have seen men who have marched all night, wet, cold, and hungry go over the top with spirit. I have seen men suffering from gas. I was at the battle front just one night and until eleven o'clock the next morning. I have seen enough to do me. Others have been here for months, some for years. Truly war is hell.

I do not know where we will go from here or what we will do. It is hard to get transportation here for anything. There has been no mail here since we came. It is hard even to get in town. Some are hopeful of being home by Christmas. The boys want to get home by Christmas. Good luck to them but I don't think they will make it.

I am in good spirits and still have a good appetite. I will be glad whenever any mail comes for me. I have moved around so much it will take it forever to come. I do not know when this letter will get out. I hope quite soon. I wish I could send you all a Christmas present.

We are all glad the war is about over, aren't we?

With lots of love,

Melville.

Writing from the *USS New Orleans*, Ensign William Czako gives his sister an eyewitness account of one of the most fateful attacks in American – and world – history during World War I.

'*Dear Sis: It is now 9:05 Sunday morning and we've been bombed now for over an hour,*' *William Czako began a handwritten letter to his sister, Helen, on a winter morning from inside the* USS New Orleans. *Czako, a young ensign from Fremont, Ohio, continued to provide his sister with a dramatic, moment-by-moment description of what he and his fellow sailors were experiencing as hundreds of Japanese Zeroes bombarded the unsuspecting US Pacific fleet at Pearl Harbor on December 7, 1941.*

Our anti aircraft guns are yammering and every so often a bomb strikes so close as to rock this ship. Again a bomb. We're helpless down here in the Forward Engine Room because our main engines are all tore down. We're trying to get underway if possible. We were just struck by a bomb near the bow. We're fighting back as much as possible because we have no power to load our guns, no power circuits to fire them. It is all being done by hand.

This seems to you like a nonchalant letter, but it's the straight dope. There is only a handful of us down here as most of our men are ashore on liberty. They really caught us sleeping this time. For a ship being in a Navy Yard for overhaul, we're putting up a good fight. The first officer has come down here now to take charge. We've lit off all the boilers that are not out of commission and are trying to get underway so that we will not be altogether helpless by laying alongside the dock and be a stationary target. Those bombs are getting closer – God grant that they do not hit that loaded oil tanker that is lying right across from us. Ten million gallons of fuel oil would bathe this ship in an inferno of fire. There are destroyers laying near us and three other cruisers. They must be the targets including us. I am on the interior communications telephone and I can hear the various stations screaming orders at one other. A man just brought us our gas masks. We have four engines but we can at the best only use 2. We're getting steam up though. The firing of the guns have abated somewhat but we've received orders to get underway as quickly as steam can be raised. The firing has continued. Wave after wave of bombers must be coming. We've figured that some aircraft carriers must be the source of these fast dive bombing planes. We've been struck several times now but fortunately there are no casualties as yet.

It seems funny to be writing like this when it may be your last. I've never figured it to be like this. The next bomb may be our last but I will keep writing until I am told to stop or am given another job. Some Battleships that are tied up to the piers near the Fleet Air Base are reported to be afire. It seems that the Airbase was their first objective and the Battleships were just too close to that field. We were really caught short this time. All the Battleships are in – they came in this week and have been laying tied up. We have a few light cruisers that are out and we hope they can keep that invading fleet at bay until our ships that are undamaged and can get underway can get out of this trap. For a trap this Pearl Harbor has become. If we can get out of here and to sea we've still got a chance. We'll have our own power then. They can't get ammunition fast enough to the guns because of no power to the hoists. There has been a lull for a few minutes but there they go again. Strangely Sis, I'm not excited but my heart is beating a little faster from all that firing. I know that this is not a drill because the concussion of exploding bombs is jarring the whole ship.

I don't know why I am writing this because if we are hit with a bomb here – they won't find enough of me and the rest – let alone this letter. I imagine it is to show myself that I can be calm under fire. A few of the boys here are white faced and their voices hushed and choked. They too know that this is no joke or mock battle – but the real stuff. For out of a cloud studded blue sky and on a Sabbath morning death comes riding unheralded to claim for its own the unprepared and unbelieving. Who thought that they would strike in such a manner when most men were ashore and spending their payday on those traditional Saturday night sprees? They would not dare to attack us, let alone Pearl Harbor, the mightiest and most fortified base in the world. They could not get within a thousand miles of this place before we'd know it. – No they dare not – but they did – Ah – there was one explosion – perilously close – Yes – we were hit but not badly. The bomb struck between the bow and the stern of another ship tied up just ahead of us. Comes the report over my phones that there are no casualties but that there is a 40 ft hole in our bow and numerous small ones from flying shrapnel. That was close and still our guns keep answering as fast as hands – and not mechanical aid can feed those guns.

There is another lull and only sporadic bursts from our pom-poms. Preparations to get underway are still continuing. It seems impossible with all that machinery tore up but still we'll do what we can. – The order has come now to secure from general quarters. We were under fire for nearly two hours and I'm going to sneak up to topside to see what happened – .

Although a short-term triumph, the attack on Pearl Harbor failed to accomplish its primary goal of neutralizing the US Navy in the Pacific. Indeed, the American public that had wanted nothing to do with the Sino-Japanese conflict raging in the Far East was now out for blood. On December 8, Japan and the USA were officially at war. Approximately 2400 Americans were killed at Pearl Harbor (almost a thousand of whom remain entombed in the USS Arizona, which sank to the bottom of the ocean). Forty-nine civilians were among the dead, including a three-month-old infant. William Czako miraculously survived and went on to fight in the Pacific. After the war, he remained in the US Navy, working at a shipyard in Norfolk, Virginia, for more than 30 years.

In a letter to his family, Soviet Lieutenant Davydovych Zemchenkov lashes out at the 'German butchers' responsible for killing his loved ones in Russia during World War II — & — A German soldier named Bruno Kaliga writes to his family as the situation in Stalingrad reaches the point of utter hopelessness during World War II.

Claiming (falsely) that the invasion of the former Soviet Union, an operation codenamed Barbarossa, was a preemptive strike to counter an imminent Soviet offensive, Adolf Hitler predicted in an address to his generals that Barbarossa would be a 'battle of annihilation.' German troops were convinced it would be, at the very least, a sound thrashing. 'The war with Russia will last only four weeks!' one officer told his men. Well aware of the Russian capacity to stave off or outlast invaders, the Germans assembled an air and land force of unprecedented magnitude. The first of 4 million troops swarmed into the Soviet Union on June 22, 1941, catching Premier Joseph Stalin and his generals almost completely off-guard. 'Today was a day of pride for us all,' a German tank commander named Karl Fuchs, serving with the Seventh Panzer Division, wrote to his wife triumphantly from the Eastern Front on June 25. 'The Russians are fleeing everywhere and we follow them. All of us believe in early victory!' Soon after, he expressed the contempt he and his fellow soldiers felt for the Russian people as a whole, a prejudice nurtured by years of Nazi propaganda. 'We're going to show those Bolshevik bums who's who around here,' he crowed on June 28.

They fight like hired hands – not like soldiers, no matter if they are men, women, or children on the front lines. They're no better than a bunch of scoundrels. The entry of Spain and Hungary on our side against this Bolshevik archenemy of the world overjoyed us all. Yes, Europe stands under the leadership of our beloved Führer Adolf Hitler, and he'll reshape it for a better future.

It was not a future Fuchs would see; during a winter that even he admitted enveloped them in a 'gripping cold not comparable to anything that we might experience at home,' he was killed in action. And the Soviet troops he and his comrades had so disparaged turned out to be indefatigable soldiers fueled by righteous anger at having their country violated. An estimated 20–27 million Soviets died in the entire war. The following letter, written by Russian Lieutenant Davydovych Zemchenkov, offers a glimpse into the state of mind of one young soldier willing to sacrifice himself for his motherland. Zemchenkov was 19 or 20 at the time, and he, too, would lose his life in the war.

Hello my Mama, Marusya, Nastya, Valya, Zoya and Ninochka!

Like a ray of sun, I send you a warm greeting from the front, where we are battling the German fiends. I wish you good health for many years, good spirits and strength to endure all the difficulties you encounter. Sweet Mama, I got a letter from Zhenya today. How terrible! The mental picture was shocking. Death bearing a fascist swastika has spread its wings over our family. It has torn our family apart and turned to ash the nest that we worked on for so many years. Death is red with the blood of those I hold dear and has destroyed all we have created and value. Can I possibly feel even the slightest pity or humanity for them after this? No! Only a bullet piercing the black heart of the German, only a pouring forth of a river of their foul blood, only their pitiless and complete annihilation can ease my soul and temper our grief.

Those damned fiends shot my beloved brother, sent my father to an early grave, burned my home and broke my mother's health. Words fail me. This grief is too great. I am crying and am not ashamed of my tears. My friends see them and grieve together with me. But I am not despairing or losing my strength. Quite the opposite: fiery hatred and revenge burn in my heart. I swear to wreak revenge on the enemy for the rest of my life. I will keep killing and killing Germans to avenge my brother's death. My comrades in arms swear to avenge my brother's death as well. We grip our weapons tighter and shoot even straighter. The damned fiends have already felt our blows. They've already tasted plenty of our lead and steel. We've already killed several thousand of the damned Germans and will kill thousands more. We've shown our skill at fighting and winning in bloody battles with the enemy. The government and the Soviet people have shown their appreciation for our deeds, We have received a great honor – the title of guardsmen. The enemy knows us and our strength.

Dear Mama and dear sisters, you are all I have left. I want all of you, especially Mama, to keep your spirits up. Don't lose the strength you have left and take care of your health. I understand how difficult it is to endure this grief, this great sorrow, but there is nothing else to do. We have to bear it. That is how life is, Mama. Your sorrow, our sorrow, is not the only one. I've seen worse during my travels. In the mines at Shakhti we found 4,500 people killed by the German butchers. There were babies and children, women and old men. The monsters didn't just kill them; they abused them and then put them down in the hole and shot them. In one of the prisons in Rostov the Germans shot 3,500 people. Wherever the Fascist monsters go, they leave behind them a river of blood and innocent Soviet dead.

Mama, be strong and believe that I will return. When I do, we will live happily again. We will rebuild what has been destroyed. It will come with time. Mama, I'm sending letters to the RK and the regional executive committee with a request that you and the girls be allowed to go stay with Zhenya. Go stay with her and rest over the summer. I will help you. I'm sending you one thousand rubles today, and in a few days will send more. Nastya, Valya, Zoya, help Mama. Don't worry about me. I'm alive and well. I'm beating the Germans mercilessly. The hour of total victory is near. We will crush the enemy and return to you victorious.

Mama, give my greetings and best wishes to all the communal farm workers. Tell them to keep their spirits up

Confronted with both an enemy filled with incandescent rage and the daunting reality of Russia's geography – a vast ocean in which conquering armies came to drown, as many have described it – the German hubris that had been so pervasive at the beginning of the offensive slowly disintegrated. In few places was this transformation more evident than in Stalingrad. On August 23, 1942, German

135

warplanes blanketed the city with bombs and strafed civilians who tried to flee, killing an estimated 40,000 men, women, and children in two days. The Germans reached the heart of the city by mid-September but found themselves mired in street-to-street, building-to-building combat. Stalingrad itself became the battlefield, and the Russians knew that by prolonging the fight into the winter months it would give their reinforcements time to build up their strength and then surround the Germans. In December, German General Friedrich Paulas and the men of his Sixth Army recognized that they were in a dire position. An urgent plea to Hitler requesting permission to withdraw was met with scorn: 'Surrender is forbidden.' As hunger plagued the troops and the sub-zero weather became as debilitating mentally as it was physically, many lost hope. One German soldier, Bruno Kaliga, wrote the following as the army was collapsing around him.

My dear ones!
It is New Year's Eve, and when I think about home, my heart breaks. How miserable and hopeless everything is here. It's been four days since I had any bread. I am subsisting only on soup, for lunch. In the morning and in the evening, I have a swallow of coffee, and every two days I get about 100 grams of meat or some sardines in oil or a bit of cheese. Hunger hunger hunger – and all that lice and dirt. Day and night, we are attacked by planes, and the artillery fire never ends. If a miracle doesn't happen within the next few days, I will go down here. The only good thing is that I know that a 2-kg. Packet with marmalade and cake is on its way to me from you. Arsand Hede and Sindermann have also sent packets with cake and other delicacies. I think about it constantly and have started to go crazy thinking that these things will never reach me. Even though I am completely exhausted, I can't sleep at night. Instead I dream with open eyes of cake cake cake. Sometimes I pray, and sometimes I curse my own fate. Everything is without purpose and without sense.

When will salvation come? Will death come through a bomb or a grenade? Will it be sickness or chronic illness? All of these questions overwhelm us to no end. And with it comes the constant longing to go home, and homesickness does indeed become a sickness. How can a human being deal

*The scattered remains of Russian troops who died at Stalingrad
(now Volograd) are constantly being found and properly reburied.*

with all of this? Are all of these sufferings God's punishment? My dear ones, I'm not allowed to write all of this to you, but I have no spirit left in my body, and all humor has disappeared. One is merely a bundle of twitching nerves. The heart and brain are sickeningly overstimulated, and you shake like with fever. If they stand me up in court because of this letter and shoot me, I would like to believe it would be a good deed for my body. I am without hope, and I ask you, don't cry too much when you receive the news that I am no more. Be good to each other, thank God for every day that's given to you, because at home, life is sweet.

With heartfelt love,

Yours,
Bruno

Bruno's fate is not known, but it is doubtful that he survived. Out of approximately 600,000 German and Axis soldiers involved in the battle for Stalingrad, half a million are believed to have perished. The Russians lost at least that many. The remaining 90,000 Germans who were sent to prison camps in the Soviet Union entered a world of immeasurable suffering. Only 5000 made it home alive after the war.

A Russian sniper named Natalya Kovshova tells her mother how much she enjoys 'Hunting' German soldiers in 1942 — & — Cambridge University student Christopher H. Smith explains to a close friend why he refuses to fight during World War II.

Nothing – not brute strength, bravado, nor impassioned declarations of patriotism – can accurately determine how a soldier, marine, air-man, or sailor will ultimately function in combat until he or she is actually under fire. The most physically intimidating and outwardly self-assured individuals can wilt in an instant, while those who seemed timid and unimposing in training can prove to be warriors of unmatched agility and aggression when the bombs and bullets start to fly. (One of the most decorated American soldiers of World War II, Audie Murphy, was a baby-faced orphan from Texas who stood barely five and a half feet tall. Murphy joined the US Army after the Marine Corps had rejected him for being too small.) Some troops not only perform confidently once in battle, they thrive on the rush of adrenaline. '[I]f you ever talk with either instructor jockeys or the jackpots [trainees] they are checking out and mention me, don't say I am a pilot, say I'm a _fighter_ pilot,' Second Lieutenant Bill Fant, a farm boy from Kansas, boasted to his mother and father on March 25, 1943. Fant had enlisted in the army in September 1941 and was called to active duty three weeks after Pearl Harbor. Assigned to the 11th Fighter Squadron, 343rd Fighter Group of the Army Air Corps, he flew P-40s against the Japanese in the Aleutian campaign. The 25-year-old Fant was killed six days after writing to his parents, but, as his letter of March 25 attested, Fant was doing exactly what he wanted. He continued:

> I'd a thousand times rather be in the air than on the ground. And if I ever do get knocked off it will be sudden and final. I'd rather go out with a wide open throttle and two wings full of guns blasting than to sink into the slime of a fox-hole with a bayonet in my guts. Things happen fast in the air – you act but never have time to worry, which is just as well. I'm doing what I want and that's worth a whole lot to me. Up here more pilots die of old age than go down in flames. I'm safer here than driving a car at home, so don't worry about me – just forget it and I'll walk in and surprize you when you least expect me sometime.

Others drew all the inspiration they needed from the fact that they were defending their homeland. 'Our detachment has moved to the other line in pursuit of Hitler's monsters,' Russian sniper Natalya Kovshova wrote to her mother. 'You can hear horrible stories from local residents who have been in the hands of the fascist pigs. The woman we live with

139

had a guest come to visit who said that the Germans shot her brother and four of his friends, 14–15 years old, simply because they went outside after 4 pm.' Kovshova was 21 when the Germans stormed into Russia in 1941, and within a year she had become a highly skilled sniper with the 528th Infantry Detachment, 130th Infantry Division. (Although most modern armies still prohibit women from fighting in frontline infantry units, women have placed themselves in harm's way during virtually every armed conflict in history.) Few of Kovshova's correspondences have survived, but the following letter to her mother, written only five weeks before she died in battle, reveals her genuine delight at tracking down and killing German soldiers.

July 7, 1942

My dearest Mama!

Please don't be angry that I didn't write to you about being wounded. But I didn't want to worry you for no reason, since nothing serious happened. Now I'm sorry that I wrote to Sverdlovsk about it. Everything ended up fine. My wounds have healed well, and, in addition to walking on the ground, I'm climbing trees as well.

The most serious wound was to my left arm above the elbow (where they stick the smallpox vaccination), and it has healed nicely. At first the scars were bright pink, but now my skin is getting thicker and darkening. My bandages are off, too, so that is that.

I've been back with my unit since June 2, 1942. Now Mashenka and I are working with the young snipers. Their statistics are looking good. In the last two weeks of June our students took down 3 Fritzes. Not bad! And if you consider that we haven't seen any fighting during this period, then it looks great. We didn't do any hunting in June, ourselves. My arm hurt, and Mashenka didn't have time. She's doing a great job – she teaches like a real professor. A few days ago five of us went on reconnaissance without saying anything to the company commander. We were under the Germans' very noses and they had no clue! They were talking, coughing, making phone calls and we heard everything. It was great. We found a whole line of reinforcements, and the location of a mortar and artillery battery. We

Russian sniper Natalya Kovshova with her younger sister Veronika.

thought, wonderful, we'll get praised, but we almost got put under arrest. 'You shouldn't be running around on reconnaissance, especially without permission.' What a nut. But we're not upset at all. Next time we get a chance we'll go again. Reconnaissance is an interesting business.

On June 5 we were read an order giving us the sniper badge – this one goes on the right side, but we'll get one for the left side, too!

Sweet Mama, don't be sad and don't worry. Everything will be fine.

Kisses and hugs to all of you!

Nata

For other World War II troops, however, especially the 'grunts' in the infantry, combat was less a sport than a prolonged, nightmarish succession of miseries, large and small. '[T]hat very sarcastic letter of yours demands a reply and eventually an apology from you,' a peeved American soldier named William Rigby wrote to his sister after she complained he was neglecting to correspond with her. (The letter was typed, and the mistakes and creative punctuation are in the original.)

> *You don't realize the effect that being in combat has on some men, . . . some men can't take it and they break under the strain, others find another outlet for those emotions. You don't seem to realize that I've been living practically like an animal for the past seven months . . . there is no glamour, or color, or dash to the life of the Infantrymen. All there is, is dirt and death. [. . .] I didn't write because I didn't want to write, all that I [wanted] to do, was to forget about what happened during the day and forget about what might happened tomorrow. I found an outlet for my emotions by not doing anything, by just relaxing . . . reading, listening to the radio, etc. Other wrote letters and obtained the same effect. I could say more, but I'll stop here and allow you to come to a new decision . . . and please. stop pestering me about w riting.*

And in many instances, young men – regardless of nationality – refused to fight. Some deserted or fled their countries out of fear, while others resisted on religious and moral grounds. A 20-year-old student named Christopher Smith, who had been studying at Cambridge University, registered as a conscientious objector instead of joining the military. But, as he emphasized in a letter to a close friend, Smith was not opposed to contributing to the defense of England or risking his life, he simply did not want to kill another human being in the process. (The RAMC is the Royal Army Medical Corps.)

16 : 4 : 43

Dear George,

Note the address please! It was grand to get your letter and the lithograph. Just like you to remember such a thing at this time!

Everybody has been so kind and helpful during the last week. Jordan Bennett, Mr Walker, my old School Chaplain & Headmaster, & Welbourne – all have been doing all they can for me. And things haven't been so black as I had expected. After enquiries had been made in London by Alex Wood and I had interviewed many people many times, I saw the Joint Recruiting Board yesterday and re-registered, this time as a C.O. I shall get a Tribunal – when, I am not quite sure – and as far as I can make out will be able to stay up here until then. Isn't that wonderful? You know, this is a remarkable country – so much so, that it is not easy to refuse the service they demand of one! But of this one thing I am quite sure, if my duty to God & my duty to my country conflict, I must obey the call of God. I know that all Christians have not been led to make the same choice as myself, and I know they are just as sincere as myself. I tried to persuade myself for long enough that my way was the same as theirs, but it isn't, and I shan't be much of a witness for Christ if I fail him now. You know, I don't think I had ever realised before what strength God puts at our disposal, but I am convinced that through those who honestly & sincerely offer their lives to him – whatever way they may be lead and however they choose to answer this particular question – God can work, God will work and is working, and through them his power, which is almighty, which changes the world.

How did I give you the idea that I could not do Red Cross work? Have I left out a negative somewhere? On the contrary, I feel I cannot stand aside from all the dreadful suffering in the world and do nothing. Since the Christ

143

upon the Cross is not suffering passively, since the cross is not the end, since the love of God is not negative, but active and dynamic and redemptive, that same action must typify our lives. To do nothing is never the right attitude for the Christian as he faces evil, sin & suffering.

But since RAMC work involves some training of a combatant nature, I cannot conscientiously do this, and have applied to the Friends' Ambulance Unit to see if I can get in there. The one thing I am anxious to avoid is comfort and security, and I can best bear my Christian witness by sharing in the suffering and pain of the world, and by doing all in my power to alleviate it.

I thank God that I can proclaim now, as of experience, the love and power of Him who says 'Follow me.'

Remember me in your prayers. I know there are many who are doing the same, and it makes all the difference.

This had to be written to stop you fainting away when next you darken the portals of C I [College Immanuel]. My training has not yet begun, and an unconscious gentleman would still be something of a load upon the hands. As for four figure references – well, I can't give it you accurately, but I could pinpoint a pretty rough idea of meeting place on a sufficient small scale map! (It's grand to know there is little immediate danger of being sent down.) So it'll probably be, at a guess, somewhere in Immanuel College precincts and – again I hazard – perhaps on Monday night? Yippee!

Last week was a great week, wasn't it? I shan't forget. But 'let me tell you', I've got a peach of a crossword for you to solve. A little too easy, perhaps, but clues very fair and every word a <u>real</u> word! This, too, is mighty fine! Cheerio for now and thank you again for writing.

Yours ever,
Chris

Smith's argument proved persuasive, and he was allowed to join the Friends' Ambulance Unit. After serving mostly in Germany, Smith returned home alive and well after the war.

American Staff Sergeant Neil Schmelz describes to his parents an unforgettable religious service he attended during a lull in the fighting in Belgium during World War II — & — In a letter to his parents, American Lieutenant James R. Penton includes a sketch he has drawn depicting faith in action in France during World War II.

Exposed to suffering on a breathtaking scale and often confronted with seemingly random deaths, especially of innocent civilians, it is not unexpected that some troops (regardless of the conflict) begin to question their faith or the existence of any divine, benevolent force in the universe. 'Damn darling, I get so mad,' an American Army lieutenant named Russ Merrell from Utah wrote to his wife, Betty, on July 5, 1944. Merrell had seen firsthand the utter viciousness of combat, and he was incredulous that human nature could be so wicked – or be allowed to be by a loving God.

> *I know for a certainty that this won't be the last war. There will be others. At the present state of civilization there just isn't any solution for all the difficulties. And yet very few people want to fight wars. Christ, a person is so damn helpless. I don't know why I worry about such things. I've lost confidence in everything... If God's chief work has been the creation of this earth and man on it, to date He and His work have been a glorious failure.*

The same disintegration of social order that can throw an individual into existential despair, however, can also strengthen the connection many feel with God or with whatever their concept of spirituality might be. This is more than wishful thinking; alongside the sadism and barbarity unleashed in all wars, there are heroic examples of selfless-ness and compassion. Servicemen and women often risk their lives for total strangers, provide comfort to those who are sick or grieving, or act mercifully when vengeance might be their first impulse. Through these sacrifices and the close friendships forged in battle, combat troops can experience a renewed sense of humanity. 'Today I witnessed the most impressive sight I have ever seen,' an American Army staff sergeant named Neil Schmelz wrote to his parents from Belgium in September 1944. Schmelz went on to write:

We had Mass in a beautiful little church in this city and, honestly, the church seemed like a little heaven in itself. The soldiers filled almost half the church and the rest of it was filled with civilians. As usual our chaplain heard confessions first and then started Mass. Before he began reading Mass, though, the Belgian priest went to the pulpit and in their native tongue spoke to his own people. His sermon consisted of, as far as I could tell, a great big thank you to the American soldiers for coming to their country to give them the freedom they have long been waiting for. It was very impressive; the women were weeping and a hushed silence fell throughout the entire congregation. I almost had to cry myself. The priest also told the people that they should understand that we, the soldiers, were making a great sacrifice in that we were leaving behind our wives and families whom we greatly loved.

The chaplain then started Mass and it seemed like out of no where came the sweetest strains of the organ and the voices of the choir. All I can say is that it was indeed heavenly music. Then came the Consecration and the organist played the 'Star Spangled Banner': something none of us ever have heard before, but it just didn't seem one bit out of place. It gave us the feeling that we were really helping those poor people and that they deeply appreciated it. It made the shivers run up and down my spine. At the end of the Mass, to make the whole event as complete as it could ever be, the organist again played the 'Star Spangled Banner' and also the Belgium national anthem. Truly you could almost see the joy popping out of the people's eyes. If I live to be 100 years old I don't believe I'll ever see anything that will impress me more.

Neil Schmelz

At almost the same time that Schmelz sent his letter, a young Jewish officer named Joseph Portnoy described the following scene in a long letter to his wife from Holland (Bobby is their son):

Today continued with not too many events, but it gave me the opportunity of attending a Yom Kippur service. The service lasted all morning. I especially took note of the yizkor or memorial service. Death over here has become such a light matter that I've almost forgotten that it was supposed to be accompanied by sadness. But at the service, the Rabbi again gave us the theme of the old attitude of returning to God and everlasting life. It sunk deeply, and made me realize that the toughness of war can easily be erased once one returns home to the churches and synagogues, and begins building the stones of civilization all over again and removing us from the callous savagery that we find here in this war. There will be a successful returning. Don't be afraid darling. Gosh how I adore you. I can tell you that over and over again, and each time I mean it. It's marvelous to have a love that's always in springtime. Tickle Bobby's feet for me. Yours Ever.

Also in September of 1944, Lieutenant James R. Penton, serving with an American tank destroyer battalion in France that was pushing its way toward Germany, sent his parents a letter and sketch he had drawn that illustrated true grace under fire. It was inspired by a scene that deeply moved Penton, a self-proclaimed 'argumentative and skeptical atheist.' (Bill Penton, whom he alludes to, is his cousin, and the long ellipses are in the original letter.)

3 September 1944

Dear Mother and Governor:

In the 'Reader's Digest' there's a monthly article entitled 'The Most Unforgettable Character I've Known,' – or something of the sort. Well, not so long ago I met an unforgettable character myself . . . .

My guns were in position in a small farmyard in the recently-wrested town of Vire, along the crest of a beautiful ridge, – and but a stone's throw from the rubble-dusty-haze rising above the warm ruins of the cities' downtown business section.

There was no 'Business As Usual' in Vire that night, – only 'Nazi-Tactics as Usual' as the Butchers of Spirit and Property harassed the town from afar with artillery shells aimed at no one spot in particular. My platoon crept into

147

town as dusk merged into darkness, – barely moving at all in the tortured streets so as to keep down dust - - - and resulting enemy observation.

And as the sun of early morning dissolved the fog, yawning faces appeared from the depths of holes in the ground, and the boys were moving about comparing notes about the night before. Considerable interest was shown in the truck, – which had suffered three gashed tires, a perforated radiator, and other numerous shrapnel holes.

In the light of day I noticed a sprawling, peaceful convent to the immediate rear of the position, – with its courtyard and spires almost miraculously untouched. And while I sat there, – in the protection of a bank, gazing at the convent and listening to the melodious chiming of its bells intermingle with the hideous wail of Jerry 88's, – a solitary nun made her way deliberately through the yard, a bucket of water in one hand. It was a shock to hear her address me in perfect English, show identification papers, and learn that she was caring for the livestock in the absence of the terrorized farmer and his family.

And that's the sum and substance of my story. All morning long, as the whine of Jerry artillery overhead kept the rest of us in our holes, that nun moved serenely and placidly about the skeleton of the burned-out barn, – and around the bodies of dead, bloated cows; - - - - - milking the swollen cows, feeding and watering the chickens, collecting eggs.

And I know that our most argumentative and skeptical atheist was duly fascinated and impressed by that display of the power and force of that Sister's faith – – and complete fearlessness . . . . . . It was not the sudden, stimulated and short-lived courage which drives a man to risk hot lead on a daring dash to aid a buddy, to me, it was far more than that . . . . . It was the picture of a mellowed and complete faith, – it was serenity of mind and soul amidst man's savagery of arm and spirit. . . . . That nun hadn't spent two years of training, and 'battle-conditioning' and crawling under gun fire . . . . . but her poise and expression and dogged pursuit of someone else's domestic duties in the midst of that inferno was something we will all remember; – as we will the quarter-hourly chiming of the convent bells, as if in patient, long suffering defiance of the high explosive shells which ripped the city . . . .

And as I sketched the nun, – some of the boys glanced over my shoulder . . . There was no title on the paper, – but every one immediately recollected . . .

THE NUN of VIRE.....

VIRE, FRANCE
August 1944

Lt. J.R.Ponton

Well, there is nothing new to say. We seem to be doing things rapidly here in France, – but don't expect that daily collapse . . . These Germans are either crazymen or madmen, – and the fact that they are being cut off into little 'pockets' does not prevent their generals from driving them to the long drawn-out slaughter . . . . .

Received a letter from Bill Penton yesterday. Hardly seems possible he's been overseas two full years. Time flies here, though, – and I rarely know what day of the week it is.

Do not worry when I don't have time to write. You know in the army – 'no news is good news.'

Love to all,
Jim

More than two months later, Penton was shot through his right shoulder. 'Well, how's this for my first southpaw letter?' he wrote in a short, surprisingly upbeat message to his parents on December 23. 'My right arm is in a plaster of Paris cast, – I'm in Paris, too – France. . . . I'm O.K., though, and will soon be in England. Don't worry over me. Love to all, Jim.' Penton would recuperate fully, return home, and continue making sketches and paintings.

U S Second Lieutenant Thomas A. Edwards writes to his parents in 1945 from the Japanese island of Iwo Jima, but says he will never mention the island again — & — In a letter from war-ravaged Germany during World War II, American Captain Roy F. Bergengren shares with a friend what he hopes will be achieved after so many years of death and destruction.

'It is with great shame that I report that despite our efforts, we will not be able to prevent this strategic island from falling into enemy hands,' General Tadamichi Kuribayashi, Commander-in-Chief of all Japanese forces on Iwo Jima, wired Imperial General Headquarters on

March 17, 1945, before killing himself. 'Please accept my most sincere apology for failing to fulfill my mission.' Three and a half years after a crippling blow at Pearl Harbor, the USA had transformed the world's 18th-largest army into one of the most powerful, and now the full fury of its military was bearing down on the islands of Japan in preparation for a full-scale invasion of the mainland. (Codenamed Downfall, the operation would have eclipsed the June 1944 Normandy landings in both size and complexity.) For five grueling weeks beginning on February 19, 1945, 70,000 American troops, most of them marines, confronted 22,000 Japanese soldiers on the tiny but heavily fortified and booby-trapped island of Iwo Jima. Using flamethrowers, grenades, artillery, machine guns, and at times even bayonets and knives during hand-to-hand fighting, the Marines successfully captured the island, but at a cost of 6800 lives and 20,000 wounded. (All of the Japanese either were killed or committed suicide.) On March 13, a Welsh-born US marine officer named Thomas Alun Edwards sent his parents a letter from Iwo Jima that, although brief, said volumes about the strain the marines were under.

Dear Folks:
Well here I am, still alive & well. Things are dragging out for a final show-down. The island has been pretty well secured, and we're all thankful. This place has been Hell and still is. It is just a hot dusty pile of sand and ashes.

It smells of death and is barren and desolate. Suribachi is bleak, and forbidding. The men sit about listlessly. Nobody is in any sort of mood for kidding. There is death all around. A lot of the boys that landed when I did, are dead. Every time the ambulance goes by, I say to myself, 'There but for the grace of God, go I.' It is the sight of our own dead that is terrible.

You see these youngsters, horribly mutilated by shrapnel, & artillery. There is no peacefulness in their death – it came on them too violently and viciously. Many of them had no idea why they fought. They were so young. I am humble and grateful for being spared.

I would rather not write anymore today, and I will not mention any more about Iwo Jima in any later letters because I am sick about my friends who died, and so please just tell me about things at home, & don't mention this campaign anymore.

All my love to you both

Alun

The battle for Okinawa, which followed almost immediately, had half as many casualties, but the combat was every bit as horrific. Describing the first influx of injured troops, a navy pharmacist's mate recalled the scene in a letter to his parents: 'They were hurt bad, it wasn't pretty & they mumbled, those who could, first eye witness reports. "Jesus Christ it's murder" said a Guadalcanal veteran, & another kid, not more than 18 kept repeating, "Oh God, oh God. . ." And some men were so traumatized they went truly mad.' J. W. Foster, captain of the USS ATR 80, related the following story in a letter home (OOD stands for 'officer on deck'):

Shortly after dropping anchor an incident occurred which left me in a physically weakened condition, and the likes of which I surely hope never happens again. I was standing out on the wing of the bridge when a Marine 1st Lt. came alongside in a small boat and wanted to take his casualties off. I told him that they had already been transferred to the hospital ship and everything had been taken care of, but this did not seem to satisfy him. At first he seemed to be normal, but the longer he stayed, the crazier he began to talk, such as: 'We're all going home;' 'All of my men have been killed;' 'The war is over;' 'I want to go with my men;' etc. Then he asked again if I was or wasn't going to give his casualties back, to which I replied, 'No.' He pulled out his .45 pistol and fired point blank at me. God's Grace prevented him from hitting, I suppose, for a marine doesn't miss at that close range. He took off toward another transport nearby, so I sent them an urgent message to investigate him . . . About five minutes later, I got this message back, 'The marine officer came aboard, shot the O.O.D., then blew his own brains out.' Well, I wasn't so scared until I heard this, and I'll admit my knees knocked together a few times when I realized what a close call it had been.

The Pacific war ended four months later in a crescendo of violence with the atomic explosions over Hiroshima and Nagasaki. As the world celebrated the news of Japan's surrender, frontline troops wrote more solemnly about the conclusion of hostilities. 'Everybody around here had a wild time for a few minutes when the news first came through about the end of war,' 24-year-old Max Peters wrote to a friend back home. 'But, although I felt just as jubilant about it as the rest, I still had the memories of the death and destruction I had seen in the last few weeks too fresh in my mind to feel like giving vent to any cheering and shouting.' After providing a litany of gruesome memories from those past few weeks as a sergeant with the Tenth Mountain Division in Italy, Peters went on to write:

> I can easily see that we can never expect the folks at home to understand what we've seen and done; so I'll skip all the rest of the things that I've done (or I'd rather say 'things that the war has made me do') - - - I'm pretty sure I couldn't even bring myself to mention a great many of them anyhow - - - - maybe if I force myself not to remember them their meaning will gradually fade away. Now that at least partial peace has been obtained I only hope that all our statesmen and people at home as well as us overseas will see that the peace we form is a real and lasting one. I and all the rest of us over here will certainly do everything in our power to preserve that peace - - - We owe that much at least to our buddies who are gone.

Peters was not alone in his yearning for something positive and enduring to be born out of the sacrifices made by those who would not be returning home. Even before the armistices in Europe and Asia were declared, servicemen and women who traveled through demolished towns and villages once bustling with life, or drove past the seemingly endless blur of homemade crosses on open fields, reflected intently on the cost of their hard-won victory. Roy F. Bergengren Jr., a captain with the Seventy-eighth Fighter Control Squadron, Second Air Defense Wing, saw combat for over two and a half years in Africa, England,

France, Germany, Italy, and Sicily. Writing to a friend in Madison, Wisconsin, Bergengren ruminated not only on the end of war, but on the human condition itself and what its future would be in the shadow of such a searing and monstrous tragedy. He passionately hoped that his generation and those to come would learn from the years of slaughter and ruin that he, like so many others, had witnessed firsthand.

Dear Don,

Having entered Germany a while ago, I feel something like the coast-to-coast marathon runner must as he crosses the New York state line.

In 28 months, I've journeyed through 11 countries to get here. It was a rather round about route, but there's never been any doubt about where we were headed. I hope I shall travel right to Berlin – and then home.

So far, it has been an interesting, if unpleasant experience. I could certainly have done nicely without it, but since it has been necessary, I'm glad to be one of those taking a share in it.

There have been a few outstanding impressions. Obvious though they may be, they are none-the-less vivid.

First is the absolute futility of war. Seen at close range, it becomes so brutal and stupid that we have to rub our eyes to believe the world is capable of it. It can't be written; samples of the death, poverty, and destruction in war's wake must be seen to be appreciated.

In a Lyons café, a French journalist asked me, 'Why is it you Americans refuse to believe the Germans really tortured and killed so many innocent people in France?'

I couldn't answer. I guess it's because we live so far from such things and we must see to believe. Words fail to make such things real.

A second impression is the fundamental similarity of the peoples of the united nations. I've lived and worked with British, French, Australian, South African, New Zealand, Polish, and Belgian soldiers to name a few. I'm convinced that we all seek the same general sort of life. We criticize one another for our little individual eccentricities; each of us thinks his is the best nation; but fundamentally we differ little. When this war is won, we must remember only the fundamentals and get together in a big way.

A third impression is that of America's own capabilities. London, Algiers,

Paris, Rome, Florence, Marseilles, and every other city and town in every liberated country teeming with American traffic. Huge depots of American supplies, throngs of American men everywhere. If we can put forth one half the effort for peace that we've expended in this war, because it was necessary, there should never be need for another war. We must realize that peace, now, is just as necessary as the war has been.

I'm now living in a half-wrenched miner's house. There's snow and there's cold in addition to other little worrisome things. I and millions of others like me aren't enjoying ourselves at the moment, but we're perfectly willing to live this way because we have faith that the peoples of the world this time are going to do a better job in fashioning the peace.

I greatly enjoyed your Christmas box which arrived before I left Italy – in fact the various pages of the 'artist's sketch book' now gaily adorn the walls of this shack and greatly add to it's livability. When I pull out, they'll go along with me. They're quite the travelled little beauties.

I've rambled on at some length and must now get a bit of shut-eye. The lessons to be learned from war are so simple and so obvious, that they have to come out. This time, dammit, we've got to remember them.

My best to the gang,

Roy

Writing from a hospital behind the front lines, during the Korean War, American Private Ted Brush gives his parents an unsparing report on how he was wounded in action — & — Lieutenant James Van Veen, an American pilot serving in the Korean War, laments to a former sweetheart that he does not feel close to anyone – but that it might be for the best.

Even before the final surrender of Japan was signed aboard the USS Missouri *on September 2, 1945, marking the official end of World War II, the long-term global peace that so many troops had prayed for was already threatening to unravel. The menace was not Japan, America's* former enemy, but the Soviet Union, its wartime ally. The mutual distrust between President Harry Truman and Soviet premier Joseph Stalin, apparent at the Potsdam Conference in the summer of 1945, better reflected the relationship between the two nascent superpowers than the image of grinning Russian and US soldiers at the Elbe River several months earlier. As the Soviets imposed Communist rule over neighboring countries and, years later, tested their first atomic weapon, many in the West perceived a larger Communist conspiracy at work to dominate the world. Their fears were bolstered on June 25, 1950, when 90,000 pro-Communist North Korean troops surged across the 38th parallel in a surprise invasion of the US-backed Republic of Korea. President Truman immediately mobilized the army and appealed to the newly formed United Nations for military assistance. By the end of July, American-led UN and Republic of Korea (ROK) soldiers were vastly outnumbered and clinging to the southeast corner of the peninsula. The tide suddenly turned, however, in September after General Douglas MacArthur, who commanded the UN forces, staged an ambitious landing behind enemy lines at Inchon. 'I will be glad when we start pushing these Gooks back across the 38th Parallel,' a young private from Ohio wrote to his family on September 15, 1950, the day of MacArthur's invasion. Like many of his fellow soldiers, he anticipated a swift conclusion: 'After we start, it won't last long & I can get home that much quicker.' The fighting would last another three years. Officially, the UN called the conflict in Korea a 'police action,' but for those on the front lines it was a full-blown war. On September 30, 1950, the North Koreans were in full retreat, and within weeks they had been driven back to the Yalu River, which marks the boundary with Manchuria. It was an astonishing reversal, and one that heralded the possibility of a unified, democratic nation. And then the Chinese attacked. In late October and early November hundreds of thousands of Chinese soldiers streamed into North Korea, and by January 1951, the Chinese and North Koreans had re-captured Seoul and other major cities. Three months later the tide turned again, and the UN troops were now on the *offensive. The seemingly endless crisscrossing over the 38th parallel continued, with hundreds of thousands of lives lost in the meantime. 'I arrived in Korea last night,' 20-year-old Private Ted Brush wrote to his parents in Richfield, Idaho, on August 14, 1951. Brush was stunned by the physical devastation of the country and the plight of the civilians.*

> It is quite a site. Every town is shot up, and most of the good buildings are all ruined. The Seoul railroad yards are a mess. There are wrecked tracks with ruined cars all over. The Korean's are in pretty bad shape. They live in bombed out houses, grass and doby shaks, and burlap houses. I don't see how some of them can avoid freezing to death.

Brush's letters, like those of his fellow troops fighting in Korea, were not censored. Combatants were instructed to use their discretion, but their letters tended to be more forthcoming about locations and casualties than those from World Wars I and II. (Many servicemen and women from the world wars related graphic combat accounts and sensitive information, too, but these letters were often written long after a battle or smuggled home by a friend returning home.) The Korean conflict had exploded too quickly for the military to implement an official procedure for checking all outgoing mail, and with the war's end always seeming imminent, such a mechanism was never put in place. There was also concern that suddenly instituting censorship would dampen morale and suggest that the government had something to conceal. (Truman's popularity was already sinking in the USA as a result of the war.) Less than two months after landing in Korea, Ted Brush sustained multiple wounds while fighting in Taejon. On October 6, he described his injuries to his parents in detail.

Dear Folks,

I suppose you have already received a telegram saying that I was wounded in action. I am now in a hospital at Tajon, South Korea, about 30 miles behind the front line. I was hit by two grenades. We went into the assault up a hill and the

Chinks just stayed in their holes and threw out grenades. I dodged around still keeping moving forward but slowing down cause grenades were all over. I was shooting at the chinks' holes to keep them from getting up and shooting and I knelt down to put a new magazine in my B.A.R. when a rocket shrapnell from a grenade behind me hit me right along the left jaw. I saw blood spurting and my face went numb so I called to my foxhole buddy (Kelly) to take my B.A.R.

I was just handing it to him when someone yelled 'Grenade!' I started to hit the dirt and Kelly kind of fell away when I felt myself get hit in the right leg. A curious feeling went up my leg and then I got hit in the right cheek. I fell down and felt blood running in my boot and looked at Kelly, he was holding his hand and motioned for me to come back where he was but I couldn't make it. I just laid there praying, half afraid I was going to bleed to death. I was calling a medic but I couldn't see one. About ½ hour later, one showed up and bandaged me, another guy had tried to move me, but I couldn't hardly move. I laid there for about another hour and ½, hollering for a litter. (I could hear my squad leader cussing and yelling to get one for me too, when I noticed bullets kicking up dust and found out a sniper was firing at me, so I crawled over the hill.)

They're about ready to put me on the train to Pusan so will close. I have a broken leg so maybe I'll get home. I am fine, but it still hurts a little. Will write tomorrow so don't worry. The medical corps is doing a good job on me.

Love,

Ted

P.S. We lost a lot of men on that hill. The # of the hill is 477.

In a foreshadowing of the Vietnam war, troops in Korea also began to communicate their frustrations about the conflict more openly. Griping about unpalatable rations, awful weather, and other inconveniences was nothing new. Combatants in previous wars had expressed bitterness toward those responsible for starting them, but had rarely opposed the objectives for which they were fighting. In Korea, the aggravations were mounting. Many blamed the president for gutting the military after World War II, and they were further incensed when he fired MacArthur in April 1951 after the general's comments about wanting to wage a larger war with China. They were furious about the outdated equipment and inadequate gear they had been issued. And they found it maddening to seize, surrender, recapture, and then lose again the same territory time after time, especially as peace negotiations were started and then abandoned because of – from the perspective of those in the field – trivial squabbles and disputes. In an emotional five-page letter about the loss of a close buddy named Robert 'Bat' Banuelos Madrid, a Japanese-American marine named Robert M. Wada vented about the war's overall aims, which he argued should be more aggressive and include advancing 'all the way to Moscow.' The letter was dated December 21, 1951, a time when UN forces had, once again, penetrated into North Korea. (Wada self-censored one word in the text.)

> *I loved ['Bat'] like my own brother and I never let him leave my heart and I never shall forget him – I think of him everyday and still can not believe he is gone – We are now waiting for the peace talks to either go through or blow up – We are preparing to move back 10–15 miles – Goddamn Rudy, we are leaving the ground we just took, the hill 'Bat' was killed on and everything – F- - - it, let's go on – It hurts me, It really does Rudy, to leave the ground so many guys died on – Especially 'Bat.'*

Other troops were nearly despondent about being in Korea. Less than a month before he was killed in action, 22-year-old Private James Arnold wrote to his family:

> *If something don't happen to me I should get to see all of you people about Xmas or I'm going to be greatly disappointed. I guess all we can do now is to pray that the good Lord will see fit to stop this mess in the near future. It looks to me like he is the only one who can stop it now. I went upon the front lines & stayed alnight & one day. I did't see any action but some of my buddies did in fact one of them is missing now. Boy that really makes a fellow feel bad, to have to go & help carry the dead & wounded out on litters when he knows they died for some*

useless cause. The hills are so steep & rough that ambulances can't get in to get the boys so they have to be carried out by hand unless they can get them by helicopters   they move a lot like that. You talk about hurting . . . if someone had of shot me it would have been a favor to me.

Even letters that articulated a sense of pride and determination revealed hints of an underlying gloom and ambivalence. James Van Veen was attending the University of Michigan's School of Business Administration on an ROTC [Reserved Officers' Training Corps] scholarship when he was called up to fly combat missions in Korea with the 310th Fighter Bomber Squadron. On April 25, 1953, Lieutenant Van Veen wrote a short letter to a woman he had dated at school named Elise Kerlin. Van Veen believed his contribution to the war effort was valuable, but he also longed for home.

25 April '53
K-2-KOREA.

Dear Elise,

It has sure been a long time since I have written you. I hope you have not forgotten me completely.

I now have 20 missions. They have taken me from the front lines to near the Manchurian border. I have certainly been lucky so far, for fate has been with me and I have gotten home after every mission.

As a pilot quite a bit is demanded. Sometimes I think too much, but actually I wouldn't be doing anything else here. It seems your part in the fight is tangible. I do not mean to slight any of the jobs that go to support the flying end [without which] not a single jet could get into the air.

So often I think of the beautiful campus and the wonderful time I had at Michigan. I wish I was back again. It always seems that no matter what you are doing you wish you were doing something else. I remember in my last semester I thought how wonderful it would be to fly a jet fighter in the cause of freedom. So here I am and [I] wish I [was] back at school. Foolish isnt it?

I often think how happy you made my last semester for me. I shall never forget it. I hope you don't feel too badly towards me for breaking it off so abruptly.

As for my love life. I can truly say I have none. At present I am writing no one, and have no ties. Perhaps it is best this way. When one prepares to be far from home he should hold no ties, for so often it can only mean more loneliness for all concerned. Many men in my line have died here or have been killed in training in preparation for war. I have seen their wives and loved ones suffer sorrow which they will never get over.

I have been talking on and on about myself and have not asked about you. Hope you will write me and bring me up to date I will be looking forward to hearing from you.

Well I sure have run out of things to say. So until my next I remain your correspondent

Love
Jim

Kerlin responded to Van Veen's letter, but her reply was sent back with the word 'deceased' stamped over his name. At the time of Van Veen's death, neither the Chinese and North Korean troops nor the UN forces were able to overpower the other decisively, and negotiations sputtered on and off again until July 27, 1953, when an armistice was declared. Neither side had, in the end, gained ground after the UN action successfully pressed the Communists back above the 38th parallel in September 1950. Millions of Koreans perished in the three-year war, along with 37,000 Americans (8000 are still listed as missing in action). The number of Chinese deaths is not known but is believed to be in the hundreds of thousands. Officially, the war is not over but merely in a state of cease-fire.

After experiencing crushing defeat at Diẽn Biên Phu, in Vietnam, French Army doctor Jacques Aulong criticizes the military leadership but praises his fellow troops for their courage and tenacity.

'*Vu Ban is in the Muong country,*' Roger Micault, a French soldier in Vietnam, wrote to a young neighbor curious about a soldier's life in Vietnam, '*a country with very rough terrain, and there's only one way to handle it: When we leave on patrol, we either crawl on all fours along the sides of the mountains in order to climb them, or we march in the valleys where the rice fields are, where we're in mud up to our knees.*' He continued:

> There's no road, trails are waterlogged by the rainy season, and you can't always use them because they're often mined by the Viet Minh communist troops. And the sun is always beating down! What a country! At night, the mosquitoes succeed in finding their way through the mosquito-netting and keep us from sleeping. Another big problem – safe drinking water. I mean there isn't any. We do have a spring beside the post with water that's nearly clean. But it's the only one, and you maybe have to go 50 km to get to the next one. So when we're on patrol we have to make do with river water or water from the rice fields (there's plenty of that) that we have to filter with a handkerchief and disinfect with chlorine. And since it's so hot and we're very thirsty, we make ourselves drink it.

Micault then went on to share his thoughts about the war from both a military and political perspective. He was frustrated by the growing strength of the Communist leader Ho Chi Minh and his Viet Minh troops, and Micault lamented hearing about the antiwar sentiment – including accusations against the soldiers themselves – fermenting back home.

> When will this war end? I admit that I don't see the solution. . . . Ho Chi Minh is getting organized and counts a lot on the Chinese Communists. As for us, we don't have enough personnel or equipment, and we're disapproved of by one segment of public opinion that doesn't hesitate to call us assassins and that glorifies Ho Chi Minh . . . We really wonder what's going to happen in the future.

*The future for Roger Micault and his comrades, in fact, was bleak.
Micault was a French soldier fighting Viet Minh forces in 1949, and
five years later the French would be soundly defeated at Diên Biên
Phu. France had begun its colonization of Vietnam almost a century
earlier, but after the French capitulated to Germany in 1940, Japanese
troops – who were allied with the Germans – occupied Vietnam until
1945. (Ironically, during World War II the US Office of Strategic
Services, which would later become the CIA, provided funding and
weapons to the Viet Minh guerillas resisting the Japanese; the Viet
Minh was the precursor to the Viet Cong, who would battle American
troops years later.) When Japan surrendered to the Allied Powers in
1945, the French began to reestablish, with military force, their
presence in Vietnam. Ho Chi Minh famously warned them, 'You can
kill ten of my men for every one of yours that I kill, but even with
those odds, you will lose.' By 1954, popular support in France for the
war had plummeted, and the most devastating loss was yet to come.
Approximately 300 miles northwest of Hanoi in a strategically located
outpost named Diên Biên Phu, the French had stationed 15,000 troops
(many of whom were colonial soldiers from Algeria, Morocco,
Thailand, Vietnam and West Africa) commanded by Colonel
Christian de Castries. On March 13, General Vo Nguyen Giap's Viet
Minh soldiers unleashed a withering artillery barrage from the
mountains encircling the valley, catching the French by surprise.
Essentially surrounded, the French relied on airdrops for food,
munitions and other dwindling supplies. Much of it, however, fell into
the hands of the Viet Minh, who were especially delighted by the
chocolate bars, candies, and perfumed love letters they discovered.
After being attacked and bombarded relentlessly for almost two
months, the starving and shell-shocked French troops raised the white
flag on May 7, 1954. More than 3000 had been killed, and more than
10,000 became prisoners of war. (Forced to march hundreds of miles
through rugged terrain, many of the wounded succumbed to disease
and malnutrition. More French soldiers died as POWs than during the*

siege at Diên Biên Phu itself.) The Viet Minh suffered tens of thousands of casualties. On May 8, a French army doctor named Jacques Aulong wrote the following letter from Hanoi to his mother and father in France expressing the grief he and his comrades were experiencing about the defeat. (General Henri Navarre, alluded to in the letter, was Commander-in-Chief of all French forces in Vietnam. When Colonel de Castries became increasingly overwhelmed by the tragedy unfolding before him, Major Marcel Bigeard assumed control of much of the tactical decision-making during the siege.)

Dearest Parents,

Diên Biên Phu fell yesterday, after heroic resistance. A day of sorrow. The atmosphere is that of a death chamber. We lived with the imminence of this fall, but we cannot face the fact that it has actually happened. It's like the long-awaited death of someone who has suffered a terminal disease, and yet we are in a state of shock and cannot conceive of this tragedy as irreparable and irrevocable.

You cannot imagine how admirably brave and clear-headed they were up until the very last moment, when the radio went definitively dead. The wire taps were recording up until 17H20; the last words were mixed with the roar of explosions. We heard 'Ah, the bastards!' And then nothing. De Castries had the pieces of artillery blown up, along with their ammunition, before the onslaught of Viets. The last explosion of ordnance was more powerful than all the rest. They used the 'Stalin's organs', six-tube rockets, for the first time.

We hear that Bigeard succeeded in getting through the lines with a few hundred men. To go where? Cost: twenty doctors and around twenty élite battalions. When I think that, day before yesterday, and the day before, the 1st BPC, our last paratrooper battalion, was parachuted in, it's insanity!

A catastrophe of this size involves immense and horrifying responsibility. Everyone here is in a state of agitation, against the government and our politicians to begin with, and against the high command, starting with Navarre, as well.

Our soldiers proved themselves blameless, and I say it without a trace of

Jacques Aulong

chauvinism. They maintained an iron morale, right up until the end, and there was an amazing flow of troops who volunteered to be parachuted in until the very last day.

And parachuted in under such conditions! It's the only remaining thing that we can be proud of. Shame and sadness for all the rest. And what will happen now?

We can't even hope to recuperate the wounded. When will they understand in France that we must have done with this at all costs, and rapidly, before we suffer a final catastrophe? I'm not talking about myself, I think I'll be capable of doing my duty up until the end, just as I volunteered for Diên Biên Phu on March 15th. I can tell you, now that it's over. The director didn't think it was up to me to do so. But I think of all that can be saved, human lives and moral interests, even material ones. We no longer have our place here, and this has been true for so many years, otherwise we should chuck the hypocrisy and send in the contingent. I'll leave you now, my heart full of immense sadness, and I embrace you tenderly.

Jacques

Two months after the surrender of Diên Biên Phu, an agreement was reached in Geneva that divided Vietnam at the 17th parallel, with the Communists under Ho Chi Minh ruling the North, and the anti-Communists led by Premier Ngo Dinh Diem governing the South. With the Cold War escalating and the possibility of Ho Chi Minh's forces overtaking all of Vietnam, President Dwight D. Eisenhower boosted military aid and ordered advisors to the region. On June 8, 1956, one of those advisors, Technical Sergeant Richard B. Fitzgibbon Jr., became the first casualty of the growing conflict in Vietnam. (Other Americans had already been killed in Southeast Asia, including pilots assisting with the airdrops to Diên Biên Phu, but Fitzgibbon's death is officially recognized as the war's earliest on the American side.) Less than nine years later, under orders from President Lyndon B. Johnson, the first ground combat unit – US Marines, 3rd Battalion, Ninth Expeditionary Brigade – came ashore at Da Nang on March 8, 1965. Fitzgibbon's son, 21-year-old Lance Corporal Richard

B. Fitzgibbon III, landed in Vietnam soon after. He, too, would be killed in the war.

A merican Lieutenant John Abrams explains to his wife how the fighting in the Vietnam War differs from past wars — & — The Vietnamese Friend of a Viet Cong collaborator named Huynh Lan Khanh tells Lan's mother how her daughter died.

'Well this war is a lot different than any other war,' US Lieutenant John Abrams explained on an audiotape he mailed to his wife, Jane. Abrams was a navy helicopter pilot originally from Milwaukee, and he frequently sent his wife audiotapes that recorded his stream-of-consciousness thoughts on everything from the snap decisions they had to make in combat and his disdain of the Viet Cong (nicknamed 'Charlie') to his comparisons between Vietnam and past conflicts. 'You could ask somebody from World War II or Korea if they ever killed anybody,' he mused,

and they'd probably say, 'Well, I don't know.' And they're probably telling the truth. They were firing at long ranges, long distances, to emplacements, this type of thing. This isn't that kind of war. This is a people-to-people war. We're firing from 600 meters away. We fire, we hit, we see what we hit. We see the results of our hit. We see the wounded, and of course we oftentimes see the dead. Of course, Charlie gives it back to us too. We take a lot of hits in the aircraft. Occasionally one of us gets it too. We've had three door gunners wounded – one of which died – since I've been here. I've been shot at quite a few times, and I think I've got a purple heart coming for a minor thing that happened here a couple weeks ago. There's nobody here that's not getting shot at, although this part of the war isn't as highly publicized as the part that's going on in the north. The part we're doing down here nobody wants to talk about. It's a dirty job. It's women, 12-, 15-year-old boys and grown men that we're killing because they're killing Vietnamese and trying

167

to kill us. Some of the atrocities that Charlie commits are unbelievable. It's really hard to believe some of the things that he does. In this thing the last few days we liberated a VC [Viet Cong] prisoner of war camp. Some of the people have been in the camp for two and a half to three years.

Abrams was interrupted by the sound of gunfire crackling in the background. 'Wish that guy would stop firing,' he muttered, 'it's making me nervous.' He continued his train of thought:

Yesterday, for example, we were cleared into an area where Charlie supposedly had an arms cache. We went into the area – sure enough, there was all camouflaged arms cache. So we went in, circled the area one time at high altitude, rolled into our strike. All of sudden, people started running out of the hootches – we call them hootches, they're grass houses – running out of the hootches that this material was all stacked around. And every one of them had a saffron robe on. A saffron robe is a bright orange robe – kind of the color of a flight suit, if you remember what that looked like – that the Buddhist monks wear, every one of them. Now, what were Buddhist monks doing where there was a large cache of Charlie equipment, and no Buddhist pagoda around the area? Charlie's not dumb, but he's not smart either, really. They ran out of the hootch, ran across the rice paddy, and they never got any further. Now maybe there were some Buddhist monks among them. Possibly there were. And Charlie was trying to escape along with them. But they all got it.

Although not a soldier, a Vietnamese woman named Huynh Lan Khanh aided the Viet Cong and was, much like the Buddhist monks described by Abrams, caught between her comrades and US forces, with fatal consequences. A close friend and coworker of Khanh's wrote to her mother to describe as best he could how Khanh had died. Other than her name, exact details about her life and where she was working are not known.

Dear Tam,

I just received your letter from comrade Dot. I know you are anxious to hear back from me, so I am responding to you now. Sister Kinh, I understand you must be very sad writing to ask about Lan Khanh, and it hurts me to write about her.

In my earlier letters, while you were at Lo Go, I enclosed personal items and photos of Lan Khanh, and when I saw brother Tam and took him to Lan Khanh's grave, I told him how Lan Khanh died, and the affection we all had for her. Her strength, frankness, ambitiousness, responsibility, and especially her courage will never fade in my mind. Lan Khanh was a great assistant in my office who I haven't been able to find for two years, and I want you to know how good she was!

Now let me tell you a story about her death. At 9 am of Jan 4th, 1968, Khanh and her 5 colleagues were delivering rice. It takes about 30 minutes to travel from the office to the depot. As soon as they arrived, they were ambushed and some were shot by enemy rangers (why did this take place? I will tell you in detail when I see you). Khanh was two meters away from an American ranger, thus unable to get away. She was accompanied by a comrade who was standing 10 meters behind and trying to return fire, but he was killed.

After the rangers had pulled out, we inspected the battle site and when her body was found, here is what we were able to determine: Khanh was wounded by a landmine, and was then immediately captured. She tried to resist but failed to escape. They took her to the helicopter nearby but couldn't get on because we had shot it to pieces. They had to call the jet fighters to protect their unit together with Khanh, and our force had run out of ammunition and was outnumbered. About 2 pm, they could communicate and were evacuated by another helicopter. When the helicopter started to climb, at about 0.5 km Khanh jumped to her death. I think she died at about 2 pm on 4 Jan 1968. It is so painful telling this.

I will tell you more when meeting you again as I can't say anything more!

Your brother

Kien

PS. It was not until 6 Jan 1968, that we found Lan Khanh's body and buried her properly.

After possibly killing a man in combat during the Vietnam War, Specialist Fourth Class Ronald 'Butch' Livergood asks his parents to forgive him.

Witnessing the killing of other human beings, particularly enemy soldiers, can become so commonplace during wartime that some combatants grow almost nonchalant about it. 'We were sitting around eating coconuts, sugercane, bananas and pineapple, plus a few other things I couldn't identify, and, in a general way, were relaxing and having a good time – waiting for orders to move on,' 20-year-old Robert Hughes wrote from Vietnam in a typed letter to his family in Columbus, Ohio. (ARVN is an abbreviation for the Army of the Republic of Viet Nam, who were allied with the Americans. VC is short for the enemy Viet Cong. The typos and spacing errors are in the original text.)

From out of nowhere there came some shots real close. We all jumped behind anything available and really didn't know what was happening – at least I didn't. I saw an A.R.V.N. running toward a clump of bamboo. There were more shots – from the bamboo – and the A.R.V.N. disappeared in the grass. I saw him again crawling toward the clump. The V.C. stood up and aimed his pistol right at the A.R.V.N. (we call him Number 10) and pulled the trigger – empty, just like in the movies. 'No. 10' jumped up and let the V.C. have a full round in the head. Pretty gruesome, but that's what happened. ('No. 10' had borrowed the lieutenent's radio man's M-16, and had it full automatic. The 20 rounds were out before he knew what was happening.) Good thing he didn't miss; he didn't know how to reload the thing There was nothing left of the V.C.'s. head – just a lot of blood, brains and shattered bone. (burp) Number 10 was pretty proud of himself. Quite a brave little guy. The excitement over, we settled down to lunch again.

But some troops were notably less casual about killing when they were the ones firing the shots. 'I'm so damn lonely, and I feel so helpless,' a soldier wrote to a female friend in the USA.

I know I can't change anything so what's the use in ever thinking about it. People killing people, that's all the whole damn world thinks about. Well they can go on killing, but I'm not going to. Do you know or have any idea how it feels to kill a person? I shot a gook 2 days ago and it really is a bad feeling.

Uncertain if he had done so or not, 20-year-old American soldier Ron 'Butch' Livergood was distressed by the mere possibility that he had shot an enemy soldier, even in self-defense, during the Vietnam War. On February 14, 1968, Livergood sent the following letter from Ben Luc to his parents in Gary, Indiana, after debating with himself whether he should tell them or his wife, Linda, what had happened.

Dear Mom and Dad

Hi folks, Well I am sorry I havent wrote to you in quite a while, but if you been listen too news you could pretty well figer out. Sigon was hit heavy and we were to. So they have been keeping us busy during day and night. We were mortared last night and about 4 days ago. Two of the fellows in the Company were wounded but nothing to serious. Now don't you start worrying about me I am O.K. a little nervos but O.K.

I am not worried that much anyway I been reading the Bible off and on and it helps a lot. I think God is protecting me as much as he can. I finally got some film for my camra and I been taking pictures like mad. Mom I don't know if I should tell you this or not, but I have to tell somebody and I can't tell Linda because she would worrie to much, and I think you might be able to take it better than her. I think I might have killed a person but I am not sure, we were fired at and I seen some men running with rifles so I opened fire on them and one of them fell to the ground. I just pray to God for forgiveness.

It shook me up quite a bit but I am feeling better now, because we went out to where I seen him go down. We found blood but nobody. I am glad of that. Well I am glad I got that off my chest I feel better now. I just hope you can forgive me.

Mom I don't know if I should tell you things that happen over here or not because not to many of the guys write home about it. But the pressure bulids up in me and I just have to tell somebody. If Linda if knew she might not be able to live with me knowing that her husband has killed a person. Well I change the subject. Hows all the kids back home fine I hope. Tell everyone I send my love and Ill be home in 327 days. I love you both, and I will write more later

Love

Butch

Your Son in Vietnam

P.S. Write as often as possible mail call is all I have to look forward to.

Love

Butch

The incident that Livergood, who survived the war, recounted in his letter occurred during the Tet Offensive, named after the Vietnamese lunar new year, which begins at the end of January. Viet Cong and NVA (North Vietnamese Army) forces launched a massive, co-ordinated blitz throughout the South on the eve of Tet, catching the Americans and their allies (many of whom were out celebrating) by surprise. Although militarily it was a disaster, failing to overtake and hold a single town or city or ignite a greater Vietnamese uprising as was intended, the attack was an enormous political victory for the Communists. Images of firefights in the US embassy compound and mayhem in the streets of Saigon, including the abrupt, point-blank execution of a Viet Cong officer, flashed on television screens throughout the United States, fueling the perception that Vietnam had descended even further into chaos. All of President Lyndon Johnson's podium-pounding arguments that the USA was winning the war were silenced by the stark, photographic evidence many Americans believed proved the contrary. At the end of March, Johnson stunned the nation by announcing he would not seek reelection.

In a letter to a friend, American Lieutenant Jerry Hill tries to answer the question: 'Why are our men over there [in Vietnam]?' — & — Former Peace Corps volunteer John Pohlman explains to a close friend, Carolyn Barber, how his views on the Vietnam War have changed now that he is under fire.

'Since I've been in Vietnam I've flown many missions that were purely for paper purposes,' a young airman complained in a letter to his family, written a year and a half before the 1973 Paris Peace Agreement. 'While I like to stay away from war stories let me just say that a person resents risking his life for the sake of logging another combat sortie for statistical purposes.' He was not alone; disillusionment was plaguing the armed forces in Southeast Asia as deaths climbed well past 50,000 and public support continued to erode on the homefront. But what was particularly maddening to many combatants – and had been for some time – was the unconventional nature of the conflict itself. With the exception of the Tet Offensive, the battle for Khe Sanh, and the 1972 Eastertide Offensive, the war was mostly an unremitting campaign of firefights with few measurable objectives other than the killing of as many enemy soldiers as possible. Servicemembers could not point to a map and see the countries they had liberated or follow the approach of victory the way World War II troops, for example, could mark their drive across Europe toward Berlin or up through the islands of the Pacific and into the heart of Japan. In Vietnam, territory was more likely to be relinquished after a hard fight than secured. (Even Khe Sanh was deserted only three months after tens of thousands of troops had fought so doggedly to prevent its loss to the NVA.) Vietnam was a war of attrition and a test of wills, but as the persistence of an inexhaustible enemy seemed only to strengthen over time, many American and allied forces wondered what difference they, both individually and as a whole, were making. For some, a sense of meaning came from helping the civilian population. Gerald I. Nelson was a staff sergeant in the US Marine Corps, and

after a visit to a village in Chu Lai, Nelson wrote the following to his wife, Victoria, back in Beaufort, North Carolina:

> One time we went into a hamlet and our 'doc' wanted to fix up some of the little children. I said 'Hell yes. Let's do everything we can.' So I was the lead man on patrol because I had the shotgun. And I stepped from behind some trees into a small courtyard. There standing were three little girls, each about 10 years old. One started crying and just stood still, afraid, and the other two took off and hid behind a hut. I couldn't blame them after seeing me. Well, we stopped there for a break and one of the girls (I fell in love with her) peeked her head out and I motioned her to come to me. She finally came over after much coaxing and I gave her some dry milk in a pack... I mixed the milk in water for her and she looked at me with those sad black eyes and drank. I couldn't help getting a lump in my throat because I think she knew (as a child does) how I felt, and yet she never said one word to me... [A]s we left I felt in my heart that we had accomplished so much and yet we did so little. But maybe this is what has to be done in this war. Show these people what we can do for them and how foolish the V.C. cause is, and then, and only then will there be peace in all of Vietnam. I pray for these people that it will be soon.

Other troops viewed the conflict as integral to a larger global fight against communism. Losing Vietnam would be a tragedy for the Vietnamese, they argued, and it would embolden the Soviets and other antidemocratic regimes. Specialist Fourth Class Jerry Hill was fully aware of the brutality of the war, but, in a letter to a friend back in Danville, Illinois, Hill tried to put their overall mission in the context of a more powerful struggle unfolding around the world.

Dear Gary,

So you want to know how it is over here in Viet Nam. I don't get to see an American newspaper very often so I don't know how bad they say it is over here but I'll tell you it's definitely bad.

Right now I have it fairly good myself but it wasn't like that when I first got here.

Had plenty of fighting in Quin Nhon but here in Ban Me Thuot where I am now things are pretty quiet.

I'll never forget the feeling I had when I killed my first man. After the first one it was easier but still not easy.

My best buddy who I've been with ever since two months in the army was killed fighting right next to me. I haven't made any close friends since for it's a hard feeling to get over.

I've seen dead Americans, some that were scalped and some that were tortured to death.

All in all Gary this is the dirtiest war of them all so the less the people back home know about it the better off they are.

The people here are friendly but you don't know who to trust. Your friend in the daytime might try to cut your throat at night.

Now I'll try to give you my feeling on being over here in Viet Nam. To start out we do have a purpose over here and we are needed here very badly. This country has been hard at war for 12 years trying to defeat Communism without any winning results till the Americans came. From the long hard struggle these people have had, its put them in a state of poverty. There is much sickness in this country from the downright filth the people live in.

The big question everyone thinks about is 'Why are our men over there?' In 1956 Hungary revolted against communism and asked for help which they definitely needed we didn't go there. When Castro turned Cuba communistic we didn't go there so why are we here?

All I can say is a person would have to be here to fully understand why we are here.

I'm no hero and I can't wait till I'm out of this army and back in the states but as long as there is a free America and there is communism there will never be world peace. Freedom and prosperity is something taken for granted back in the states but over here there is very little. Prosperity and freedom are what the Vietnamese are fighting for, and as long is there are people who want freedom I will try to fight and help them have it.

Jerry

For the average soldier in Vietnam (and arguably in most wars), there were two objectives that ultimately took precedence over any humanitarian, philosophical, or long-term geopolitical concerns: looking out for one's buddies and getting home alive. The troops were not uninterested in or oblivious to the domestic and international policies at stake or the larger ethical issues of the war, but their priorities in the field were simply much more pressing. In April 1970, just as overall troop levels were being reduced, Warrant Officer John H. Pohlman wrote a letter to a close friend named Carolyn Barber reflecting on his contribution to a war in which he had had, before being drafted, no desire to participate. The 25-year-old Pohlman had left the beautiful island of Fiji, where he was teaching children as a Peace Corps volunteer, to hump through the oppressively humid jungles of Southeast Asia at a time when his own government was signaling its intention to pull out of the region. The perspective he articulated in his letter was shared, either in word or in spirit, by many of his comrades in Vietnam.

April 15

Dear Carolyn,

It would be interesting to know first what you're expecting me to have to say. Or what you want to hear me say. Either to confirm your suspicions that the army has begun to make a conservative establishment tool out of me, or else to bolster your own anti-war feelings by hearing first-hand that the whole mess over here is the royal shits. I'm afraid you're going to get neither.

My outlook, though not my actual perception, has narrowed considerably in the last month. It matters very little what my views are on the war. It doesn't make a bit of difference whether I feel it is just or unjust, politically or morally. The fact is that I'm here, and will be for the next eleven months. And as terrible as the war may be for you to contemplate, it is far more difficult, for me, to live with, and, as things look now, through. That is my own very selfish compulsive interest right now. Survival.

I developed this mental tunnel vision during a mortar attack the first night I was here. Something happens to your mind when you realize there are people out there who don't like you. And they aren't trying to make you get a haircut, or bust you, or pave your park. They're trying to kill you. It doesn't matter that it isn't me, it's what I represent that they want to stamp out. When somebody shoots at me, I take it personally. It's a weird experience.

To be continued.

Love + kisses, John

Pohlman was killed later that day.

—— FEATURED SERIES ——

'Last Letters Home'

Scottish Highlander William Paterson, 'On the Eve of a Great Battle, at Cambrai during World War I,' cautions his parents that they might never hear from him again — & — Australian soldier, H. W. Crowle, fatally wounded in France during World War I, finds the strength to tell his family how deeply he loves them — & — Before leaving on a secret mission to kill a high-ranking Nazi during World War II, Czech soldier Jan Kubis expresses his true emotions to a young woman — & — On the eve of a Kamikaze mission during World War II, Japanese pilot Ichizo Hayashi encourages his mother to 'Cheer up' and accept what he is about to do — & — Twenty-three-year-old American Sergeant Josh Harapko, fighting the war on terrorism with the 10th Mountain Division in Afghanistan, in 2002, sends an unexpectedly reflective and emotional letter to his mother.

Ideally, the letter would never have to be sent. But if the worst should happen, young Second Lieutenant William Paterson, fighting in France during World War I, wanted his parents in Scotland to understand that he was fully aware of the peril he faced and would be thinking of them until the end. From Wick in Scotland, Paterson was serving with the Seaforth Highlanders, who in mid-November 1917 were preparing to punch through the German line at Cambrai, France. From the very first line, Paterson chose to be as straightforward as possible.

France. 16/11/17.

My Dearest Father & Mother,

I feel it my duty to write you this last message of love, which will only reach you in the event of my death.

The fact is, we are on the eve of a great battle or advance, & with my platoon, I have been detailed to go to the furthest objective 3,500 yards from our own trenches. I need not tell you what this means – you know well enough.

Well, I hope this message never reaches you, because if it does not, then I come out of the fray alright. However, so many are bound to fall, & perhaps I amongst the rest. If such should happen, remember that the sacrifice has been made in a good cause. I do not want to leave you, far from it, but whatever happens, dear father & mother, I am prepared to go forth with a clear conscience, and the knowledge of always having followed your example of uprightness & purity of word & action, so don't worry about me; but think of me as having gone forth into a purer & more peaceful world, where I will meet you all some day.

And now I must thank you all for all you have done for me. My whole life has been centered around you, and any little success I may have made is the outcome of your generosity, so you deserve to reap the benefit. My one aim was to see if I could not help to get you settled down comfortably, and then, after that had been done, I might have thought of doing the same myself, so if anything should happen to me, I hope you may derive some little help from my unfinished work, & that it may continue to be successful. We have been a happy family, much thanks to the sacrifices you have made for us, & the many times you have gone without, yourselves, that we might be satisfied.

I look back on my life – mostly spent at home – and I feel that sometimes I have given you cause for regret, but I know, if such is the case, you will forgive & forget. I knew that when I joined the army I caused you much worry & anxiety, but I think you will admit I did the right thing. If I had not done so, I should never have been satisfied, & perhaps you won't think it credible, but I was satisfied & content when wading through muddy Flanders, & sitting under earsplitting shellfire, – satisfied, because I knew it was where I ought to be at this time.

Well, I sincerely hope Johnnie, Donnie, Alex & Eddie may get successfully through their careers, and it must be a great pleasure to you to watch their welldoings. I'm proud to be your son & their brother. I hope Lizzie & Bella, & Jeannie & her family may spend many happy days & be a comfort to you always.

Well, dear father & mother, I have written at greater length than I intended. Now, whatever you do, don't worry. I am not worrying – except for your sakes –, and ready to carry out the stern duty that is before me, prepared, & calm in body & mind.

So in wishing you goodbye, remember that life at best is one long journey of toil & strife, & that if I go under, I have reached the goal to which we are all passing day by day.

May God, the Father of us all, guide & comfort you, until the joyful day when we will all meet again in the Promised Land where all is joy & gladness, & where suffering & sorrow entereth not.

Your Affectionate & Ever Loving,
Willie.

A sniper's bullet ended Paterson's life only days later, and Mrs. Paterson received her son's letter along with a sincere expression of condolence from his commanding officer. Mr. Paterson did not learn of his son's fate; he himself had died, presumably of natural causes, before the news was received. For frontline troops, death is always a possibility and, depending on the hazards, even a likelihood. It is rarely, however, an absolute certainty – with one exception. Combatants who have been mortally wounded and realize they have little time to live will often dictate to a close buddy or the medic treating them a final message home. Those who are physically able will hurriedly write as much as they can before losing consciousness. Second Lieutenant H.W. Crowle, an Australian serving with the 10th Battalion, AIF (Australian Imperial Force), was critically injured in Pozières, France, on August 21, 1916. As gangrene ravaged his body and his strength began to flicker, Crowle tried to be optimistic but recognized, even as he was writing to his wife and son, that his time was all but finished.

Dearest Beat and Bill,

Just a line you must be prepared for the worst to happen any day. It is no use trying to hide things. I am in terrible agony. Had I been brought in at once I had a hope.

But now gas gangrene has set in and it is so bad that the doctor could not save it by taking it off as it had gone too far and the only hope is that the salts they put on may drain the gangrene out otherwise there is no hope. The pain is much worse today so the doctor gave me some morphia, which has eased me a little but still it is awful. Tomorrow I shall know the worst as the dressing was to be left on for 3 days and tomorrow is the third day it smells rotten. I was hit running out to see the other officer who was with me but badly wounded. I ran to far as I was in a hurry and he had passed the word down to return, it kept coming down and there was nothing to do but go up and see what he meant, I got two machine gun bullets in the thigh another glanced off by my water bottle and another by the periscope I had in my pocket, you will see that they send my things home. It was during the operations around Mouqet Farm, about 20 days I was in the thick of the attack on Pozieres as I had just about done my duty.

Even if I get over it I will never go back to the war as they have taken pounds of flesh out of my buttock, my word they look after us well here. I am in the officers ward and can get anything I want to eat or drink but I just drink all day changing the drinks as I take a fancy. The Stretcher Bearers could not get the wounded out any way than over the top and across the open. They had to carry me four miles with a man waving a red cross flag in front and the Germans did not open fire on us.

Well dearest I have had a rest, the pain is getting worse and worse. I am very sorry dear, but still you will be well provided for I am easy on that score.

So cheer up dear I could write on a lot but I am nearly unconscious. Give my love to Dear Bill and yourself, do take care of yourself and him.

Your loving husband,

Bert.

Just outside of Berlin in the scenic, leafy suburb of Wannsee, 15 high-level German officials gathered together in an elegant villa on January 20, 1942, to coordinate the Final Solution, a euphemism for the genocide of Europe's Jews. The Nazis had already begun murdering Jews and others – gypsies, people with mental and physical disabilities, gays, Catholics – whom they regarded as 'undesirables,' but the purpose of the Wannsee meeting was to expand these efforts and ensure that the various government ministries were working in harmony with one another. Every aspect of the Wannsee proposal was carefully analyzed and discussed, from the legality of rounding up and killing innocent men, women, and children (many of whom were German by birth) to the precise logistics of executing them as efficiently and inexpensively as possible. Reinhard Heydrich, chief of the Reich Security Main Office, was tasked with leading the conference and directing the implementation of its proposals. Heydrich was nicknamed 'The Blond Beast' and 'Der Henker' (hangman), as well as 'The Butcher of Prague' for the brutal means of oppression he employed as the Reichsprotektor of Czechoslovakia, which had been seized by Germany in March 1939.

Allied forces were determined to assassinate a leading Nazi in one of the occupied countries, and Heydrich seemed a deserving target. On May 27, 1942, two Czech soldiers – Josef Gabcik and Jan Kubis – approached Heydrich's chauffer-driven car as it slowed down through a sharp curve on a road near Prague and machine-gunned and threw several grenades at the vehicle. Both men were able to escape. Two weeks before the potentially suicidal mission, the 28-year-old Kubis had sent a letter to a young woman named Marie Zilanova, whom he had fallen for several months earlier. Kubis could not in any way divulge what he was about to do, but, knowing he might never see Zilanova again, he had wanted to express his fondness for her as discreetly as possible.

Prague May 12, 1942

Dear Marie:

I have received many wonderful messages from you, and I have such fond memories of you. Please accept my cordial greetings and know that you are always in my thoughts.

I apologize for not responding to you for so long. I think of you every day, but I was unable to write to you because a friend of mine, without asking me, borrowed the book in which you wrote your address, and then he left for Moravia. So I had to wait for him to return, and I was very glad that he brought the book back with him. I hope that you won't be angry with me because of this and will forgive me.

You will forgive me, won't you?

You have to, otherwise I won't be able to fall asleep at night if I know you are upset with me. . . . We soldiers also have our feelings and hearts that want to beat for somebody, but we have to hide it.

Marie, I'm not sure if it will be possible for you to write to me. I would like to give you the address of a place where you could send me a few lines, but it would not be possible for me to receive anything there now. I will send you the address next time.

Marie, I will finish even though I have more to say in my heart, but it is not possible to express it with words.

With best regards, you will forever be in my memory.

Yours

Initially it appeared the daring attack by Kubis and Gabcik had failed; the shots fired at the car all missed Heydrich and the grenades exploded well behind him. But as it turned out, Heydrich had indeed been injured by flying shrapnel, which ripped into his back. He was rushed to the hospital and, due to an increasingly painful infection that spread throughout his body, died a week later. (After Heydrich's assassination, Jan Kubis and Josef Gabcik were tracked down by the Nazis and killed. An estimated 1300 Czechs in all were executed in reprisal for Heydrich's death. One small village, Lidice, was wiped out entirely. Based on inaccurate reports that its citizens were protecting members of the assassination plot, the Nazis surrounded Lidice, just outside of Prague, and shot virtually all of the village's men and deported their wives and children to concentration camps. The Nazis then dynamited, burned, and bulldozed the village to the ground.)

No warriors, are more associated with 'last letters' than World War II Japanese kamikaze pilots. Even as the defeat of their country seemed inevitable in early 1945, thousands of these young pilots flew themselves into enemy warships in a last, desperate act of aggression. It was customary for them to write to their family before they embarked on their mission, and the language they used to convey their emotions was rich with metaphor and lyricism. They compared themselves to cherry blossoms that would be reborn at springtime and rays of sunlight that

Jan Kubis

would forever warm the faces of their loved ones. 'We are fifteen warriors,'
one pilot wrote simply, 'may our deaths be as sudden and clean as the
shattering of crystal.' Like many of the suicide pilots, Ichizo Hayashi was
young (23) and prepared to give his life for the Empire. But he was unique in
that, while most Japanese are followers of Shintoism or Buddhism, Hayashi
had converted to Christianity. His final words were addressed to his mother.

Mother,

The time has come for me to write you a sad letter. I have truly been happy in my
life. I have been a spoiled son, haven't I? I know you will forgive me for being
such a child.

I am glad that I have been chosen to be a Kamikaze pilot, but I cannot stop
from crying when I think of you. You have raised me the best you could, and I
am sorry that I must die before I can show my love for you in return and make
you happy. How can I tell you to let go of me or be proud of my sacrifice to the
country? Mom, I shall not speak of this anymore, since you know how I feel.

When I received your second letter regarding the girl you intended for me to marry,
I could have refused because I already knew about my mission. But I wanted to be your
little boy just like I used to be, and the letters I received from you made me so cheerful.
I wish I could see you again and had enough time for a quiet talk with you and rest in
your arms just once more, but Moji was the last place we could be together. I leave the
day after tomorrow. The day after tomorrow I must die. I am looking forward to flying
over Hakata, and I will silently say good-bye to you from above the clouds.

I am sorry I could not see Chiyoko to thank her. Everyone in our family was so
supportive and helpful when I had my high school exams. I miss our house in
Miyazaki-cho. Mom, I know you had great dreams for me and I have disappointed
you. I wish I could say that I was right, but I should have listened to you. Please
take comfort in knowing that I have been selected as one of the best pilots to
accomplish the mission, and I am especially honored to lead other students.

After I die, you will still have my brother Makio, and although you may love
me more than you love him, I know he will be able to provide anything you and
our family might need in the future. You also have my sisters Chiyoko and
Hiroko, and your grandchildren, remember? I promise I will always be with you
in your heart. I want you to live in peace, and thinking of you being happy
makes me happy, so please do not be sad.

From time to time I am tempted to come home to you. But I cannot because it would be cowardly. When I was baptized, the priest said to me, 'Renounce your own life.' I am committed to our Saviour, even if it means being struck down by the American bullets and sacrificing my life. Everything is in God's hands. Our life and death on this earth should not matter to us who live with God. Jesus has said, 'Thy will be done.' I have been reading the Bible every day now, because I feel close to you when I do. I will fly and crash to my death with the Bible and the Book of Psalms in my aircraft. I will also take along the mission badge which the schoolmaster gave me and the charm I received from you.

Regarding marriage, I never intended to take it lightly, but it would be better if you explained the circumstances to the girl and her family. I really wanted to get married and please you. It is just not possible now.

Forgive me, and I know you will as you always have. Mother, I admire you so much. I could never be as good and courageous as you are. You have never hesitated to sacrifice yourself and you bear so many burdens, and I find it so difficult to do. The only fault I have found in you is that you loved me too much. But how can I blame you? For I needed to be loved by you.

I can die peacefully knowing that you, my sisters and brother, and my friends will always remember me. I will pray to you when I crash into the enemy, and pray for me after my death because all of your prayers are heard and accepted by God.

I have asked Umeno to deliver this letter to you. Please do not show it to anyone else. I am ashamed of it. It's strange, as it does not feel like I am the one who is going to die. It feels as if I can see you anytime again soon. I suppose it is because I am overcome with grief when I realize I will never see you again.

By the time of the invasion of Afghanistan in October 2001, American and Coalition troops had at their disposal more ways to communicate with the home front than any other generation of combatants. Although not everyone had access to the technology in all parts of the region, many troops could make satellite phone calls or send emails, text messages, faxes (although even those have now become antiquated and are rarely used), and audio and DVD recordings back home. These transmissions from the war zone let anxious family and friends know almost instantaneously that their loved ones on the front line were alive and well. But when an especially intimate or personal message needed to be shared, many soldiers sat down with pen and paper and handwrote a letter that they would later mail or have mailed in the event of a worst-case scenario. In early March 2002, Coalition forces began to gear up for Operation Anaconda, a major assault on Taliban and al-Qaeda strongholds in the mountains of Afghanistan. Josh Harapko, a 23-year-old sergeant and platoon leader with the US Tenth Mountain Division, rarely sent letters to his mother back in Arizona or opened up much about his feelings under any circumstances. But with great care, Harapko neatly handwrote the following letter to his mom before advancing into what would be one of the worst firefights of the Afghan campaign. (Peg was a very close family friend who had died of cancer; Marcie and Dave are her children; Jake is Marcie's son; Nikki, Lauren, and Steve are Josh's cousins; and Sean is his brother and Heidi is his sister. She, too, was in the military and would go off to serve in Iraq two years later. KIA means 'killed in action'.)

Dear Mom,

I'm writing this letter before I leave. I couldn't say what I wanted to over the phone. First I want to say I love you so much. You were always there for me even though I would never talk about my problems. Second you gave me the options to be a man giving me slack in the rope to try to make the right decisions. No matter what you always believed in me, no matter how much of a punk I was to you. We are leaving for Bahgram to flush out 600 Taliban soldiers from the mountains. This is the biggest battle of the war on terrorism. We already sustained 30 casualties and one KIA. I never thought war was fun. It's hard to see all the guys who were shot or wounded and to know your going right back in there. I thought you should know where I am.

I don't want you to worry about me. (I know you will cause I'm your son). Mom I'm not afraid to die for something that is right. I'm more scared of being wounded like most of these guys and not being able to walk again. I just hope that I made you proud, and if I don't come home for any reason I just want you to know I'll always be with you. Really you shouldn't worry though. My guardian angel (Peg) is with me. I didn't get ahold of Sean, but please tell him I love him. I remember when I used to tell him to stop acting like my Dad. Well tell him I really respect him for that. I wish I could have told him myself. I wish we could have hung out together more and I regret not being able to.

Sergeant Josh Harapko

I want you to know you raised the cream of the crop. I haven't been able to contact Heidi so please tell her I love her so much. I'm so proud of her. I want her to know that. I wish I wasn't such a brat when she was around. These are just some things I needed to justify before we move out. Tell Aunt Kathy my prayers are with her and Uncle Joe. Tell Nikki I hope to be there for her wedding. Tell Aunt Barb and Uncle Kevin I love them. The same to Aunt Sharon and the kids and Uncle Bob. If you go to Steve's graduation tell him how proud I am of him. For Lauren tell her I liked hanging out with her and her roommates. Also good luck and congratulations. To Marcie and Dave you were just like a blood brother and sister and I love them like family, and to little Jake happy birthday.

Well Mom I have to go now, all that I have said here are words from my heart and I mean every last one of them. Tell Aunt Joyce I said hi and I love her. I hope to see you soon but if that doesn't work out I just needed you to know how I felt. I Love you and Miss you. Take care your always in my thoughts.

Your Loving Son Josh.

Harapko survived Operation Anaconda and returned to the USA alive and well. In an awful irony, however, he and ten other soldiers died one year later (March 11, 2003) when the UH-60 Black Hawk helicopter they were flying in crashed during a routine training mission at Fort Drum, New York.

In a letter he considers almost a 'confession,' a US marine writes to his priest back home about the opening weeks of Operation Iraqi Freedom during the War in Iraq — & — Lieutenant Colonel David Bellon provides his father with a graphic depiction of the fighting in Fallujah and the ruthless tactics used by the insurgents in the aftermath of Operation Iraqi Freedom.

'VICTORY!! As of 0800 our time it's over,' Master Sergeant L. Vincent Francese declared triumphantly in a letter of February 28, 1991, to his wife, Rhonda, in South Carolina. Francese was a US

marine serving in Kuwait during Operation Desert Storm (ODS), in the Gulf War, and, like the other 500,000 troops in the region, he was elated that the war had ended swiftly and with minor American and allied casualties. The shortest major conflict in US history (after a 43-day air campaign, the ground assault lasted only 100 hours), Operation Desert Storm was not only a resounding military success, it ushered in a restored sense of confidence within the armed forces, as well as a new generation of highly sophisticated instruments of war. From the B-2 'Stealth' Bomber that was virtually invisible on radar, to laser- and satellite-guided missiles that could strike a target with pinpoint accuracy, not since World War I had there been such dramatic advancements in weaponry. Military planners envisioned future conflicts that relied less on live ground troops and more on automated and robotic weapons systems, including remote-controlled reconnaissance devices and unmanned tanks and warplanes.

The US-led air strikes against Serb forces in the mid- and late 1990s further demonstrated that battles could be won with minimal casualties – or, as with the Serbian campaigns, no combat fatalities at all – for the American servicemembers involved. During a speech in February 1996, Air Force Chief of Staff General Ronald R. Fogleman remarked that the USA was on the verge of 'a new American way of war' that focused more on air power and less on 'placing thousands of young Americans at risk in brute, force-on-force conflicts.' Advanced capabilities will, General Fogleman predicted,

> *help minimize casualties on both sides, reduce the 'CNN effect' [i.e., bringing the horrors of combat into people's homes via live television], and allow us to wage war in a way that corresponds to what appears to be the values of American society – that is, what the American people are willing to accept on the battlefield. Air power will also provide tremendous leverage to resolve future crises – rapidly and at low cost.*

The earth-shaking 'Shock and Awe' barrage launched against Iraq on

March 20, 2003, at the outset of the War in Iraq, demonstrated how overwhelmingly destructive a massive air campaign with technologically superior weapons could be. (More firepower was unleashed on Baghdad in the first twenty-four hours of Shock and Awe than during the entire Gulf War.) American and Coalition troops encountered pockets of resistance during the ground invasion that followed, but major clashes or a prolonged standoff with tens of thousands of Iraqi troops did not occur. The Iraqi army, in the eyes of many, seemingly melted away. But even in the first few hours and days of the war, US and Coalition servicemembers noticed that the paramilitary forces loyal to Saddam Hussein were employing unconventional tactics that unnerved some troops and infuriated others. One F-18 pilot, Captain Travis Russell, alluded to what the Coalition was up against in an email to family members back home in Washington, DC.

We launched on a mission this morning where we found and employed on our targets. We did a tag team with a flight who was already working these guys over pretty good and we just added to the punch.... I had to pause there for a second to put on my gas mask and chemical suit, those silly Iraqis keep launching scuds this way. Anyway, we put a hurting on some guys earlier today and we hope it did some good. Amazing, they are certainly taking advantage of our humanity by faking a surrender to set up an ambush. You can bet those who were alive to start the ambush were not alive much after.

Another combatant, a US marine captain (whose name is being withheld in the interests of privacy), handwrote a short but emotional letter to his priest back home in the USA about his first combat experiences in Iraq. Although he was heartened by the welcome response he and his fellow marines received from many civilians as they advanced toward Baghdad, he was haunted by the retaliatory measures the marines had to take against Iraqi forces who hid themselves behind innocent men, women, and children.

Easter
20 April 2003

Father Bob,

With religious banners flying, truckload after truckload of cheering Iraqis pass our position. After decades of religious oppression, the Shi'a muslims are now free to worship as they wish. Old men have tears of joy and the younger generation try to thank us the best they can in their broken English. 'Thank You America' and 'Mr Bush. . . good' are about all the Marines can understand, but the sight of the liberated people is an incredible gift to all of us on this most wonderful Easter.

What a difference a month can make. Thank you for your prayers during the darkest days of the war. Even though I had a front row seat to man's inhumanity to man, I believed that good would prevail. I never thought that man could be so cruel. My time in An Nasiriyah will hopefully be forgotten. Never have I felt so angry before, a kind of anger that I never knew existed. I never felt joy in my actions, nor regret. The paramilitary forces which we faced shielded themselves with civilians. The blood of the innocent was spilled and will forever stain my hands. My actions were just and had to be done, but that doesn't make it easier and I will just have to live with it. This letter is turning into more of a confession than a greeting, but maybe that's what I need.

Thank you for watching over my family and the families of others who proudly wear the military uniform. Despite all the ugliness that I've seen, I still believe this world is beautiful. I look forward to standing before the St Rose altar with my fiancée in August. It will be a time that will only have room for love. Only through love will there be peace! Please continue to take care of St Rose. You are a good man, Father Bob, a very good man!

God Bless.

The Lord is my light and my salvation; Whom shall I fear? The Lord is the stronghold of my life – of whom shall I be afraid?

Psalm 27:1

(special words during a trying time)

On May 1, 2003, President George W. Bush announced that 'major combat operations in Iraq have ended,' but went on to say that he recognized there was still difficult work to do in Iraq. We're bringing order to parts of that country that remain dangerous. . . . The transition from dictatorship to democracy will take time, but it is worth every effort. Our coalition will stay until our work is done and then we will leave, and we will leave behind a free Iraq.

In the months to follow, the conditions became significantly more threatening as a full-scale insurgency began to take hold. Unable to match the air power or heavy artillery of the US and Coalition troops, the insurgents waged guerilla – also known as 'asymmetrical' – warfare, both to kill their enemies and terrorize anyone associated with them. The United Nations closed its Baghdad office after it was partially destroyed by a car bomb on August 19, 2003, and many aid workers and civilian contractors fled the country after their colleagues were kidnapped and executed, either by a shot to the head or decapitation. The epicenter of much of the violence was Fallujah (also spelled Falluja), a city just west of Baghdad and in the heart of the Sunni Triangle, where Saddam Hussein remained a popular symbol of anti-American resistance. In November 2003, insurgents shot down a US Army CH-47 Chinook helicopter, killing 16 soldiers. On March 31, 2004, in an incident that startled the world, four American civilian security workers were pulled from their car in Fallujah and beaten to death. Insurgents then set fire to their bodies and dangled the charred remains from a bridge over the Euphrates. 'The Falluja fighting is intense, up close and personal,' a 38-year-old US Marine Corps major named David Bellon emailed his family on April 13, 2004. Bellon, who was serving as the First Marine Regiment Intelligence Officer, was especially revolted at how viciously the insurgents were targeting other Iraqis.

I cannot tell you how many reports I have gotten about insurgents threatening civilians at gunpoint telling them that they will be killed if they try to leave the city or do not let the enemy use their land/homes for attacking us. The enemy takes over houses at gunpoint and tries to draw fire hoping that we will kill innocents so they can exploit it. I sincerely doubt that the Marines have passed by a mosque/minaret where they have not taken fire. We return fire and it is the lead story. The hypocrisy and lies are exasperating. . . I could go on and on about the treachery of our enemy here, smuggling weapons in humanitarian rations under Red Crescent banners, moving arms and ammunition via ambulances, bombing civilian vehicles in order to alienate the people from the coalition. . . However, the worst are reports that these foreign fighters have snipers in the city that engage the women and children as they try to escape the fighting. It sounds too horrific to be true but nothing is off the table to this enemy. Daily, they fire unguided rockets into the city and then get on the mosque loud speakers to blame the US. On, and on and on. . . .

Bellon and his fellow marines had been gearing up for an all-out assault on Fallujah that spring, but it was eventually called off. Seven months later, Bellon – who was now a lieutenant colonel – emailed his father to let him know that they were preparing, once again, to take over the city. (IED stands for improvised explosive device, and 'muj' is short for mujahidin, a military force of fundamentalist Muslim warriors engaged in a jihad against those whom they believe to be enemies of their faith.)

Dear Dad –

As you have no doubt been watching, we have had our hands full around Fallujah. It would seem as if the final reckoning is coming. The city has been on a consistent down hill spiral since we were ordered out in April. Its siren call for extremists and criminals has only increased steadily and the instability and violence that radiates out of the town has expanded exponentially. If there is another city in the world that contains more terrorists, I would be surprised. From the last two years, I just don't see a way that we can succeed in Iraq without reducing this threat. The cost of continuing on without taking decisive action is too high to dwell on.

The enemy inside the town have come to fight and kill Americans. Nothing will sate their bloodlust and hatred other than to kill everyone of us or at least die trying. It is hard to fathom as a Westerner as rational thought would dictate that we will only be here for a relatively short blip in their history and while we are here, billions of dollars in investments will pour in and opportunity that is beyond comprehension will open up for anyone willing to work. This is not Kansas and this enemy does not think like that.

If we build a school or clinic, they destroy it. They would rather deny medical care or education for the children of the citizens who live nearby than to have any symbol of the West in general and America specifically among them. It is hard to comprehend. Frankly, we are done trying.

For eight months, we have been on our chain. The enemy has fooled itself misinterpreting our humanity and restraint for lack of will and courage. For eight months, we have watched Marines, Soldiers and Sailors maimed and killed by invisible cowards hiding behind some wall or in a canal as he detonates another IED. For eight months, we have been witness to suicidal sociopaths driving vehicles laden with explosives into crowds of Iraqis and into our own convoys.

Just last week, we lost another nine Marines killed and an equal number of wounded as the result of some ignorant extremist who was able to convince himself that killing himself and as many Americans as possible would send him to paradise where he could finally get his virgins.

Now, their own ignorance and arrogance will be their undoing. They believe that they can hold Fallujah. In fact, they have come from all over to be part of its glorious defense. I cannot describe the atmosphere that exists in the Regiment right now. Of course the men are nervous but I think they are more nervous that we will not be allowed to clean the rats nest out and instead will be forced to continue operating as is.

Its as if a window of opportunity has opened and everyone just wants to get on with it before it closes. The Marines know the enemy has massed and has temporarily decided to stay and fight. For the first time, the men feel as though we may be allowed to do what needs to be done. If the enemy wants to sit in his citadel and try to defend it against the Marine Corps and some very hard Soldiers . . . then the men want to execute before the enemy sobers up and flees.

It may come off as an exceptionally bellicose perspective but where the Marines live and operate is a war zone in the starkest reality. When the Marines leave the front gate on an operation or patrol, someone within direct line of sight of that gate is trying to kill them. All have lost friends and watched as the enemy hides within his sanctuary that has been allowed out of what one must assume is political necessity. The enemy has been given every advantage by our sense of morality and restraint and by a set of operational rules that we are constrained to operate under. The Marines feel like their time has come and we will finally be ordered to do what must be done and be given the latitude to do it. Even though the price will be high, there is not a man here that would chose status quo over paying the price.

Every day, the enemy takes more hostages, assassinates developing Iraqi leaders and savagely beats suspected collaborators. I will give you just one recent example that happened last week. One of our patrols was moving down a street when they saw what looked like a fight. The Marines closed with the scene. It was a family that had come to Iraq on religious pilgrimage that was taken hostage and was being taken into Fallujah. The muj stopped for some reason and the father began fighting. The Marines interdicted and captured two of the kidnappers. Two more ran and the Marines could not get a shot without fear of killing/wounding others.

Every day, insurgents from inside Fallujah drive out and wait for Iraqis that work on our bases. Once the Iraqis leave they are stopped. The lucky ones are savagely beaten. The unfortunate ones are killed. A family that had fled Fallujah in order to get away from the fighting recently tried to return. When they got to their home, they found it taken over by terrorists (very common). When the patriarch showed the muj his deed in order to prove that the house was his, they took the old man out into the street and beat him senseless in front of his family.

Summary executions are common. Think about that. Summary executions inside Fallujah happen with sobering frequency. We have been witness to the scene on a number of occasions. Three men are taken from the trunk of a car and are made to walk to a ditch where they are shot. Bodies are found in the Euphrates without heads washed downstream from Fallujah. To date we have been allowed to do nothing.

I have no idea the numbers of beheadings that have occurred in Fallujah since I have been here. I have no idea the number of hostages that have ended up in Fallujah since we have been here. I just don't know that Americans would be able to comprehend the number anyway. Unfortunately, the situation has only gotten worse. There is no hope for any type of reasoned solution with an enemy like this.

Once again, we are being asked by citizens who have fled the city to go in and take the city back. They are willing for us to literally rubble the place in order to kill the terrorists within. Don't get me wrong, there are still many inside the town that support the terrorists and we cannot expect to be thanked publicly if we do take the city. There is a sense of de ja vu with the refugees telling us where their houses are and asking us to bomb them because the muj have taken them over. We heard the same thing in April only to end up letting the people down. Some no doubt have paid with their lives. The 'good' people who may ultimately buy into a peaceful and prosperous Iraq are again asking us to do what we know must be done.

The Marines understand and are eager to get on with it. The only lingering fear in them is that we will be ordered to stop again. I don't know if this is going to happen but if it happens soon, I will write you when its over,

Love,
Dave

With AC-130 Spectre gunships providing support from the air and Abrams tanks and Bradley vehicles leading the drive in, 15,000 US marines, soldiers, Navy SEALS, and Iraqi security forces attacked Fallujah on November 7, 2004. During the weeklong, building-to-building battle for the city, an estimated 1200 insurgents were killed and wounded. Some of these, it was discovered, were not Iraqis but Afghans, Egyptians, Saudis and Yemenis. US casualties totaled approximately 500, including more than 50 fatalities. Dave Bellon himself survived.

An Iraqi woman describes for a relative in Cairo a fatal encounter between her family and a group of American soldiers during the War in Iraq — & — US Army Specialist Gary Chandler assures his aunt that he was not injured by a recent bombing near Baghdad during the War in Iraq but reports on the condition of those who were.

For innocent Iraqis who have wanted nothing to do with either side of the fighting, remaining neutral has still not guaranteed their safety. Many have been blown up by the same crude bombs meant to kill US and Coalition forces, and some have been shot by troops who have mistaken them for insurgents. In September 2003, an Iraqi woman named Shayma (last name withheld for reasons of privacy) was the victim of a misunderstanding that had tragic consequences for herself and her family. In the spring of 2004, when she was able to establish email communication with relatives in Egypt, she described the traumatic event, which had happened the previous fall.

Dear Aunt Khadija,

I was so happy when I received your message last week. We were all destroyed and hopeless after the incident, but Mother is better, and I believe she will overcome the pain. Faris is getting better, and the doctors say he will be able to walk in two months.

You asked me for details of the accident, and I am going to tell you about it, but it is painful. It is hard to remember, and I was trying to forget it all.

It started at 10:00 in the evening that night last September, and I was at my family's home with my two babies. You know about the continuous cutting of electricity, so we were all sleeping on the roof of the house. Father used to put his gun under his head since the situation was, and still is, dangerous.

We heard knocks on the door, and there was a noise out in the street. We heard people shouting, and we couldn't recognize what they were talking about. Suddenly we started to hear shooting in the air, and father got up and went down. Faris went after him. I told him not to go out, but he wouldn't listen.

It turned out it was an armed robbery from a gang in the neighborhood.

197

Father heard steps, voices, and thinking that they were from the gang, he began shooting at them with his gun. They weren't the gang, they were American soldiers, and when they heard the shooting, they fired at father. Their bullets struck him in his neck, lungs, heart, kidney, legs. Faris was shot in his right leg by three bullets. There were three holes in his leg, but he is better now.

I'm sorry to tell you all these things, but you asked me to.

Now we are ready to come to Cairo, because we cannot live here anymore; it is hard to do.

Yours,
Shayma

As the fighting intensified, many US soldiers became less sympathetic with the plight of average Iraqis, whom they sometimes referred to as 'Hajis' or – more disparagingly – 'ragheads.' (Conversely, many Iraqis privately began referring to all US troops, regardless of their faith, as 'Jews.') But from the very beginning of the war, one of the sentiments expressed most commonly in letters and emails by American troops was how deeply affected they were by the Iraqi children and the suffering they have had to endure. When Sheri Travillian heard over the news that a bomb had exploded near a base outside of Baghdad, where her nephew Specialist Gary Chandler was stationed, she frantically dashed off an email to make sure he was all right. Chandler emailed the following reply.

Im fine.the bomb was off post but there were a lot of civilian casualties.the bomb was at a school.a lot a little kids were killed.they brought the victims here and we helped them.it was bad.all these little kids missing hands and feet.one little boy had half his face missing.the dead ones were the worst.im not gonna go into detail about them.i still see their faces.eyes still open starring off into space.ill never forget that,ever.well im fine not hurt.there was a bomb on post but we found it before it exploded.they cought the guy and he told them that there are more bombs on the way.well we hope none make it here.weve had some firefights at election sights they were'nt very long but just enough to scare people.its getting warmer out so the enemy starting to come out of hiding again.well I gotta get back to work. love gary

Some troops found hope in the prospect of younger generations of Iraqis growing up in a country free of Saddam Hussein. In the middle of an effusive love letter to his fiancée, Danielle, a US Army Ranger, Captain Jason Ritter, commented:

> [P]erhaps we are making a difference over here. I think that we are. I did have an experience the other day that helped put it into perspective. I watched as a dozen or so little girls hurried past us on their way to school. I would like to think that you and I are directly responsible for allowing them the opportunity to even go to school in the first place. And maybe when it is all said and done the place will be changed for the better. I think so.

Other troops wondered, with tensions and hostilities appearing to become more aggravated with every passing day, if the cycle of violence would ever stop. 'Yesterday a kid, who couldn't have been any older than 4, pointed a stick at me like a rifle and pretended to shoot me,' a US marine, Lance Corporal Stephen Webber, wrote in a long email from Iraq to classmates at Saint Louis University, where he had been a junior before being called up for active duty. 'I wonder if someday my kids will meet him on some distant battlefield. I pray to God that if I ever have a son, he never has to go to war. That would tear my heart out.' After describing the bloody aftermath of an explosion that killed 20 Iraqis, the 20-year-old marine reflected on life back home and the psychological toll that the war was taking on his loved ones – and him.

> I feel very bad for my family. I know that I am putting them through hell. Sometimes I feel guilty for not just studying abroad. If you get a chance, hug your mom – for me. My mom is 9,000 miles and six months away. I would do anything to give her a hug right now... It feels that everyone back in the world is getting on with their lives, finishing school, getting jobs or internships, making friends, planning their future – and we are frozen in time. When I get back, friends will be gone, innocence will be lost, and things will have changed.

Webber concluded: 'I just want things to be the way they used to be.'

A sign at the Filipino Cemetery in Manila sternly warns against the following activities on the grounds: PRACTICE DRIVING, BIKING, DATING. *According to a local tour guide, "dating" was a euphemism for "something else". And apparently "something else" had been going on quite a bit there.*

LAUGHING THROUGH THE TEARS

Humorous and Unusual Letters

Just a wee note. I am 'going over the parapet', and the chances of a 'sub' getting back alive are about nix. If I do get back, why you can give me the horse laugh. If not this'll let you know that I kicked out with my boots on. So, cheer up, old dear, and don't let the newspapers use you as material for a Saturday magazine feature. You know the kind: where the 'sweet-faced, grey-haired, little mother, clutching the last letter from her boy to her breast, sobbed, " 'e was sich a fine lad", as she furtively brushes the glistening tears from her eyes with a dish rag, etc. etc.' Your son is a soldier, and a dog-gone good one, too, if he does say it himself as he shouldn't. And if he gets pipped it'll be doing his blooming job. S'there y'are.

Canadian soldier Hart Leech, writing to his mother during World War I. Leech was killed soon after.

Every able bodied man who can hold a gun is now a parashot. I don't think, as a matter of fact, that the able bodied with the guns are going to be the only people to attack the parachuters, if they should attempt a landing here, for the country people are waiting for them with scythes and clubs. Myself, serious as I know the parachuter danger to be, can only find them funny. The thought of a German descending through the skies, disguised as a clergyman, even perhaps as a bishop, with his machine gun under one arm, and his bicycle under the other, is hard to take seriously. The wireless broadcast a description of how the parachuters will be dressed, and in spite of the fact that the country is grimly determined to exterminate the lot, everybody died with laughter. One of the comforts of war seems to be that when one horror piles on another there comes a point when a great deal of what is happening makes the public laugh.

Noel Streatfeild, writing to 'Binkie and Champion' on June 13, 1940, about a possible German invasion of England, during World War II.

I've got plenty of everything else (food). My assistants take care of me. We live well together. When I am gone they fall into a funk, but as soon as I appear they start working full steam. On holidays we drink 100 grams or so. As Markov always says, 100 grams isn't enough, but 200 grams is too much. Let's drink 150 grams. Twice.

Soviet soldier Kotka Gofman, writing to friends on November 3, 1941, during World War II.

Had a few scary weeks during the last days of November. Was it the AAA [Anti-Aircraft Artillery], surface to air threat, night tanking, night traps? Nope – we almost ran out of piddle packs. My squadron, in keeping with the theme that desperate times require desperate (i.e. moronic) measures, survived these dark days by adopting a completely unsafe dehydration plan coupled with the procurement of several emergency inflight relief vessels/urine storage devices – Gatorade bottles – for those times when bladder evacuation at 32,000 feet was just plain unavoidable. As an aside, donning the ever reliable DEPENDS undergarment was momentarily discussed but instantaneously dismissed. We were all in agreement that the image of a downed Navy fighter pilot in Afghanistan, paraded in front of the cameras of CNN, wearing only DIAPERS would only serve to heighten the fighting spirit and resolve of the Taliban and Al Qaida network worldwide.

An American Navy pilot, emailing his family on January 2, 2002, in between combat missions over Afghanistan during Operation Enduring Freedom.

Tadeusz Kosciuszko, a Polish-born colonel serving with the Americans in the American Revolution, sends a teasing letter to his friend, Major John Armstrong.

Early American war-related humor manifested itself in many ways – satirical political cartoons (known then as caricatures), editorials, speeches, songs, and lines of verse. ('When perched on your charge on dress parade / You looked as brave a soldier as ever was made. / If you look but as brave when the bullets fly / Your Country will love you and so will I,' reads one poem titled 'The Colonel.') But levity was rarely evident in the letters of the common fighting man. Writing paper, especially in the 18th century, was a precious commodity for the average soldier, and when given the opportunity to send a letter to loved ones back home, necessity compelled him to report relevant war news and his own condition and well-being. Describing funny incidents or practical jokes played on comrades (which certainly occurred) was not a priority. Officers were more likely to be witty or facetious in their correspondences.

One young officer, a Polish engineer named Tadeusz 'Thad' Kosciuszko (pronounced ko-SHOOZ-ko) came to America in 1776 and was greatly admired for his service to the Continental Army during the American Revolution. He was also known for his sense of humor. When one American general complained that his name was difficult to pronounce, Kosciuszko retorted good-naturedly that 'Knickerbocker' and 'Schenectady' didn't exactly roll off the tongue for him, either. Writing on March 3, 1779, from West Point, where he was overseeing the construction of fortifications against a British attack, Kosciusko sent a short letter to his friend, Major John Armstrong, poking fun at Armstrong and his staff for neglecting him. (William Claijon and Colonel Troup, whose names Kosciuszko misspells, were aides to General Horatio Gates. 'Bob' is most likely General Gates's son. 'Priapus' is the Greek and Roman god of procreation, renowned for being endowed with a large phallus.)

West Point 3 March 1779

Dear Friend,

I do not tax you with want of Friendships in not writing to me knowing that you have a good reason to give, that the handsome Girls ingross the whole of your Time and attention and realy If I was in your place I should of Choise do the same. But you Col. Clairjon can give me no Reason but your Laxiness. I have ben told you are about Marying a Young girl and mean to exert yourself that the name of Clairjons may not be extinguished. You Col Troop as a good officer of Artillery will make use of you Activity and prove the Goodness of your Cannon on the wedding Day of Col. Clairjon. Your help Doctor Brown will be wanted with all your Surgical Faculities to promote so laudable a design for the interest of Mr. Clairjon and administere such Medicine as will make him Strong and Fameus as Priapus. You Bob will take exemple from the misfortune of Mr. Bucks and not be so imprudent as to get the clap. Send me one pound of green Tea. The Officer who bears this will pay for it.

Your affectionat Friend

Thad Kosciuszko Col.

A Russian soldier, fighting on the Eastern Front in World War I mails a (sort of) heartfelt letter to his wife — & — A British soldier drafts a multipurpose love letter for his – or anyone else's – spouse during World War I.

The letter, beautifully written in cursive handwriting, was tender and impassioned. Although not dated, it was sent by a Russian soldier during World War I.

My Dear and Beloved Wife!

I am sending you, my dear, a little note about myself from far away. I am, thank God, alive and well and feel good about myself. Write me about your health and the health of our dear children. If only you knew, how my heart longs for you and the children, if only I could hold you to my chest and kiss you from the bottom of my heart.

I ask you, my darling spouse, write me even more often. I live by your letters alone. As soon as I receive communication from you, I read it through and through several times, and it's as if I see you and the children, as if I am right next to you.

Every day I pray to our Good Lord above for you and for our children, and I ask Him, so that He, the Merciful, would let us meet again. And I believe, that happy day is not far off. Or, my dearest one, do not despair but instead as soon as you receive my letter, write me back about everything in great detail, for I eagerly await your note. I rely on the Lord, Our God, that I will find you and the dear children in good health and happiness.

I am sending heartfelt greetings to all our friends and family. Let them not forget me, for I shall not forget them.

I remain your loving and faithful husband.

What is unique about the letter is that the government, not the soldier, authored it. Recognizing the importance of mail to bolster spirits on the home front as well as the battlefield, the Russian government provided these prewritten letters, which soldiers could simply fold up and send to the designated recipient. (There were effusive letters for mothers and other loved ones, too.) The Russians were not alone in encouraging their troops to write home – or 'suggesting' topics for discussion. During World War I, the US military distributed mass quantities of Christmas cards to American troops for them to fill out and send home: 'NOTHING is to be written on this side except the date and signature of the sender,' the instructions on the card exclaimed. 'If anything else is added the post card will be destroyed.' This was followed by a preprinted list of statements a soldier could mark to update his family about his condition without accidentally disclosing information that might prove useful to the enemy. (One could select, for example: 'I am well' or 'I have been admitted to the hospital.') In 1917, a British soldier – or soldiers – created a tongue-in-cheek, preformatted 'love letter' that poked fun at the impersonal nature of the official messages and the limits imposed by censorship. The letter also revealed a cynicism and irony many soldiers had

developed in response to a war they felt had reached the point of
absurdity; the British lost approximately 1 million soldiers in World
War I; the United States, by comparison, lost 63,000. (The Xs at the
end of the letter are assumed to represent kisses.)

In the Field.
/ /1917.
————————

    (Dear,
My   (Dearest,
    (Darling,   (overworked
  I can't write much to-day as I am very   (busy
                                    (tired
                                    (lazy

      (CORPS)
      (G.O.C.)
and the (G.S.O.I) is exhibiting intense activity.
      (A.A. & Q.M.G.)
      (HUN)

                      (quite well.
Things our way are going on (much as usual.
                      (pas mal.

We   ) put up a bit of a show (last night) with (complete
The HUNS)   (yesterday)   (tolerable
                                        (-out any
                                        (success

Our   The French   )
The Russian   The Belgian   )
The Italian   The Serbian   )
The Montenegrin   The Roumanian)
The Monagasque   The Portugeese) Offensive appears to be doing well.
The United States   The Japanese)
The Brazilian   The Cuban   )
The Panama   The Chinese   )
The Bolivian)

<pre>
                        (obviously   )
The German offensive is   (apparently   ) a complete failure.
                        (we will hope)

                                        (this year.
I really begin to think the war will end (next year.
                                        (some time.
                                        (never.

The   (flies   )   (vile.
The   (rations) are   (execrable.
The   (weather) is   (much the same.

                (cheery.
                (weary.
The [   ] is (languid.
                (sore distrest.
                (at rest.

                    (Chateau
We are now living in a (ruined Farm.
                    (Hovel.
                    (Dug-out.

        (hoping soon to come on   )
I am   (about due for   )   (on.
        (overdue for   )   leave, which is now (off.
        (not yet in the running for)

I am suffering from a (slight)   (Fright   )
                        (severe)   wound (Shell-Shock)
                * ....
</pre>

....   (sent him   )
.................'s Wife has just (presented him with) ....

What I should really like is ....

                      (letter.
Many thanks for your (parcel
                      (good intentions.

          (poultry including cows)
How are the (potatoes   ) getting on?
          (children   )

                (well.
                (better.
I hope you are (bearing up.
                (not spending too much money.
                (getting on better with mother.

Insert here protestations ....
of affection – NOT TO ....
EXCEED TEN WORDS. ....

Ever........................... (State what ever)
....

XXXXXXXXXXXXXXXXXXXXXXXXXXXXXXXXXXXXXXXXXXXXXX

A German wife urgently appeals to her husband's commanding officer insisting that her husband be allowed to return to her and provide the 'Satisfaction' she can no longer go without during World War I — & — The commanding officer replies to her request.

The absence of husbands from millions of homes during World War I left their wives with the enormous burden of maintaining their households by themselves, which often included raising children and, in more rural areas, tending to farmland and livestock. But there were other, more personal needs that required the presence of a husband as well. These matters were usually addressed euphemistically or delicately in the private letters between spouses, each stressing how much they 'longed to be back in the arms' of the other or looked forward to 'making up for lost time' once they were together again. And then there were those who simply could not hold out any longer and didn't care who knew about it. One German woman, whose name (as well as that of her husband) has been deleted in the interests of privacy, sent the following plea to her husband's commanding officer (CO).

Treuen, January 2, 1917

Dear Leader of the Company!

I, the signer below, have a request to make of you. Although my husband has only been in the field for four months, I would like to ask you to grant him a leave of absence, namely, because of our sexual relationship. I would like to have my husband just once for the satisfaction of my natural desires. I just can't live like this anymore. I can't stand it.

It is, of course, impossible for me to be satisfied in other ways, firstly, because of all the kids and secondly, because I do not want to betray my husband. So I would like to ask you very kindly to grant my request. I will then be able to carry on until we are victorious.

With all reverence,
Mrs. S

The CO who received the letter, Kurt Zehmisch, was not unmoved by her plight, and responded on January 8.

Honorable Frau S   !
With this letter, I confirm the receipt of your friendly letter from January 2, 1917. I can certainly sympathize with you and understand that you would like to see your beloved husband come home, and I will do everything in my power to fulfill your wish. But you must also realize that I have many men in our company at the moment who have been away from their homes for nearly a year. To be fair to these men, I ask you to be patient for another 1–2 weeks. Then, I will be able to add your husband to our list of men going on leaves of absence.

> With friendly greetings,
> K. Zehmisch

Royal Air Force Captain George Huckle records in his logbook excerpts from actual letters sent to his fellow prisoners of war during World War II.

'I wish you could picture the faces when letters arrive for us who are so far away from home,' an American soldier wrote to his wife on March 27, 1944, echoing the sentiments of all servicemen and women about incoming mail. '[E]verything stops so the letters can be read, each reading a portion of his letters to the others, telling something that a child or children said or did. Letters are the breath of life.' And when a month later he, himself, received letters, the reaction was rapturous: 'Tonight I hit the jack pot! Mail! Mail! Oh, what sweet music to a home sick soldier.' The significance of letters as a morale booster was especially great for those confined as prisoners of war (POWs). Letters were one of their few tangible connections to family and friends and helped break the maddening boredom of camp life. This made it all the more devastating when those back home seemed oblivious to the

harsh circumstances, both physical and mental, prisoners endured. Shot down over Germany in August 1941, a Royal Air Force (RAF) captain named George Huckle spent more than three years as a POW before returning home. During his imprisonment he kept a journal that recorded what he called 'mespots' – letters to his fellow POWs from wives, sweethearts, parents, and siblings that included unwelcome information, ridiculous comments, or curt rejections. The following – again, all written to men being held in an isolated camp and subsisting on meager rations – represent just a sampling. (The succinct descriptions and dates before some of the letters were added by Huckle himself. The references to '5/-' [five shillings] and 5/6 [five shillings and sixpence] relate to British currency at the time.)

Darling I hope you are behaving yourself and not drinking too much.

–

Darling, I've just had a baby, but don't worry, the American officer is sending you some cigarettes every week.

–

Jan '44. – Darling I was so glad you got shot down before flying became dangerous.

–

Darling in your letter you ask for slippers. What colour would you like?

–

The words after lousy describing your new camp were obliterated.

–

To P.O.W. shot down '43 – I'm sorry you were shot down so early in the war.

–

Darling, I hope you are staying true to me.

–

Can you buy beer anywhere or do they only sell wine.

–

Darling the first batch of repatriated prisoners arrived recently, they looked terrible. I hope you're on the second party.

–

Letter from fiancée to P.O.W. – Dear John, you were missing a month, so I got married.

–

I have a grandmother in Germany, have you met her?

–

From a wife – Dear, I'm going to have a baby by an American, brother has forgiven me, I hope you do.

–

From home – I find I can't get any sandals here so am sending out the coupons and perhaps you can get them in the shops over there.

–

If your skates have arrived, only go where it is shallow enough, so you can get out easily if you fall through.

–

From Best Girl – So you're in perfect health are you? Wait till I get you home. Then you'll know the meaning of bags under the eyes.

–

You will be satisfied to hear that I'm getting married next week, but you can look forward to our happy reunion when you come home. It will be too bad if my husband doesn't agree, because I'm going to see you anyway. If he's away you can stay at my home, and if he's at home we can go to mother's and not tell him. We can give the family 5/- each to keep their mouths shut.

–

Comparison – I'm on my honeymoon, so like you I'm in captivity.

–

From fiancée – I do appreciate your allotment as a chap I go with is only a private on 5/6 a day. Please increase it.

–

From girl-friend – Darling, I married your father. Signed, Mother.

Filipino Native Marcial Lichauco describes in a secret letter to an old friend some lighter moments during an otherwise fearful time during World War II.

'Dear "Mother" Putnam,' 39-year-old Filipino Marcial Lichauco began a letter to a close family friend on December 12, 1941, just days after the Japanese attacked the Philippines. 'I am writing during a period of great uncertainty. I do not know whether or when I shall be able to contact you.' After the strike on Pearl Harbor, which had occurred only hours before, the Japanese launched a full-scale invasion of the Philippines. Lichauco, a highly educated lawyer, knew that if his letters to Mrs. Putnam were discovered he risked being imprisoned, tortured, and even executed. But he wanted to record for his children an eyewitness account of the Japanese occupation, and the letter, written on scraps of paper, became a running narrative of the dangers he and his family experienced for almost three years. It also chronicled how many Filipinos used humor to alleviate the unbearable strain they were under on a daily basis. In early July 1942, Lichauco wrote of several bold actors who subversively mocked Japanese authority. (Fort Santiago, which Lichauco refers to, was a Manila prison notorious for its harsh treatment of inmates.)

Friday, July 10, 1942:

The few remaining American films which our movie houses still have on hand are being released at the rate of about one each month. They are, of course, very carefully censored. This shortage has been a god-send to the local vaudeville talent. Four comedians, however, have been recently taken to Fort Santiago by the Military Authorities who failed to appreciate the Filipinos' sense of humor. The scene which brought about the arrest of two of these men was as follows:

One comedian approached the other and, in a very respectful tone of voice, asked a simple question. The one addressed thereupon slapped him severely on the face. The audience burst into laughter because it reminded them of many cases they had witnessed in which Filipino civilians were slapped by Japanese sentries for no apparent reason at all. But the Military Police stopped the show and arrested the two men.

The other scene which occurred in another theatre was even more timely. After the Japanese entered Manila last January we soon found that they were very interested in wrist watches. The jewelry shops in town then still had a large supply on hand which Japanese officers were quick to purchase, but it was well known that many soldiers simply confiscated wrist watches from pedestrians whom they accosted on the streets and it was not uncommon to see a soldier with two, three or even four watches strapped around his wrist. In this particular scene, one of the Filipinos, dressed in khaki uniform but without any insignias on his coat to indicate his nationality, asked his fellow comedian to try and guess what kind of a soldier he was trying to impersonate. The conversation was more or less as follows:

'You are trying to simulate an Italian?'

'No.'

'Russian?'

'No.'

'Hindu?'

'No.'

'Chinese?'

'No.'

'Nazi?'

'You are getting warmer.'

At this point the comedian dressed as a soldier scratched the back of his neck and, in so doing, his right sleeve was pulled up revealing three watches strapped around his wrist. There was no further need for his companion to say anything because the audience howled with glee. These two comedians also found themselves that evening in Fort Santiago.

In late January of 1943, Lichauco related an incident where an exchange of 'letters' themselves played a crucial role.

Monday, January 25, 1943:

Here is the latest story that is sweeping the city concerning guerilla activities: Jorge Vargas, head of the puppet government which the Japanese have organized here is said to have sent a letter through an intermediary to one of the most active guerilla leaders hiding in the mountains of the Island of Panay. 'It is useless and cruel for you to continue your resistance,' said Vargas in his letter. 'Cruel because the civilian population in the villages near you suffer terribly as a result of the fighting that takes place around them. And useless because you will, sooner or later, have to give in. America cannot help you. What remains of her army here surrendered long ago. The Japanese fleet is master of the <u>Pacific and no supplies</u> from the United States <u>can possibly reach these shores.</u> American sovereignty is gone from the Philippines, never to return. If you and your men, however, will lay down your arms and report to the nearest authorities, the Japanese who are merciful and generous will pardon you for your stubborn resistance.'

The guerilla leader did not reply in writing to Mr. Vargas. Instead he sent back a small package inside which were four juicy Delicious apples. As you probably know, apples do not grow in the Philippines.

In October 1944, the Americans, led by General Douglas MacArthur, initiated a ferocious naval, aerial, and then ground assault against Japanese forces in the Philippines as part of an overall campaign to retake the Pacific and, if necessary, invade Japan. Although Lichauco and his wife, Jessie Coe, watched with great anticipation as the Japanese were finally put on the defensive, they also feared that they – or, more important, their two children – could be killed by a stray bomb or artillery fire. In the following letter, Lichauco described a discussion with their youngest child about what life would be like after the occupation had ended. Like so many wartime correspondences that alluded to lighthearted moments, this one included a searing reminder of the terrible human cost of battle.

Sunday, October 15, 1944:
American dive bombers came over again today. The alarms sounded at 9.30 and, almost immediately afterwards, about three dozen fighter planes took off from Nielson field. This airport is about two miles from our house. The real show did not begin until an hour and a half later so that the Japanese had

plenty of time to get ready. This time they were certainly not caught napping.

When the guns were popping loudest we tried to amuse baby Cornelia.

'As soon as the war is over,' said Jessie, 'I will take a vacation in America. Wouldn't you like to come to America with me?'

Cornelia was pensive for a moment or two. 'Is there candy in America,' she finally asked. She has been getting very little of it here.

'Yes, plenty of candy,' I replied.

Cornelia then looked at her locally made shoes which are pretty shabby and worn out.

'Do they have shoes in America?' was her next query.

I laughed and said, 'Of course.'

'Can I get two pairs of shoes there?' And when I laughed again and said she could have all she wanted, she very solemnly gave us her decision.

'All right, I go to America.'

The worse part of the raid did not last more than forty-five minutes and we were out of our shelters in time to see the machine gunning of a helpless American flier who had bailed out over the city. He seemed to be heading for the river at first and to be making desperate efforts to avoid falling in the water. Then, when he was perhaps only two hundred yards away, a burst of machine gun fire was heard. The aviator who up to that moment had been kicking his feet and straining at the ropes suddenly went limp. The housetops around us concealed him from view as the chute neared the ground. It was an awful sight to witness.

Marcial Lichauco and his family survived the war, and he had five more children (there are now 18 grandchildren). After practising law in the postwar years, Lichauco would eventually become a distinguished statesman, serving as the Filipino Ambassador to the United Kingdom, Denmark, Sweden, and Norway.

A Californian insists to his local draft board that he really, truly wants to serve in World War II – if only it weren't for a few minor medical problems.

The December 7, 1941, attack on Pearl Harbor and Germany's declaration of war against the USA two days later ignited a patriotic fervor that prompted American men and women from coast to coast to enlist in the armed forces. There were, however, those who did not want to volunteer, and, if drafted, tried any number of pleas and schemes to secure a deferment. One young Californian assured his draft board that he absolutely wanted to join the military, but probably could not – or at least should not – for the reasons articulated in the following appeal. (His full name is not used in the interests of privacy.)

Draft Board No. 240
5507 Santa Monica Blvd.
Hollywood, California

Dear Sirs

This is to notify you of the symptoms I have Swelling of ankles & feet. Right eye effected & ear by bells paulsia. Right eye discharges white matter. Both eyes water on contact with wind.

Left great toe not active of operation from secondary infraction from bad case of athletic feet. Left great toe develops fever on too much pressure on i and fever's left leg to knee. Left chins bone pains from sunburn two years ago

Left leg & arm cramps or rheuatism ashama and synus. Believe have touch of T.B. in lungs frequent coughing and spitting of matter and substance very gluey and color brownish black and vomatory in morning some times blood

Stomack tender & pains. Burns like fire if drinkin orange juice fo breakfast. Believe I have ulcers or cancer right large intestance have frequen pains. Have had doctor's treatment for it. Piles sometimes bleed.

Continus colds, and head pains. fevers. High or low pressure probably heart. spine in back pains & itches. frequent back of neck pains and sever headache.

All teeth ache very bad at times. Have infieorior complex and nervous conditions.

Perspirationn of forehead. Painful bunions on right foot & left bottom foot, right foot pains and have fever.

95% of my aquantancies claim that I'm mentally unbalanced. Worries me at times if its not so. Was kicked on head by a horse when very young.

James

P.S. am patriotick man & dont want you should think I'm trying to get out of draft. If was would exagerate a litle.

J.P.

The draft board's response, alas, is not known.

A young German soldier called Willi describes the 'fun-filled activities' that keep him and his fellow soldiers amused during World War II — & — Lieutenant Florene Thelma Keik, serving with the US Army Nurse Corps in World War II, shares a somewhat risqué letter with her family in Texas.

Thrust into extremely stressful and often life-threatening situations, confronted with the horrid sights and sounds of battle, and given enormous responsibilities (most notably the power to take another person's life), many combatants mature rapidly during their time of service. But the vast majority of troops, regardless of the war, are in their late teens or early twenties, and it is not uncommon for them to talk of things that tend to amuse young minds – including, as evidenced in the following letter by a young German soldier, deeply profound discussions relating to bodily functions. (Please note: this letter is not for the scatologically squeamish.)

219

10, July 1943

Dear Magda and Bert!

Please note my new address!

Please do not be angry for not hearing from me in such a long time, which really wasn't so long, because I'm always thinking of you all. Perhaps you think that it's easy to say that and why bother coming up with such lazy lame excuses. But you know, a soldier has very little time, and I'll prove it to you straight away.

05.30 wake up call, wash up, make bed, clean up sleeping quarters, breakfast
06.30 roll call
11.30 lunch
13.00 receive orders for the day
13.15 line up for service
17.00 clean and polish gear
18.00 dinner
19.00 clean weapons
20.00 inspection of cleaned fire arms
21.00 a letter to my wife
21.45 blackout
22.00 bedtime

From 22.00 until 05.30 air raid alarms whenever the Tommies feel like it. You see how day and night are packed with fun-filled activities.

In spite of all this, I'm fine and the boot camp drill has just brought me an advanced course in the bakery to fine tune me for a profession that I've been working in for the past sixteen years! Apart from that, I've become a real soldier. I can stand still, keep my trap shut, shout 'shit' in a loud voice, behave like a 'Johnny be good,' and zap like a bolt of lightning about the parade grounds. In addition, they taught me not to steal any silver spoons and not to rape women, because this behavior is unworthy of a soldier.

I'm with twelve others in one barrack, and I'm probably the youngest. All are sacrifices for the total war. Among them, a doctor of chemistry, a middle-school principle, a diploma engineer, a blacksmith, a musician, farmers and craftsmen. In the evening, when we're all sitting around the table, the middle-school principal might tell us about something, and the blacksmith lets off a loud fart, purely out of excitement. The chemist mumbles a chemical formula and swears that there was some sulfur involved. The musician awards a B-major or a C-major, according to the tone of the fart. The engineer calculates the rate of dissolving in the air, and the blacksmith even thinks: 'It smells just as if it came from a horse itself.' I, however, think that it's a little 'Johnny be bad' finding its way out again. Apart from all that, we get along just fine, because we're all struggling for one common goal – home leave. But up until now, the enemy proves stronger. I wonder who'll be the first to get through.

I like Bremen very much, but it would be even nicer if Tommy couldn't fly. Köln has been hit very badly. It's horrible how everything looks. I think the frontline isn't as bad as either of these cities. I heard from Mutz that you sent her two pictures, for which I thank you very much. I hope that you are all coping well under the circumstances, and hope for a quick peace for all of us.

Warmest greetings and kisses.
Your Willi

Women, not surprisingly, tended to be less uncouth in their letters, but they were not immune from enjoying the occasional bawdy story or joke. US Army Nurse Corps Lieutenant Florene Thelma Keike, who served for more than two years in the Pacific during World War II, came across the following letter that had been passed around for amusement and shared it with her family in Austin, Texas. (Preceding the letter is a brief introduction explaining that an American soldier, hoping to impress his beloved, bought her an elegant pair of gloves. His sister offered to help him shop for the gloves, and, at the same time, she purchased a pair of silk bloomers for herself. The two packages got mixed up, and the young man unknowingly sent the underpants and not the gloves with the letter to his beloved. The typos are in the original.)

My dear sweetheart,
This little token is to remind you that I have not forgotten your birthday. I wish to express my appreciation of your friedship during the past year.

I chose these becouse I noticed that you had not been wearing any when we go out evenings. Had it not been for my sister, I would have bought long ones with one button. These are very delicate, But the ladey in the store whare I bought them showed me a pair she had been wearing for three years and they were hardly soiled at all.

How i wish i could put them on for the first time, No doubt many other gentleman's hand's will come in contack with them before i can see you in them, But I hope you will think of me everytime you take them off and put them on again. I had the clerk put them on and they sure looked good on her, I wasn't sure of the size but i feel that I should be a complete judge if any one is. When you put them on the first time, Sprinkle a little powder into them and they will go on easily. When you take them off blow in them as they will naturally be damp from wearing.

I hope you will accept them in the same spirit they are given, And wear them to the dance saturday, when I come to see you be sure to have them on. I would like to count the number of times that I will kiss the back of them during the coming year.

YOUR'S AFFECTIONATILY,.

C anadian field censors report to their superiors about a variety of insulting and prohibited letters they have intercepted during World War II.

'They are censoring our letters right here in Camp now so I will send this by civilian post,' wrote a Canadian soldier from England during World War II, 'as I don't want any fat son of a bitch reading my mail.' Of the many bureaucratic and official procedures disdained by servicemembers in World Wars I and II, few inspired as much contempt and ridicule as censorship. Most understood the necessity of protecting sensitive information – indeed, their lives depended on it – but they nevertheless resented having their intimate correspondences read by total strangers and the seemingly willy-nilly manner in which letters

were returned to them without explanation, cut to pieces, or, according to loved ones back home, delayed for months. Stories abounded as well about censors filching souvenirs and small gifts sent from the front lines, or candy, money, cigarettes, and baked goods sent by the family to the front lines. (One censor even wrote on the bottom of an unsuspecting soldier's letter in the soldier's handwriting, 'Hey mom, how about that fruitcake you promised me?' and then copped the fruitcake when the mom dutifully sent it on.) The censors, from their standpoint, were exasperated by the carelessness of the writers in revealing specific locations, ship and troop movements, casualty estimates, and other details that could prove useful if they fell into enemy hands. Field censors apprised their superiors of the overall mood of the troops, and, in one report compiled by Canadian censors in England during World War II, of how the different Allied troops were getting along with one another. The Canadian soldiers, for the most part, were less than complimentary about their British counterparts:

The Scotch like us better than the English do – the English don't like us much, and we don't like them either.

–

A lot of the people at home have been sending presents with the Limies, who are returning to England, for the Canadians over here. But oddly enough these presents never reach their destination. So that doesn't make us like them any the more. One of the chaps wife sent a wrist-watch over to her husband this way a few months ago, (it was a Bulova too) and he never got it . . . He says if he ever catches an English soldier wearing a Bulova watch he's going to lick the tar out of him.

–

The English call themselves reserved but I should call it hypocrisy. They are underhand. We have been warned not to mix too much with them because they are only trying to look down on the Canadians. There are, fortunately, Canadians here in large numbers. Also they (the English) are very slow to act and take a long time to make up their minds. Canada is heaven compared with England. They are very cold and consider us Colonials, coming from an uncivilized country.

—

I've always imagined the English army to be all military and neat but they're really the sloppiest slovenliest bunch I've ever seen. They never are neat or have any press in their clothes, just a bunch of bums, so we call them. The slouchiest Canadian is really tops compared to some of them.

One soldier wrote what might be the worst insult of all:

The beer here is rotten like everything else.

Sometimes the feelings were mutual, as indicated in the following British letter:

We are all in the barracks tonight, as we have had to scrub the place out today as the place is filthy, the Canadians have just left here.

Censors were also on the alert for letters that could affect morale, either in the field or on the homefront. The following nasty letter, supposedly from 'a friend' sharing unwelcome news to a complete stranger, was held by the censors, with an attached comment stating, 'Perhaps retention of this mail will eliminate further correspondence . . .':

Dear Mrs. Johnston,
Just a tip from a friend, as you know, no doubt, that your husband is in love with another woman, and I am afraid it is kind of heavy and I think that if you both want to be the happier, you will both go your own way. I am writing this, just from what I myself have seen, and I know how your husband is with this woman.

As a matter of fact he can hardly get away enough to see her.

tip from a
friend

Even if the grievances were true, letters that severely criticized commanding officers, military strategy, or anything integral to the overall mission at hand were also prohibited, as they could be used for propaganda purposes by the enemy. They could also dampen morale back home. Censors recognized the need for combatants to vent, and they often grappled with the question of what constituted an acceptably mild outburst and what was truly objectionable. 'If we are fighting for democracy and freedom of speech,' one censor noted after reading a short diatribe about the lack of food and ammunition, 'can we take disciplinary action against the writer of this letter?' The following letter, however, was a prolonged rant that the field censors believed might warrant serious attention.

Just a line and card to wish you all the best for Xmas and the New Year. How are you all keeping these days, just fine I hope. I'm feeling O.K. – no thanks to the damned army. I hav'nt been able to get home since Oct. but was hoping I'd be able to get home for Xmas but that is washed out as our unit (the 5th Gdn. Reg. R.C.A's colonel has decided that we shall not proceed farther than 40 miles from camp at Xmas on our 3 day leave – and we must not travel by train. The rotten old! x !! x We have 7 days leave coming to us – we are entitled to 7 days leave every 3 months in England and our time was up on 5th Dec. – and we can't get that. Other units have started their 10 day leave already – it is just a matter of getting the worst of a rotten bunch of officers I guess.

By the Great God above Win – I hate the army worse than I dreamt possible to hate anything. The army does everything humanly possible to break a man and talk about rotten – it is worse if that is possible – than the present day political set up. Can you imagine it – last Xmas they took us away from home 8 days before Xmas and now chaps who hav'nt been home for Xmas for years can't go now. Mark my words there will be a revolt or something of the kind in the army before this Winter is over. All the boys are completely dissatisfied. Now our rations have been cut 20 per cent and heaven knows the boys don't get too much to eat now. I'm cooking for the officers so I get all I can eat. We are living in quarters that have not been occupied for 10 yrs and were condemned years and years ago. They are damned lousy. There is no reason for it either. We are not needed over here – there is'nt food, accommodation or equipment for us.

There was a revolt so to speak in one outfit – comprised solely of Westerners – they have more guts than this Eastern trash. They were like us – fed up with the way things were going and when Gen. Odham came up for inspection they refused to go on parade. Conditions for them were improved in an awful hurry – believe me. If God and his almighty justice has anything to do with winning a war I don't see how the army can win it – it is too rotten and corrupt. Alice and her mother have given money, blankets, socks etc. to the red cross – another army racket and I have yet to see the first goods from the Red cross. A friend of one of our boys from Toronto received a letter from a trapper in Northern Ontario saying if she could let him have the same kind of socks for 55 c/s a pair – he'd take 6 pairs. She had donated the socks to the Red Cross, put her name on a paper in the toe of the sock – as I believe many women do – and that is how the soldiers get the Red Cross clothes and comforts. It is just a racket like it was in the last war.

The same with our mail. There are millions of cigarettes not reaching the addressee and thousands of parcels and they <u>don't</u> go down in the boat. There are too many light fingered guys handling the mail. Alice sent me a big parcel on Nov. 3rd and a letter on Nov. 4th and 11th. I received the letters but no parcel. Somebody figured they had more right to it than me. That is what is happening to thousands of the boys and the army doesn't do anything about it. They must know what's going on. I don't think even the army is that stupid. Thank God we have the U.S.A. on our side – if it was'nt for her the war would have been over. When I get back I plan to stop at Montreal – buy a motorbike and see some of the U.S.A. and to see you before heading back for S'toon. Joan started kindergarten on Nov. 5th at a convent. I hope they don't try and make a catholic out of her. God help them and Alice if they do. I hear from Alice fairly often she has sent me money several times and some parcels. Her mother tho' can't do enough for me always sending me stuff and papers letters socks, eatables and sweaters. I've told her lots of time not to bother as I don't need them but you know her – she's got to have her own way. But still it's very good of her – she couldn't treat a son of her own any better.

How is the weather where you are? It is nasty here. Cold and frosty one night and raining and blowing the next. I sure don't like England or the people in it. What the hell Hitler wants this country for beats me and all the Canadians. I don't believe there are 20 men out of every 1,000 that are not sorry they ever came to this country. I know I am. I would'nt trade one square foot of Canada for this whole damned country. Jerry sure is making a mess of some of the places over here. Just wiping the places out. But he has'nt dropped many bombs near us yet. I guess he knows he does'nt need to bother about us with the quarters we have the kind of horse doctors we have. As long as one is able to walk they tell you you are not sick you're just swinging the lead. Several chaps have died of pneumonia already because the doc. said they were <u>not</u> sick. How is Ben doing – is he still working at Kohler? The Greeks sure are giving the Italians hell, I only wish we could get close to the jerries – we'd soon have them on the run. I've heard from Eric and Bert but hav'nt seen them. I saw Dolly, Tom, Conie and Jim besides Mum and Dad. I saw Vi – and she has grown to be a lovely girl. Not a bit course like Jim, Nell and young Jimmy. You'd hardly think she came from the same family. She works in a radio factory at a place call Woking – not very far from here, about 27 miles. We moved to this blasted plasted place on Oct. 10th from Mons barracks at Aldershot. Well I guess I'll ring off for now Win, be sure to write soon, Best of Luck and Wishes.

'Pigs is pigs and freedom of speech is freedom of speech,' a censor wrote in his report, 'but there are limits to both. We should pass this on to Corps for their necessary action.'

The Parents of US Private First Class William Lee Kyzer receive a 'censored' letter from their son serving in the Pacific during World War II.

Censorship could also prove frustrating for family and friends desperate for information about their loved ones serving far from home. William Kyzer, a young farmer from Jacksonville, Arkansas, was drafted into the army after the outbreak of World War II and became an infantry rifleman in the Pacific. Kyzer's father and stepmother were eager to hear how William was faring, but they would mostly receive letters like the following, which appeared to have been cut up entirely by the censors:

Dear Dad & Carmilita
I'm OK, days flies by here in

Well maybe it can be all again soon. I'm praying for it. Write soon
Nothing like getting a letter from home. Here on

Love
Bill

P.S. They may censor this letter

In fact, Kyzer's mail was not edited at all; he simply hated writing letters and only penned the few sentences at the top and the bottom so that his folks would believe that the censors were responsible for slicing out the rest.

Lieutenant Commander JJ Cummings describes his missions over Afghanistan and the inevitable rivalries between US Navy pilots and their USAF and RAF counterparts during Operation Enduring Freedom.

Just over one month after the September 11, 2001, terrorist attacks on the USA, a multinational force was deployed to Southwest Asia to battle al-Qaeda and Taliban forces and hunt down Osama bin Laden. Operation Enduring Freedom, as the mission was called, represented the first major American conflict where email was utilized by the troops – perhaps with even greater frequency than traditional mail. Owing to concerns about biological contaminants, Operation Enduring Freedom was also the first conflict in a generation that prohibited 'To any soldier' letters – i.e., messages of support written by total strangers and mailed to troops abroad. (In September and October 2001, envelopes containing weaponized anthrax had been sent through the US mail, killing five people and infecting many more.) The tone of the emails and letters by the troops who were serving in and around Afghanistan was reminiscent of messages sent in the early days of World War II – defiant, determined and fiercely patriotic. But they were not without humor. No matter how unified the different services and nations involved in Operation Enduring Freedom were, high-spirited and time-honored rivalries could not be easily overcome. A Navy pilot aboard the USS Theodore Roosevelt, *Lieutenant Commander JJ Cummings, wrote the following email to his family back in the USA, updating them on his activities and adding a comment, here and there, about other pilots in the American (USAF) and British (RAF) air forces. (The USN refers to the US Navy, and the USMC to the US Marine Corps. The ellipses are in the original text.)*

Happy Thanksgiving (belated) everybody!
For Thanksgiving, the ship dressed up the wardroom, dimmed down the lights and put out a nice T-day spread and, for a brief moment, it was almost

like being home. Sure it was. I don't know too many folks who live in a gray tin can with 5,500 other roommates but what can you do! We had flights later in the day scheduled, so scores of aircrew had to fight off the triptofan nods during their 6 hour flights over Afghanistan. Can you see the headlines now? 'US Fighter Down Over Afghanistan. Turkey Overdose Suspected. Should Have Gone For The Dry Ham.' I was able to call home and chat briefly with Mackenzie (and Sara and Delaney, of course) who filled me in on the untimely passing of her second fish. 'It's OK Daddy. We'll get another one.' It was a great day.

The flights over Afghanistan continue. The country's landscape reminds me of northern Nevada (without the casinos). As you cross over the southern border with Pakistan, you are met by hundreds of miles of desert. After the 'Desert of Death' (as the charts call it), you get into rolling hills and occasional 2000' mountain ranges. From about mid-Afghanistan and north, the country turns into dark brown mountains that max out around 13,000 feet. Snow tops a majority of these peaks which remind me of the area surrounding Fallon, NV (one of our training areas). As you near the northern border by the -stans (Uzbeki and Turkmeni), the mountains start easing off and work down back into light brown, sandy plains. Off to the northeast are big snow-capped ranges that reach up to 25,000 feet. Overall, extremely rugged looking terrain in Afghan. To date, I have not seen one tree. The rural areas are littered with villages that are filled with collections of roofless, four walled structures that appear to be abandoned. The 'cities' are completely unremarkable and colorless with no structure being any taller than 2 stories. The only color I've seen in these cities besides the ever present light brown hue is the occasional red streak coming from the Taliban gunners as they open up with their anti aircraft artillery. There is some farm land present, but it is infrequent and minimal. In a nutshell, Afghanistan is a giant pile of brown to light brown rocks that is bordered to the south and north by huge deserts and bordered to the east by an even bigger pile of rocks. The only signs of life that I have seen are vehicles (Toyota appears to be the SUV of choice) moving on one of the country's three main highways, some lights in the smaller towns at night and Taliban tough guys running from their convoy of military vehicles right before multiple weapons impacts.

The bombs keep falling on the Taliban. Sometimes you get in country and drop, sometimes you can't. As you can gather from all of the news coverage, the ground picture is changing radically and as a result, the air strike players are a bit more restrained. That's OK though because it serves to further cut the Air Force out of the picture. Designed to fight a war against an immobile enemy with fixed targets, the USAF is having a hard time with this fluid battlefield stuff, scenarios to which the USN/USMC routinely train. I'm sure they'll do fine when they get their 13,000 foot runways built in . . . . . oh, that's right they don't have any runways nearby. Guess those boys should have invested in some carrier decks a few years back. Realize that the previous statements are heavily biased and ridiculously true.

A few funny stories for you before I sign off. Talked previously about the air to air refueling that goes on over here. Over time, you get a feel for who the cool tanker drivers are and who the dolts are. The dolts? Air Force guys, of course. Love all the gas they carry, but they have no personality whatsoever (big shocker there). Cool tanker guys? The Royal Air Force! Love these guys. They will always go the extra mile (literally) to make sure you get your gas when and where you need it. The RAF tankers are ALWAYS on station and on time. Apparently, the F-14 is their favorite platform so as an added benefit post tanking, you can pull up along side the pilot's window and he'll shove some literature up against the window for your perusal (your guess on the type of literature displayed).

A few days ago, we were directed to hang on this RAF tanker's wing until we received mission tasking. After about 10 minutes, I decide to strike up a conversation with the crew (we monitor the same frequency while getting gas) to kill time. Thus began the comedy. After a 30 minute exchange of good hearted jabs, the pilot delivered a challenge to our flight of two.

But first, let me explain a little bit about inflight refueling. As I have mentioned earlier, to get gas airborne we have to put out a refueling probe which extends out from the right side of the jet about 2 feet outboard and forward of the pilot's head. The tanker is dragging a 20 foot hose which ends in a basket that looks similar to a badminton 'birdie'. The basket is about 2 feet in diameter. Now the hard part of tanking at 300 MPH is getting in the basket, because as you near the basket, the air disturbance created by the nose of your jet causes the basket to move up and away from you. Also thrown into the moving basket equation is general air turbulence, as well as the 'ham fist' of the pilot who is flying the tanker.

Sometimes you get in the first time, sometimes it takes a couple of stabs.

Where was I? Oh yeah, so this RAF guy says, 'If you F-14 chaps are truly America's Finest Fighter Aircraft (my quote from a previous discussion), then you should have no problem getting into the basket first time, right?' I respond with, 'Yeah, I usually bat about .900 with these poorly designed Brit baskets. The problem is that when I get in close, I find myself thinking about Margaret Thatcher naked, get sick to my stomach and miss the basket. Tell you what, we'll put a case of beer on both Tomcats getting in the first time.' Did I mention that he's flying a DC-9 type tanker where a basket comes off of each wing tip which exacerbates (thankyou thesaurus) the turbulence problem by virtue of the rough air flow over the wingtip? Screw it. Bet's on.

The call finally comes for us to go hit some targets and it's time to get topped off. Pressure's on. I head over to the tanker's left wing, my wingman over to his right and as we are closing in I tell my wingman, 'Now Moses, as you get in close, try not to think about all of the great English warriors of the past: the Spice Girls, Boy George, Wham UK and Dame Edna. Just free your mind and be the basket.' A couple of corrections later and just as I plug (on the first attempt) I scream over the radio, 'Revolutionary War, baby!' 'Moses' was good on his first attempt so the final score was US-2, England-0. I doubt we'll see the beer but who would want a case of shitty warm Brit beer anyway.

Speaking of beer, somewhere in the Navy regulations it's written down that for every 45 consecutive days that you spend at sea without a port call, you rate two beers. Two weeks ago, they broke out 10,000 beers for the crew to tear into for this deployment's first of many 'beer days'. With beer day fast approaching, multiple discussions erupted in the Ready Room over how to best maximize the beer day allotment. Do you starve yourself for two days to increase the 'buzz' potential? How about giving blood 2 hours prior to assist in decreasing the amount of blood in your alcohol system? Do you nurse your two beers over a two hour span or just chug 'em and ride the wave? Which type of beer gives you the most bang for the buck? Fosters? Yengling? MGD? All very important and crucial questions. After much mental anguish and repeated calls to the flight surgeon inquiring about blood donor opportunities, I decided on the 'full fed, Fosters chug' gameplan. Rumor has it that over 22,000 beers were killed. Hmmm . . . . 5,500 person crew, 2 beers per person . . . . hey . . . . . . someone went through the line more than once! No comment. Only 20 days until our next beer day, so I will take inputs on any improvements to my gameplan!

One last thing before I complete my novella . . . . . . Please remember in your thought and prayers every single enlisted Sailor that is slugging it out here on the *USS TR*. The aviator types have it easy in that we get to leave this ship for 6 fun filled hours to fly into a foreign hostile land and blow stuff up. We have variety and excitement in our days. Think of that 19 year old kid up on the flight deck 17 hours a day, fixing the same jets day in and day out while maintaining the same daily routine. Imagine doing that for over 70 days straight (only two days off in the last 6 weeks). He looks forward to 4 things: 1) getting off his feet for 5 minutes, 2) eating bland Navy chow, 3) sleeping in a cluttered space shared by 239 other Sailors and 4) port calls. His variety and excitement comes mainly during inport visits and, to date, we have had none and oh, by the way, there isn't one in the near or even distant future. They are the real heroes of Operation Enduring Freedom because it is through their efforts that we are able to launch and ultimately defend American shores. Through it all, you rarely hear one complaint from these kids despite the fact that they are working harder than anyone on this planet in the most dangerous 'office space' on Earth, the flight deck of an aircraft carrier.

Hope this email finds you all safe and having a great Holiday Season. Don't worry about us, we are doing great out here. I can honestly say that there is no other place in the world I'd rather be than right here, right now, sticking it to the Taliban.

Later, JJ

—— FEATURED SERIES ——

'Animals in Wartime'

The carrier pigeon Valiant delivers a final plea from French Troops, trapped at Fort Vaux in Verdun, France, during World War I — & — In a letter to a young friend, General John Monash writes from France about a German messenger dog that deserted his platoon to join the Australians, during World War I — & — Three young members of the Hewlett family implore Lord Horatio Kitchener, Secretary of State for War during World War I, not to draft their pony Betty — & — American Lieutenant Junior Grade BJ Armstrong emails his family about two military dolphins that have gone AWOL during Operation Iraqi Freedom.

After being notified by an aide-de-camp that some of the troops were abandoning the army on horseback, General George Washington replied, in letter of January 8, 1777, that his officers needed to be vigilant about preventing these desertions – because they couldn't spare the animals. '[T]he loss of a worthless soldier,' Washington stated bluntly, 'will occasion less regret when it is not accompanied with that of a Horse.' Since the first warriors clashed thousands of years ago, animals have played an integral role in the defense and conquest of armies and entire nations. Among many other duties, they have served as sentries and alarms, hauled munitions and men across seemingly endless and insurmountable terrain, parachuted into enemy territory, traveled hundreds of miles to deliver urgent messages, detected buried explosives, and assisted in search and rescue missions. In a pinch, some have had the added bonus of being edible. ('This day Capt Goodrich's Company Kill'd my Dog, and another Dog, and Eat them, [and] I remain unwell,' a starving and heavy-hearted Captain Henry Dearborn wrote while on the brutal 1775 march to Quebec during the American Revolution.) But for the most part, military animals are valued not for their nutritional benefits, but for their service and sacrifices. Messenger pigeons used in times of war have often been gunned down in midair or torn to pieces by hawks specially trained to find and destroy them. And some literally flew themselves to death. Trapped inside Fort Vaux during the ferocious, ongoing battles in Verdun, France, during World War I, Major Sylvain Eugene Raynal and his men had reached the limits of human suffering. There was no clean water to drink. Raynal had shut off the fort's ventilation to prevent the Germans from gassing them, and the air became saturated with the stench of human waste and the decaying bodies of men who had been killed during the relentless bombardments. The Germans breached sections of the fort and sent streams of fire into the narrow passageways with flamethrowers. Realizing defeat was all but imminent, Raynal tied a desperate note to a homing pigeon named Valiant and released him into the sky. The message read:

We are holding, but are under a very dangerous attack of gas and smoke. Relief is urgently needed. Send a visual signal through Souville, which is no longer answering our calls for help. This is my last pigeon.

Wounded and nearly asphyxiated by poison gas, Valiant nevertheless made it to a command post in Verdun – and then dropped dead on the spot. Although Fort Vaux would ultimately fall, Valiant was lauded as a symbol of courage, posthumously receiving the prestigious Legion of Honour. Almost 40 years later another carrier pigeon, Gustav, would become a national celebrity for bringing back one of the first reports of the D-Day landings in Normandy on June 6, 1944. An English 'grizzle cock,' Gustav flew 150 miles in about five hours, earning him the Dickin Medal. Unlike Valiant, Gustav survived the flight. Ironically, though, he met a tragic fate after the war, when his breeder, while cleaning the pigeon's loft, accidentally stepped on Gustav, killing him instantly.

Dogs have also been used as messengers, darting through minefields, destroyed towns and dense forests, all the while trying to avoid being shot or captured. In World War I, a German dog named Roff became famous for 'switching sides' in early May 1918. Just days before General John Monash would be appointed Commander of the Australian Corps, he sent the following short letter from Villers-Bretonneux, France, where his men were locked in a fierce battle with German forces trying to march on Paris. (It is not known for certain who Susan is, but she is believed to be a young friend.)

May 26, 1918

My Dear Susan,

In France here the weather has been very warm, and this has brought out all the beautiful wild flowers. The other day we took prisoner a beautiful German messenger dog. He is a beautiful Alsatian wolf hound, and he is very friendly. He has learned to speak and understand English, and is very faithful to us, and we all pet him so much.

In fact, Roff was a Doberman, and he was not taken prisoner by force; he voluntarily trotted over to the Australian side. The container in his collar still held the note intended for a platoon of German troops cut off from food and other necessary supplies. They had asked for relief, and, had Roff continued with his mission, they would have received the following snippy reply from their commander: 'Weber has been in longer than you and he does not complain. We will send you food tonight. Give Roff any further messages – he does not complain.'

In World War I alone, an estimated 8 million horses were shot or blown apart in combat or died of disease or exhaustion. Demand for the animals was so great during the war that horses were taken from families who owned them as pets, and this proved especially heartbreaking to children who had grown attached to the horses. Even before they received notification that their own pony, Betty, had been 'drafted,' three young members of the Hewlett family – Poppy, Lionel and Freda – wrote directly to Lord Horatio Kitchener, Great Britain's Secretary of State for War, to ensure that Betty would be safe.

Aug: 11th 14

Dear Good Lord Kitchener,

We are writing for our Pony which we are very afraid may be taken for your Army! <u>Please spare her</u>! Daddy says he is going to be a Mother early next year & is 14 years old – it would break our hearts to let her go – We have given 2 others & 3 of our family are now fighting for you in the Navy.

Mother & all will do anything for you but <u>do do please</u> let us keep old Betty & send official word <u>quickly</u> before anyone comes.

Your troubled little Britishers

P., L. & Freda Hewlett.

Several days later the Hewletts received a note from the War Office proclaiming that 'Lord Kitchener has decided that no horse under 15 hands shall be requisitioned belonging to the British family P. L & Freda Hewlett.' A second message was attached that stated:

13th August 1914.

Dear Miss Freda Hewlett

Lord Kitchener asks me to say in reply to your letter of the 11th August, that if you will show the enclosed note to anyone who comes to ask about your pony, he thinks it will be left to you quite safely.

To the dismay of many an animal lover, creatures large and small have also been 'weaponized' in times of war to attack military and civilian populations alike. In World War II, Soviet troops regularly tied explosives to dogs that had been trained to run toward enemy soldiers and tanks, with fatal consequences for the targets – and, of course, the dogs.

Winged and footed creatures are not alone in being called into service; aquatic animals have been employed as well. Bottlenose dolphins were first used in Vietnam to hunt for mines, retrieve inaccessible equipment on the ocean floor and serve as guards, protecting warships from attack by enemy agents. Sea lions and other marine mammals are now being trained to perform similar feats. Extremely intelligent, playful, and social, dolphins exhibit many humanlike characteristics; they can also be mischievous, aggressive, moody, and stubborn. In the buildup to Operation Iraqi Freedom, a team of dolphins was sent to the Middle East with Commander Task Force (CTF) 55, a group of American, British, and Australian sailors and marines whose mission was to clear the northern Persian Gulf, which the US military refers to as the Arabian Gulf, of mines. The dolphins accomplished their assignment admirably, but in a few cases they demonstrated that they had minds of their own. Twenty-six-year-old Lieutenant Junior Grade BJ Armstrong, a HH-46D Sea Knight pilot stationed on the USS Kearsarge *as part of a search and rescue (SAR) detachment, emailed to his family about one such incident. (EOD stands for Explosives Ordnance Disposal.)*

Just wanted to drop everyone a note and say hello. Things are going out here. I wouldn't say going well, or badly, they are just going. The sandstorm has hit us after a frontal passage yesterday and even inside the skin of the ship our noses are filling with dust. No flying today but its just the kind of day that we need to be ready for SAR work. Nobody ever seems to go for a swim during good weather. I'm on the Alert Crew most of the day so I'll probably take in a lot of CNN while we sit around waiting (Ed . . . Alert 15, not bad since we don't have to be in the bird and we can even access one of the det's computers).

Just a funny story to pass along. A little over [a] week ago, before this had all started getting real, we got a funny call from Tower while we were out flying. We were told to report all Dolphin sitings. We didn't see any for the couple hours I was up but we did think the call was rather odd. When we hotseated the bird to the next crew we asked about it and they had been briefed more specifically on what to look for. Apparently the EOD guys had lost one of their male mine hunting dolphins. It had just swum away. They had sent out a couple others, trying to lure it back (presumably females) with no luck. All the SAR birds out here in the Gulf were alerted in case we saw a lonesome dolphin swimming around. Apparently there was a happy ending, flipper showed back up a couple days later. I guess even our finned friends get a little weary of life on (and around) the boat.

Love to all,

BJ

The search for innovative ways to employ animals in both combat and peacekeeping efforts continues. In Mozambique, Gambian giant pouched rats are being trained to sniff out land mines left over from the country's vicious civil war. (Dogs are commonly used, too, but the rats' sense of smell is just as perceptive, and the rats themselves are cheaper, easier to care for, and lighter – and therefore less likely to set off a mine accidentally.) Bees are also being tested for mine-hunting activities; their bodies pick up all types of airborne particles, and if residual TNT is found mixed in with whatever pollen they are carrying, it can confirm the presence of land mines in a specific area. Similarly, entomologists are researching if bugs can be used as tiny sentinels that can be collected and then tested for toxins in the air, water, or soil during a possible bio-terror attack. Insects are not new to warfare. Glowworms were used in World War I to help soldiers read maps and other documents at night. Even plants are being enlisted. Biologists are working to determine whether i is possible to create genetically engineered plants that will quickly change colors in relation to poison gases or other life-threatening agents. And these, of course, only represent the ideas that the military is able to make public.

Second Lieutenant Barbara 'Heiny' Demetria, US Marine Corps, serving in Operation Iraqi Freedom, explains to her family how she got her call sign.

Much like a civilian nickname given to a close friend, family member, teammate or coworker, a soldier's informal 'call sign' might be inspired by any number of factors. It can be an abbreviation of or play on someone's name, or a reference to a physical characteristic, personality trait or military specialty. And in some cases, as 23-year-old US Marine Second Lieutenant Barbara 'Heiny' Demetria discovered, it can be prompted by a single unfortunate incident that draws the attention of the chain of command, from top to bottom – literally. (MOPP refers to chemical-protection suits, DASC is the abbreviation for Direct Air Support Center, and COC is Combat Operations Center. The ellipses are in the original text.)

Hi everyone,

I was sitting on crew today and realized I hadn't shared the tale of my callsign with you. It is one of danger and embarrassment. I will try not to be too lengthy, but it takes some explaining . . . Everyone knows that all pilots have a callsign. Well we work pretty closely with the air officers and pilots so we all eventually get a 'callsign', usually inspired by something you have said or done. Well I didn't waste any time in getting mine. I think it was our third location where Liza and I had to share a tent. There was a terrible sand storm that day – the worst one we've seen so far. The sky was orange in the hours before it started and we were sleeping before our crew. The wind was so violent it woke me up. It wasn't until I felt my face and realized there was a thick layer of dust on it. The sand was so fine and the wind blowing so hard that it went through the rain cover over our tent, through the actual tent walls and covered EVERYTHING in the tent – including us! It was absolutely disgusting. We were thinking it couldn't possibly get any worse . . . and then it did.

The torrential downpours ensued shortly after and completely drenched everything that was covered with dirt. What was great about this was that all of my gear (helmet, flak, MOPP boots, camelbag) was outside. Normally you put all this gear on to walk over to the system, but my flak vest was actually one with the ground and my helmet filled with mud. So I left it behind and hoped that day wasn't the day we took mortar rounds. Turns out we were located right in the middle of a dried out river bed – great place to be when it rains. So we all trudge over to the DASC in ankle-deep mud in the middle of the night with hardly any illumination from the moon. We get to the DASC and the tent is a total mess. Mud had been tracked all over the place. I was a liason that day between the DASC and COC. The COC tent was a big round tent we called the 'Thunderdome' and it had several small off-chute tent (the DASC being one of them). So there is a little passage way that connects our tent to the Thunderdome and it was particularly slippery with all the mud that had been tracked in by traffic and I had come close to slipping several times . . . You probably think you know where this is going and you may be partly correct but it is much worse.

Shall we continue? OK, so the admin folks have a table set up in the COC just to the right of the passage way. General Mattis, as in the Commanding General of the entire 1st Marine Division, was using the phone at this table. I need to give the Air Officer in the COC some information so I start heading through the passageway and I felt myself slip. At this point one of those slow motion moments began and I thought 'Noooooooo!' . . . I could feel myself falling and knew I couldn't stop. I was trying not to completely fall so I was on my hands and feet tumbling full force into the COC. The General's back was to me and I couldn't stop myself I went head-first into his butt. Yes, my head; his butt. Thus marked the birth of 'Heiny'. Since then I think I have heard about every joke there is about 'kissing the General's ass' not being taken literally. Luckily the man was talking on the phone and was kind enough not to berate me. Everytime I see him and say good morning he smiles (Thinking, 'Yup, that's the girl') and returns the greeting and I'm positive I blush (Thinking, 'All he's thinking is "that's the girl who rammed my butt with her head, I mean there are other ways of getting my attention"'). No he's really very nice. When we were back at Matilda I also used to put the frozen slices of butter under my leg to thaw while we ate, and they always used to joke that one day I would forget I put it there and get up to walk out of the chow hall with butter on my butt. So I think this one is going to stick :) I've gotta go for now but I thought you would enjoy that one. I'll write more as soon as I get a chance.

I love you guys,
Deme

Dayna Kennison receives an email from her husband, a US Air Force major, suggesting what family members can do to help returning troops adjust to civilian life after Operation Iraqi Freedom.

Long before the advent of email, servicemen and women composed amusing and satirical letters that lampooned military life and were copied (usually on mimeograph machines) and then widely circulated to friends and loved ones. One of the earliest of these parodies was an official-looking document instructing World War II combatants on what to expect and how to behave when they returned to their normal lives. 'The United States is composed of land,' begins the memo for American troops heading home in 1945, millions of whom had been away for years. The letter continues:

Bisecting the center is the Mississippi River. Everything east of the river is known as New York, while everything west is simply called Texas. There are a couple of other states, but they are not important . . . Food is generally plentiful [and in] many restaurants you will see an item called 'steak' on the menu. This dish is to be eaten with knife and fork. Steak has a meaty taste and isn't too revolting after one gets used to it. Of course, it doesn't come up to the luscious delectability of our own Bully Beef... One must be very cautious when ordering drinks in bars and saloons. Bartenders try to sell old, aged stocks of Scotch and Bourbon. Don't be taken in by such practices. Some of the whiskey is twenty or even thirty years old, and obviously spoiled... The country is run by Republicans, Democrats and Frank Sinatra. It's a big place because it stretches all the way across the country. Keep on your toes and you will get along alright.

German soldiers on the brutal Eastern Front fighting the Russians during World War II had their own version, titled 'Notes for those going on leave,' which was considerably darker.

Curfew: If you forget your [house]key, try to open the door with the round-shaped object. Only in cases of extreme urgency use a grenade.
Defence against Partisans: It is not necessary to ask civilians the password and open fire on receiving an unsatisfactory answer.
Defence against Animals: Dogs with mines attached to them are a special feature of the Soviet Union. German dogs in the worst cases bite, but they do not explode. Shooting every dog you see, although recommended in the Soviet Union, might create a bad impression...
General: When on leave back in the Fatherland take care not to talk about the paradise existence in the Soviet Union in case everybody wants to come here and spoil our idyllic comfort.

During the Vietnam War, the 'coming home' advice was addressed to friends and family back in the USA who were about to receive a returning serviceman: '[S]how no alarm if he insists on carrying a weapon to the dinner table... If it should start raining, pay no attention to his joyous scream as he strips naked, grabs a bar of soap and runs outdoors for a shower... Pretend not to notice if at a restaurant he calls the waitress "Numbah One Girl."' Despite the coarser language, the mock instructions end on a rather poignant note

Above all, keep in mind that beneath that tanned and rugged exterior there is a heart of gold (the only thing of value he has left). Treat him with kindness, tolerance, and an occasional fifth of good liquor, and you will be able to rehabilitate that hollow shell which was once the happy-go-lucky guy you once knew and loved.

More good-natured than bitter, 'Instructions for a smooth homecoming' was written just before the first rotation of troops began returning from Operation Iraqi Freedom. Dayna Kennison received the following version via email from her husband, a major in the United States Air Force, Air National Guard. ('FNG,' mentioned at the end of the letter, stands for 'F - - - ing New Guy.'

These instructions are intended for the spouses and loved one's of deployed troops to help provide a smooth transition back to civilized life.

1. Leave a flashlight near your spouse while they are sleeping. It is possible the returnee may need to use the bathroom in the middle of the night. While they are walking around your backyard trying to find the bathroom, they may need a flashlight. Don't be alarmed if your returnee is more comfortable walking to the nearest gas station to use the restroom.

2. While your returnee is sleeping, it is imperative you make as much noise as possible. You have many options on what kind of noise to make. For instance run the lawn mower just outside the bedroom door. Hold conversations with people within 2 feet of the sleeping person. Play recordings of jet engines taking off at the highest volume your home stereo will allow. Your loved one is not used to sleeping in complete silence and could possibly suffer from severe insomnia if extreme noise is not maintained during the hours they try to sleep. Also keep the shades on all windows in the bedroom open. If the individual is sleeping at night, keep the lights on. Your loved one is not used to sleeping in the dark and may be very disoriented without a blinding light in their eyes.

3. Keep several boxes of bottled water near every water faucet in your house. The returnee will be scared out of their mind to drink or use the water from the faucet for brushing their teeth and will need the bottled water.

4. Under no circumstances is your returnee allowed more then 2 boxes of cereal. This could potentially lead to violence. However, they will adjust.

5. Be sure to place a cup of sand in front of an oscillating fan on high . . . enough said!

6. You might notice obsessive-compulsive behavior in your returnee due to the ever-present Hennessy Disease rampant at their deployed location. Simply provide your loved one with antibacterial lotion and they will be fine.

7. Don't be embarrassed if at your local bar your returnee pulls out his/her beer card. This will pass. If your returnee sneaks off to the bar and tries to bribe the bartender for a fourth beer, let them go – they need it.

8. Twice a week your returnee will be looking for the laundry turn-in point. Set up a tent in your backyard where laundry can be dropped off. Make sure not to use any type of laundry detergent or fabric softener, as the good clean smell and the softness of the clothing may confuse and frighten your returnee and cause them not to wear those articles of clothing. Also, be sure to put stickers on your returnees clothing. Ensure they are placed where they will irritate the hell out of them.

9. Only offer meals at certain times of day and ensure they sign for EVERYTHING. DO NOT under any circumstances allow the individual to eat at a time when the 'chow hall' is not open. If they are permitted to eat during these times, it is very possible that the feeling of not being hungry could cause their bodies to go into shock. Additionally, ensure they stand in a line for at least 10 minutes and give them a large tray that you cleaned off with dirty dishwater to set their plates on. Find at least 10 or 15 of your friends, dress them in blue coveralls, and ask them

to talk incoherently while they act unhappy to slop the food on the dishes ensuring to give them twice what they've asked for. Pile the food together in the middle of the plate – they'll think it tastes better that way.

10. With every meal ensure that there is plenty of fluffy steamed white rice. If this is not provided, your returnee will be unsure exactly what to do, and could possibly starve to death. Always offer salad, but sometimes don't use lettuce – instead substitute old cabbage and limit their selections of dressing to 1000 Island, Ranch, and Italian if you decide to provide it. Additionally, you must buy all plastic silver wear and Styrofoam plates.

11. Have your loved one bag the trash and then explain where you want it taken. It might be easier and preferred by your loved one to drop it off on the way to the gas station for a bathroom break.

12. Finally, your loved one may count the days he's been home and call everybody that visits the house 'FNG'. If this occurs, tell him he's leaving every few weeks and to keep counting – remind him he's making history.

These instructions are meant to help ease your returnee back into life at home. It will take some time and extra care on you part, but after 30–60 days, your loved one should be good as new. Just in time to return. Good luck.

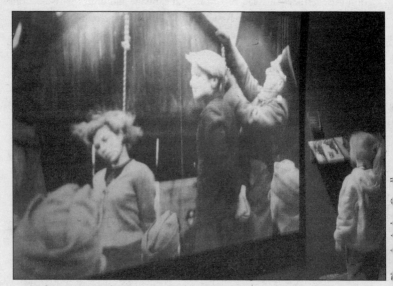

At the Memorial of Caen in Normandy, France, a young girl (far right) looks at a wall-sized photograph of two teenage Polish civilians being hanged by a German officer.

CAUGHT IN THE CROSSFIRE

Letters By and About Civilians

In place of a dutiful and grateful return to your King and Parent state, you have been guilty of the most unpardonable Rebellion, Supported by the Ambition of a set of designing men, whose insidious views have cruelly imposed on the credulity of their fellow creatures, and at last have brought the whole into the same Dilemma, which leads me to feel not a little for the Innocent of them, in particular on the present occasion, having it in orders to execute a just Punishment on the Town of Falmouth.

> *British Navy Captain Henry Mowatt, ordering the citizens of Falmouth, Maine, on October 16, 1775, to evacuate their town before he burns it to the ground during the American Revolution.*

On the 18th Octbr last a Fleet under the command of Capt Mowatt burnt the Town of Falmouth as you've undoubtedly heard – . Your House Barn Out Houses, Fences & Office are all in Ashes. – I was obliged to flee for my Life – and my wife & I were forced to foot it with large Bundles on our Arms about 6 or 8 Miles & abused as we passed the Road . . . am Still in the Woods, where if I cant get off either to London, Boston or Hallifax, I intend to remain till Peace be restored to this infatuated, this distracted Country –

> *A citizen of Falmouth reports to a friend that the town is destroyed during the American Revolution.*

Dear Ning: It is my greatest regret that I failed in my duty to provide you with the education and upbringing you deserve. I will never see you again in this life, my dear son. I hope you will grow up fast so that you can comfort your mother at her grave. I cannot teach you with my words anymore, but I can educate you with what I have done, which you will better understand when you are older. Please remember always that your mother sacrificed her life for the future of our country.

> *Zhao Yi Man, one of millions of Chinese women who assisted the army in resisting the Japanese, sending a final farewell from prison to her young son before her execution.*

London is the best place to be in. Marguerite tried hard the other day, to satisfy Cevil, to get herself to Canada, and it's absolutely <u>impossible</u> to get a passage unless you are either under 16 or over 60, and I don't think that however skillfully I disguised myself I could pass as either of those age groups –so stop fretting about me – anyway my blood is up & I'm dying to take a poke at the Germans – if one has the mischance to land in the garden he's going to have a hot time before I'm through with him – and I'm glad to be Johnny on the spot with a chance of taking a crack at them with saucepans of boiling water aimed with great precision from the kitchen window – My best love to you, and don't believe people who say that British morale is low – we're just spoiling for a fight – so here's cheers till next week – It hasn't rained yet! Papoose.

> *Yvonne Green, a Canadian woman living in London, writing to her anxious mother back in Canada on July 4, 1940 about the Blitz during World War II. Green was killed nine months later during an air raid.*

We have passed a couple of hot points initially, the first one is right when we crossed the border for the first time. The city is called Safwan and 50% of the population are children who are starving. The rest are men and women who might snap at any time. The city is now under the protection or security of the Brits. The Brits are doing an outstanding job. Now we don't travel through the city, instead we have to travel through an alternate road which is much safer. Basarah is not far from the road we travel on. On the sides of the road there are kids who beg for food. We give them our MRE's [Meals, Ready to Eat] and water. I have had poverty stare at me dead in the eyes, these eyes that stare are from kids who do not deserve these harsh conditions. They are beautiful kids who need love, need shelter, and freedom. It breaks my heart to see them begging, soon they will be free. I've taken pictures of their faces to remind me that there are places in this world where people suffer, especially children.

US Marine Corporal Denis Silva Torres, writing from Iraq in early April 2003 to his future parents-in-law.

It is hard to tell you the situation here, it is bad, very bad. I can't even get out with my own car, as I may be killed by the robbers, or by a mine put to the side of the road, or by a firefight between Americans and some people. Death is not an accident here, no, it is the only real, stable, possible thing here. I was trying to find a job, but no work is available. You know that I was forced to leave working with Americans. My home had become a target for those who are pretending to resist the invasion, and they had kidnapped my brother, sent me a message to quit or they would kill him, so I did. I don't know what to do. I think I will work as a taxi driver, but it is not easy, you know the traffic probelms, the dangers of being robbed by someone. Write to me about you . . . I need to hear from you.

Iraqi citizen Khadum A., writing from Baghdad, Iraq, to a relative in August 2004.

The brother of a German soldier fighting in Belgium, during World War I, advises him to 'have no compassion for these cut-throats,' referring to Belgian men, women, and children — & — An Irish woman, Alice S. Green, shares with a friend stories about German war crimes against the Allies, both soldiers and civilians, during World War I.

Hand-delivered on August 2, 1914, the letter from the German government to the Belgian Minister for Foreign Affairs was as cordial as a friendly note passed from one neighbor to the next about a potentially troublesome matter. Marked 'Very Confidential,' the message claimed that France was plotting to invade Germany through Belgium, a neutral country. The Germans asserted that they 'cannot but fear that Belgium, in spite of the utmost goodwill, will be unable, without assistance, to repel so considerable a French invasion.' The Germans offered a solution: they would strike France first. A preemptive attack, however, would require allowing the Germans to march through Belgium, and they hoped the government would turn a blind eye and grant free passage. The Germans would, they added, 'feel the deepest regret' if Belgium rejected their proposal. And then for a brief moment, the open hand of brotherhood clenched tightly. 'Should Belgium oppose the German troops,' the message warned, 'Germany will, to her regret, be compelled to consider Belgium as an enemy . . . [and] the relations between the two States must be left to the decision of arms.' With that unpleasantness out of the way, the letter concluded on a genial note:

> The German Government, however, entertains the distinct hope that this eventuality will not occur, and that the Belgian Government will know how to take the necessary measures to prevent the occurrence of incidents such as those mentioned. In this case the friendly ties which bind the two neighboring States will grow stronger and more enduring.

Belgium had 12 hours to respond. At 9:00 P.M. that same evening, King Albert met with the Council of States and declared emphatically what the country's answer would be – ' "No," whatever the consequences.' His military advisers and ministers agreed, and a reply was drafted. Like the German message that prompted it, the Belgians' letter was not entirely perfunctory. 'This note has made a deep and painful impression upon the Belgian Government,' it began. But nor was it timid.

> *The Belgian Government, if it were to accept the proposals submitted, would sacrifice the honor of the nation and betray its duty towards Europe. . . . [The] Belgian Government is firmly resolved to repel, by all the means in its power, every attack upon its rights.*

The Germans were incredulous. Belgium had no formidable army to speak of, and to confront German troops would merely incur their wrath, inevitably costing innumerable Belgian lives while accomplishing little more than temporarily slowing down the German advance. Belgium was not, of course, alone in the struggle. Great Britain was bound by treaty to come to its aid, France had been preparing for a confrontation with Germany since their last war ended in 1871, and Russia – a French ally – would be pressing Germany from the east.

The growing tensions were all part of a larger drama unfolding throughout the region. On June 28, 1914, just over a month before Germany's appeal to Belgium, a 19-year-old Bosnian Serb, Gavrilo Princip, had shot Archduke Franz Ferdinand, the heir to the Austro-Hungarian empire. When Austria-Hungary threatened Serbia in retaliation, the Russians vowed to protect their fellow Slavs in Serbia, with the larger aim of expanding their influence over the Balkans. Germany, an ally of Austria-Hungary, declared war on Russia. With its defiant refusal to let German forces cross its borders, Belgium – along with England – was now drawn irrevocably into the escalating conflict. (*The USA would not send troops for almost another three years.*) True to their word, and less than a day after their ultimatum was rejected, German forces bore down on their tiny neighbor, clashing with outnumbered Belgian soldiers and terrorizing civilians in every town and village they trespassed en route to France. The burning of Louvain on August 25, 1914, and its world-renowned library, with almost a quarter of a million volumes and 750 medieval manuscripts, provoked international outrage. A Paraguayan priest named Manuel Gamarra, who was studying in Louvain, wrote to the Belgian Minister in Buenos Aires:

> The burning began at half-past seven in the evening of the 25th August. Whilst the town was burning on all sides the Germans shot the unfortunate people as they fled from their burning houses. It was a night of unimaginable horror... At Héront, five kilometres from Louvain, I saw in a corner of the wall the body of a little girl of 12 or 13 years of age burned alive.

But for each accusation, the German military, from Kaiser Wilhelm II on down, responded that their troops were fired on first or that every Belgian was a potential franc-tireur – a guerilla fighter – and needed to be dealt with mercilessly. (*Thousands of the Belgians killed by the Germans in the opening days of the war were indeed soldiers, but many were also women, priests, and children.*) The Kaiser even sent a telegram to President Woodrow Wilson lamenting the destruction of Belgium, but blaming it on the resistance of its 'bloodthirsty' citizens. German propaganda pervaded deep into its own population. Afraid for the safety of his brother, a soldier marching into Belgium, a young German named 'Willi' sent him the following advice. (*A 'Lazaretto' is a hospital that cares primarily for patients with contagious diseases.*)

Schleswig, 25.8.14.

Dear Brother,

I lately obtained your address through Frederick, and I trust that you will receive the present letter in good time before your regiment leaves for Brussels. No doubt should you have already started my letter will be forwarded.

As you know I am attached to the Lazaretto here and I shall remain here for a long time yet, perhaps altogether, although I should much like to go with a field ambulance, as an Inspector of ambulances. But I shall certainly remain here until the middle of September.

You will shortly go to Brussels with your regiment as you know. Take care to protect yourself against these Civilians, especially in the villages. Do not let anyone of them come near you. Fire without pity on every one of them who comes too near. They are very clever, cunning fellows these Belgians, even the women and children are armed and fire their guns. Never go inside a house, especially alone. If you take anything to drink make the inhabitants drink first, and keep at distance from them.

The newspapers related numerous cases in which they have fired on our soldiers whilst they were drinking. You soldiers must spread around so much fear of yourselves that no civilian will venture to come near you. Remain always in the company of others. I hope that you have read the newspapers and that you know how to behave. Above all have no compassion for these cut-throats. Make for them without pity with the butt-end of your rifle and the bayonet.

You will have learnt the news of the great victories. When you arrive in Belgium our soldiers would probably have crossed the Franco-Belgian frontier. Keep well. I hope that you will come back to the house in good health. May you prosper. Best greetings.

Your brother,

Willi

In a long, somewhat rambling diatribe to an English friend, a German mother, whose son, Franz, was fighting at the front, expressed similar disgust with the British, whom she now considered 'vile traitors' for siding against Germany in World War I, a war that was spreading swiftly throughout Europe and other regions of the world.

> *We do not hate and despise the French, for they are in their right when they seek revenge from us, and try to reconquer Alsace and Lorraine; we do not hate the Russians, a poor, misguided people, who are led like sheep to the slaughter without knowing why; but we hate and despise the English who make war against us from mere mercenary reasons; a brother-people, who have been lying and intriguing against us for years, while, to our face, they are making believe friendship, desire for peace, good-will and what not. . . I, for my part, I have to strike out something in my life; my love and respect and gratitude for the English, amongst whom I've lived and been happy. Never again will I seek their society, as I have done all my life. I shall shun them like dirt and poison. . . And now, dear Bessie, good-bye. After this, you will not want to have anything to do with me again; and I don't blame you, for I will neither have anything to do again with an English person, if I can help it. Thank you again and again for your lifelong friendship, for which I've ever been very, very grateful. If Franz falls, you shall know of it. My existence is terror, fear, anxiety, yet, if I could gain my country's victory by my boy's death, I would sacrifice him ten times over again, and so every woman thinks with me in Germany.*

The feelings were mutual; English soldiers who had been fighting in Belgium and France came home with horrifying tales of German cruelty against innocent civilians and Allied soldiers alike. The British were aghast that a so-called civilized nation could commit such acts, especially a country so enamored of its supposedly advanced culture (or Kultur, as the Germans called it). The following letter, believed to have been written by a respected Irish author and scholar named Alice S. Green, articulated the sentiments of many in Great Britain whose contempt for the Germans was absolute. (Regarding several allusions in the letter: Theobald von Bethmann-Hollweg was the German Chancellor; the Emden *was the German light cruiser* SMS Emden, *renowned for both its proficiency at sinking Allied ships and its crew's humane treatment of enemy POWs; and Hermann Sudermann, who penned the poem from which Green quotes at the end of the letter, was a noted German playwright and novelist. There is no salutation or signature to the letter, which appears to be a typed transcript of the original.)*

I am glad you thought my last letter fair and above racial prejudice. But I don't wish you to think that my small trumpet gives any uncertain sound as regards the German principles of warfare, and principles of conquest. No words would be strong enough, condemnatory enough, to say what I think of those principles; and the seal of 'Kultur' with which the Germans seal their atrocities, makes those atrocities worse. The Frederician tradition that the conqueror must subdue a people by all kinds of horror, torture, and cruelty, – that he must terrify and enslave it into submission, – before he <u>begins</u> to be kind and fatherly to it: it is <u>this</u> tradition and principle that Europe is up against. It is to Germany's eternal disgrace that she has allowed her 'Kultur' to be identified with such a system; she will and must reap the reward. I suppose for a century or so, no one outside the Fatherland, will mention 'Deutsche Kultur' without a smile! One really can't help smiling a little even now, when each fresh batch of attested horrors, or exactions on little towns already bled white, coincides with some swaggering remark by Bethman-Hollweg or others, about establishing 'unsere Kultur' among poor ignorant foreigners. The indictment against the Germans is steadily growing in gravity; it is no question of horrors such as are committed by the scum of every army in every war, even the most civilized. It is something worse than that.

I don't want to speak of the enormous number of atrocities attested by witnesses, and certified by inquiry, that fill the documents of investigation by State authority; you have all, no doubt, seen Lord Bryce's report. But I wish to tell you of things I have heard privately from my relations and friends who are in active service. My own nephew has just been at home on leave from the French trenches for a few days, and came to see me. I hoped he would reassure me about German atrocities, but alas! no. He told me many horrible things which I will not write down. Among other things he told me of an incident which took place in a German trench which he and others afterwards took; he had bomb-throwers (people who carry bombs, grenades, and throw them, – otherwise unarmed), and those men were about to throw their bombs on to the Germans in the German trench, which would have killed them all, of course, when the Germans threw up their hands to capitulate; whereupon our bomb throwers desisted, did not throw, and came quickly forward to take the Germans prisoners; as they approached, several German bomb throwers sprang up from behind, threw their bombs on to our men, and killed nearly all of them. Can you wonder that my boy says, 'I don't want to take German prisoners now; I don't believe it when they hold up their hands, nor when they show a flag of truce. You can't trust them.'

He told me that when the Germans took some of our men prisoners, they in cold blood, stripped them naked, and then bayoneted them to death. The only comment my nephew made was, 'I can't understand Germans, Aunt – ; I can't understand a civilized people doing such things.'

A friend of his in another regiment after the battle of Mons missed his sergeant, and went to look for him; he found him inside a farm-house, dying crucified against a wall with a nail through each hand. He was told of half a dozen Highland soldiers who were going through a ruined Belgian village at dusk; they saw a child looking out from a cottage window; they saw that there was something queer about the child; it was so stiff and still, with its arms stretched out; they went into the cottage and found the child was dead; it had been impaled and stuck up in the window to terrorize the inhabitants, I suppose. On the floor lay the dead naked body of the mother, mutilated. These Highland soldiers were so moved, that they stood in a ring around the body of the dead woman, clasped hands across it, and swore to each other never to take a German prisoner.

A Belgian lady to whom I talked, replying to some one who said, 'The Germans may come here,' said excitedly, 'If the Germans came to this town, I would fly and go anywhere to escape from them; they are terrible.' Her hostess was present and tried (I tried too) to reassure her, we saying, 'Oh, no, you would stay with us; it would be unsafe to fly; you would suffer for want of food and shelter; you might die of starvation.' She answered, 'I would risk all that; I would leave you and go into the wilds of Wales, anywhere, anywhere, if I heard the Germans were coming.' Why did she speak so? Because she had experienced a German occupation.

The brother of my chief friend here, who is just home from France on a few days leave, says that English reprisals on the things that the Germans do would be impossible, – that when he marches his troops through villages where the Germans have been, the sights are such in the houses (mutilation of the bodies of helpless victims, etc) that his roughest and coarsest Tommies are revolted. He says the Germans set fire to all churches, – that he has been through villages with all the churches blazing. He says English instructions are a great contrast; they are not allowed to set fire to a church; they do not do so, even if the church is being used by an enemy.

These things I have written down have come directly to my knowledge; you could multiply them a thousand times by interviews with English or French soldiers, or with Belgians throughout the country. The cruelty has been systematic, organised cruelty and ruthlessness, not accidental. I consider that the Kaiser is unfitted for his post; in war time he cannot control his impulsiveness, which in peace time is part of his charm. When just before Mons, in a moment of tense excitement among his soldiers, they listened for a message from their Emperor, and received a vindictive message from the Kaiser that they must 'annihilate the English miserable little army'; when he said this and other foolish things, he did not mean 'crucify the prisoners'. No doubt he would regret that this was done, but the fact that he was so careless and heedless and given over to the fierce impulse of the moment, or knew his men so little as not to know that the effect of vindictive messages from their Kaiser would be to make the coarsest of them wreck tortures on helpless prisoners, – this quality of ignorance of his subjects on the part of the Emperor has repeatedly shown him unfitted for his post as war-lord. How different the really great leaders are! Such as Nelson, who in a moment of equal excitement, said, 'England expects every man to do his duty.' I think the German officers are worse than the soldiers, especially the Colonels, who could have stopped the cruelties and murdering.

Now I must end, and I don't wish to moralize or comment, but if the Germans had fought on other and nobler principles, how we should all have admired them. Especially we English, who are so ready to admire an enemy. (We lavished so much praise on the Captain of the Emden, that the Germans thought we couldn't mean it). Do you remember what Sir Philip Sidney called France years ago: 'that sweet enemy'? We cannot call Germany that.

What do you think that all this Deutsche Kultur amounts to? I think it amounts to a great power of scientific organisation. But one of its worst sides is, that it enslaves its subjects to such an extent that they obey orders to do evil as readily as they obey orders to do good. 'Obedience may be a spiritual virtue, but only if you still keep a will beyond the will to obey. The vice of the German obedience and its terrible power is that there is no will in it beyond the will to obey.' In any case Deutsche Kultur can never attain to civilisation; it is too cramped, too caged, by the irons of its own making. If we want justice and refinement in its truest sense, we must look for those things where they grow. We look in vain for them inside the fence of Deutsche Kultur. Did you see Sudermann's Hymn? That wonderful poet of better things!

> O God, I pray
> That the Briton
> Like Judas perish.
> Let mine eyes see him
> Before I die,
> Grey in a hempen ring
> Dangling from on high.
> And as he swings
> Let him descry
> The German eagle
> Wheeling in the sky.

In more than four years of fighting, approximately 8–10 million troops were killed in World War I. Estimates of civilian deaths vary widely, from the low millions to numbers that exceed military fatalities. Some historians suggest, as well, that since the increased poverty and deprivation caused by the war hastened the spread of the influenza virus near the end of the conflict, the tens of millions who died in the

1918 to 1919 pandemic should also be considered casualties of World War I.

An American missionary, James H. McCallum, writes to his family from Nanking about the vicious treatment of Chinese civilians during the Japanese invasion of Nanking in 1937.

Before the surprise attack on Pearl Harbor, before the brutal invasion of the Philippines and Malaya, before the Bataan Death March and the 'hellships' that transported countless Allied POWs to Japan as slave laborers during World War II, there was Nanking (now known as Nanjing). After waging a fierce battle to capture Shanghai in November of 1937, an estimated 50,000 Japanese troops stormed the Chinese capital of Nanking one month later and, with unrestrained savagery, began murdering and raping Chinese civilians until the following March. 'It has been just one week now since the collapse of the Chinese Army in its Nanking defense,' an American named James Henry McCallum began a letter to his family on December 19, 1937.

> *It is a horrible story to relate; I know not where to begin nor to end. Never have I heard or read of such brutality. Rape: Rape: Rape: We estimate at least 1,000 cases a night and many by day. In case of resistance or anything that seems like disapproval there is a bayonet stab or a bullet.*

Contemporaneous journals, photographs, correspondences and other materials, both private and official, all attest to the enormity of the tragedy, and many of the most detailed firsthand accounts come from the letters by more than two dozen Western missionaries, like James McCallum, who stayed in the city despite the urgent appeals of their embassies to evacuate immediately. (All the missionaries would

*survive. One missionary, Wilhelmina 'Minnie' Vautrin, however,
would take her own life a year to the day after she left Nanking to
return to America. Many believe her suicide was caused by the trauma
of having witnessed the massacre.) The missionaries put their own
lives at grave risk, sometimes literally placing themselves between
drunken, belligerent Japanese soldiers and trembling Chinese citizens.
They also helped to create a Safety Zone within the city that offered
some protection for residents who had no other means of escape. James
McCallum, a 44-year-old American missionary working in Nanking,
sent the following to his family, who were living in Kuling, China.
(Please note: the letter, which does not have a salutation and ends
abruptly, contains graphic descriptions of civilian deaths that might be
unsettling for some readers.)*

Have been so busy every day and five nights of the week that I've had no
time to write. A foreigner must be on duty 24 hours here at the hospital in
order to deal with the Japanese visitors. It is snowing and bitterly cold; our
hearts ache for the thousands who have poor shelter and who are cooped up
in such close quarters. Our hospital is full and the lighter cases fill the
University Dormitory building. Some we cannot dismiss for they have no
place to go. Have had fifteen or twenty babies within the last week; six on
Christmas Day. It is easy to find Miss Hynds; she is always in the nursery
mothering the whole crowd of babies.

Thought of you all on Christmas Day and hoped it was a happy time for
you. We presumed you were still in Kuling. The rumors are reaching us that
Kuling may be evacuated. We have been completely out of touch with the
rest of the world. No one can get into Nanking and it seems very difficult to
get out. We have talked of sending some one of our group out to carry the
news of the terrible things that have been and still are happening here, but
know that person would never get back if he once left.

I have been living with Mills, Fitch, Smythe, Sone, Wilson, Bates, and
Riggs here in the Buck house. All of us have been doing double duty. We
scarcely sit down to our meals without someone coming in every other five
minutes or so to call for help. Food is swallowed whole and hurried exits are

made to save a truck from being stolen or more often to protect women from soldiers. Seldom do we all sit down to eat at the same time. We dare not go out alone after dark but go in twos or threes.

Every day or two I have gone out for an inspection of our mission property. I have found visitors in our house at Peh Hsia Rd. Every time I have gone there. Every foreign house is a sight to behold; untouched until the Japanese army arrived, nothing untouched since. Every lock has been broken; every trunk ransacked. Their search for money and valuables has led them to the flues and inside pianos.

Our phonograph records are all broken; the dishes are in a broken mess on the floor along with everything else that was discarded after each looting. The front of the piano was removed and all the hammers struck with something heavy. Our house being outside the Safety Zone, this was not to be unexpected but houses within the Zone have shared a like fate. Two of our boys' school buildings were set fire to, one a complete loss. Nanking presents a dismal appearance. At the time the Japanese Army entered the city little harm had been done to buildings. Since then the stores have been stripped of their wares and most of them burned. Taiping, Chung Hwa and practically every other main business road in the city is a mass of ruins. In south city much of the area back of the main street was also burned. We see new fires every day and wonder when such beastly destruction will cease.

But far worse is what has been happening to the people. They have been in terror and no wonder. Many of them have nothing left now but a single garment around their shoulders. Helpless and unarmed, they have been at the mercy of the soldiers, who have been permitted to roam about at will wherever they pleased. There is no discipline whatever and many of them are drunk. By day they go into the buildings in our Safety Zone centers, looking for desireable women, then at night they return to get them. If they have been hidden away, the responsible men are bayonetted on the spot. Girls of 11 and 12 and women of fifty have not escaped. Resistance is fatal. The worst cases come to the hospital. A woman six months pregnant, who resisted, came to us with 16 knife wounds in her face and body, one piercing the abdomen. She lost her baby but her life will be spared. Men who gave themselves up to the mercy of the Japanese when they were promised their lives would be spared, – a very few of them returned to the Safety Zone in a sad way. One of them declared they were used for bayonet practice and his body certainly looked it. Another group was taken out near Ku-ling Sz; one who somehow returned, lived long enough to tell the fate of that group. He claimed they threw gasoline over their heads, and then set fire to them. This man bore no other wounds but was burned so terribly around the neck and head that one could scarcely believe he was a human being. The same day another, whose body had been half burned over, came into the hospital. He had also been shot. It is altogether likely that the bunch of them had been machine-gunned, their bodies then piled together and then burned. We could not get the details, but he evidently crawled out and managed to get to the hospital for help. Both of these died. And so I could relate such horrible stories that you would have no appetite for days. It is absolutely unbelievable but thousands have been butchered in cold blood – how many it is hard to guess – some believe it would approach the 10,000 mark.

We have met some very pleasant Japanese who have treated us with courtesy and respect. Others have been very fierce and threatened us, striking or slapping some. Mr. Riggs has suffered most at their hands. Occasionally have I seen a Japanese helping some Chinese or pick up a Chinese baby and play with it. More than one Japanese soldier told me he did not like war and wished he were back home. Altho' the Japanese Embassy staff has been cordial and tried to help us out, they have been helpless. But soldiers with a conscience are few and far between.

Now it is time to make the rounds of the hospital. There are a hundred on the staff. When we have water and lights again it will be much easier, for the lamps to look after and water to pump each day increases our labour considerably.

Many ultra-nationalist Japanese politicians and their supporters still strenuously deny that widespread atrocities and killings occurred in Nanking, insisting that the numbers have been exaggerated by China and the USA, allies in World War II, to justify the use of atomic weapons against Japan in 1945. The Chinese – and most historians, American and otherwise – have well documented that an estimated 200–300,000 innocent people were butchered and tens of thousands of women were raped. The issue remains a source of tension between China and Japan to this day.

The parents of Beryl Myatt send their daughter a cheerful letter as she embarks for her 'Big Adventure' in Canada far from the German Blitz on England during World War II — & — Elizabeth P. Hudson describes for her parents in South Africa the courage and resolve of her fellow Londoners after months of bombings during the German Blitz in 1940 — & — Hans Schröter informs a neighbor in Dresden how her parents and his family had died in one of the worst air attacks on Germany during World War II — & — After almost five months as a POW during World War II, an American soldier writes to his father about being imprisoned in Germany and surviving the firebombing of Dresden in 1945.

'*Dear Mummy & Daddy how are you getting on[?],*' six-year-old Leila Rothstein wrote to her parents on March 24, 1941, from the English countryside. Rothstein had exciting and undoubtedly surprising news for her parents:

> *I have got a husband and his name is Keneth Farrow, when I come home do you think There will be any room for my ~~hub~~ husband, Please send me a scarf because it is verry cold. Pamala Portuies has moved because she was unhappy. my birthday is the same day as my husband's brother's birthday, his name is Ronny. When I am reddy to marry kenneth he'll be 27 and I will be twenty. Kenneth is a nice looking boy love to all Leila*

Rothstein was one of millions of children temporarily evacuated from England's major cities during World War II to safeguard them from incessant bombing campaigns by the German Luftwaffe. (Rothstein would survive the war and, later in life, get married – but not to Kenneth Farrow.) Two days after the German invasion of Poland on September 1, 1939, Great Britain and France declared war on Germany. Over the coming months, wartime leader Winston Churchill repeatedly warned the British people that a massive bombardment of their country was imminent. In his first speech as Prime Minister, on May 19, 1940, Churchill sought to embolden the French – already being hammered by the Germans – and also to prepare his own countrymen for the adversity to come. 'This is one of the most awe-striking periods in the long history of France and Britain,' Churchill stated.

> *Side by side, the British and French peoples have advanced to rescue not only Europe but mankind from the foulest and most soul-destroying tyranny which has ever darkened and stained the pages of history. Behind them – behind us – behind the armies and fleets of Britain and France – gather a group of shattered States and bludgeoned races: the Czechs, the Poles, the Norwegians, the Danes, the Dutch, the Belgians – upon all of whom the long night of barbarism will descend, unbroken even by a star of hope, unless we conquer, as conquer we must; as conquer we shall.*

France surrendered a month later in June 1940. Relishing the opportunity to humiliate the French as he believed his own country had been more than 21 years earlier at the end of World War I, Adolf Hitler ordered the armistice-signing on June 22 to take place in the very railcar in which Germany had capitulated on November 11, 1918.

Operation Eagle, the Luftwaffe's effort to dominate the skies of Great Britain, commenced less than three weeks later, on July 10, and would last for almost four harrowing months. Although vastly outnumbered, the tireless Royal Air Force (RAF) pilots – with a little help from the recently developed radar system – thrashed the Luftwaffe, preventing them from gaining air supremacy and, it is believed, ultimately staving off a full-scale ground invasion of England. Questions remain as to whether Hitler ever intended to carry out such an operation, which the Germans had codenamed Sea Lion, or was merely engaging in one of the greatest bluffs of the war.

Regardless, had the Luftwaffe gained control of the British skies, the Allied cause in Europe would have sustained a crippling, if not fatal, blow. The RAF could not stop all air raids, however, and on September 7, 1940, Hitler ordered major residential areas to be pounded almost without interruption for nearly two months. Tens of thousands of British men, women, and children were blown up or burned to death in the ensuing fires during what would become known as the Blitz, the German word for lightning. Aerial attacks would continue throughout the war but dropped off significantly after the Germans invaded the Soviet Union in June 1941 and concentrated their forces in the east. Many parents feared that their children would be casualties of such a widespread assault, even outside the cities, and they felt the safest course of action was to send their children to Allied countries far from danger. For the parents of Beryl Myatt, relief came on September 9, 1940, just days after the Blitz began: 'I have to inform you that your child, <u>Beryl Myatt,</u> has been accepted for the evacuation overseas,' began the letter to Myatt's parents from a local government official. Their young daughter would be allowed entry into Canada, where she would stay with relatives, and Mr. and Mrs. Thomas Myatt were instructed to arrange for her departure immediately. A variety of obstacles, including immigration quotas, prevented entire families from joining their children. The confidential letter continued:

I have enclosed two labels for your child's luggage and a tie on label which should be fixed on an outer garment. . . . She should carry a sufficient supply of food and thirst quenching fruit to last 12 hours. No bottles should be carried. No chocolate should be included. It will be appreciated that it is the utmost importance in the interests of the children that the least possible publicity should be given to the port of embarkation and commencing date of the voyage.

It was an excruciating decision for the Myatts – or any parents – to make, but one with the best interests of their daughter in mind.

Hoping to keep her spirits high through what would undoubtedly be a difficult separation for a young child, Myatt's mother and father sent her enthusiastic letters about the new home she would soon be visiting and emphasized how much they loved her. But their daughter would never receive the letters; Beryl Myatt and almost 300 other passengers (including more than 80 children) on the SS City of Bernares *perished in the waters of the Atlantic 600 miles from land after being torpedoed by a German U-boat. On September 21, Mr. and Mrs. Myatt wrote the following letter to their nine-year-old daughter, unaware that she was already dead.*

Our Dearest Beryl,

This is our second letter to you since you set out on your big adventure Dear, and we suppose you were very surprised when you arrived at Auntie Emmies to find a letter and your Dandy and Sunny Stories waiting there for you. We will send them each week.

We expect that you enjoyed your voyage on the boat across the wide Atlantic Ocean, and your long journey on the train to Winnipeg. We don't suppose you saw any icebergs during your voyage across, as it would hardly be quite cold enough at this time of year. How would you like to be a nurse on a big Ocean Liner when you grow up Dear?

Now, sweetheart, don't forget what we told you. We want you to let auntie and uncle see that you can be a great help to them about the house by helping to the best of your ability, such as running errands, & helping auntie with her housework and her baking, and above all dear, keep your bedroom tidy and always hang your clothes up in their right place, and this will show Auntie and uncle that you really appreciate the opportunity they have given you to have a grand holiday in one of the most interesting countries in the World – CANADA – the home of the Maple Leaf. You haven't forgotten, have you, 'The Maple Leaf for Canada, The Rose for England, The Leek for Wales, The Thistle for Scotland, and the Shamrock for Ireland.'

You remember the photograph you had taken at Christchurch School, Killburn – well, Mummy wants to know if you would like us to send it on to you. Let us know Dear, will you?

267

How are Pat and Sue. We hope they are O.K. and that they were not seasick or in any way upset by their journey.

The weather here is still fairly nice – what kind of weather are you having?

Well Dear, please give our Love to auntie & uncle & when you write you must tell us all about what you are doing.

Everybody at home sends their Love. Must close now with Tons of Love and Heaps of Kisses. God Bless You.Mummy & Daddy.

XXXXXXXXXXXXXXXXXXXXXXXXXX

Far from regretting the 'collateral damage' – (a euphemism for civilian death), caused by the Blitz, the German high command welcomed civilian casualties as integral to their overall strategy. 'The Fuerher declared that he would repeat these raids night after night until the English were sick and tired of terror attacks. He shares my opinion absolutely that cultural centers, bathing resorts, and civilian cities must be attacked now; there the psychological effect is much stronger,' Joseph Goebbels, Adolf Hitler's diminutive, almost skeletal minister of propaganda, wrote in his personal diary. He added:

> *The English, I suppose, will have occasion to be surprised when this undertaking is launched on a big scale. There is no other way of bringing the English to their senses. They belong to a class of human beings with whom you can talk only after you have first knocked out their teeth.*

The bombings, however, would have the opposite effect. Despite the relentless explosions, fires, blackouts, and food shortages, the English people – especially those who did not have country homes to escape to and slept in subways ('tubes') and makeshift bomb shelters – demonstrated extraordinary grit and perseverance. Elizabeth Pritchard Hudson, a South African woman residing in London at the time, was awed by the resilience she encountered throughout the city. On May 1, 1941, she sent the following to her parents in South Africa.

[Hudson frequently used 'wd.' for 'would,' and the '(?)' and other parenthetical additions in the text are her own. Jan Smuts, whom Hudson refers to, was a prominent South African statesman. The account below represents the bulk of a two-part letter, and there is no signature for the first section, which is printed here in its entirety.]

My darlings,

<u>More</u> letters from home today, one from each of you. This has been a rich week for mail. They were both written in March, Dad's on the 17th & Mom's on the 26th & talked about such recent things that they sounded quite normal. It was delicious. The box you are sending me is causing an anticipatory stir in our house, you know I have always enjoyed food – well everyone is as bad as I am now – in fact it has quite replaced the weather as the Englishman's topic of conversation. You overhear at bus-stops & in tube trains snippets such as: 'Have you tried the new eggless cake made with honey instead of sugar & oil instead of butter?' – to which the reply is: 'Well, my children eat my honey ration & my grocer can't get any oil' – or house-wives exchanging gossip about the latest discovery on the kitchen front (I believe they all enjoy it enormously) – instead of the old: 'Unusual weather for the time of year, isn't it?' To which the reply should be: 'Yes, it always is.' I have never before heard so many people, or been myself so thankful for this country's climate: it rains (as tonight) & you say: 'Thank God, there won't be a big blitz.' It wd. be hell at home with those long, lovely, clear nights. Fog means no siren at all & even very great cold & frost, & of course wind, will keep them away.

I have just come back from Potten End today leaving Harley & Little Wilf in fine health & spirits in spite of our second evacuation. Winston's recent speech cheered everyone up about it, he is a wonderful old man to make such a heartening tirade out of such unpromising material, isn't he. I imagined you listening to him just before going to bed as we were doing at 9 o'clock. We also listened to Smuts, who went down very well too.

You both keep saying things about the air-blitz being such an ordeal. Well, it sometimes is, but you know these things sound much worse than they are. I am continually thankful that I don't have to sit & listen to reports of raids on you, & see pictures which show only damage & fire & leave out (naturally) the masses of untouched houses. I think you are the brave ones to write so cheerfully & sweetly. I am sure I should get querillous (?) & nerve-shattered in no time. Things happen to people & unthinkably horrid they are, but it is roughly localized & very seldom are there more casualties than there are from ordinary road-accidents. That is how you must think of it – for a shorter period the danger is greater – there is no danger, so to speak, of being run over in the day time. Proportionately blitz-life is only as dangerous to us as this world of motors <u>wd.</u> have seemed to are great-grandfathers. A motor accident seems horrid when you're there but there are such millions of people who don't have them. Remembering this perhaps you can bear to read the report of a taxi driver given at our post police station. I think it is most wonderfully typical of the Cockney at his laconically matter-of-fact best, & shows how simply & unmelodramatically they take these things – comically so, & I don't think it's callous to find comedy in the tragedies because we have adjusted our minds to the fact that the tragedies do happen we accept them & look at them in the same light as we do the rest of life. Thank God for the adaptability of the human mind, for to continue to be overwhelmed by (or even to allow oneself to examine) each horror would most certainly lead to insanity. If you continued to think of each motor accident as a ghastly & horrible thing you wd. soon be a nervous wreck.

Well, our Wardens have not yet traced the body of Dr. Snaith's house-keeper. Everyone else has been accounted for in our area. Because of this, our rescue-squad is compelled to continue digging in the wreckage of Ebury Street, where she lived, until they are sure she is not there. It is over two weeks now since the bomb fell there & it wd. be a waste of time to go on digging if she wasn't there, so we are trying every ally to trace her body somewhere else. We found one unidentified one in the street, but the Doctor, her employer, cannot definitely say this is ~~her~~ she. One Warden heard a taxi-driver mentioned in a conversation & traced him up to Kennington, near Fulham, & brought him here to be questioned. I will now copy for you the report he wrote: –

'Statement taken from John H. Davies (No.1116) taken at Gerald Rd. April 26th 1941. 20.00hrs. On the morning of the 16/17 April between 12:00 & 12.15 hrs. my cab was stationary at the corner of Eaton Terrace & Chester

Row. I was preparing to change a wheel. (This was in the midst of fire &
brimstone hailing all round him) This necessitated me going into the back of
my cab to get the jack out. At the precise moment of lifting the back seat the
explosion of the bomb took place, throwing me out into the middle of the
road. Recovering, I decided to carry on changing the tyre & did so. (!!!) I
then replaced my tools carelessly (!!!!) into the back of the cab, having
decided to take my cab home (he means instead of going on cruising about
for passengers as he had been doing; God knows who he expected to find
hailing a taxi at that hour in the hell that was going on, but, as you will see,
he found the only passenger he might have expected)! On stepping forward
towards the Driver's seat, my right foot came in contact with human
remains. I then proceeded home to Kennington to my garage, which had
been bombed & was burning at the time. I then looked into the back of the
cab with more care & discovered the pelvis section of a human body I then
decided to go home feeling rather exhausted (this is beyond comment). The
following day I reported the matter to the district Inspector Fury,
Kennington Lane Police Station. The section was taken to the mortuary in
Kennington & there I was told the matter ended. Hanging on to the rear no.
plate were the light under-clothing usually worn by an elderly person
(female). Signed by John M. Davis, we believe that this 'section,' as he calls it,
is part of another 'section' found in the bombed street because his cab was
just outside the street, & that the two together make Dr. Snaith's house-
keeper, if we can prove this we can stop digging. She might easily have been
blasted into his cab as he was blasted out (that he is alive is a miracle & he
must have been badly wounded in spite of the fact that he continued to look
after his cab & his livlihood instead of dashing to the nearest shelter as one
might expect) because blast does the most extraordinary things, such as
killing many people by the impact & force of air in the stomach, through the
mouth, without doing them any visible damage except that it <u>always</u>
removes their shoes. One doctor was blown out of his bed-room, with his
bed, right out of his house, over the next row of houses & into the gardens
beyond. It sounds fantastic but is quite true because he was seen, in that bed,
a couple of hours earlier by his maid, & the next morning was found quite
near it in the gardens. Blast can also shred a pair of curtains to ribbons &
leave them hanging. It is unpredictable & uncanny.

271

Darlings, I hope these things will not sicken you. I don't know whether being at a distance from them will make you more or less sensitive about it. Having had my bad shock & recuperated I can & must now find them interesting. If you don't, just forget it as you forget the motor accidents. Or regard it as impersonally as one does a murder story. The memorable thing is the impeturability of that taxi-driver. Needless to say that story is not for publication & I'm not even sure whether I ought to send it to you. Our logbook will make some reading after the war!

As enemy warplanes killed the British and destroyed their towns and cities, Britain did not merely stay on the defensive. Much to the surprise of Air Marshal Hermann Goering, who had assured Hitler that the British were not capable of infiltrating so deeply into German territory, the RAF bombed Berlin in late August 1940. Two and a half months later, they hit Munich, the birthplace of the Nazi Party. On November 14, Hitler retaliated by ordering Operation Moonlight Sonata, a ferocious nighttime raid on Coventry. Wave after wave of German planes, nearly 500 in all, swarmed over the city, dropping bombs and incendiaries specifically orchestrated to ignite a firestorm. The barrage would continue without pause for almost 11 hours. The RAF struck back – and hard, attacking Hamburg, Cologne, Hanover, and Berlin multiple times. Their most devastating and, indeed, controversial raid on Dresden came near the end of the war. Churchill would deny that the firebombing of Dresden was revenge for Coventry (which suffered more than 40 raids in all) or any other British city, but for Air Marshal Sir Arthur Harris, vengeance was justification enough:

> *The Nazis entered this war under the rather childish delusion that they were going to bomb everyone else, and nobody was going to bomb them. At Rotterdam, London, Warsaw, and half a dozen other places, they put their rather naïve theory into operation. They sowed the wind, and now they are going to reap the whirlwind.*

The whirlwind descended on Dresden on the night of February 13, 1945, less than three months before the war ended, and lasted for 15 hours. Emulating the attack on Coventry, British and American warplanes carpeted the city with thousands of tons of high explosives and incendiary bombs, and Dresden – a pearl of architectural beauty – was soon engulfed in an ocean of fire. Residents of the city, including countless refugees, were burned alive, crushed by falling debris, killed by shrapnel, or suffocated in a thick, all-encompassing shroud of smoke. Some who sought relief from the scorching heat in water fountains were boiled alive. Approximately 100–200,000 people were initially believed to have died in the attack, and the name Dresden has since become synonymous with the slaughter of innocent civilians. Recent scholarship, however, based on newly released British and German documents, argues that Dresden was a legitimate military target and the estimated number of casualties has been wildly inflated, with 25–40,000 fatalities being a more realistic count. A final consensus is unlikely ever to be achieved.

In the following letter to a female acquaintance whose mother and father were killed in the attack, a native of Dresden named Hans Schröter describes in obvious despair how his friend's parents and his own family had died. (The '20th of July' refers to the failed assassination attempt in 1944 on Adolf Hitler led by Colonel Claus von Stauffenberg and other high-ranking members of the German military.)

August 5, 1945

Dear Mrs. Ganze,

I only just received your letter with its sad contents – my belated, heartfelt sympathy to you. But so many are experiencing the same. Fate's turn was the worst for me. I don't have any interest in living longer. I stand completely alone in a miserable world – no purpose or sense anymore – because what is there to work for? I have had to sacrifice my family and seven friends to Hitler's crazy idea. If only the 20th of July had been successful! But you are

273

happy – you still have your husband, your child, your home – I wish you the best from all of my heart, but now I want to describe the events on February 13th and 14th to you. It was terrible and I will never forget it for the rest of my life.

Saturday evenings and Sundays, I was at Marienstraße 38–42. This brings up powerful memories of my loved ones – hopefully, I will be taken soon – all I am lacking is opium. I will tell you the story: we were all in the cellar, we in 38, your parents with Eulitz in 42, had all survived two attacks successfully and thought we would live through this one. But that would unfortunately not be the case. With the second attack, the door of #38 was destroyed, so that only the emergency exit for 40 and 42 was left. As we got to #40, the flames from the stairwell hit us in the face, so to save our lives we had to move quickly. Everyone acted very calmly. The electric lighting failed, but we had flashlights and petroleum lamps at hand. To get through the exit required great courage, which many could not seem to muster, and perhaps this was the case with your parents. They thought, perhaps, we would survive in the cellar, but they didn't factor in running out of oxygen. When I ran out, I saw my wife and son standing in Marienstraße 42 so helplessly, but I had an older aunt from Liegnitz, and I wanted to save her, so I said to my wife, I'll be back in 2 minutes. But when we came back in just that amount of time, my loved ones had disappeared, and I searched for them in the cellar, on the street – they were nowhere to be found. Everything was in flames, and it was almost impossible to go anywhere. Since I couldn't find my family, I summoned once more the little bit of courage that I had and went over to the Bismarck memorial and waited an hour across from the little house until the roof caved in. Then I went 30 meters along the Ringstraße and waited there until daylight, and everything that you saw was so grotesque that you can hardly describe it, everything was covered with burned corpses.

I went with great haste to my home and office, hoping to find my loves still living, but that didn't happen. They lay on the street in front of house 38, so peaceful, as if they slept. You can imagine what I was going through. At that point, I determined to go where my in-laws and close friends were and help them get out of the cellars. For this, I summoned two men from the Wehrmacht since none of my associates were there. When we opened the emergency exit to #38, such a tremendous heat came out that it was impossible to go inside. So we went in the entrance to #40, through the bathroom, and down into its cellar to get to #42. The cellar in #42 was full of corpses. I counted 50 of them. Eulitz was there, but I couldn't recognize your parents since everyone was on top of each other. Just seeing it was terrible.

Afterwards, I described everything to the local commando in the Leskästen on the street. Then I got sick with a respiratory infection and couldn't be present at the burials, so I cannot write to you about what happened there. One more thing remains to tell you. The cellar stairs of #42 had caved in, so the people couldn't get out. I am certain you can imagine for yourselves how gruesome this was. I greet you and your family,

Yours,

Hans Schröter

Ironically, a group of US prisoners of war (POWs) imprisoned in Dresden lived through the firestorm virtually unscathed. When the air raid sirens began to blare, the American POWs and a handful of German guards were hurried into a giant meat locker underneath a Schlachthof (slaughterhouse), which protected them first from the bombs and then from the raging inferno above. One of these prisoners, a 22-year-old army private first class from Indianapolis, sent the following letter to his father back in Indiana chronicling his time as a POW.

Dear people:

I'm told that you were probably never informed that I was anything other than 'missing in action.' Chances are that you also failed to receive any of the letters I wrote from Germany. That leaves me a lot of explaining to do – in precis:

I've been a prisoner of war since December 19th, 1944, when our division was cut to ribbons by Hitler's last desperate thrust through Luxemburg and Belgium. Seven Fanatical Panzer Divisions hit us and cut us off from the rest of Hodges' First Army. The other American Divisions on our flanks managed to pull out: We were obliged to stay and fight. Bayonets aren't much good against tanks: Our ammunition, food and medical supplies gave out and our casualties out-numbered those who could still fight – so we gave up. The 106th got a Presidential Citation and some British Decoration from Montgomery for it, I'm told, but I'll be damned if it was worth it. I was one of the few who weren't wounded. For that much thank God.

Well, the supermen marched us, without food, water or sleep to Limberg, a distance of about sixty miles, I think, where we were loaded and locked up, sixty men to each small, unventilated, unheated box car. There were no sanitary accommodations – the floors were covered with fresh cow dung. There wasn't room for all of us to lie down. Half slept while the other half stood. We spent several days, including Christmas, on that Limberg siding. On Christmas eve the Royal Air Force bombed and strafed our unmarked train. They killed about one-hundred-and-fifty of us. We got a little water Christmas Day and moved slowly across Germany to a large P.O.W. Camp in Muhlburg, South of Berlin. We were released from the box cars on New Year's Day. The Germans herded us through scalding delousing showers. Many men died from shock in the showers after ten days of starvation, thirst and exposure. I didn't.

Under the Geneva Convention, Officers and Non-commissioned Officers are not obliged to work when taken prisoner. I am, as you know, a Private. One-hundred-and-fifty such minor beings were shipped to a Dresden work camp on January 10th. I was their leader by virtue of the little German I spoke. It was our misfortune to have sadistic and fanatical guards. We were refused medical attention and clothing: We were given long hours at extremely hard labor. Our food ration was two-hundred-and-fifty grams of black bread and one pint of unseasoned potato soup each day. After desperately trying to improve our situation for two months and having been met with bland smiles I told the guards just what I was going to do to them when the Russians came. They beat me up a little. I was fired as group leader. Beatings were very small time: – one boy starved to death and the SS Troops shot two for stealing food.

On about February 14th the Americans came over, followed by the R.A.F. their combined labors killed 250,000 people in twenty-four hours and destroyed all of Dresden – possibly the world's most beautiful city. But not me.

276

After that we were put to work carrying corpses from Air-Raid shelters; women, children, old men; dead from concussion, fire or suffocation. Civilians cursed us and threw rocks as we carried bodies to huge funeral pyres in the city.

When General Patton took Leipzig we were evacuated on foot to Hellendorf on the Saxony-Czechoslovakian border. There we remained until the war ended. Our guards deserted us. On that happy day the Russians were intent on mopping up isolated outlaw resistance in our sector. Their planes (P-39's) strafed and bombed us, killing fourteen, but not me.

Eight of us stole a team and wagon. We traveled and looted our way through Sudetenland and Saxony for eight days, living like kings. The Russians are crazy about Americans. The Russians picked us up in Dresden. We rode from there to the American lines at Halle in Lend-Lease Ford trucks. We've since been flown to Le Havre.

I'm writing from a Red Cross Club in Le Havre P.O.W. Repatriation Camp. I'm being wonderfully well fed and entertained. The state-bound ships are jammed, naturally, so I'll have to be patient. I hope to be home in a month. Once home I'll be given twenty-one days recuperation at Atterbury, about $600 back pay and – get this – sixty (60) days furlough!

I've too damned much to say, the rest will have to wait. I can't receive mail here so don't write.

May 29, 1945
Love,
Kurt - Jr.

Kurt Jr. is, in fact, Kurt Vonnegut Jr., who had been captured by the Germans during the Battle of the Bulge and returned to the USA in the summer of 1945. Vonnegut went on to become one of the world's most esteemed and influential writers, and his experience in Dresden inspired the literary classic Slaughterhouse-Five. *Fourteen years after the war, Dresden and Coventry became 'sister cities' (also referred to, especially in Europe, as 'twin towns') promoting cross-cultural events and exchanges with one another to foster reconciliation and mutual understanding.*

A doctor serving with the Polish Armia Krajowa during World
War II explains to his fiancée the grave challenges they are
facing but assures her that 'Warsaw will be free of Germans' — &
— In letters to loved ones, two Dutch resisters reflect on faith and
forgiveness before being executed during World War II — & —
The mother of Elaine Vagliano, a heroine of the French Resistance
in World War II, recounts to a family friend how the Nazis treated
her daughter after they captured her.

*Many civilians fought back. Regardless of age, gender, or ability, and
lacking military training and stockpiles of weapons, average citizens in
nations conquered by Germany and Japan employed both nonviolent
and lethal means to destabilize the occupation of their towns and cities.
They created underground radio programs to keep morale high and
disseminate essential information. They served as spies, providing critical
updates to Allied intelligence on enemy troop levels and movements.
They cut communication lines, disabled military vehicles, and sabotaged
railroads, airfields and ports. They assassinated high-ranking officials
and collaborators. And in some cases, they even launched large-scale,
coordinated offensives. After German troops blitzed into Poland on
September 1, 1939, Polish citizens battled the highly trained German
soldiers throughout the war. Armia Krajowa (the Home Army, also
known as AK), was the largest underground resistance army of World
War II. Beginning on August 1, 1944, the AK waged a ferocious
counterattack against the Germans in what would become known as the
'Warsaw Uprising.' The AK was led by Polish military officers, but much
of the fighting was done by civilians. Tadek J. (his last name is not
identifiable) was a 21-year-old medical student who offered his expertise
to treat wounded members of the AK – a 'crime' punishable by death. In
a letter to his fiancée written at the beginning of the uprising, Tadek
described the threats they were facing, but also their determination to
counter the Nazi invaders. (Jurek is his younger brother, and PASTA
refers to Warsaw's telephone exchange building.)*

Dearest Dzidziunia!

I am terribly worried about you, but the fact that your home is on our territory brings me some solace. I tried to reach you three times already, but failed. Once I was forced to turn back as my comrade was shot as we were crossing a street. It is supposedly safer to cross there now, but unfortunately I cannot leave my post at the hospital. I have been made (imagine that) the commander of a military hospital, a small one, which only has 25 beds, but I am the only one here who knows anything about surgery.

The first three days of the Uprising were the most trying for us (that is for me and Jurek, as we failed to reach Zoliborz). Jurek is a member of a detachment assigned to capture the PASTA building.

Don't worry about me, as for the past two days I have not left the hospital and have no need to be close to the front line. Jurek miraculously survived the collapse of a building. Bombs keep falling all around us, but our spirits are high. The horrors I saw are difficult to imagine. There are huge numbers of injured. Only recently have I been able to sleep 4–5 hours a day, which is more than before. In Wola I saw an American airdrop.

The fervor among our soldiers is tremendous. All we need is more weapons, as ammunition is plentiful, and Warsaw will be free of Germans.

I have to end this letter now and go back to my duties.

I kiss you dearly and love you so much

Tadek

Bolstered by the assumption that the Allies would come to their aid, the Poles, outgunned and surrounded on all sides, fought aggressively. But the desperately needed support did not come. Joseph Stalin, intending to dominate Poland for his country's own territorial purposes, wanted the AK and Germans essentially to wipe each other out before his troops marched into the city. Soviet soldiers on the other side of the Vistula River from the Warsaw Uprising were ordered to stand down, and Stalin refused Prime Minister Churchill's persistent appeals to allow Allied warplanes to refuel in the Soviet Union and provide the Poles with ongoing assistance. (British and American warplanes nevertheless attempted airdrops, but the missions were extremely hazardous and the containers often fell into German hands.) On the ground, the outlook grew bleaker with every passing day. Writing again to Dzidziunia, Tadek was candid about the precariousness of their situation and the scarcity of clothing and other essential supplies.

Dearest Dzidziunia!

I received your letter. It gave me lot of joy. I would like to see you as early as possible. I was planning to visit you tonight (because I am to busy during the day), but never left because an injured soldier who was brought in from Aleje, said that the passage would be to dangerous. I may possibly visit you tonight if I find somebody to fill in for me. I have missed you so much that when I see you I will embrace you like never before. It is peaceful here now, bombing has stopped. Jurek has been assigned to a company protecting the General Staff. They are being fired upon by tanks and grenade launchers. When I was there yesterday, a grenade exploded and injured three soldiers.

We have just received new underwear and socks. I also have a raincoat and one that belonged to a German military policeman. I got hold of it at a hotel on Widok Street. The German was shot in the head and the raincoat was blood stained but the rain washed it down and now it is first-class. The German died on me when I was changing his dressing.

I will try to see you as soon as I can. In the meantime I send you a long and passionate kiss. I love you so much.

Tadek

Without the Allied support anticipated by the Poles, the Warsaw Uprising was crushed with brutal finality 63 days after it started, leaving an estimated quarter of a million civilians dead. The AK was, however, successful in killing upwards of 150,000 Wehrmacht and SS soldiers during the war. Tadek and Dzidziunia both survived and married, but Jurek was fatally wounded during the Uprising and, after being rushed to Tadek's hospital, died in his brother's arms. As Stalin had hoped, Soviet troops swept into Poland the following winter and soundly routed the Germans. Poland would be oppressed by the

Soviet Union for more than five decades; the country's first free elections would not be held until 1990.

Although not as organized or extensive as the Polish resistance movement, tens of thousands of Dutch citizens also banded together to undermine the occupation of the Netherlands after the German invasion on May 10, 1940. The German files on individual Dutch resisters condemned to die, which were preserved during and after the war, include copies of their last letters, many of which emphasize the profound sense of religious conviction that influenced their actions. One Dutch resister facing death, Henk (last name unknown), seemed truly at peace in his final moments – even to the point of forgiving his captors. 'When you receive this letter, I will not be alive anymore,' he began a letter to his father.

> *This evening at 8 o'clock I was informed that I will have to depart this earthly life tomorrow at seven-thirty. Do not be sad, it just has to be. We mortals often cannot understand it and rebel against it, but we have to realize that 'God has given, therefore God also has the right to take away'. A German priest came to see me tonight and we have talked for several hours. He is a fine man, even if he is someone who belongs to the people of our enemies. Therefore, I ask you as my last wish: do not bear hate, even if that will sometimes be hard for you, and be tolerant. Perhaps he will visit you in a while, receive him hospitably and amicably. That will give me great pleasure. . . [I]t is regrettable that I will not live to see the peace, as I had always hoped to be able to participate with all my strength and energy in the reconstruction, not only materially but also spiritually. Our real work will not actually begin until after the war. We must take away the hatred between the Nations, because only if that disappears can there truly be peace.*

The details surrounding the sentence of a Dutchman known only as Harmen are unclear, as civilians could be executed for anything from hiding Jews and protecting them from persecution to reading unsanctioned newspapers. When writing from his prison cell to his pastor, Harmen's thoughts see-sawed between different emotions as he

struggled to maintain his faith through an agonizing delay. (The letter,
which was in fact Harmen's last before being executed, has been
edited slightly in the interests of privacy. 'Br.' is his abbreviation for
the name of a cellmate.)

Dear Pastor and Friend,

The things we have gone through! Last Friday, the four of us were first
transported to Amsterdam and we were extremely cheerful in the car. One
of us had been told that we would be interrogated again and that could be
favorable after the death sentence. So the blow came all the harder. We had
three hours to live and could start writing our farewell letters. I did so, while
awaiting your visit. I had a brief talk with Father Ferwerda and could assure
him that I was doing fine. I couldn't have said otherwise; I was incredibly
peaceful and courageous. That was God's work, where else could I have
gotten such cheerfulness? I could peacefully say farewell to everyone and
everything – only, that broke the last tie with this earth.

Then, fifteen minutes before the time, there came the news: post-
ponement. That completely shattered me. While I was looking Death in the
face, I did not have a single rebellious moment; my trust in God remained
strong. When I was locked up in that horrible death cell with its heavy bars,
there was even a moment that I felt the urge to start singing. I looked at that
mass of iron with a smile. When the door slammed shut, I thought: that's the
door to earthly life closing for good. But this was followed immediately the
clear and steadfast thought: 'If He so desires, God can even redeem this', but
not the slightest sadness or disappointment in that, not the slightest desire
that He would actually do so. Only when I was plunged back from the
certainty of death into doubt and fear, into having to wait again, my faith
gave out. I remained assured of God's unfathomable goodness in Jesus
Christ, of his forgiveness for sin, I remained certain that He knows better
than I, but I had to appeal for His special aid, weeping and sobbing, to be
able to bear this new shock. I suffered for two days, with my cellmate; at
times we could talk about God's rich mercy, but my own certainty about
salvation was gone. I did not rebel against God about this – I just fought that
last battle to the end in that first sleepless night from Friday to Saturday and
only now have learned, before all else, to pray: Thy will be done. I have said:

Lord, I can't go on anymore, here I am, utterly powerless and beaten. Now, I await only Your mercy. . .

Dear friend, in this miserable prison there is really only one thing we can do with great, liberating conviction with our hearts and mouths: to praise God for His miracles. The daughter of Br. wrote to him: as God wants it, so it is good. How does the child come up with that? he said. God plows the world deeply. Let us pray that after these horrible times, the New Order come closer to God's light, closer than our dead, saturated past. Give my regards to your wife, the members of the Church Council and the Congregation and accept my, perhaps next-to-last greeting in Jesus Christ our Lord from

your loving
Harmen

Only weeks after they had vanquished the Netherlands and Belgium, German troops rolled into Paris on June 14, 1940. Just four days later, a lone voice broadcasting from BBC Radio in London beseeched the French people not to yield without a fight. 'Has the last word been said? Must hope disappear? Is defeat final? No!,' he exclaimed. 'Whatever happens, the flame of the French Resistance must not be extinguished and will not be extinguished.' The speaker was General Charles de Gaulle, the former French Undersecretary of War, who would emphatically reject the armistice that ceded half of France to Nazi Germany. (Ironically, the new French Prime Minister appointed to lead the Vichy regime, which would collaborate with the Nazis to rule occupied France, was Marshal Henri Philippe Pétain – the 'Hero of Verdun' who had defended his country so tenaciously in World War I.)

Encouraged by de Gaulle's words, countless French citizens risked their lives over the next four years to subvert the Vichy government and aid the Allied effort as it prepared for the liberation of France in June 1944. Born to Greek parents who had homes in both France and England, Elaine Vagliano was inspired by de Gaulle's call to arms and joined the Resistance. After the Germans had been driven from France by the Allies, and when it was safe to write freely about the occupation, Elaine's mother, Danae, wrote a long and intensely emotional letter to a friend in Great Britain about what the past four years had wrought. She focused particularly on the barbarity of the Gestapo soldiers (the Nazi secret police), and the fierce courage of the men and women, including her daughter, who actively served in the Resistance.

Dear Mr. Andrews,

With all our hearts we want to thank you for your wonderful letter and Mrs. Andrews. We are so touched by your great and sincere sympathy. Please thank your daughter from me for her dear, beautiful letter! I hope that a friend will send you this letter for I cannot write to each one of you yet! It would take six weeks at least by post and I should like you to know the details now! Will you also thank Miss Norman for her kind nice letter and Ellen Wicks and Florence. I want them to know quickly how <u>much</u> we appreciate their sympathy and their thought of us. Later, I shall write to them all by ordinary post as I cannot trouble too often this kind friend of mine, who is doing such fine work in Paris. She is English and has a heroic husband who is 'somewhere' near the front lines. They are a fine pair. I need not repeat to you all our agony and suffering. We were luckily arrested the same day as our daughter, though not at the same place. We had the great luck of seeing Elaine three times during our arrestation. Once in the courtyard outside the Grasse Prison before leaving for Nice and twice in the cellar at the Gestapo's Headquarters at Nice or rather at <u>Cimiez</u> above Nice.

In the Nice prison we were separated and each of us was pushed into different cells with three other occupants. No murderers and criminals in England would be put into such filthy places; full of bugs and with hardly any food. No one could endure such treatment for long and many prisoners died after a couple of months. The Gestapo knew that we were pro-English and pro-de Gaulle and perhaps they knew that we did propaganda work. The real reason for our arrest I think was to torture my daughter still more and hurt us to make her break down. We were beaten in front of her and though she adored her father and me, she <u>never</u> gave away the names of her comrades. Even now I can see her poor little shrunken face with two big burns on it, and the anguish in her eyes. Tears rolled down her cheeks but she was silent. I prayed that she would not give way through her love for us. She never did for you see, if she had betrayed the names of her fellow workers or indicated where their Headquarters were, most of the Resistance groups would have been found and tortured and shot. She told me this very quietly and simply in the Gestapo cellar at Cimiez. We spoke in whispers for we knew that the Germans kept us all together and had microphones in the place. It happened so at the Cannes prison.

She told me also the name of this 'great friend' who had denounced her. Elaine was so loyal to her friends and could not believe this fact, until she saw this woman's signed statement and a list of names. I was also given this list of the people on it who had come to see me on Sunday and this woman had also come on that day! I refused to sign it and denounce them <u>of course.</u> This cost me four teeth because the Gestapo man thought I could give details concerning them which this vile woman did not know, though she knew that they were violently anti-German. But she gave away those she knew. Luckily she was not aware of the Resistance organizations (their headquarters) and some of the agents' names. She gave away those she was acquainted with and said that Elaine had sent her twice to various places with letters. Elaine trusted her, but she never told her of her 'Big Work'.

On the 25th of July my daughter became anxious and burnt <u>all</u> her papers and warned her fellow workers. (She told me this in prison and added '<u>Nothing</u> could ever have been found or used against me, for no <u>proofs</u> existed. It was only through Antoinette R.C. that the Gestapo found out that I had sent these letters. It was only through Antoinette that they knew that I had helped people to escape. She had begged me to save her son from the Germans and I had him sent away. <u>This</u> was the first thing Antoinette put on her deposition and she added (to impress the Germans, I suppose) that her son's departure had been <u>against her wish</u>!!!) Then my darling cried and said to me 'Oh Mamma, I was fond of her! <u>Why</u> did she do such a thing to me?' I could answer that Judas still exists and has some followers on this earth.

This horrible woman is now in prison in Cannes since the end of August. She is to be judged one day. She told the French Interrogator that she had denounced my daughter (after she [Mme.R.C.] had been taken by the Gestapo, on a minor charge) because she was 'Mentally tired' (!) She added that she had not been tortured. Some of her family say: 'Poor Antoinette'!

She was so tired – 'mentally'! It's not a good excuse, for Mme. R.C. is a very strong woman and not a tender rosebud! Through her I have lost my darling and without her our house is empty. Poor Stephen is sweet, but he is a man, and young, so he is gradually getting over it. It's natural but for Marino and I it is different. Elaine was the mainspring in our house. She was so full of life, so unselfish and for us more than a daughter – a friend, who always helped me and kept me alive during these last four dreadful years. My husband has suddenly become an old man and I feel a hundred! I shall never forget those awful days, my child's torture, her last words! 'Goodbye, Mamma darling' and her gallant little smile. She told the lady in her cell that she was so happy, so relieved, that we had been released, but she sobbed all night. We were not allowed to stay in Nice. On our return to Cannes we moved Heaven and Earth to get her out of prison. We even offered bribes, sometimes money tempts these Nazis! I was very ill on my return as my face was in a mess and had been cut open, so blood poisoning set in and reached my eyes. All this did not bother me, for I kept thinking of my darling, alone with those Nazis! I kept on hoping that Elaine would return; that it was all a German bluff; that they could not hurt her any more, as no proofs existed (even then, I could not believe that they could murder her!).

The landing took place (it's all over so I hope I can mention it now). We were cut off from everything. We had no light (only 4 candles!) no water, not much food and we lived in our cellar – but we were so thrilled! We kept on saying how delighted Elaine would be. She wanted so much to see all our flags on the roof of our house! The bridges were down, the roads were bombed. No news came through at all. We waited and Nice was taken! We waited, but Elaine did not arrive. The police knew the truth and some of our friends too – until on the 22nd Stephen came in sobbing and told us that Elaine had been shot! On the 3rd October her body was brought back as it is against the law in France to transfer bodies from one place to another. (We had to fight the police and at last they gave way and we got our child back. It was dreadful!) We had to wait even for that!

She was brought back like a soldier on a gun carriage and her coffin was covered with a French flag. (It still is, as she is lying in a vault!) She never came home to us. She was taken to the Mairie and all night she had a guard of honour around her and soldiers stood at attention. Next day she had a State funeral, so grand and they gave her 'tous les honneur'. 'Un salut d'honneur' and the 'Last Post' and so many, many flowers! We all stood near her like stone statues, for we could not even cry. Cannes had taken her from us. She was <u>their</u> heroine. 'Notre Helen!' (A street near the rue d'Antibes is called 'rue Helene Vagliano – Herione de la Resistance'). The <u>only</u> person who helped me was a woman of the Resistance, when she came to see me after Elaine's funeral. She had fought <u>with</u> the soldiers and she had, earlier, hidden arms. She was arrested, but escaped by a miracle. Her husband was taken, tortured and killed. On the day before Elaine's funeral, she heard that her only son had been shot by the Germans. She told me all this so simply and, when I tried to console and said she was so brave, she answered 'C'est affreux – mais je n'ai pas le temps de pleiner'! (It's dreadful, but I have no time to cry!) I saw the anguish in her eyes! We became great friends. She belongs to 'Les Femmes de France'. I am their President, as they call it over here. We have to find clothes, etc. for the families of the Resistance; for the families or only the children of the victims of the Gestapo and for the families of the men who were forced to go and work in Germany. It's good work, for these women are wonderful! For Christmas we arranged parties and a Christmas tree for all these children, over a thousand; one for Elaine's pets (the Prisoners' children). (She had worked so hard for them.) and a party for the children of the soldiers who are 'somewhere' in the mountains. It is good to be occupied, but when one returns home the wound re-opens!

We were asked to send the photos of the victims who were killed by the Gestapo to England. We had to collect these. First of all we went to the Mont-fleury prison in Cannes. There, on the 14th of August, these creatures of Himmler's, had a champagne party – (one of them is now arrested and confessed) then these <u>Herrenmensch</u> took off their coats and went into the basement. There they shot down all the helpless prisoners, amongst others, two young girls of 19 and of 20 years old. We saw blood on the floors – on the mattresses (the one I had occupied on July 29th, 30th and 31st was steeped in blood!). We saw over-turned stools, bloody fingerprints on the walls. On the 15th of November, we went to L'Ariane, near Nice, where my child had been murdered! We found the farmer who had been the only witness as the land belongs to him. On the 15th of August he saw a lorry drive up. He saw prisoners descend from it. He saw the Gestapo agents and

German soldiers push these prisoners over the high bank on to the strip of land by the river edge. He heard these brutes laugh as these helpless people fell. He rushed over the bridge leading to his house on the other bank. Near it he saw two machine guns. Before he shut his shutters he saw all the prisoners in a row facing these machine guns across the narrow river. He heard the guns fire three times, and soon after the sounds of revolver shots. Much later a neighbour came to him and said a dreadful tragedy had taken place and both men rushed across the bridge. There they saw a horrible sight. Bodies of men and women all over the place. Some had tried to escape and had been horribly murdered and even stamped upon as they lay!

My daughter had not tried to escape for she lay on her side. Her face was covered in blood (even her pretty hair!) and at the back of her head there was a huge hole made by a revolver. (When she was put into her coffin her little head was detached!) To return to the horrible photos, amongst them we found my daughter's, taken after death! When she left my room on the 29th of July at 10.30 a.m. she looked so fresh and gay. Her pretty hair was especially arranged; she had a new dress on and she asked me if I liked it! I only recognised the <u>dress</u> in her last photo, for the Germans had destroyed her face! We <u>had</u> to see all these horrors, because in this way we can tell the truth and not be accused of exaggerating these things. If any man and woman in England ever see these photos let them think that <u>this</u> girl – <u>this</u> boy might have belonged to them if Germany had won the war! These horrible murders would have happened over there in towns and villages, too! One does not need to exaggerate in France and I suppose in all countries which the Germans occupied.

The people here do not ask only for sympathy. They want to be believed, because what they have suffered happens to be true! We hear on the radio people make speeches on 'We must be kind to the Germans after the War'. 'There must be no hate!' After all, the Germans are human!' I can answer <u>No!</u> I am not a hysterical woman, mad with hate because my child was murdered by the Germans! I simply state that if you do not and have not lived in towns <u>occupied</u> <u>by the Germans</u>, you cannot understand what it means! 'Be kind to the Germans' sticks in our throats!!! These Germans are not human! They voted for Hitler; they did not protest against the Gestapos even in their country! They shouted with joy when Hitler told them in his speeches that he meant to burn every town and village in England! Kindness to them, even beaten – is weakness.

When they left the towns over here and in Cannes, they deliberately fired in each window they passed. In ours too, and we hid in our cellars! They fired on civilians and burnt houses and entire villages. They behaved like savages. We still look over our shoulders when we speak to a friend and still shake when the door bell rings too loudly! The German cars came often to our house. Twice to arrest us. (The first time they pretended that my husband was a Jew!!! The charge was too ridiculous and he returned, but how we suffered until he did so.) They came twice to take the house and tramped all over it and said they would return. Luckily, next day they found houses near us which suited them better. They became our neighbours – all around us and down the road. The German soldiers prowled in our garden night and day. They cut down our trees; stole our fruit; broke stone benches and we could not complain!

The German women were as bad; they used to roar with laughter when they saw prisoners in lorries! I know that suffering exists in every country. In England you were bombed, and everyone was so brave. It must have been awful and yet you all stood up to it. All honour to England. What you do not know, thank God, is to be tortured slowly, to be dying and to see, at the last, sneering German faces, or laughing ones as you die! My daughter was always called the 'sale Anglaise' (the dirty English girl) by the Germans. She had a strong English accent when she spoke French and that infuriated them. It was owing to her English upbringing and to her English education that Elaine learnt self-control, determination and the courage that leads to endurance and to sacrifice. I should like people in England to know about her, and to understand why she 'stuck to it' (her job) up to the end! She would not want honour or decorations, only the remembrance of her friends. She told me, to please give you all her music; and especially Bach's (as Mr. Andrews admires him so much). She had collected lots of old musical scores! For Sue Harvey she said to me 'Please give her my silver fox skin – in case! I answered 'of course I will – in case'! We never finished the sentence.

On the 13th of August she smuggled out two letters from her prison by a released prisoner. One was to us and frantic! She wrote to say that the Germans were coming to fetch us and keep us till the end of the war, as we had complained! (We had not done so, or seen friends or left the house, but people in the bus had seen our faces and talked about us in Cannes). Luckily the roads were being bombed and the Boches did not come for us. The other letter was sent to her 'Chief'. She wrote 'Do not be anxious I shall <u>never</u> speak'! When he showed it to me, he cried like a child.

Would you send a copy of my letter to Sue Harvey, 46 Godfrey Street, London, S.W. 3., and say I thought that the details about Elaine might interest her, as she loved my child. I should like to hear from her too, as she was my daughter's friend. (Please ask Sue Harvey to show this letter to <u>Uncle Bill</u> – Marino's Uncle.)

Would it trouble you too much to send some details to Ellen and to Wicks? Where is Cliffe? He used to be so fond of Marino! We were so sorry to hear that you had both been so ill. What bad luck you had!

We send you both our best wishes for a Happy New Year and the best of health. <u>When</u> shall we meet? Our best and most affectionate regards.

Danae Vagliano

P.S. Mamma is well and was as courageous as a lion even with the Germans!! Shall we ever get <u>books</u>? How we long for them!!

Please excuse this badly written letter, but memories come back when I mention these events! <u>I do hope you will get it soon</u> as you knew Elaine since her birth – so these things will interest you I hope!

Six weeks after Charles de Gaulle had first transmitted his rallying cry to the French population in June 1940, he was tried in absentia for treason by Vichy France and condemned to death. When Paris was liberated more than four years later, General de Gaulle triumphantly marched into the city with Allied troops and became head of the provisional government. Marshal Pétain fled the country weeks after de Gaulle's arrival, but returned to France in April 1945. He defended his wartime collusion with the Nazis as an effort to save France from being destroyed (as Poland was), but the argument proved unconvincing, and the almost 90-year-old Pétain was sentenced to be shot before a firing squad. De Gaulle commuted the judgment to life in prison, and Pétain died behind bars in 1951.

ARussian boy named Slavik provides his Aunt Natasha with
an account of how wretched life has become during the siege
of Leningrad in World War II — & — Slavik's sister Galia, also
trapped in Leningrad, in 1943, begs her aunt to come and find her,
now that everyone in her family is gone — & — Private First Class
Harry Zaslow depicts for his parents the hellish existence of a
group of girls he met who had been enslaved by the Nazis during
World War II.

*Of the more than 50 million people killed in World War II, the
majority were believed to have been civilians – many of whom were
children. Russian boys and girls fared among the worst. Rural and
peasant families were either massacred by invading German troops or
expelled from their homes only to perish from exposure. Those trapped
in the cities of Moscow, Leningrad (now St. Petersburg) and
Stalingrad (now Volgograd) suffered through some of the most
punishing bombardments and blockades of the war. The siege of
Leningrad alone lasted nearly 900 days, from September 8, 1941, until
the end of January 1944, extinguishing the lives of at least 600,000
Russians. Some estimates put the number at over 1 million. (Subsisting
each day on, at best, one small loaf of 'bread' made of flour, sawdust,
and paper, hundreds of thousands of Russians died of hunger alone.
Starving the Russians to death was precisely what Hitler had
intended. Two young siblings trapped in Leningrad, Slavik and Galia
(last names unknown), were orphaned during the assault and, in
March 1943, they pleaded to their aunt to come and care for them.*

Hello dear Aunt Natasha. A salute from Leningrad.

Oh, aunt Natasha, Galia and I have lived through so much in this war.
Bombings, hunger and again, filth and epidemics. If I wrote about them all, I
doubt you would believe me. 27 September Uncle Lyosha is wounded. 24
November Papa is buried. 15 January we buried Liza. 28 February we buried
mommy. Kostya was killed. Sashka is in shell-shock. Galia and I are alone

together with no relatives. Oh it's lonely, aunt Natasha. All hope lies with you – please come soon, we are waiting for you.

I kiss Aunt Natasha warmly. Slavik.

Weeks later, Galia wrote to her aunt with news of a terrible development.

10 April.

Greetings from Leningrad. Hello dearest Aunt Natasha.

This morning we received a letter from you dated 1 March. You write that you have no letters from us. After mother's death I gave you 2 telegrams – and Slavik and I wrote four letters – this is already the fifth. They say that the letters do not reach their destinations. So here:

16 February mother died

16 November father died

10 January grandmother died and

15 January Aunt Liza died

21 March our room was destroyed and Slavik received a wound to the head.

23 March he died in the hospital at 9 o'clock in the morning.

And I found myself alone.

Dearest Aunt Natasha my hope now rests on you and I wait for you to come like a guardian angel. I think that you will not abandon me. I am left all alone, without neither relatives, nor relations. Mother's and father's acquaintances have all been either evacuated or won't show their noses. The streetcars have not been running all winter. And there is not a single person who could really take pity on me and help me out.

It's true, Uncle Lyosha came as soon as he heard about these horrors. But he was allowed in for only fifty hours, worse still he did not make it onto the train and had to walk to Alexandrovka on foot. He and I met for only a few hours, but I was so glad (you must understand this yourself, dearest aunt Natasha).

He brought me some groceries. They were not much to be honest, but still, they helped me out greatly. My mood, aunt Natasha, is very grim. The large room is destroyed. All our things are covered in filth. Everything is covered in slaked lime from the walls. And that is the kind of dirt that you cannot clean up without water – and there's no water. And it's far to go and get water, and to stand around an hour for one pail, and then to carry the dirty water out to the dumpster is also not easy. So, I have not the energy to clean.

As soon as it is warm and the water is running again and I am still alive, I will clean up everything. Now the letters travel better – you will probably receive this one. But for now, good bye. Warm kisses to you.

Galia

It is not known what happened to Galia during or after the Siege of Leningrad. Young girls of any nationality – Russian, Polish, French, Dutch – captured by the Germans faced the possibility of a fate worse than any other, except death. Two weeks before V-E Day, a 19-year-old private first class from Philadelphia named Harry Zaslow wrote a letter to his parents from Germany after a heartbreaking encounter with Russian girls, the teenaged victims of Nazi depravity. Zaslow's father, himself, was a Russian immigrant, and the 'blue envelope' Zaslow refers to was a special letter servicemembers could write that allowed them to bypass their unit censors. The letter would still be checked before being posted to the USA, but only by a total stranger, enabling the troops to raise personal matters they did not want, for whatever reason, revealed to buddies or commanding officers who might have access to their mail.

Thursday, April 26, 1945

Dear Mom & Dad,

I havn't written you in the past three or four days simply because I have been moving around so much. I wrote a letter to you in a blue envelope about five days ago and just now I got a chance to mail it with this letter. So you can see how busy I am. But incoming mail is coming in pretty good. I received letters steadily from Dorothy and Norm, from Sam Mills, a nice letter from Lorraine and one from Stanley. It usually takes from 10 to 15 days for your letters to reach me.

Its an easy life now Mom, believe me. All this war is in my estimation is mopping up operations. I do expect to get into one more big fight before this war is over. We are headed for that place now. Where, I cannot tell you but by the time you receive this letter it will be all over. I imagine its going to be the last big fight too. But dont worry about it because I have been in them before and I know the art of war.

The other day I walked into a slave camp. They were still living in there, Russian girls. They had no other place to go. No sight of pity ever hit me so hard as when I entered that door. It was not the filth because there was none, they kept the place pretty clean. It was not the crude furniture and beds because one sees that all over Europe. What made me and a score of other fellows boiling mad was the condition of the women, girls and – babies. Babys, babys, all over the place. Their mother's faces were weary and tired and they were feeding their babies with what they had left of themselves. One Polish girl, she must have been about 15, 16 years old told me the same story that I have been hearing since I crossed the Rhine. They worked hard during the day with not much food and at night, German soldiers. She said, 'Look what a German soldier gave me.' I asked her if the baby was just born. 'NO, five days ago' and it was no bigger than a kitten. 'Ten babies died in the past week,' she said. I was glad to get out of that sad and gloomy maternity.

It's not like America. Yet I wonder if American woman appreciates their high morals and respect given to womankind. The Germans don't.

I received two letters from you dated April 5, and 7th. Take advantage of staying at Aunt Annie's place for awhile. It will do you and Jerry some good. Did you become a citizen yet Dad? I hope you make the grade because it will help you a lot if you do become a citizen! Nothing more to write.

All my love,
Harry

Lisa Rosenblum, a French Jew being deported to Auschwitz-Birkenau, during World War II, bids her family good-bye — & — A Polish teenager imprisoned in the Pustkow Labor Camp, during World War II, sends word to his parents that he 'Won't get out of here alive' — & — In a letter to her husband, a Hungarian doctor, Anna Koppich, relates what happened to her and their

young son at the Auschwitz-Birkenau Extermination Camp during World War II.

In letter after letter after letter about the concentration camps, the sentiments expressed were remarkably similar: utter disbelief, rage, sorrow and a desire to communicate what they had seen. On April 13, 1945, Major Malcolm Leon Downs wrote the following to his wife:

> I have heard and read of things like these but you cant believe it till you see it and I have seen some awful things but this is past belief. We came right into this city on the heels of the Army with orders to hit the Gestapo Political Prisoner Camp. We went there about noon. We got up at 4 AM and drove hard all morning for nearly a hundred miles when we hit the Camp it took your breath away. People lying on the floors in Barns shriveled up. Just skin and Bones. Absolutely starved to death and tortured. Hundreds were dead in their beds, just skeletons . . . Another Camp on the other side of town has about 900 Hospital Cases but only a few bodies because they have a large Crematorium and they burned the dead and sometimes the live ones. There were 40 bodies piled up waiting and the ovens were full. There were huge pits in back filled with ashes and parts of bones. A Polish Doctor told me that the ashes in the Pits represented 13,000 People . . . I thought for awhile that maybe the people were not all bad but they are a race of madmen and not fit to live. The longer I stay here the worse I hate them and I dont believe I will ever be able to have any use for them again.

On June 28, 1945, a British soldier named Ralph Walsh sent the following to his family in Headley, England.

> About 2 miles from the camp were notices 'Typhus area' and before you reached the camp itself you could smell 'death'. However we 'rolled' into No 3 and a half of the blocks were barbed-wired off labelled 'Typhus' and the poor devils at the windows were full grown men & women weighing no more than 4 or 5 stone . . . just bones covered with

parchment, eyes open sunk 1½ inches into their heads, sores in most cases over their bodies. . . One poor devil still clutched a lovely crucifix & another had tried to end it by cutting her throat . . . It's a pity everyone couldn't have seen those bodies then I don't think there would be a chance of any more wars.

Uncensored letters from those imprisoned by the Nazis are extremely rare. Some inmates were able to smuggle messages out of the camps or toss them from trains while being deported, but the risks were enormous, and the likelihood that their correspondences would reach their friends or loved ones was scant. Lisa Rosenblum was a French Jew arrested in Paris for not wearing the mandatory yellow Star of David patch designating that she was Jewish. In late October 1943, she was condemned to Auschwitz-Birkenau, where she would eventually be killed. On October 30, she scribbled the following note to her family while en route to the extermination camp. How the message got to her husband, Henri, and their children, Paulette, Edouard and Bernard (a POW who had been serving in the French Navy) is unclear, but they received it at the end of the war.

Wednesday

My Dearest,

The day before yesterday I received your letter. I have no more strength to cry. Tomorrow Thursday at 3 o'clock after midnight they will finish us up. We are here a 1000 people. Among us are many old people and small children. Where they are going to take us, we do not know.

My Dearest Henri, Paulette, son, and my elderly mother, I clasp you to my heart. All of you should pray to God for me. I would like to live to see all my children. I am kissing all my family and all our good friends. I plead with you, do not go out any place, because every day new prisoners will arrive. I do clasp you to my heart.

Do not forget Bernard. Zalman and Esther and their son are also on the same train.

Lisa

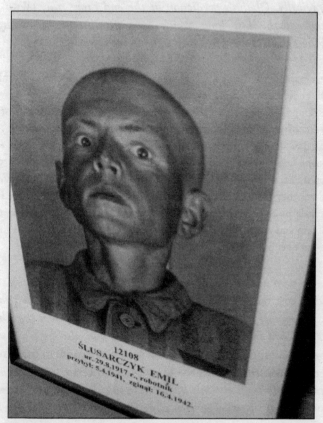

Emil Slusarczyk, one of more than a million individuals killed at the Auschwitz-Birkenau extermination camp.

A 14-year-old boy named Chaim (last name unrecorded), confined at the Pustkow Labor Camp in Poland, was able to slip a short message addressed to his mother and father through the camp's barbed-wire fence and into the hands of a local peasant. The note made it to them, but, tragically, Chaim's prediction at the end came true. (With the exception of the last line, which cuts off abruptly, the ellipses throughout the letter are believed to be in the original.)

My dear parents, if the sky were paper, and all the seas of the world an inkwell, I could not describe my suffering and all that I see around me.

The camp is located in a clearing. From the morning they make us work in the forest. My feet are bleeding because they took away our shoes ... We work all day almost without eating and at night we sleep on dirt (they took our cloaks away too). Every night drunk soldiers come and hit us with wooden sticks, and my body is black with bruises like a piece of burnt wood. Sometimes they throw us a raw carrot or a beet and it is shameful: We fight over a little piece or even a leaf. The other day two boys escaped, so they lined us up and every fifth person was shot ... I was not fifth, but I know that I won't get out of here alive ... Chaim

For many who did survive the camps, freedom came at a devastating emotional cost. They would be plagued by depression, lose their faith, or become unable to establish lasting relationships – for fear that these, too, would end in tragedy. The converse would also be true: some discovered that their belief in God and their connections to friends and loved ones only deepened. In the worst cases, however, solace from the haunting memories could only be found in suicide. Others experienced 'survivor's guilt,' convinced that they should not have lived when, from their perspective, so many stronger or nobler or kinder souls did not. The degree of pain may have varied, but no one came through the camps entirely unscathed. Little is known of Antoni Kropielnicki, the Polish writer of the letter below, or of the recipient, Helena Lubke, except that she was a family friend who lived in Switzerland. On May 9, 1945, Kropielnicki wrote to Lubke of that unforgettable day when he was released from the Murnau Concentration Camp in Germany, and he asked Lubke to inform his wife that he was still alive:

> *On April 29, 1945 at 16:30 hours, a Polish-American soldier drove his tank through our gate and machine-gunned a group of SS officers who were just arriving at the camp. What an irony of fate that an SS general – Brigadefuhrer Fink and three of his officers – lay dead for half a day at the gate to the Polish camp, killed by bullets aimed by a Pole who arrived from across the ocean. . . We still sleep in barracks without sheets and pillows, bitten by bed-bugs. Please let my wife know, since I don't have her address, that I am healthy and free, but this barbed wire is still mangled into our hearts.*

Two months after the Nazis evacuated Auschwitz-Birkenau and as Soviet troops advanced into Poland, a Hungarian physician named Anna Koppich, who had been deported to Auschwitz for being a Jew, wrote a series of letters to her husband, Ferri, recounting all that had transpired since he had left home. (Like many of the country's Jews, Ferri had been forced by the Hungarian military into providing manual labor for the army.) Anna began by describing how their young son, Gyurika, had been distressed by his father's departure.

> *We tried to play act, make believe that somebody brought news from you. We didn't spend too much time together except after lunch. He asked lots of questions, and he did not mind if sometimes I didn't have answers. He loved to eat at Mother's or at the Hausmann's, and claimed that kosher food is better. He even wrote to the relatives in Vasarhelj that he would only come to visit if they would cook kosher. He was a devout little soul, and he blamed me for not lighting candles on Friday night. . . He was happiest when we ate at Mother's on holidays. If we had noodles with poppy seeds, he didn't want to eat; he wanted to save his share for you. It took a lot to convince him that we had plenty left before he was willing to have some. If we made cookies to send to you, he wouldn't even touch them, since it was 'more important for Daddy.'*

On May 9, 1944, Koppich and her son were forced from their home and into the Ghetto. Six-year-old Gyurika was almost paralyzed with fear.

In the ghetto, the Nazi (SS) murderers reigned. We stood in line for medical examinations, and when one SS killer kicked an old Jew who fell, Gyurika was squeezing my hand, kept his eyes looking at the ground, and his entire little body was shaking. I was only afraid of what we would have to see and witness before our own death. I managed to send word to Buchler to try to help us. The ghetto was in the brick factory. There was a roof but no walls on two sides, only dirt and dust and cold wind. Somehow we built our tent and got settled. I tried to prepare our darling before we left our house. I told him that the soldiers needed our house and we'd just go camping. Didn't he love excursions? He said no, not this kind.

Their situation, however, was about to change dramatically for the worse. Koppich, her parents and Gyurika were all loaded into a cattle car and taken to Auschwitz. Within moments of arriving at the camp, Koppich was separated from her family and, because of her profession, ordered to work in the camp's 'hospital.' This led to an extraordinary brush with one of the vilest members of the Third Reich – Dr. Josef Mengele became infamous for his heinous experiments on inmates, especially children. On March 12, 1945, Koppich wrote to her husband:

The number of sick people increased every day, the first dysenteries appeared, an epidemic of scarlet fever started. We did not know how to deal with all the illnesses, and at that time, we still did not believe the horror stories that the Blockalteste [barracks elder or leader] told us. Our chief murderer, Mengele, appeared, thirty-nine years old, good looking, elegant with pleasant features. He was so kind and considerate; he was concerned about everything. He came because the first death occurred; a young girl who committed suicide in the bathhouse at her arrival died a day later.

In one of her final letters to Ferri before they were reunited, Koppich summarized her final days at Auschwitz before being moved to a woman's concentration camp or 'FKL' (Frauen Konzentraton Lager), as she referred to it. With enormous difficulty, she shared her anguish about the suffering that her only child, who had turned seven while at Auschwitz, had had to bear in a place more sinister and frightening than any nightmare. (Rozsa was a 24-year-old relative who died from an illness Koppich does not name. The letter, dated March 19, 1945, and translated years later by a cousin, Agnes Kun, does not include a salutation or signature. Eva, alluded to at the end, is another cousin.)

Today is the anniversary of Rozsa's death and also of the German invasion of Hungary. I have to finish my letter for now, since the Red Army is leaving, and I don't want to stay behind. I have two important jobs to do: one, to give a physical checkup to all the women; and two, to gather some more data that will be useful for us in our future fight against fascism.

My dear, the following is strictly for you. I'd like to describe to you my horrible suffering for a period of three months, without actually relating all the chronological events. On October 13 they 'liquidated' the hospital. In two hours, they loaded 530 of a total of 600 patients on the 'death trucks.' These were mainly strong, recovering young girls and women, since the ones that were really ill were 'liquidated' previously. I had to just stand there and observe how all those for whose lives I fought, all those whom I managed to save several times from being taken away, all those whom I managed to heal were gone. We were taken to the FKL, and here I lost my last glimmer of hope the same way as all my work in the hospital went down the drain. This was the end of the camps – the 'other side.' There was nothing beyond it. So all the stories that there are huge camps beyond were untrue. I had to face the horrible reality that my darling child and my good parents are no more. Please forgive me for causing you so much pain, but you are the only one I can be weak with, you are my only solace, you're the only one I can lean on. Everybody else, family and friends, always expected me to be the strong one. My only consolation is that you are there and I can talk to you about my feelings.

And now I have a confession to make. For many, many years, even after I gave birth, I thought that being in love is the most formidable, the strongest feeling in the world. Later I realized, however, what being a mother means. I found out that motherly love is way above any other kind, a kind of love that is so little talked about, so little written about.

When I finally found out with certainty what happened, the world just stopped existing. I myself felt like I stopped living. Husband or sister could not make a difference in my state of mind. I did my work mechanically; the patient and her illness, life or death, didn't mean anything to me. Luckily I was assigned to a ward that only contained old Polish women, most of them suffering of rheumatism or just old age. I only lived for my sorrow. I cried all day long, I stopped eating, and didn't even have the energy to wash up. I couldn't even keep the appearances up. My patients liked and understood me even though I neglected them, but the staff despised me because of my desperate attitude. I envied those mothers who died with their children. I did not want to live any longer, and a death wish was my only emotion. On November 20th they took Eva to Germany. This was the last straw. I totally collapsed. I could not stop crying any more. I cried while I worked; I cried all day and all night. I relived every mistake that I made raising my child. I did nothing but torture myself. My left hand got infected; that caused physical pain for weeks.

I thought I was stronger and more resistant emotionally (mentally). People coped better with the loss of their loved ones in the camp. Only I, who was stronger than the average person, broke down totally. I was on a roller coaster that seemed infinite. My dear Gyurika, my child that meant life and joy and sorrow to me, was no more. Everything ceased to exist. I stopped existing myself. When I was at the end of my rope, I came down with a very serious case of hepatitis. I had no strength left, but I welcomed death; I was happy that I'd share his (Gyurika's) fate. When I thought the end was approaching and I thought of you, my darling, and my dear Eva, all of a sudden I realized that both of you will need me. So I started to fight for my own life, and as I improved physically, my mental and emotional balance started to improve too. And now that I am free, I thank you, dear heart, that you saved my life.

So now I started to worry about you and Eva, but I hope that we'll be reunited. I am not broken anymore. I have energy and goals, my dream came true: the Red Army liberated me. I want to live and work for you and Eva, but the loss of my dear child left such a tremendous vacuum that can never be filled.

S urvivors of the Japanese takeover of the Philippines during World War II share with the American ambassador, the Honorable Emmet O'Neal, personal stories of the terror and abuse suffered during the three-year occupation.

After five months of intense fighting against Japanese troops, Filipino and American soldiers (initially led by General Douglas MacArthur and then by General Jonathan M. Wainwright) surrendered the Philippines on May 6, 1942. For those forced to live under Japanese occupation for the next three years, even their worst fears could not prepare them for the unrelenting brutality to come. Writing letters or any other accounts that recorded Japanese atrocities was punishable by death, and very few contemporaneous journals or correspondences by Filipinos exist. But after the war, the newly appointed American ambassador Emmet O'Neal actively encouraged Filipinos to write to him about their experiences. Almost everyone in the country had been scarred by the occupation, and Ambassador O'Neal received thousands of letters describing everything from mass executions of innocent civilians to isolated acts of humiliation and torture. The following letter is just one example of the latter. (The texts, which were transcribed for the ambassador, do not include salutations.)

Cotton growing was forced among the people of Calumpang and other neighboring barrios. There were Japanese inspectors who went around to visit the cotton fields. The people worked from early morning to late afternoon. In spite of this the people were not properly treated.

There was a poor worker, Timoteo de Gracia, a thin man of 41 years of age. He was a lone worker for he was a widower. When Okada, a cruel Japanese inspector visited this poor man's cotton field, he found that a few plants were not yet sprayed with insect poison. Very early the next morning he [Timoteo] was called to the office. He was sent to a dark room with his son, the inspector following him. He trembled because of the danger before him. At the command of Okada, Timoteo lifted a bar of iron about fifteen centimeters in diameter and three feet long. He held it high in the air with his straight, slim arms while his eight-year-old son with tears in his eyes looked pitifully at his father. Because of the steady weight of the iron bar, Timoteo lowered his arms a bit, but Okada whipped him with a piece of wood that forced the poor fellow to raise the bar again. The punishment lasted for a day with tears in the eyes of both father and son. Since that time Timoteo remained silent, dull and stupid but worked hard due to fear perhaps. After a month he became insane always calling the name of Okada.

When the Americans arrived a year after, he was sent to Mandaluyong Psychopathic Hospital where he spent his last days.

Crispina de Garcia

Many Filipinos discovered that trivial misunderstandings could have horrifying consequences, as evidenced in a letter by Genciana Paipan. (The guerillas were native Filipinos fighting the Japanese.)

San Luis, Batangas

One early morning on August 28, 1944, a man by the name of Esco was assigned as a 'Segidan' or a Japanese guard post at Tang, a barrio of Lila. In the afternoon he went home to Calvario, on his way near Sacsac spring, he met a troop of Japanese soldiers. The head of the troop asked him where he came from. Esco with fear and respect replied that he came from his duty as a 'Guardia'. Esco did not know the meaning of Guardia and segidan. Guardia means a Bohol Guerilla Guard and a Segidan means a Japanese Guard. The Japanese troop upon hearing that Esco have been a Guardia seized him, beat him and took him to a lone place. There he was tied to a tree and was beheaded.

304

Children, too, were the victims of barbaric punishments, no matter how insignificant the matter.

A boy about twelve years old was caught stealing nails in a factory in Grace Park. The factory was managed by the Japanese. The boy was tied and brought to the cemetery. While a Japanese was digging his grave, the boy did not stop saying bad words to the Japanese soldiers. He even spit on their faces. The Japanese beheaded him. But before they buried him they got his heart because they said he was a brave boy.

J.N. Falcon

Masao Yamaguchi writes to his sister explaining how her mother, brother, sisters and nephew all died in the atomic attack on Nagasaki, Japan, at the end of World War II — & — After a tour through what was once the city of Yokohama, Commander Walter C. Michels urges his young daughter to 'not forget the capacity for destruction that exists in man'.

When no immediate word of surrender came from Japan after Hiroshima was hit by a four-ton atomic bomb, on August 6, 1945, US President Harry Truman ordered a second strike, three days later, on the city of Kokura. Early on the morning of August 9, a B-29 Superfortress, piloted by 25-year-old Major Charles Sweeney, approached Kokura, the site of one of Japan's largest munitions plants. But thick clouds and smoke hampered visibility, preventing the crew from locating their target. They tried several times before heading to their alternate target: Nagasaki, home to weapons factories and the Mitsubishi shipyards. Nagasaki, too, was obscured by haze, and with fuel running low, Sweeney and his crew were close to aborting the mission. Suddenly, there was a break in the clouds. At 11:02 am local time, a plutonium bomb detonated 1500 feet over the heads of the city's

240,000 residents. Approximately a third of them were killed, and another third were critically injured. Those closest to the blast were literally vaporized. Twenty-nine-year-old Masao Yamaguchi was the only member of his family living in Nagasaki who did not perish in the attack itself or from radiation poisoning. After the Japanese surrendered on August 14, 1945, Yamaguchi wrote to his sister Yae, who lived in Chigasaki, to inform her that their entire family, including his three-year-old son Masakatsu, was gone. (Tadao was their brother, and Ine, Kie and Yoshi were their sisters. There is no greeting to the letter.)

I must tell you about what happened in Nagasaki on August 9th. At the time, people were constantly anxious because of the threat of daily air raids by the enemy. That's why I decided to evacuate Mother and Masakatsu on the 8th to Kie's place in Katabuchi, but they didn't feel comfortable there, so they came back home to Takenokubo that evening. I sent them to Katabuchi because they have a secure air raid shelter there, and I had heard that the enemies had announced at the time that they were going to burn down Nagasaki on the 8th, so I took them there early morning on the 8th.

Also, the 8th was the day when Tadao was going to get married into the Tani family in Inasa (the Tani family had a daughter who was 19 and a mother) but Mother was busy taking care of Masakatsu who was sick, so Ine and I took Tadao to Tani family's place, and the wedding took place at around 8 pm. An air raid warning siren started blaring, and the lights went out, but everything went smoothly, and after celebrating their wedding, we arrived back home in Takenokubo at around 9:30 pm.

The following day was the 9th. Since Masakatsu was ill at the time, I had taken a day off of work, so I woke up at around 7 am on the 9th. As always, the preliminary alert was issued starting at 6:30 am that day.

On August 1st, the shipyard that I was working for in Akinoura was attacked. Luckily, I wasn't killed, and since then, I've been very careful about listening for the the warnings. Whenever the preliminary alert was issued, I changed into the air defense clothes. And because Mother forgot to bring Masakatsu's medicine with them when they returned from Katabuchi, I left for Katabuchi at 7:30 am.

In the meantime, the air raid warning had stopped, so I left Katabuchi a little before 11am, and took the train to Uragami. When the train was around Hamanomachi, there was a flash and a crashing sound, so I jumped off the train and lay down on the ground. When I got up after a while and looked around, I saw a massive fireball that was coming up from Uragami, and all the houses along the roads had been completely destroyed. I couldn't go further toward Uragami from Gotouchou, so I went back to around the prefectural office, and I'm not sure how I arrived there, but before I knew it, I was at the top of Tateyama. When I looked down the waterfront to Chikuchou, Uragami was engulfed in flames. Because of the winds, the fire was spreading toward the top of Tateyama. I couldn't keep my eyes open, so I followed a path to the top of Zenza School. The school was incinerated. The blaze started to die down, so I left from there and came out by the Honren temple.

In the midst of all this, I stepped over several dead and injured people. The parts of the body that were exposed were bright red and burnt very badly. There were people screaming, 'Help' from everywhere, but I was concerned about getting home, so I dared not to stop for them and dashed through the fire to get to Takenokubo.

There was nothing there. Our house, which was by the middle school, had been completely blown away. I had followed the road as best I could, and when I came across the area that I thought was our house, I found Mother and Masakatsu lying in agony. I didn't see Ine around, and when I picked up Mother, her injury was so severe that her spine was exposed, and her face was swollen. There was dirt in her eyes, mouth and nose. I can't even describe what I saw. As for Masakatsu, he just lay there motionless. When I picked him up, his body was stiff and his eyes were caked in dirt. The only thing he was able to do was to close and open one of his eyes, but he didn't say a word. Mom kept repeating, 'Give me water, give me water,' but if I gave her water at that moment, I was afraid she was going to choke, so I carried her to the side of the road, and took just Masakatsu to Katabuchi.

When we got to Katabuchi, the sun had set, and the enemy planes were flying endlessly above us. The bell announcing the attacks rang incessantly. While we were in the air raid shelter, I worried about Mother, but there was nothing I could do. Masakatsu was suffering and kept asking for water. His condition was getting worse, and on the third day, the 12th, as he called out for Mother, his short life came to an end. There was no place to cremate him, so I buried him in the ground, in the Kie family's grave.

Also, Tadao, who had just got married the day before the bombing, came to visit me clinging a pillow. Yoshi had just come by from Shimabara, so I decided to stay in the care of Yoshi's family with Tadao. After four days, Tadao developed a fever and diarrhea, and he died on the 18th. The only thing we were able to do for him was to help him find a doctor and have prayers read for him.

I was concerned about Mother, since I had left her, so I took the first train out to Nagasaki on the 19th, and went to Takenokubo, but she was nowhere to be seen. The only thing I saw was the cloth she uses as a pillow, and one rice ball that the rescuers had given her. I didn't find Ine either. I searched the shelter and Inase School, but it was no use.

Going back to Tadao, according to what he had told me before he died, he, his wife and his Mother-in-law were visiting Takenokubo on the 9th. Because it was so hot, he had taken off some of his clothes and was in his underwear when everything started crashing down. He escaped from underneath the house and rescued his Mother-in-law, wife, sister Ine, Mother, and nephew Masakatsu. At that time, there was blood coming out from Ine's mouth and nose, and she was mumbling something, but she started running around hysterically as she suffered, and then she died. I found out that Mother had passed away in the street, so the rescuers most likely cremated her. Tadao had found Mother and was giving her water until the afternoon of the third day, the day when Tadao visited me in Katabuchi. Mother thought he was me, and kept calling him 'Masao, Masao'.

It is all so tragic. Even as I write all this, my hands shake and my heart aches; the scenes of that day appear before me. They're driving me crazy. Images of Mother lying on the road covered with dirt and blood as she groaned, of Masakatsu, of blades of grass dyed in red, tree after tree torn from the ground, countless people injured and killed. I really thought that the world was coming to an end.

Shimo no gawa area was the worst of all. Many people inhaled poisonous fumes. Even though they didn't have any wounds, a lot of people died. That was the case of Tadao. In the place of Mother and Ine's bones, I took back the burnt dirt of our house and buried it. Tadao's wife and Mother-in-law were able to go back to their home in Inasa, but they did not survive.

What a tragedy. I heard you were injured by the bombing, but keep your spirits high. Rest well, and I hope you will recover soon. I'd like to visit the doctor at your hospital and thank them, but it's not that easy right now, so I send all my love. Take care.

Masao

Critics have argued that President Truman authorized the use of atomic weapons not only to compel an unconditional surrender from Japan, but to intimidate the Soviet Union, which, although an ally of the USA at the time, was threatening to become its principal opponent after the war. But Truman, a veteran from World War I, familiar with the horrors of combat, remained adamant throughout his life that his aim in striking Hiroshima and Nagasaki was to end the war as swiftly as possible.

For the American pilots and crews who had, throughout the war, watched from miles above as bombs demolished Japanese towns and cities, even before Hiroshima and Nagasaki, there was a feeling that justice was being served, not only for Pearl Harbor, but for the millions of lives lost in the war resulting from Japanese aggression throughout the Pacific.

But when some of these servicemen saw the extent of the damage on the ground firsthand, their reactions were tempered. For Paul A. Reitz, who flew in raids over Japan, the human cost of the air strikes came to him after the war and in his very own hometown: by an incredible coincidence, a Japanese woman who had lived in one of the cities he had bombed moved into a house just a few blocks from his. After the two realized their extraordinary connection, they talked at length about the war and eventually developed a strong friendship. Reitz remained proud of his contribution to the Allied victory, but later expressed regret about the deaths of innocent civilians.

Servicemen who visited Hiroshima and Nagasaki were especially thunderstruck by the enormity of the destruction. 'Hiroshima is something

I never hope to see again,' Colonel Hubert A. Schneider wrote to his wife, Mary, on September 6, 1945, after a visit to what remained of the city.

> *The damage there is so extensive, so complete, that it frightens you. They say Hiroshima was Japan's most modern city and very much like an American city with American type office buildings, apartment houses, etc. Today not more than 5 or 6 of these are standing and every one of these is completely burned out . . . The whole place looks just as if a giant hand had pressed down on the place and then set fire to it. Houses way out of town have caved in, roofs and trees in the same area lean away from the city having been pushed over by the blast. A few people poke around among the ruins but even these are taking a chance of being burned by the radio activity which still remains. Hiroshima burned for 8 hours after the bomb fell and people who went in after the fire for rescue purposes died days later from the effects of the rays.*

Serving on a hospital ship that arrived in Nagasaki's harbor just weeks after the city was obliterated, Pharmacist's Mate Second Class Donald West related to his wife, Elizabeth, his experiences treating victims of the radiation. (The long-term effects were still unknown to doctors and scientists at the time.) On September 15, 1945, West sent the following to his wife:

The radio activity of the atomic bomb hasn't been positively identified. That's one reason we were to take x-rays, to see if we could find anything on the film that would throw any light on the cause of death. The other doctors with us were specialists, too. While we were upstairs they were elsewhere in the building, watching a post mortem of one of the victims that had just died (a fifteen year old boy), and getting slides and samples and other things for study. The victims of that mysterious energy, whatever it is, just wilt away and die very quickly, once the symptoms begin to assert themselves. These were all injured with that one bomb – the second one – but the symptoms are just now showing up. It's apparently very much like a radium or x-ray burn, but it's so much more widespread that it's very nearly 100 percent fatal, or at least is proving so here. The victims look weak and ill, they aren't visibly injured at all, but the effect is there, and there is no cure. . . . The women and children stared at us with frank curiosity and some bowed politely to us as we passed. But the men, apparently mostly discharged soldiers, ignored us, or looked at us out of the corner of their eyes. We took the opportunity of looking out of the vacant windows to where the town had been around us, but there was nothing there but a rubble of broken bricks and concrete. All the wooden things had been burned up when the fire swept through in the wake of the bomb. I have never seen such complete and thorough destruction before and hope I never do again.

While the almost apocalyptic force of the atomic weapons that exploded over Hiroshima and Nagasaki stunned the world, conventional and incendiary weapons dropped on Japan in the latter part of the war ultimately killed and wounded more civilians. The firebombing of Tokyo alone, on March 10, 1945, claimed more lives than Nagasaki. On September 9, 1945, exactly one week after the Japanese surrender was signed on the USS Missouri, *an American commander named Walter C. Michels had the opportunity to visit Yokohama, which had been decimated by aerial bombings. Michels, 39 years old at the time, was so shocked by what he encountered that he felt compelled to write the following letter to his 12-year-old daughter, Leslyn, back in Strafford, Pennsylvania. (Nan was his wife and Leslyn's stepmother.)*

Aboard the U.S.S. Teton in Yokohama Harbor

Dear Leslyn,

It isn't often that I ask you to save one of my letters, but I am going to ask that you save this one. The reason is that I took time this afternoon to walk about Yokohama for a couple of hours, and what I have to say tonight may be useful to show to someone else in some future day when war again threatens the world and it is up to your generation to stop it.

I don't know whether to be glad or sorry that you weren't able to see the city with me. I'm sorry because the shear awfulness of it all is something that is worth burning into the memory of everybody; I'm glad because I would hate to have you feel as dejected and sick with the human race as I felt when I finished.

Here is a city, or rather was a city, comparable in size with Philadelphia or Baltimore, – one of the leading ports of the world, – so nearly completely destroyed that it will take months just to clean it up, to say nothing of starting reconstruction. Around the edges of the city something is left and looks pretty decent, but in the center nothing but a few buildings stands. And the ones that are still there have been so thoroughly gutted by the intense heat that they will probably be useless.

When I say nothing stands I mean exactly that. It isn't a matter of roofs gone, or broken walls, for all that is left is a pile of the metal parts of the buildings, scattered over the original sites. One can walk down a street and say, 'This must have been a pottery shop' because of the broken masses of china left, or, 'This was a store,' because of the quantities of burnt and scorched tin cans. But those are the only remnants of what were once, houses, offices, work shops, and stores.

I think I felt most depressed when we passed through the remains of a stone wall, of which parts of the gateposts still remained. It had obviously been built around a private residence and the owners name 'SENZAKI' was still readable to our interpreter. Inside there were just enough things left to indicate the presence, at one time, of a walled garden, one of those gardens of minature trees and plants, with little pools carved from stone, of which the Japanese people were so fond. Even in its present state there was something about the place that carried the idea of loving care and of a happy family. I could only think of how I would feel had the same thing happened to Strafford!

You understand, dear daughter, that I'm not saying that the incendiary bombing should not have been done. Once the horrible inhuman and ungodly war had started, the consequences could not be avoided. That is why I'm writing to you so seriously tonight. I believe that my generation can help peace for awhile, if we work at it hard enough, but your generation must not forget the capacity for destruction that exists in man, and must somehow see that neither you nor your children face this again. I don't want your sons, if you have any, to look upon the sight that I saw today, or on the even worse sights which another war may bring, with improved technical means of killing and maiming the bodies and souls of other men.

In order to accomplish that, you, I, and everyone else who believes in the Christian ideals by which we supposedly live must get into the political race and fight for right, even though it inconveniences each of us and interferes with the things that we want to do. That thing that appears on your report card at Baldwin 'Good Citizenship' is very, very important.

I hope that you'll show this letter to Nan and that you won't think that your Daddy is being too impersonal and serious in writing this way, but I feel very keenly tonight that we all have a big job ahead, which we must tackle in the spirit of my favorite quotation from Lincoln, 'With malice toward none, with charity for all, and with a firm determination to do the right as God gives us to see the right.'

Love and goodnight to a dear daughter from,

Daddy

The impact of Michels's trip to Yokohama was not fleeting; after the war he converted to Quakerism, a denomination of Christianity that advocates nonviolence as one of its fundamental tenets.

Lieutenant Colonel W. L. Larson tells his daughter Antoinette about a horrific accident involving several Korean children during the Korean War — & — British, Major P. A. Angier writes to his family about the Korean War's impact on innocent Korean men, women and children.

Although servicemen and women usually refrain from sharing vivid depictions of violence in correspondences to younger family members, they will occasionally – perhaps for cathartic reasons or to remind their children of the realities of warfare – detail gruesome incidents with surprising bluntness. Letters written by troops during the Korean War, in particular, tended to be more candid than those from World War II veterans because there was virtually no censorship. In a short, jarring letter to his 10-year-old daughter in Fredericksburg, Virginia, Lieutenant Colonel W. L. Larson described the awful outcome of the discovery by some inquisitive Korean children of unexploded artillery. (The letter, apparently handwritten in haste or under duress, is missing words in several places.)

Dear Toni:

How's my big pretty girl this evening?

Some small Korean children picked up a live ammunition on our test range which hadn't gone off or exploded. These children took large shell home and started hammering on it with a rock and it exploded. It killed one or two and wounded about three other children. We expect none of them to live. One piece of shrapnel went right through ~~her~~ stomach of one of young girls. The Air Force and other unit used this range so we don't know whether it was our ammunition or some one elses.

Such things are terrible particularly when they are young children.

A Big Hug & Kiss,

Daddy

Major P. A. Angier, a British officer serving on the Korean peninsula with the 1st Battalion Gloucestershire Regiment, also wrote to his family about the degree to which civilians, and especially children, were victimized during the Korean War. (The percentage of non-combatants killed in North and South Korea is believed to have been even higher than that of World War II.) Angier muted the severity of what he saw in his letters to his daughters, Rosalind and Priscilla, but nevertheless attempted to convey to them some idea of the hardships that the Koreans had to endure. 'I am very busy looking for some Communists who have been unkind to some of the children out here,' he wrote to Rosalind.

Their school was burnt down also which was a pity. They have still got some of their school books though and I expect they will build a temporary school with wood and straw for the summer. I am looking forward to doing lots of gardening with you when I come back, but I expect to be away very much longer. I do not know how long, but very long. Lots of love my dear and kisses. We shall be able to play all sorts of games when I come back to Mulberry Tree – perhaps I'll even be a civilian, who knows. Daddy.

In his letters to his wife, Angier was significantly more explicit about the images he and his fellow U.N. troops were witnessing on a regular basis. '[There were] dead babies everywhere abandoned by their exhausted mothers,' he wrote in early January 1951. 'We had done a lot of unofficial medical aid. These people are very tough and I have seen a mother with two bullet wounds pick up her baby and walk off after her wounds had been dressed.' The humanitarian crisis was fraught with danger for Angier and his men as well. 'At 3 p.m. today I could see at one glance a multitude of five thousand [refugees] within my own positions. It is a considerable anxiety to us tonight as we know not who they are. The enemy can easily swarm our positions in this manner as he has done elsewhere.' The possibility of such an attack forced Angier to take drastic preventive actions. But on January 6 he lamented to his wife that he was painfully aware how these measures would only compound the misery of innocent families.

This evening I had to give orders for the burning of four or five occupied houses which had to be cleared for the field of fire of my supporting machine guns. None of us liked doing it at only half an hour's notice to the inhabitants. Imagine if someone came to you to burn down our house at half an hour's notice. My men helped to get the furniture out, carried the babies and soothed the frantic old women. It was a horrid sight next morning to see the charred remains of these innocent homes consumed in the reckless fury of the nations.

By the next day, January 7, Angier's frustration had only grown, and *he sent the following to his wife. (Transcribed years after the war by his wife, many of Angier's letters do not include salutations or sign-offs.)*

When we stood to at dawn this morning, the noise as of a bleating heard of sheep was coming from the area in front of my positions. As the light came one could distinguish the black mass of a great assembly of persons, this time nearer ten thousand strong. I had patrols out by night for protection but now there was nothing but this great crowd between my positions and the enemy. In the half light I pushed out small patrols and after twenty minutes I had canalised the movement of the hordes down the one prescribed road.

I mingled with the flowing multitude and saw again many of the same pitiful sights. Heavy laden mothers, feeding a child at the breast as they were swept along by the tramping column. Wee kids with dirty little mouths being sustained on the road side with tiny brews of vegetable porridge. And where will they all land up? How will they feed and live as they accumulate against the sea barrier of the south coast? What a target for disease! What a terrible failure of the expedition that came here to protect these people and establish the rule of law among nations. It would seem we have failed because UN is not yet strong enough to back its law by force.

I must get this into an envelope before it is lost in the confusion of retreat.

Approximately four months after writing this letter, Major Angier, himself, became a fatality of the war.

Cecilia Reed, serving as a nurse during the Vietnam War, sends a note to relatives about attacks on US Army hospitals by pro-Communist collaborators pretending to be civilians — & — The younger sibling of a North Vietnamese soldier implores his brother to avenge their family members killed by enemy bombings during the Vietnam War.

From British soldiers battling ragtag American minutemen in the late

18th century to Coalition forces clashing with insurgents in Iraq more than 200 years later, it is a dilemma that confounds and infuriates almost all troops who fight in a foreign land: how does one distinguish between harmless civilians and enemy combatants, who often wear no uniforms and can instantly blend into the native population after hiding or discarding their weapons? American troops have faced this threat in many conflicts, but during the Vietnam War, the confusion proved especially tragic for both sides. 'Let me tell you what goes on around here,' a US soldier wrote to a buddy back in the USA, 'over here you have to watch everbody.' (The letter has numerous misspellings and almost no punctuation.)

> *One of my friends was walking through the jungle and a women picked up her skirt and fired him twice She was up in a tree hiding my friend saw her – shot back once and killed a little kid about 5 year old – We were fighting so one sargent pulled out a [grenade] and through it at some soldier The little kid ran out picked it up and threw it back at the sargent and blew up the sergeant. . . . When you fight over here* ~~most of~~ *a lot of time these Viet Congs will bring there wives and children and walk behind them and at the same time shoot at you. . . . The only people I feel sorry for is the little kid because the don't know better.*

Even medical facilities, which treated both Americans and Vietnamese, were targeted by the pro-Communist forces with make-shift explosives carried or planted by presumedly innocent citizens. Cecilia Reed, a 49-year-old nurse from Milroy, Montana, updated family members about her service with a US Army evacuation hospital near Pleiku. 'Everyone has great respect for these people,' Reed said of relations between her staff and the Vietnamese. 'There is a very extensive program going on in helping the people as well as the war.' But several months later a flurry of bombings would make it impossible for the Americans to help the locals who depended on their care. (Reed's letter contains many typos, which are likely the result of the poor quality of the typewriter she was using. The reference to 'svcm' is an abbreviation for serviceman, and CO for commanding officer.)

Sunday morning 8/24/69

This is a nice Sunday morning, beautiful weather and a good rest last night. Was talking to a young svcm who was down at the 6th convalescent Center the day after the attack and he said that it was an inside job as well as from outside and that there were sachel charges planted all over the place. and at least twelve wards and other bldgs blown up. Almost a hundred injuries and two deaths. So guess we are not being any too careful. IN fact the CO told me the other day that they found on one of the visitors, Vietnamese, the making of one and when they found it on her, the patient who, she had been visiting departed the hopsital the next day.Our CO is gradually weeding out all of the Viet. and Montonyards patients from the hosp. which is very sad in one way because it is the only medical care available to them.On the other hand, we must prtect our own US patients and staff.In deed, it is a strange type of war.The gate between us and the Air Base is now open and it is just about two blocks to their club which makew everyone happy again. Should wind this up and beleive I'm at the bottom, about.

Love, Ceil

As with any major conflict, determining the exact number of civilian casualties in Vietnam is nearly impossible. Estimates for the 'American period' of the war range from hundreds of thousands of deaths to 5.1 million, a figure announced by the Vietnamese government in 1995. (This number is significantly higher than what the pro-Communist forces reported 20 years earlier, but in 1995 Vietnamese officials conceded that a lower number had been manufactured during the war so as not to demoralize their people.) There is little debate, however, over the fact that the war inflicted widespread suffering on civilian men, women, and children throughout North and South Vietnam, as well as in Cambodia and Laos. Civilian deaths also, not surprisingly, fueled hostility toward the enemy. Little is known about the North

Vietnamese soldier, Thou, whose body, along with a letter from his younger brother, was found on the battlefield by a US Soldier. Much of Thou's letter concerns everyday family matters and clearly reflects the sentiments of a sibling on the home front longing for the safe return of a beloved elder brother; but it is also an impassioned reminder as to why he is fighting.

Vinh Yen, Nov. 1967

My dear brother,

This is your little brother! Do you miss me? Since I was back in the country and met you while you were on leave, I have not received any letters from you. I am working hard and time passes by quickly. I am also helping with the re-construction of many collapsed bridges. I have transferred to a Middle Transport Professional and Technical School. Today, I am taking time to write a letter to you.

My dear brother, our grandparents, aunts, and I are all well. Our family is okay. I want to inform you briefly about my job and I hope that you will not worry about me, 'All to serve our country.' I also want to tell you to revenge our father!

Regarding my job, I am teaching at the Middle Transport Professional and Technical School of Ha Noi. There are 120 instructors and 1,257 students in my school. I am responsible for training 120 students in technical skills. My students are all different ages, the eldest is 30 years old and the youngest is 18; they are staff officers. Also there are some international students from Laos. I am helping 5 Laotian students in studies.

Life at my school is relatively poor. As you know our country is at war; the American army is losing, so they have gone crazy and have been dropping bombs everywhere. Therefore, my school has had to evacuate to a forest location at the Vinh Phu province. As a result, our accommodations and classrooms are in need of improvement.

Regarding my studies, I am now in school till June-1968 and I am planning to study at a University after that. Now, my salary is VND 50 per month including 0.5 kg sugar, 18 kg rice; it relatively good for me.

My dear brother, I have traveled to many places and many cities. Every time I go to either Ha Noi, or Hai Phong, or back to our town, I always think

319

of you – I miss you so much. How wonderful it would be if you would have accompanied me on those trips. Oh! I would like to share with you my good news; our grandparents and parents will buy me a bike either in coming May or June-1968. I hope that you will be happier knowing this news.

Next I must tell you the bad news, that on 22-August-1966, an American airplane bombed the city of Ha Noi, and they killed our uncle's wife. She dies leaving behind four children for uncle Can. Our grandmother has to help him to look after his children. She is exhausted.

Regarding uncle Do, uncle Ha, and their wives, they are doing well. They love to share the happiness with you. And Mrs. Ngoat has graduated, but she is not sure which school she will be assigned to for teaching. She is doing fine though.

Dear brother! Living at this time, we need to strive for the ideals of our youth; I am also serving our country diligently.

My brother, this letter is quite long already. I promise that I will write you more next letter. Now try to focus on your job: kill more American soldiers to revenge our father and for many other people who have died.

With the love from the bottom of my heart, I wish you health, and happiness. Remember to write a letter to our grandparents so that they are not so worried about you. Once again, I wish you all the best, and more successes in fighting against the American empire invading our country.

Hope to see you soon. In a warm and welcoming home.

Love your younger brother.

Sarajevo resident Mevlida Pekmez expresses to her sister and mother the anxiety she feels as the siege of their beleaguered city continues in 1992 — & — As Serbian troops assault the UN 'safe haven' of Srebrenica in July 1995, a Dutch army medic named André Dekker sends his girlfriend Ingrid a 'farewell letter' — & — In a terse, fragmented letter, Dekker shares with Ingrid his impressions of the fall of Srebrenica in 1995 during the civil war in the former Yugoslavia — & — As NATO warplanes bomb Belgrade, in 1999, Patricia A. Andjelkovic emails her family and friends abroad about the degree to which she and her neighbors are trying to maintain a sense of normalcy.

On November 2, 1991, a group of Serbian soldiers entered a hospital in the town of Vukovar, Croatia, and rounded up approximately 260 patients, both civilian and military, along with doctors and members of the hospital staff. The Croats were taken to the neighboring town of Ovcara, where many were beaten. (A small number were released.) Under cover of darkness, the Serbs then drove the Croats to a pig farm, lined them up side by side, and mowed them down with machine guns and automatic rifles. The corpses were tossed into a mass, unmarked grave. The Vukovar Massacre, as it would be remembered, was merely a prelude to the bloodshed that would envelop the Balkans in the years to come. After Yugoslavia's Communist ruler Josip Broz Tito died in 1980, tensions flared between the republics that constituted Yugoslavia, and in 1991, Slovenia and Croatia officially proclaimed their separation from the federation. Slobodan Milosevic, the Serbian President of Yugoslavia at the time (Serbia was home to the Yugoslav capital, Belgrade, and was the largest of the republics, both geographically and in terms of population), dispatched ground and naval forces to halt the secession as aggressively as possible. Dubrovnik, considered one of the most picturesque cities on the Adriatic coast, sustained a three-month bombardment from the sea – a display of brute force by Milosevic intended both to intimidate Croatia into submission and to serve as a cautionary example for other republics considering a move toward autonomy. Refusing to be threatened, Bosnia and Herzegovina declared independence in March 1992. Bosnians of Serb ethnicity began to fight with Bosnian Muslims, with the most volatile area being the nation's capital, Sarajevo, a multiethnic city of almost half a million people. Thousands of peace demonstrators spontaneously took to the streets in the beginning of April 1992, only to be gunned down by Serb militants. President Milosevic and Radovan Karadzic, leader of the

Bosnian Serbs, blockaded all roads leading in and out of the city and closed down the international airport. The citizens were trapped, and no outside aid – including food and medicine – could come in. Serb artillery and sniper units moved into position on the hills and mountains that surrounded the city, and by mid-April, the thunder of incoming shells announced that the Siege of Sarajevo had begun. As the Serb stranglehold tightened, residents assumed that the world would be outraged and press Milosevic to withdraw his forces. (Bosnia's own army was no match for the Serbian troops.) Week after week, they waited. No help came. Months turned into a full year, and then another. United Nations resolutions were passed, an arms embargo on all the republics was imposed, as were economic sanctions, but little of it staunched the violence. Thousands of people were dying – shot by snipers on their way to work or school; killed in the daily mortar attacks on apartment buildings, busy thoroughfares, parks, and even cemeteries where families had gathered to bury a loved one; or became victims of malnutrition and cold. The number of miscarriages and deaths by suicide soared, while birthrates plunged. Traveling anywhere in the city, even just a few blocks, could be fatal, and people depended on letters either carried by loved ones or delivered through the Red Cross to check in on each other's well-being. The following message was sent by Mevlida Pekmez to her sister Raza Durakovic, who was caring for their mother. Like many letters of the time, it accentuates the despair experienced by so many residents of Sarajevo as the siege wore them down mentally and physically. (Although not everyone mentioned in the letter is identifiable, Enes is their brother, Selma is his daughter, and Avdo is Mevlida's husband. The paper is in poor condition, making the text illegible in parts.)

My Dear ones,

I am losing hope that I will ever see you. My dear mother, I cry every day. Every day, every moment... These letters are very slow in getting to you. I see that you have written on January 3rd but I got it only on April 2nd. I have no idea what is going on with you. I know mom is ill, I know you are desperate, I know you don't have anything, like us, but all this can be overcome if these atrocities would stop so we can get together again. My dear mother, I beg you to hold on, don't give up. The children dream about you all the time. I don't dream about you, I'm with you twenty-four hours a day. . .

I've moved three times so far. You can survive for only five days from the humanitarian aid. We went into this war without money. . . Mubera has made the children very happy. She has sent them 200 marks, and Ajko 100. One relative sent me 100 marks. That's all I have for this year. A pack of eggs costs 50 marks. Sugar is 80. Imagine how happy the kids are when I'm able to get that for them. They're wonderful. They're not kids anymore, but old people. They don't go to school. It's too far away and it is dangerous to take them. Also, they don't have any clothes or shoes to put on to go to school. What can I tell you about Enes? Should I write to you about what he has been through? Selma has unsurprisingly taken the whole thing well. . .

Avdo has changed drastically for the worse. He is fighting like a lion, but this situation seems an eternity. He's dreaming of taking us somewhere out of here. Where?! There are no roads around us. Some cry to come back, while others try to run away through the airport and die like chickens. Oh God, you have loved all these people for all of us. There's no space in this letter for Emir to write you. He will write you through the Red Cross.

I love you and kiss you. Say hello to Nada, Jelha, Dzemo.

As Serbian atrocities against Bosnian civilians escalated, pressure on Europe and the USA, in particular, to end the siege was also mounting. But there was still reluctance to get involved (or, in the words of some anti-interventionists, 'entangled') in the Balkans crisis. Everything changed after Srebrenica. Located in the easternmost part of Bosnia and Herzegovina, Srebrenica was designated a UN 'safe haven' and protected by Dutch peacekeepers. The lightly armed troops were ordered not to engage the Serbs except in self-defense. On July 7, 1995, thousands of Serb forces descended on Srebrenica. The Dutch urgently requested air support but none came. As the sound of gunfire and shells exploded all around them, death seemed a certainty. André Dekker, a 20-year-old army medic, frequently updated his girlfriend, Ingrid, on the rising tensions in the region. On the evening of the 6th, fearing for his life, Dekker dashed out a final letter to his girlfriend. In the heat of the moment, he addressed her as his wife, although they were not married. (OP is an abbreviation for Observation Post, QRF stands for Quick Reaction Force, and YPR for an armed, personnel carrier.)

20:00 To my dearest wife

During this moment of great uncertainty, I am writing you a farewell letter. Since four-thirty this morning, our enclave has been under fire from tanks, artillery, and mortars. Since then we have been cooped up in the bunker, allowed only to go out sporadically and in full gear. OP Foxtrot, which was closest to OP Echo, took three direct hits. No casualties, only damage to the OP. There were several detonations of unclear origin. The question is whether OP Foxtrot has to leave now or not.

At any rate, I told Alex that I wanted to go with him on the YPR in case something went wrong, but Willem came up to me and told me I was to take over the QRF from Jasper, whose grandfather had just passed away. Stands to reason, and I didn't mind, but the situation is growing steadily more threatening, and combined with the fact that my rotation has been moved up again and it is not clear what is going to happen next, there are a few things I must tell you. On TV they say that Foxtrot was only hit once and that we are not under fire ourselves. However, the opposite is true.

I am a medic with the QRF (1900) until the day after tomorrow. Two whole days. Things may change then, but I'll cross that bridge when I come to it. It's just that the feeling I have now is not good. And with the threat of an attack, I am fearing for my life for the first time. It may be because the tour is coming to an end. It doesn't matter what brings it about, I'm having a bad premonition. I'm hoping that I am not good at this sort of thing and everything will turn out all right, but it's very depressing.

I will sleep in the bunker with my colleagues of the QRF as well, so we'll be the first to know if something happens. For now, enough of this.

My point actually is that I have come to the conviction that you were the woman I wanted to marry. I am eternally grateful to you for all the support you have indirectly given me and my family these past months. So grateful that I would turn the world upside down if I ever had to go and look for you. Perhaps you received some comfort from me, as I certainly got it from you. You're everything to me, my confidante, my shoulder to cry on, my love nest, and everything you give to me exceeds my expectations. I feel good when I'm with you, I can be myself and together we are invincible.

Ingrid, you really were my wife.

Do not be sad for what has happened
Think with pleasure of all that we were able to do
And the good times we had.
Look ahead with your head held high
And set course for your future
You, the strongest, the most joyful and loving woman in the world
Find peace within and go on.
Do this for me, then I will have done this for you.

André

The Dutch troops were taken hostage by the Serbs but later released, and Dekker made it through the attack uninjured. The remaining residents of Srebrenica were not so fortunate. Beginning on July 10, the Serbs surrounded an estimated 12,500 Bosnian Muslims, almost all of whom were men, including many young boys. Over 5000 were able to escape to safety, but the remaining 7000 or so were enfiladed with machine gun fire, mortared at close range, and positioned in groups directly in front of tanks, which then fired on them point blank. Almost two weeks after his farewell letter, Dekker was far from Srebrenica and able to inform Ingrid he was alive. But he was deeply shaken, and on July 19 he composed a somewhat disjointed letter that listed images and observations that had stuck in his memory. 'I couldn't write in the last few weeks, it was just too much, too terrible to put into words,' he began. 'Therefore, I will use catchwords and try to clarify everything a little more. . .'

I am writing this letter to you on one of the evenings preceding our departure.

The planned itinerary is to go to Split and next to Belgrade, but all of us prefer Zagreb.

The reason is very simple. We do not want to run the risk of having to cross through Muslim territory and to come under fire again as yet. Having to pass along sniper alley south of Sarajevo and to put our lives in the balance. Not only that, but it's also a three-day drive and all we want, when we go, is to get home as quickly as possible. Isn't this what the politicians wanted as well: 'We want to get our Dutch military personnel home as quickly as possible.' Of course.

Both of us will have learned plenty, and certainly the fact that waiting in uncertainty supercedes the facts as established by either the politicians or Defense or any other agency, and certainly in view of the past half year.

As it turns out, the reunion with family and friends is not all that important, as evident from the TV news, where it was said that hundreds of family members were still waiting for their returning soldiers. Luckily, we haven't had all that many bad experiences here and so we don't want to go home yet.

No, the decision was made that we can leave with all materiel we have here. Because relocating by convoy would be far to slow, we need transport materiel which should arrive tomorrow.

- Under fire at Foxtrot, seized the next day
- Multiple o.p.'s threatened and seized subsequently
- Foxtrot colleague killed during retreat
- Nights, days in the bunker
- Stood in the middle of town for one day with the YPR, Alex and Willem
- Mortar and rocket strikes at 50 meters from the YPR
- The next day, hundreds, thousands of refugees in and around the compound
- Horrible scenes
- Cowardly enemy fighters scream like everybody else
- Another day later, thousands of refugees in compound after the town came under fire
- Hysteria
- Request for air support

- Mortar/rocket on compound
- Wounded people in our buildings, boy with injured arm, girl with injured leg, both wounded by grenades; old woman with hole in hip
- Total hysteria
- Keep head cool, am the last returning medic
- Signal to take down compound, ran to the YPR under fire and unprotected
- Drive to Potocari
- Emergency aid refugees, wounded
- Coffee in bunker, then slept
- Had to burn letters
- Tending to the wounded
- Half of the wounded transported Kladanj, Tuzla, crippled people, dead people
- Had to leave behind lad with broken pelvis in Bratunac
- Doc Schouten remained with the Serbs voluntarily
- Girl with injured leg, and old woman in truck
- Saw refugees pass by during traffic jam. Familiar faces
- Had a break-down with Willem
- Maximum engagement for taking care of the wounded and the sick
- Little guy with smiling eyes, man with black eye and stick, man with cigarette and aching back, the two gals, the woman who had just had an abortion, the singing man, the boy without parents, the foul-smelling man next to the screaming woman, I.V.s, catheters and injections
- Farewell?
- TV images arrival in Tuzla
- Rest, talk, sleep and come to our senses, think a lot and hope for a speedy return to The Netherlands

Considered the worst wartime atrocity in Europe since 1945, the massacre at Srebrenica, and subsequent mortar attacks on market-places in Sarajevo itself, triggered the USA and its allies to launch NATO airstrikes against the Serbs. Now facing the military might of the West and a rebuilt Croatian army (which Milosevic denounced for committing atrocities against Serbs), Milosevic agreed to a cease-fire. In December 1995 a peace treaty, based on negotiations the month before in Dayton, Ohio, at the Wright-Paterson Air Force Base, was signed by Milosevic, President Alija Izetbegovic of Bosnia and Herzegovina, and President Franjo Tudjman of Croatia. NATO forces were then dispatched to the region to implement the agreement.

Just as the Balkans were struggling to establish a semblance of calm and stability, another region of the former Yugoslavia was disintegrating into turmoil. The ethnic Albanians who lived in Kosovo, a province of Serbia, were now pushing for autonomy as well. Although most Kosovars were ethnic Albanians, a minority of ethnic Serbs controlled the government and the military. During the mid-1990s, the Kosovo Liberation Army began clashing with Serb forces, and by 1998 President Slobodan Milosevic was once again accused of initiating a campaign of ethnic cleansing to crush the independence movement and to make Kosovo ethnically 'pure.' Exasperated with Milosevic and the orders emanating from his administration in Belgrade, NATO began an intensive air war against Serb positions in Kosovo. But this time NATO warplanes also struck Belgrade itself, hammering military and government installations in the Serb capital. Patricia A. Andjelkovic, an American teacher in Belgrade, began to send emails to family and friends abroad after the first bombs began to fall on March 25, 1999. Andjelkovic loathed Milosevic (as did many Serbs), but was furious about the air raids, convinced that while what was happening in Kosovo to the ethnic Albanians was an injustice, the crisis was an internal matter in which the world had no right to meddle – and one that potentially could have been averted if the West had supported the Serbs who had demonstrated en masse against Milosevic in 1996 and 1997. What especially angered Andjelkovic was the NATO tactic of knocking out bridges, factories, power grids, and other facilities on which the people of Belgrade as a whole relied. 'Before I lost the lights this morning, another satellite reporter literally gloated over the strikes on power plants,' Andjelkovic wrote on May 25.

328

I think strikes against targets which heavily affect the civilian population cannot, in any terms, be condoned. They are cruel, inhumane, and show a definite lack of respect for human life. Do they care how many people have already suffered or died because there's no current or water? . . . There are people who depend on dialysis machines, those who must use absolutely sterile equipment, and those being otherwise cared for in hospitals.

Her outrage culminated on April 12, when a precision-guided missile struck a train dead-on as it crossed a bridge, killing or wounding about two dozen passengers. A NATO spokesperson expressed regret over the loss of life, but insisted the bridge itself was a legitimate military target and the train was not meant to be hit. Andjelkovic had her own views on the subject. (The pronunciations added parenthetically are Andjelkovic's own.)

Just a few minutes ago I heard on the news (local and foreign) that an international passenger train, bound for Greece, was bombed around noon as it passed over a bridge near Leskovac (LES-ko-vahts), about three hours south of Belgrade. Eight people or so were killed, some apparently children. These lives, unsuspecting passengers, people like you or me, were the 'collateral damage' (sounds so much better than 'deaths', doesn't it?) that NATO speaks of. Why, for God's sake, would a pilot bomb a bridge with a train on it in broad daylight? . . . What in God's name went on in the pilot's head? I imagine that even with high-tech warfare, it still comes down to a human being to push the button.

Andjelkovic tried to focus on positive stories, too, most notably the efforts of the city's residents to band together and persevere during the blackouts, water shortages, deafening explosions and constant fear of being in the wrong place at the wrong time. Three and a half weeks into the NATO campaign, Andjelkovic related an annual event in Belgrade that she had assumed was going to be cancelled under the circumstances.

April 19, 1999
Monday

Dear Family/Friends,

I hope my several days silence hasn't troubled anyone. We are still here, relatively safe and sound. I spent Saturday continuing to do spring cleaning around the house, interspersed with long dog walks, and cruising the grocery stores for things I may need. There are still no shortages, but to the trained observer (i.e. anyone who survived the sanctions imposed on Yugoslavia during the Bosnian War), it's obvious that there will be. Grocery stores are beginning to rearrange items on the shelves, spreading them out, rows of products are no longer 3–4 rows deep, and more expensive, imported items are more predominant, the local ones having been all but bought up. I don't have the natural instinct to lay in great amounts of necessities. Some people are buying large sacks of flour, liters and liters of cooking oil. Perhaps I should.

A few letters back, I mentioned that I had noticed that the city's white traffic lines and pedestrian crosswalks had been repainted, and that this was usually done in April because of the yearly Belgrade Marathon, open to runners from all over the world. I had doubted that this event would take place this year, but sure enough, last Saturday, 15,000 runners from Yugoslavia and 10 foreign countries, including the US, braved a torrential downpour worsened by hail, to complete a shortened route of the marathon's 46 km regular course. If they had run the full course, the participants would have passed in front of our building, but this year I had to watch on tv.

Usually, the Belgrade Marathon offers a cash prize and a car to the winner, but because of the exceptional circumstances this year, Belgrade's 12th marathon was transformed into a 'fun run'. Indeed, the theme was 'Stop the Bombs, Run the World'. Before you read too much of the last part, know that it is a poor translation of 'Trcite Svet' (run around the world). No double-entendres intended; the other meaning would have required a different verb. Instead of an official number, the participants, ranging in age from 70's to babies in pushcarts, had targets pinned to their shirts. Because of the pouring rain, onlookers didn't have to offer water to the runners, but encouraged them by waving peace flags and cheering. The circuit was not

330

only shortened, but also slightly rerouted to show television viewers the damage done to several of the city's buildings.

I am a strong walker, but I've always admired the stamina of runners, and I always watch the marathon both on tv for the downtown part, and often outside my building or by the river park where I can watch in person. This year, the marathon meant something more to me and, I'm sure, to all of those watching and participating. Gone were the cash and the flashy car prizes, gone were the fame and glory of winning, but people ran as if the laurels still awaited them. (Again, it's the teacher in me, but in the past few years, it's hard to get kids to do anything above and beyond the call of duty without their asking, 'Do we get candy/stickers?' Gone is much of the intrinsic value of 'just for fun'.)

To be truthful, I had to admit that running a marathon in the midst of war, be it a de facto one as if that makes it any less of a war, appeared to me at first as absurd. However, as I watched these people, Yugoslav and foreign, running their hearts out, the race made more and more sense.

For both participants and spectators, it was a chance to do more than run or cheer. It was an opportunity to show the world in some small way their opposition to the bombing. Physically for them and for the spectators, the race purged their anxiety, frustration, and anger in a healthy, non-violent way. Their enthusiasm was not dampened by the rain, which beat down for a greater part of the race. Nevertheless, I had to suppress a fleeting thought about the rain, which still emerges as I watch local vegetable and flower gardens grow each day – what's in the rain?

Bombs have fallen on chemical factories in nearby Pancevo (PAHN-cheh-vo), releasing amounts of chlorine, ammonia, and other chemicals into the air. The rain falls onto earth and whatever's on it, in it. Don't talk to me about using or not using chemical warfare. It's the same thing to drop a bomb with dangerous chemicals as it is to hit factories that produce chemicals, and allow them to spread. And spread they do, far and wide.

A few days back, President Clinton spoke to the nation, reiterating that he had nothing against the Serbian people, and that we Americans shouldn't either. I don't think the Serbian Americans believe that, nor do the Serbian people here. As the cliché goes, actions speak much, much, louder than words. It's hard to believe the President's statement when your husband has

331

lost a leg, your son has been called up, when your house no longer exists, when you jump when a car backfires, or when you have to explain to small children why they are being bombed.

On Saturday during the day they ran in Belgrade for fun. At night, many flee to the shelters. In Kosovo, villagers run for their lives. All of this could have been prevented, resolved in a peaceful, humane manner, and long before it came to this humanitarian and ecological catastrophe, which directly affects not only Serbia (and I'm including Kosovo, which is part of Serbia), but all of Europe.

Until next time.

On June 9, after 78 days of bombing, President Milosevic relented, and agreed to allow UN peacekeepers into Kosovo. Sixteen months later, he lost the presidential elections to Vojislav Kostunica. Milosevic initially refused to accept the results and holed up in the presidential compound, where he stayed for six months. He finally surrendered himself in April 2001 and was later taken to the Hague to stand trial for war crimes. Despite the seeming irrefutability of his guilt, Milosevic remained a hero to many Serbs, and only two and a half years after his arrest, while he was still in jail awaiting trial, he was elected to a seat in Serbia's parliament.

Once safely back home in North Carolina, Anna Miller tells her loved ones about an unprecedented act of violence that occurred right before her eyes on 9–11.

'First, let me say that I would not have or be making it through experiencing this trauma without all of the incredible support, care, concern, and love I have felt poured on to me,' 22-year-old Anna Miller began a deeply heartfelt 'thank you' letter to her family and close friends. 'I realize this letter is arriving to you all almost a month late,' Miller went on to say,

but it has taken me time – time to express my thoughts and emotions – sometimes I would start to write and just get too emotionl, or feel like I needed a break. So I apologize – but here it is . . .

Miller had returned home to North Carolina several weeks before from what was supposed to have been a routine business trip, and she wanted everyone close to her to know exactly what had happened and that their thoughts and prayers were truly appreciated. In 10 handwritten pages, Miller went on to describe how, while attending a business seminar in a Lower Manhattan hotel, she and her co-workers suddenly became eyewitnesses to – and almost victims of – one of the most catastrophic attacks in USA history. (The letter is uncut; the ellipses are in the original.)

My hotel room was on the 30th floor; therefore, waiting on the elevator seemed like an eternity. I walked to the window and looked at this beautiful building next door to us that was having all of this construction and rennovations done to it. We started our meeting just after 8:30 – after telling everyone that when we had our lunch break at noon, the best place to go was across the street to the world trade center – they had a great food court. My co-worker Paige & I were sitting in the back of the room and she was telling me how good the shopping was there & that we also <u>had</u> to go eat at the Windows on the World restaurant at the top of the w.t.c. At this point, I remember hearing this really loud noise, which I now realize was the first plane flying overhead, and then <u>loud</u> crashing sounds. I remember thinking to myself 'Oh gosh – some of the construction from the building next door has fallen & hit our building.' Bob, my other co-worker who was instructing the class at the time, thought/said the same thing and we continued on with business. Because we were on the 3rd floor & almost directly under the W.T.C. we could not see/realize what had happened. There was a gap in the curtains and I couldn't help but peering out to see if I could determine what had happened. I saw people beginning to gather on the street corner & noticed that they were all looking & pointing up. Bob was having to raise his voice because suddenly all you could ~~wh~~ hear were sirens.

At that point, I tried to subtly motion to Bob that something was definitely going on out there & a man in our class said, 'I don't mean to be rude, but can we stop for a second and look out the windows to see what's going on?' At that point, everyone rushed to the windows. I remember looking down and seeing no cars on this normally busy NYC street except for a few scattered down the street, stopped in their tracks, pan caked by the fallen debris; And every kind of emergency vehicle you can image coming from every direction. More and more people were gathering on the street, but because we were directly below it, we still could not tell what had happened. Paige & I went down to the lobby to try & figure out what was happening and that's when I realized it was something major. They were not letting anyone out of the hotel and the lobby was becoming a medical station. People were coming in or being brought in off the streets, some were what seemed to be going into shock, others covered in blood, others even worse – EMS people were setting up medical stations and I decided we'd better get back up to the room, get Bob (our other co-worker – older man – Paige & I are both in our 20's) and figure out what we should do. We got back up to the conference room where everyone was, still faces plastered to the window. Just as I got to the window to look out again someone screamed Holy Shit, (sorry) I could hear another loud noise, and looked up to realize that it was a commercial airliner swerving around a building in front/diagonal of us. Then it disappeared. Then another boom & our building shook. Still, no idea that the WTC had been hit – just very aware that something terrible was happening and having no idea what to do.

I remember as I was looking out the window I turned to the guy Brian beside me & said 'Brian, I really think that's blood & flesh, in the street.' After which, I ran for the pay phones outside of our room to call my family and tell them I loved them because I had no idea what was about to happen to me. No luck – not a single phone – regular or cell, was working. Then an emergency intercom system came over and said that the New York City police department was evacuating the building. I was petrified to go out there. After a team of Marriott grey-suited workers led us through stairways, offices, a kitchen, and I couldn't really tell you where else, we made it to a back emergency exit. None of the normal exits/entrances were open because the debris was falling there, blood/flesh was in the street, rescue cars were everywhere, etc. So, we got to this exit and another Marriott worker, who obviously had not heard NYPD announcement said 'you musn't go out there – it's terrible, you don't want to see what's in the streets.' Someone yelled to him that we had been told to evacuate & he commanded that we all keep our heads up, <u>don't look</u> at what is in the streets, and <u>RUN,</u> RUN in the same direction as everyone else. We got out & did exactly that. (At this point I was with Paige, and 3 men from our class Bryan, Jack, and Gier – who I will never forget as long as I live) We held hands & ran with the screaming masses of paniced people. I noticed though that everyone kept turning around & looking up – we all did too – And that's when I saw both WTC bldgs above me in flames and someone jump from I have no idea what floor.

I didn't look back again until we got to the point where we couldn't run any further, Battery Park. We figured it was the safest place because if they were going to attack again, there were no buildings in the park. I stood there in absolute shock, terror, and disbelief as I watched the towers burn. Black smoke was billowing out from the buildings and more & more people were running into the park for safety. It was so petrifying to be in the middle of it all because all that you know of what is happening is what you're seeing right before your eyes – which is horrific – and what all of the paniced people are screaming. 'America's under attack.' 'All of New York is going to be blown up.' 'We've gone to war.' and on and on. . . . I was frantic to get in touch with anyone in my family because I knew they probably knew by now what was happening and that I was in the middle of it. I wasn't sure if I was going to live through that day and wanted to be able to let anyone and everyone know how much I loved them. I was afraid it was going to be my last chance. Every time I tried a cell phone all I could get was a busy signal . . . No one could get a cell phone, or any phone for that matter, to work. But I was bound & determined to get through to someone. I was shaking so badly I could barely dial the numbers. Finally I was able to get through to my Dad and the sound of his voice, while it was exactly what I wanted to hear, made me all the more afraid. Afraid it was the last time.

Just as I hung up the phone, ~~and start~~ I watched the first building fall. There was so much commotion, screams, noise, confusion – that even though I had known the building had just fallen and that's what was filling the city air with the overhead intense sounds – I couldn't make clear reasoning and I thought it was more planes flying over to wipe out New York. The air around us was starting to get darker and massive herds of screaming people starting running – I realized they were running from this black wall that was quickly approaching – I remember thinking 'This is it. This wall of I don't know what that is moving towards me has poison in it that will kill us all.' All 5 of us got down and put our faces to the ground and the men covered us with their jackets/shirts I just broke down into tears, so terribly frightened. And although we couldn't look at each other, Paige grabbed for my hand and said 'Anna, this is not our time to die. We will make it through this.' We stayed in that huddle for I don't know how long – what seems like forever, until finally we realized that people had begun to move around us. I stood up to a shower of soot. Literally, it was pouring soot. We couldn't really open our eyes and I had covered my mouth and nose with the man Jack I was with's jacket. ~~That's when~~ We were all huddling there, I guess just stunned not knowing <u>what</u> to do and that's when I saw Bob (our co-worker we had left at the Marriott). I started screaming his name. I wouldn't have recognized him if he hadn't of taken his shirt off & wrapped it around his face. It was a distinctly patterned shirt – he was maybe 3 feet away and I still had to call his name (first & last) 5 times before he registered. Everyone was in such disbelief and shock – nothing was registering or making sense. Out of no where emergency vehicles were pulling up with water & masks to breathe through. Men were shirtless every~~one~~where because they had taken them off to give to people to breathe through.

The six of us just stood there holding each other not really knowing quite what else to do. I remember planting my face into Bob's chest because it was so hard to hold my eyes open they burned so badly & I really couldn't breathe – but he just wrapped his arms around me and when he did it – his strength made me realize how terribly I was shaking; my entire body just shook in his arms. Then came the next set of intensely loud crashing noises booms, bangs, screams and each of us grabbed each other by the hands and ran for better shelter. I wasn't even thinking about what was happening – just keeping focused on holding onto hands and each other staying away from the paniced seas of people, and breathing through my mask. We found a restaurant patio and all of us closed one of the huge table umbrellas over us and we watched the pile of soot grow around us and listened to people shouting out the names of what I assume to be people they could not find. A man & wife came and got under an umbrella next to us with their baby in it's stroller. I had a little of the water I had gotten from a rescue worker left and reached out from under our umbrella to hand it to them. The wife grabbed my arm and said Oh, we were so desperate for water for our baby. I think that maybe this was the point that I told myself – Anna, you must not panic. Everyone is so frightened, but if we remain calm, we can help each other. We made our way into the restaurant where they were shredding their table clothes into squares for people to breathe through. It was still very difficult to breathe in there because so much had come in through the doors.

A̶ I looked around at all of us packed into this restaurant with grey hair, bloodied clothes, masks on our faces – we all looked the same, I just recall thinking – everyone looks the same and we're all going through the same thing – Each of us – black, white, Japanese, business persons, daughters, mothers, children – we're all the same right now.

And everyone was trying to get through to their loved ones on cell phones. I think we all just felt – there's no words to appropriately convey it – the preciousness of life, the importance of expressing of love, the desperateness to be with those who we care about – I know I̶ ̶k̶e̶p̶t̶ ̶t̶h̶i̶n̶k̶i̶n̶g̶ all I wanted to do was hear the voices of those that I love. I'd never t̶h̶o̶u̶g̶h̶t̶ felt so real s̶e̶r̶i̶o̶u̶s̶l̶y̶ ̶a̶b̶o̶u̶t̶ the thought/feeling/fear of never speaking to them again. Jennifer is the next person that I got a hold of and I remember when I said 'Jenny' – the impact of love, relief, fear, I felt when she said 'Oh my God Anna' as we both burst into tears. (I had many memorable, unforgettable phone conversations that day and since that day which I won't write to each of you about – but please everyone know that they are all ingrained in my heart and soul and are so special and I have written them down in my own personal journal.)

T̶h̶ We were at the water and could see boats coming from all around to get people out of the city. Finally I guess sometime around 1 we took a ferry over to Jersey City. They packed as many people as they could onto the boat, yet it was stunningly quiet. We all stood and looked towards New York City – a smoldering cloud of o̶f̶ ̶b̶l̶a̶c̶k̶ ̶s̶m̶o̶k̶e̶ ̶&̶ ̶d̶e̶v̶a̶s̶t̶a̶t̶i̶o̶n̶ catastrophe and devastation, – in disbelief. ~~and~~ As we got off the ferry onto the dock in Jersey City, ~~the~~ it was lined with first emergency medical workers to take those in shock or injured, then a row of police men & women and volunteers with trash cans of bottled water and buckets of rubber gloves – for those of us who wanted to help others, but to protect ourselves from diseases transmitted through blood. There was a large office building there that had opened it's doors to everyone coming in from the city. They were bringing desks, phone lines, phones, chairs, food, water coolers, – anything they could into the lobby to help us coming in from the city. The had their employees taking people upstairs to use restrooms, phones, etc.

I remember going to the bathroom where many women all stood soaking paper towels and trying to clean off all the soot from our hair, faces, and necks because it was so irritating to the skin. My skin itched so terribly it felt like it was on fire. I volunteered to call our office and let them know we were okay & try to figure out what we were going to do next. I had pulled out a notepad & pen out of my purse in Battery Park and gotten the first/last names of everyone we were with, our room # at the Marriott, our company names, and emergency family #s – so it made sense that I be the one to go use the phone. Now what made me think to do all that in the midst of such a crisis – I have no idea – good parenting, life experiences? I was calm at this point – so calm I was surprising myself – and spoke with our office to deliver the message. I remember I was on speaker phone with our CEO, VP, CFO, and office manager and Keith – our CEO said to me – 'Anna you sound remarkably calm.' I told him that I just knew that now was not the time to allow myself to become emotional. I had to remain focused so that we could help each other and get through this. I felt so proud of myself – if you can believe it, during the middle of everything – but Keith said to me 'Young Lady, I am certainly impressed with and appreciate your maturity and we will do everything in our power to get you back to us safely.'

I met my group back at the meeting pole in the lobby and tried to figure a plan of what to do next. The room was packed with people. I helped a woman who came in with blood dripping down her face & her baby in her arms. This old man, ~~came~~ struggling to walk & even had soot in his eyelashes came in & I had paper towels & water and helped him. What was so beautiful at such a horrendous time was that everywhere you looked, that's what you saw . . . People helping people. No matter who, what – I think everyone there just loved each other like each stranger was a family member. I always had my pen & notepad in hand just because I felt like we were all too stunned to think clearly, so anything important that we/I needed to remember, I was writing down. At least 3 people came to me in that lobby asking if I was a reporter! The word was already widespread that all flights were grounded and hotel rooms booked. All nearby streets, even in New Jersey were closed to all traffic except emergency vehicles. The sound of sirens was constant. The six of us walked to a location where the busses were operating to pick people up and help them get away from the wreckage.

On the street masses of people were lined up, caked in soot or blood, some without shirts, or shoes, all of us trying to get further away from the city. We decided to make our way towards Newark because our company was trying to get us rental cars there and also my co-worker Paige had family friends that could pick us up there. We finally got a bus to the train station. ~~Wh~~ We were standing as a group trying to figure out which train to get on and I realized there were men in orange vests helping everyone. Since I had my notepad and was writing all of our directions down, I said y'all wait right here under this pole and I'll go ask one of these men what the best route for us to take is. As I was writing down directions, the police came rushing through screaming for everyone to evacuate. Terror more than ever rushed through me – I thought – 'how smart – they new everyone would come to the train stations and now they're going to blow them all up.' I just covered my head and ran as fast as I could, along with thousands of other terrified people out onto the streets. I got pretty far, to the next street corner, and they were shouting it was a scare and for everyone to come back. I couldn't move – I just stood there, exhausted of fearing for my life so many times. And I was by myself – I had lost my group members. Just as the tears started gushing, I remember a rescue worker – and I honestly couldn't tell you if it was a man or a woman – I just remember their blue outfit – coming and holding me and walking me back to the train station to help me find my co-workers/family. I remember saying to look for blue shirts b/c almost all of us were wearing blue shirts and that's when I heard them yelling out my name.

To quickly summarize the rest of the day because I do now realize I've written you all a book – We got on a train & finally made it to Newark where this incredible family helped us & took us to their home. We stayed the night there. Even though they had many bedrooms, Paige and I slept together and held each other the entire night through. We were able to get a rental car and drove the whole 13 hrs. back to Charlotte on Wednesday.

'It is weird now the way that everytime I hear a plane fly overhead, I stop and feel a quick jolt of fear. Or everytime I hear a siren – it triggers a flashback for me. But I realize now that it will take time,' Miller concluded her letter of gratitude. *'I appreciate so very much the constant network and outreaching of support and love I have felt. My Love to each of you – Anna.'*

—— FEATURED SERIES ——
'Iraq'

Commanding Officer Abdul-Mohsen Salman Kazem, serving with Iraq's Sixty-fifth Special Forces Brigade during the Gulf War, outlines the 'Burn and Destroy' tactics his troops must use against Kuwaiti civilians — & — Iraqi officer, Shawai Helu Shamkhi, instructs his comrades to take 'appropriate measures' against a boy caught carrying the Kuwaiti flag during the Iraqi occupation of Kuwait in 1990 — & — Before his hand is cut off in 1995, Nazaar Joudi, detained in the Abu Ghraib Prison in Iraq, assures his wife that 'something good' will come from his punishment — & — Nine years later in 2004, an elated Joudi writes to his wife from Washington DC with a new (prosthetic) hand, attached in the USA — & — After Operation Iraqi Freedom in 2003, an 11-year-old Iraqi girl named Sana begs her aunt overseas to help her leave Baghdad as soon as possible — & — An Iraqi student in Baghdad emails a friend in the USA to convey to him what life is like in Baghdad after Operation Iraqi Freedom in 2003.

What shocked so many who arrived at the scene after the shooting had stopped was the span of the carnage, a seemingly endless procession of scorched vehicles, dead bodies, and millions of dollars' worth of plundered goods scattered in every direction. There was also the smell – a nauseating, sickly sweet combination of smoke, decay, and perfume, tons of it (all stolen from Kuwait), saturating the desert air. The 'Highway of Death,' as it became known, was the result of a massive bombardment by Coalition warplanes on Iraqi troops fleeing from Kuwait in the last days of the Gulf War in February 1991. But despite the casualties, there was little pity from some of the observers. 'We got there after the inferno,' one US Army staff sergeant wrote on March 22 to a friend named Laurie Frost back in the USA.

> *Everything was burned black, The metal of the vehicles and guns rusted where the fire melted the paint and the Humid Gulf air hit the Naked metal. Amid all this was color. Suitcases had burst and bright clothing was scattered everywhere. It's almost impossible to describe. It's something you had to see. They're cleaning it up now. I took some Arab head Scarves off the bodies. I don't know why. But I felt revenge I guess.*

At another point in his letter, which recalled his conversations with Kuwaitis about the Iraqi occupation, the soldier explained to Frost the reason for his anger. (Please note: the following excerpt describes acts of torture in extremely graphic detail.)

> *Saw a lot of horror. Kuwaitis brought pictures to me. Horrible pictures. I saw bodies in the hospital morgues where the Iraqis dumped them – There was NO Refridgeration – NO electricity – I saw thing I will never forget. Things that will be with me forever – Such horror. The IRAQIs were Animals. Not at all human. They'd torture women in the most perverse, sick, ways and then kill them and children– They'd torture babies in front of thier parents – Then kill the parents by torture – What's the point? For what?!*

They took a little girl about 3–5 years old . . . took a drill and drilled holes into her starting at the feet, a hole every 2 inches. The final hole was through the forehead. That one is with me. In my dreams. And I cry for her – even NOW. I don't think I'll write anymore about this cause it hurts too much.

Thousands of Kuwaiti citizens were killed, tortured, raped, and imprisoned by Iraqi troops (primarily the elite Republican Guard), all of which President Saddam Hussein dismissed as lies and propaganda. Some accounts of atrocities disseminated early in the Gulf War were disproved, but the photographs and documents – many by Iraqis themselves – discovered in the detritus of the almost seven-month Iraqi occupation attested to the sanctioned brutality inflicted on the Kuwaitis. Postwar interviews with returning civilians provided further confirmation. Less than a month after the Iraqi invasion of Kuwait in August 1990, as protest rallies and declarations of national pride by the Kuwaitis continued, one Iraqi commanding officer, Abdul-Mohsen Salman Kazem, instructed his troops in no uncertain terms how the citizens should be treated.

In the Name of God, Most Gracious, Most Merciful

Secret and Personal

65th Special Forces Brigade

Date: 1 September 1990

In accordance with the instructions issued by the authorities, please take the measures required by the items below:

1. Burn and destroy all the homes on which there are slogans hostile to our leadership, the pictures of the defunct al-Sabah dynasty, or Kuwaiti flags. This is to be done after evicting the inhabitants.
2. Burn and destroy every district in which any military, security, or Popular Army individual is martyred.
3. Arrest any person who owns, or keeps at his home, a weapon. Post him, along with the weapon, to our headquarters.
4. Annihilate any hostile demonstration.

Notify all officers and fighters of this matter.

Brigadier SF Staff

Abdul-Mohsen Salman Kazem

A message by another officer, Shawai Helu Shamkhi, reveals that Kazem's orders were being followed, regardless of the age of the 'perpetrator.'

Popular Army Command in Kuwait

Kerbelaa II Command

Date: 1/11/1990

To: Sulaibikhat Section

Subject: Information

Comradeship greetings,

At 5:30 p.m., the guards of our HQ gate saw a child carrying a flag of the defunct regime. He was arrested as he was trying to fix it at the Main Street. The flag is fit to fix. We therefore post to you Najiya Hemeid Selim, the child's mother, who lives at a house close to the Main Street. Kindly take them over and take the appropriate measures.

Comrade

Shawai Helu Shamkhi

No one suffered more at the hands of Saddam Hussein, however, than the Iraqi people themselves. He raided Iraq's treasury as his citizens starved; he built palaces as hospitals, schools and electricity and water treatment plants fell into disrepair; and he dragged his country into two major wars during the 1980s and 1990s. An estimated 2–3 million Iraqis in all were killed by Hussein's dictatorial regime, hundreds of thousands of them discarded in unmarked mass graves throughout the country, many of which were unearthed by Coalition troops during Operation Iraqi Freedom (OIF) in 2003. Countless videotapes and documents detailing the executions of Iraqi citizens were also found in captured government offices during the OIF invasion. After learning about one such discovery, a 27-year-old US Army sergeant named Mark Rickert sent the following email from Iraq to his girlfriend, Jennifer, in Tennessee.

A few months ago, [a major with the 490th Public Health Team and his men] explored a building once owned by a special Iraqi police force from the old regime. In this building, the soldiers found a room as big as a movie theater with shelves lining the walls from top to bottom, filled with jars of bundled paper. The old regime evidently used these jars as a filing system. The civil affairs team had a translator with them at the time, and so the major pointed out a jar, opened it, and read the paper inside. The document had a detailed account of one interrogation. Apparently, during the Iran/Iraq war, they captured an Iraqi accused of selling information. The Iraqi police couldn't get any information out of the guy, so they brought in his brother and put a gun to his head. The suspect still refused to talk, so they shot his brother in the head. While his brother lay bleeding on the floor, they brought in his sister. The guy remained silent, and so they sent her to an adjacent room with three or four others where they raped her just in earshot. After that, they brought in the man's mother and little brother. One by one, the Iraqis killed the suspect's entire family, until finally putting a bullet through the suspect's head. The fact that they documented this account is disturbing, but the true horror is that this jar was pulled from thousands of others. The whole place was filled wall to wall, floor to ceiling, with these jars, and each contained a documented case of torture, murder and rape. The major said that this was his defining moment, and he knew he was doing a good thing by being here.

Even before the scandal in 2004 over American abuse of Iraqi inmates at Abu Ghraib, the prison had become notorious within Iraq as a symbol of everything savage and tyrannical about Hussein's dictatorship. Vicious beatings, lynchings and many other forms of torture and execution were conducted on a daily basis. Amputations of hands, feet, tongues and ears were also common, and eyes were frequently extracted as well. In 1995 an Iraqi money exchanger named Nazaar Joudi was arrested for dealing in foreign bills, in violation of Hussein's decree that only Iraqi dinars, although practically worthless, could be used as currency. Joudi was sent to Abu Ghraib, where his right hand was removed and his forehead marked with a black cross, identifying him as a criminal. Joudi was then charged the equivalent of 50 US dollars to cover the cost of the procedure.

On the night before the amputation, Joudi wrote his wife Um Furqaan the following letter. (There is no salutation.)

To every believer there is a sacrifice and there is a price to every sacrifice. The price for this is my right hand. Freedom also has a price and freedom is more valuable than anything. Do not be sad because of what happened to my hand. Hopefully Allah will replace it with an even better one.

I hope you understand that this is Allah's will, so bear with this. God will reward you for standing next to your husband and being my right hand. Behind every great man there is a great woman. Hopefully, something good will come out of this amputation for me and you.

Nazaar Joudi

Miraculously, Joudi's wish would be realized. In June 2003, the journalist and independent documentary producer Don North was working in Baghdad when he heard about nine Iraqi businessmen, including Joudi, whose right hands had been cut off. (One of the men had since died and two had emigrated to Europe.) After a tip from a Texas oil engineer who overheard North talking about the story in a Baghdad café, he contacted the prominent Texas reporter Marvin Zindler, who was known for his philanthropy. Zindler promptly called two local surgeons, Dr. Joe Agris and Dr. Fred Kestler, who agreed to donate their services. Houston's Methodist Hospital volunteered their facilities. The Coalition Provisional Authority, which was governing Iraq at the time, and the Pentagon secured the Iraqis' exit from Baghdad to an airbase in Germany; Continental Airlines let the men fly from Europe to America for free; the Otto Bock Co., which produces prosthetic limbs, provided the men with highly sophisticated bionic hands that normally cost $50,000 each; and Dynamic Prosthetics helped the men learn how to use their new hands. After the operations and two months of physical therapy, the Iraqis traveled to Washington, DC, and Arlington, Virginia, where Joudi placed flowers on the Tomb of the Unknown Soldier. While still in the nation's capital, he wrote the following letter to his wife.

In the name of God, the compassionate, the merciful.

After more than nine painful years, I am able again to use my right hand to write those words to my dearest wife, Um Farqaan. However, this time it is different. I wrote my first letter at Abu Ghraib prison, a few hours before my hand was cut off. That bleak and horrific place. This time I am writing my letter from the most beautiful place in the world, Washington, D.C, the capital of the United States of America. I wrote my first letter back in 1995, full of sorrow and pain. I asked God to provide me with another hand. God responded to my prayer and gave me a new hand. Actually God has given me more than one new hand. He has given me the hands of American friends who offered their friendship, hands of the people in Houston, who assisted us, and the endless care and kindness provided by the best physicians in the world.

Now I am writing these words with happiness, where grief has been converted into joy and gladness. This happiness was provided to me by the people and the government of the United States. Moreover, by their removal of that tyrant Saddam Hussein. So look my wife to the justice of God, how I was in the worst place in the world, and now I am in the most beautiful.

Thank you God.

Nazaar Joudi

May 28, 2004

At almost the exact same time Joudi was composing his letter to his wife in Iraq, an 11-year-old girl in Baghdad was writing to her aunt living in the USA. 'Greeting to the smell of the spring flowers and the beauty of lilies,' the young girl, Sana, began her handwritten letter. But despite the young girl's anticipation of spring, her world – as indicated in the very next line – was one of fear and violence.

I need you to help us move from here because we are dying here and bomb blasts are taking place every day in our neighborhood. The other day there was a bomb blast in front of my school and I almost got killed.

I need for you to save us, and I beg you and if you really love us and care for us as relatives, then you will save us from here. Please call us; it has been days or months that we haven't talked on the phone.

Please, don't come back here because bombings are everywhere. Save us, save

Nazaar Joudi at Arlington National Cemetery in the United States, after his surgery.

us and don't even think about coming back here and stay where you are. For the sake of our family please save us.

Best regards and hoping to hearing from you soon.

Sana

Love you

For countless civilians like Sana (whose fate is unknown), life had become both hopeful and terrifying after Saddam Hussein was forced from power in April 2003. Gone was the ruthless Baathist regime that had murdered millions. Electricity, water and other utilities were gradually being restored and their levels even improved. Schools and hospitals were being rebuilt and repaired. But while the blanket of oppression had been lifted, bombs, shootings, kidnappings and other dangers were becoming everyday occurrences. The most conservative estimates have reported that thousands of innocent Iraqis have been accidentally killed during Operation Iraqi Freedom, and many human rights groups counter that, beginning with the Shock and Awe airstrikes that preceded the ground invasion, the number is in the tens of thousands and possibly over 100,000. Iraqis who supported the removal of Hussein were nevertheless frustrated with the multinational Coalition's inability to establish security in the major cities. 'I think you have heard about the bombing in Kerbala and Al-Kadhim,' an Iraqi high school student emailed an American friend, named Mark von Sponeck, 'those were the most horrible terrorist actions ever.' (His email was written in English and is printed here verbatim. The ellipses are also in the original.) He continued:

> [W]hen we saw the victims on TV, I could see tears in Mom's eyes . . I remained silent and filled with anger . . I was worried about all my friends who could be there too . . our neighbor was worried about her husband who luckily didn't get hurt. One thing is that those attacks failed to start violence between Shia and Suna . . in fact it has caused them to unite . . because everyone realized that this wasn't resistance at all . However many people including me blame the Coalition for all this . . where were they when it happened?!

The student, who wishes to remain anonymous, voiced his fiercest resentment, however, for the Iraqi insurgents and foreign terrorists coming into Iraq through neighboring countries. In a message rife with anguish and bordering on resignation, he vented his feelings about another series of attacks that prompted him to wonder if there would ever be an end to the chaos.

Dear Mark ,

This week has been a week full of pain , difficulty , terrorism and anger .

This week was one of the hardest weeks , probably the hardest of them all .

We have been taking our first quarter exams , in which our teachers are trying to give us questions with a level higher than the other schools, to make us final grade students study hardest .

My daily studying routine starts with returning home at 3 pm because of all the traffic mess . . . and then I would have a nap , watch TV a little . . . then I would study from 7 pm to late night times exceeding 2 am.

The situation has become more tense in Baghdad than ever . . . all I hear is the consequent explosions that come from either Iraqi or American sides against each other.

The worst started on Sunday , when electricity was off , and came after 2 days and a half , leaving Baghdad in darkness all this time.

What made all that was when some 'bastards' hit an oil tube feeding Baghdad with oil, including both fuel for its power plant and its gas stations.

The blackout had a terrible effect on our studying for the exams. I and many other students had to study using oil lamps when our generators are off(because of the lack of fuel , the have to lessen the work hours), while others went to mosques, which have generators .

My school even cancelled an exam on Tuesday because of the students' situation, and because they couldn't copy the exam papers.

The lack of fuel caused the black market of fuel jump with its prices crazily . . .

But the meanest of all these terrorist operations, was putting a bombed bag in a primary school in Karbala (in the south) which exploded killing two children and injuring many . . . is this going to free us ? is it going to let the ones who did go to heaven? Did it at least touch the Coalition ?! No . . . they are a group of ignorant, infidel, wicked and cowardly murderers who love blood and pain. Who refuse to let us live without their master , Saddam Hussein , who is no less than them .

Another thing was putting explosives near the main communication tower in Baghdad. Luckily it was discovered before exploding .

All these attacks ensure that Iraq is becoming a 'Terrorist Hole' in which terrorists are a mixture of Saddam's guys, Foreign extremers and others .

And after all this suffering, still some 'people' are considering all this as resistance! I wonder how could hurting us all that bad is going to 'free' us ! and after all that, the Arab news channels stay silent, not wanting to confess that this is not the resistance they keep talking about , like they did during all the terrorist attacks .

The power finally came on Tuesday, at a bad, yet better than nothing, rate. (2 hrs on – 4 hrs off).

The traffic mess is more and more terrible, my school's minibus was even hit by another car, and you should have seen the peaceful me yelling at the driver of the car which hit us, in a manner that I couldn't believe . . . but I and our driver kept ourselves from saying any bad things, or quarreling, until the IP (Iraqi Police) came . . . they finally took our side and the car is still unrepaired.

The traffic mess is partly caused by the huge number of cars bought and taken to Iraq , and because many of them were bought by people are unqualified for driving , who don't know any driving rules but taking the wrong side, and yelling ! Not to forget the blocks put by the troops for security.

All this has made getting to school very difficult . . it takes the driver an hour and half to come and take us , and the same time to take us home . while it took half an hour to come or to take us home .

The situation been having a very negative effect on us . . . people now would keep wondering about the future, and how will all this end ? what will come out of it? When will we have a day with no explosions, no power off, bad traffic and no lack of security. When will we look at all this and say 'that was in the past'?

We are all waiting for the Festivals following Ramadan . . . which are going to be a good rest for us . . . I hope.

AFTERMATH

Postwar Letters

Elaine Lucille Banks

Towards the end of the War in the Pacific, we were taken out of the classroom under the Student Mobilization Act and sent to a war plant to build balloon bombs. After defeat, we were told that only some of the balloons reached the United States and were useless as weapons having caused but a few forest fires. Then, 40 years after the war, we learned for the first time about what is known as 'The Oregon Tragedy,' involving the loss of six lives. We who at the time were school girls, only 16 years of age, were nevertheless full participants in the war, bringing pain and hardship to others. Such a realization truly sent a chill down my spine. My heart pains to learn that the six victims were Sunday school children on what was meant to be a joyful picnic with a newly-wed minister's wife. These 1,000 cranes were folded one by one by some of us who made the balloon bombs, seeking forgiveness and with a prayer for peace and a vow that the error of the past shall never again be repeated. We pray from afar in Japan that the six victims rest eternally in peace.

> *Tetsuko Tanaka, writing in 1987 to the surviving members of the Mitchell family. In May 1945, during World War II, Mrs. Archie Mitchell and five children were out picnicking on Gearhart Mountain, near Bly, Oregon, when out of curiosity one of the children picked up a 'balloon bomb.' The incendiary devices had been built by the Japanese and floated across the Pacific to start forest fires in the USA. All five children and Mrs. Mitchell died when the bomb exploded in the child's hands.*

On the 26th of April 1937, Guernica was the victim of an aerial attack by the Condor Legion squad, which converted the name of this town into an emblem of belligerence and caught the defenseless population by surprise, turning them into victims of a terrible atrocity. The day of Guernica and the human suffering that its name symbolizes since then form part of the collective memory of our peoples. I want to acknowledge this past and recognize expressly the fault of the German planes involved. To the survivors of the attack and witnesses of the horror, I offer my message of condolence and sorrow. I wish to remember those people whose happy lives were shattered on that day in Guernica, whose families were massacred, whose homes were destroyed. I share your mourning for the dead and the injured. I offer to you all, those who still carry the wounds of the past within them, my open hand as a prayer for reconciliation.

> *Dr. Roman Herzog, President of Germany, writing to the survivors of Guernica, Spain, 60 years after German airplanes had bombed the defenseless city, killing and wounding thousands of men, women, and children.*

Sixty years ago we in Guernica had an unexpected visit. Many of us were still children when men from other lands came, and they dropped a rain of fire, shrapnel and death. And they destroyed our town. That unbelievable act did not leave with us a feeling of hate or vengeance but an enormous, an immense desire for peace that such incidents should never happen again. And that from the ruins of what was our town should surge a symbol of peace for all nations of the world. Today we have another perspective. Once again people from other lands have come to us. They come from the front and with hands extended. Although we speak different languages, we can understand each other. And we are able to do now what then we could not – open our arms and say to them: 'Welcome to Guernica, let us walk together in peace. Ongi etorriak.'

> *Luis Iriondo, representing the survivors of Guernica, Spain, bombed by the Germans in 1937.*

It is a serious experience to be in occupied territory. Immediately the country falls to our arms, we set about establishing a state of just government, order, security and well being. This is no easy job. There are lots of hostile influences at work. The Arab is divided in his allegiance. He will know that any encouragement he gives to us will be repaid by merciless punishment if a turn in fortunes of war should reinstate the Turk. Then again, the Turk is a hard taskmaster but he is a Moslem. Religion has a great influence over the Arab; but our policy is right and must win in the long run. The Turk's plan was to destroy both life and property. Ours is to build up and as time goes on and freedom and security and prosperity are firmly established the old prejudices will die a natural death.

> *Robert Stewart Campbell, an officer with the British Royal Engineers, writing home to his family in 1917 from Mesopotamia (modern-day Iraq) during World War I.*

Lots of very bad people here coming in from other countries with no other purpose than to kill Americans. It is good that they are here and we are keeping them busy so they don't feel that they need to come to the U.S. and kill innocent people. Every military person here is a volunteer and knew (or should have known) what they signed up and were getting paid to do. I am glad that we are here and able to grab some of these creeps before they can do more damage to innocent civilians. Whatever the news says about Weapons of Mass Destruction and lack of evidence, bears little relevance on the dangers that this country posed(s) in the war on terrorism. The focus is misplaced by people who have no idea what is really going on over here. Sorry to wax political. . . . we are doing good stuff here. Getting creeps off the streets and making the world safe for Starbucks. Gotta go babe. . . . Thinking of you Love you!

> *Tyler (last name withheld), a US Navy Seal in Iraq, writing to his wife back in the USA after Operation Iraqi Freedom in 2003.*

British Commander-in-Chief, Guy Carleton, writes a short note of condolence to the mother of one of the last casualties of the American Revolution — & — A French woman who cared for a US soldier felled by disease at the end of World War I assures his mother that he will not be forgotten.

No letter, with the exception of the last message written by their son or daughter, causes more heartache for parents than the one notifying them that their child has died. But this grief is all the more compounded when it comes after major military operations have ended. Accidents, disease, and scattered fighting inevitably claim the lives of troops who had assumed that since they had survived combat, they would be heading home. General Guy Carleton, Commander-in-Chief of all British forces in the Colonies at the end of the American Revolution, is not likely to have known personally the soldier surnamed Freemantle who was killed in October 1782. Nevertheless, he was aware of how the young man's mother would feel on learning that her son had died when the conflict was all but over. (Although the Treaty of Paris, in which Britain agreed officially to end all hostilities and remove its troops from America, was not ratified until January 1784, the British, under General Charles Cornwallis had surrendered to American forces more than two years earlier in October 1781.) On November 8, 1782, Carleton expressed himself with brief but sincere sympathy:

Camp at Long Island

Madam

It is with unfeign'd regret that I must convey to you the melancholy Tidings of your gallant Son's death on the 20th Ultimo. He was perhaps the last Victim of this unhappy Conflict, being slain in a skirmish by a band of Marauders near Charleston in South Carolina while guarding the King's Stores.

Your Son was a good Soldier & an exemplary Youth & the whole

Regiment deplores his loss.

> I am, Madam, with great
>> Respect, Your most Obedt Humble Servt
>> Guy Carleton
>>> Commander-in-Chief

The death of Corporal Carl C. Saunders, who served with the American Expeditionary Force (AEF) in World War I, was doubly tragic; it came just as the war was ending and was the result not of combat, but of a prolonged illness. Recognizing the overwhelming despair his mother would feel on hearing the news, a French woman who had cared for Carl in his last illness sent his mother a heartfelt assurance that her son's contribution was as meaningful as any other, and that his sacrifice had not been in vain.

Vals-les-Bains, France

Dear Madam,

It is a mother who is writing to you, a mother who has been with your dear child in his last days; and it had seemed to me that to tell you a little of his last acts and gestures may soften the bitterness of your grief.

Your son came with the 310th Band to pass a few days at Vals-les-Bains, in the Paris Hotel, of which my husband and I are the proprietors.

The first week I noticed him but little, as they all wore the same uniform; I scarcely distinguished them one from the other. At the end of a week; as a result of an epidemic of grippe, there were many sick in the house who stood about the fireplace, for it was very cold at the time. Then I noticed the little blond, as we called him, not knowing his name. I made hot drinks for him and his comrades, but after two days he preferred to stay in bed. The doctor, at his first visit, did not consider his condition serious, but at a second visit, in reply to my question, he answered, 'It is serious, very serious.' It appears that your dear child had a fall two months before on getting upon a train (or truck) and very serious disorder in the vertical column resulted. After this second visit his condition grew worse, though he was without great suffering. The poor little fellow was drowsy and we had to shake him and talk to him to get him to take liquid.

His comrades were admirably devoted and cared for him as no nurse would have done. He was for them a little brother, whom they petted and spoiled to quiet his pain. He was never left alone day or night and when they saw him depart, they wept like children. How I have regretted that I did not speak English! The doctor having decided an operation was necessary, they decide to take him to Montelimar. His comrades put him into the conveyance, but the poor boy no longer knew what was going on about him so was spared the anguish of saying goodbye. An hour before he left, my husband and I went up to see him and I kissed his forehead in his mother's name, then cut off this lock of hair as a last remembrance, but he noticed nothing.

Well, one thing certain is that though your son was deprived of his mother's care he did not know the commonplaceness of a hospital bed and so long as he was conscious saw about him the faces of devoted friends. The chaplain came to see him before he left.

The American authorities had his body brought back to the cemetery of Vals-les-Bains, where he rests beside several of his comrades.

When I go to see the graves of my own family, I assure you, Madam, that he will have a visit for his mother's sake.

If I can be of any service to you I am entirely at your service. With all my sympathies, I am yours,

> Mme. J. Armand
> Hotel de Paris,
> Vals-les-Bains
> Ardèche

As Europe explodes with joy after the armistice is announced on November 11, 1918, Lieutenant Frank Charles Miller, a Canadian airman, sends a solemn letter to his mother about the costs of World War I.

On the 11th hour of the 11th day of the 11th month in 1918, the war in Europe ended. The jubilation, as recorded in letter after letter, was palpable: 'At about one minute past 11, a yell went up, and our boys and the Germans cheered till they were hoarse. It just echoed through the woods and over the fields,' an American private named Maurice Barnett wrote to his family on November 14, 1918. He continued:

> *Five other boys and myself went over to the German lines to talk with the men we tried to kill and those that tried to kill us. They met us with a salute and a more tickled crowd of men then were those Germans. Some were fifty and sixty years old, some were only young boys.*

A French soldier named Maurius Maillet sent the following to his wife:

> *It's all over, peace has been signed – no more killing – the bugler is playing ceasefire. I'm in Ormont in the Ardennes. I'm leaving this moment for the border. Don't worry anymore. I'm out of danger now. Can't write any more today. A thousand sweet embraces for all of you. And a big kiss for you and see you soon.*

Back on the home front, the celebrations began almost immediately. Just after 2 am (California time) on November 11, an American woman, June Clevenger Miller, sat down and penned a letter to her sister in Illinois:

> *The bells are ringing, the whistles are blowing, the guns are firing, every noise is doing, and every body is out... My! What a peace! What a wonderful consummation. The scope! The millions it effects!... The*

*whole world is shouting tonight, sick or well. And well it might, there
never has been a brotherhood like this before.*

*But amidst the excitement, there was also a somber realization of the
staggering cost of the war to millions of families throughout the world.
Lieutenant Frank Charles Miller (no relation to June, above), a
Canadian who served with the Royal Flying Corps, was in London
recuperating from the flu when the postwar festivities began. In a
letter to his mother, Miller shared his impressions of the days
immediately following 'the war to end all wars.' (Miller's comments
about the Red Cross, who apparently gave his mother erroneous
information about the mail situation, were not consistent with those of
most troops, who expressed a generally favorable opinion of the
organization and its workers.)*

22-11-18

Dear Mother: –

Should you have to decipher this illegible writing it is due to my writing it in
bed. For the past few days I have been an invalid in the camp hospital.
Nothing serious – only a slight touch of the Influenza and a cold in the head.
I was to London last weekend and believe I caught it there. Tomorrow or
perhaps the day after I'll be out flipping about normally again. The only
reason why I told you this, that the character of my handwriting would
create a suspicion and you would accuse me of drunkenness.

Last Friday just before going on leave I received your letter written 21-10-
18. After carefully reading it many times I find answers to the few questions
you ask. Yes, I should be grateful to receive the old Sat. Even. Posts father
discards. And about the Red Cross. It is composed of old bats who have not
sufficient sense to stay at home and attend to their own business. For some
ungodly reason they pretend to know it all regardless of what is asked them.
In the first place I am in the British service – not American; and secondly I am
stationed in England and not in the trenches in France. Why these old fools
give out information that is all wrong is beyond me. Besides, the war is over –
Yanks going back means less mail and packages from America.

Altho the war is over and the Yanks are returning home – two left from our camp – we in the British air service have heard nothing of returning to 'civvies'. It was hinted to us while on parade not long ago that we would be expected to relieve those air men who are at the Front now. Great Britain has an aim towards a large standing air force perhaps on the same scale as her 'silent navy'. Of course I don't mean to say we will be detained for years, but may hold us for six months after duration of the war service. In the army one never knows, you know.

We all want our ticket. The sooner the better. Army life isn't so bad, but one can become so fed up with it. Ever since the Armistice was signed – which means Peace for it leaves the Boche helpless to carry on hostilities, one sees a much more pleasanter Tommy, Bill and his bitter ale, and the big mustache Bobbies on the corners. There's a smile on their faces the first time in years.

One sees all this on visiting London for a weekend. There in Trafalgar Square where stands the Nelson Monument, I saw a merry mob having one hilarious time. They started a small bond fire but it was not very long when the vicinity had been stripped of wood that the flames became a nuisance to neighboring office buildings. I suppose you picture bldgs. such as those downtown fifty stories et cetera. No! Nothing like that here. A six story bldg is considered quite a gigantic affair. Then from Trafalgar Square stroll up along Haymarket or Regent to Piccadilly Circus. There you will find the joy making at its highest. Tommies, New Zealanders, Australians, South Africans, and Canadians, dancing arm and arm with what they have picked up. The girls exchange and wear the soldiers hat and the soldiers wear the girls' hat. Fireworks are displayed frequently, horns shouting freedom, street lamps and show windows show life again, and the people smile, rejoice, a coat perhaps over their suffering.

Now and then one does run up against a most pitiful sight. I was slowly wandering down Pall Mall about to turn into Trafalgar when something attracted my attention in the shadow of a door way. I naturally kept on walking but I curiously watched the object. It was a woman in mourning standing alone weeping softly. She was silently watching the merry making in the Square. Perhaps jealous of those living, enjoying freedom again, while she suffered the loss of her husband, boy, or sweetheart. Sad.

And so it goes. I see that for the short time America has been in the war she has lost 100 000 men. But the American women will not begin to feel the loss of these men like the women of Europe and their losses. Just think mother, over, mind you, over 3 000 000 men gone! Half of New York. A country annihilated. I could never begin, even attempt to write the sacrifice women have made over here. The men have fought the battle at the Front, in the air and at sea, but the biggest battle of all is the one fought at home. The anxiety of every casualty list, starvation, and coupons for cubic inches of fresh air. What a burden the folk of Europe have shouldered! And for what? For what?

To write like this you have just cause to accuse me of melancholy. No! It is not so. But at times I sit in a corner, suck my thumbs, and wonder the why and wherefore's of things.

It is now becoming frosty. I looked out the window not long ago and beheld the roofs and roads were coated white. For the past few days since being in the hospital feeling a wee bit miserable I have observed foggy days. I suppose this is the foggy seasons and if such is the case there won't be much flying. Flying in a fog is no more joyful than sailing the high seas under similar circumstances. Should one ram a boat there is chance of floating but absolutely none should one collide in midair. So flying under misty conditions is not popular among pilots either observers or instructors. So far I have twenty hours to my credit flying time. That is my time over here. Friday I had two forced landings that I will endeavor to narrate in my next letter. You will enjoy reading about them.

> Love to all,
> Your son
> Frank.

> This fountain pen is not doing its bit.

W est Point Superintendent Douglas MacArthur describes to his fiancée an incident that prompted vivid memories from World War I.

To ensure the confidence of the men and women who serve with them, it is considered imperative for those who send troops into battle to project, at all times, a sense of calm and control. 'An officer can <u>have</u> no feeling,' one lieutenant explained to his family in a letter home. 'It is awful to see men you like drop by your side and not be able even to feel sorry. You can't stop for mercy – as the greatest good for the greatest number must be thought of first. If you do stop to think, you become unnerved.' Publicly, few military leaders exuded more strength and authority than Douglas MacArthur. Son of a famous American general, graduate of West Point, and combat veteran of World War I, MacArthur achieved the five-star rank of General of the Army in December 1944, governed the US occupation of Japan, and led all American and United Nations forces in the Korean War from 1950 to 1951. (MacArthur's boldness – or, to many, his brash arrogance – would eventually get him fired by President Truman.) But privately, in the immediate aftermath of World War I, MacArthur confided to those closest to him that the horrible memories of combat haunted him. During World War I, while still in his 30s, MacArthur had served as Chief of Staff of the 42nd (Rainbow) Division, and then commanded the 84th Infantry Brigade as a brigadier general. After the war he became Superintendent of the United States Military Academy at West Point. In December 1921, Ferdinand Foch – the French general who, in the spring of 1918, was given control over virtually all Allied forces – paid a visit to West Point. Foch's arrival provoked a rush of emotions that MacArthur shared in the following letter to his fiancée, Louise Cromwell Brooks.

Douglas MacArthur (centre) and Ferdinand Foch (left)

Winter, 1921

Dearest of Women:

Today Came France – and once more the echo of battle. As he stepped from his train and came forward with the old twist in his eyes, the old bristle in his hair, I felt the clutch at my heart, the thrill in my veins; – it almost seemed as though I could smell again the smoke and blood of my glorious Rainbow! He took me in his arms just as he did of yore, – and for a fleeting flash we were back again in the poppy fields of Flanders.

We have honored him – and he has gone – but my thoughts are back tonight around those stark white crosses where I left my children forever. Bitter, scalding thoughts of those men who were, who followed me to the end with dogged, patient eyes, with white scared faces, with shaking wobbling knees, but coming on, and on, and on to my shout until the red smear stretched them clawing in the mud with my name on their lips, my voice in their ears. How gladly would I lay down my own life if I could only bring them back! My poor, faithful, devoted men! I am on my knees tonight praying God that in His pity He will redeem their souls and bring them at last to that peace which passeth all understanding. And may He be merciful to me who took them to their death.

Douglas

L ila Oliver writes to a friend about the attitudes of the wounded soldiers she sketches as a volunteer artist with the United Service Organisation (USO) during World War II.

Along with the estimated 25 million troops killed in World War II, millions more were forever disabled. Although they made it home alive, they faced a difficult period of rehabilitation that often involved excruciating physical therapy and numerous operations, especially if they were blinded or paralyzed, severely burned, or had lost a limb (or limbs). Confined to a hospital bed for days, weeks, or months at a time, away from friends and loved ones, they also had to overcome constant boredom. Lila Oliver, a 22-year-old graduate of the Philadelphia College of Art, recognized that there was nothing she could do to alleviate the physical suffering of the wounded young men, but through her skills she hoped she could at least help them pass the time more enjoyably. In 1943 she volunteered for the USO's 'Sketching Unit,' which traveled to military hospitals throughout the country to create portraits of the GIs (soldiers). In a letter to a female friend named Terry, Oliver responded to the question of whether or not the patients appreciated her work.

> I suppose they know little about its artistic value, and from that angle I might say no. They care little about a delicate, sensitive line. On the other hand, they do value my coming to the hospital and drawing them. They think the idea is 'swell' and they enjoy the likeness as well as the fact that I draw them in uniform when they are really wearing pajamas. My favorite quip, 'You know, I've dressed more GIs than anyone around here,' always gets a laugh. That's what I am here for, not to be 'arty' but . . . to give the kids an extra chuckle, take their minds off being sick, and maybe flatter them a bit. Nearly everyone confides, 'You know, this is the first time I ever had my pitcher 'etched – hope I don't break the charcoal. . . .'

Oliver was also moved by the way in which the men coped with their ailments. In a letter written just after the war to Terry, whose husband, Allan, was in the service, she commented on the different attitudes she encountered in the wards. She was especially taken by one young corpsman who had been a medic before getting shot in battle.

Dear Terry,

Time skips by. My work, photography, the canteen, and the local hospital sketching trips, all conspire to keep me busy.

That was a grand long letter. More of the same, please. You're thinking, of course, of Allan when you ask if the boys have changed much. Funny thing

– but I don't think they do. Some, having had experiences enough for a lifetime, are older, even have gray hairs. They are a little older, yet have a greater zest for life. Sound contradictory? T'isn't. They've seen much, so they are older, but what they have lived through makes them appreciate each day and each hour. To be sure, I never before knew these individual kids, but among my models are the kind of people I knew. There are the students and jitterbugs, the smart kid, the man-about-town, the college smoothie, everybody's kid brother, the pessimist and optimist (more of the latter), and even Mamma's boy has retained his individuality.

You ask what I think of the boys' coming home changed and different, and, truly, I don't think it happens. They have new ideas, more mature outlooks, enough to make an adjustment a real consideration, but it's my conviction that most GIs bring back the same essential structure of character with which they joined the service. I s'pose others will disagree. Really, the reactions of their families when the boys first come home creates as many problems as the kids bring with them. They want to be treated as normal and left alone. They haven't forgotten what home is like, or how to act among civilians. From the time they shipped over, all the little memories they could gather were held carefully together. The kids haven't forgotten. They'll offer a woman a seat in the streetcar as quickly as some of the people who never left town, without lectures, books of instructions, or ten easy lessons in how to be a civilian. Most of them can't understand why people think they need hints on what to do on their first furlough in the States. They've told me so.

The disabled ones? They want to be treated squarely and honestly. Most of the boys have more courage than I knew existed. If we don't pity and stare sideways with long sad glances they'll be O.K. They need a chance. I say we shouldn't pity them; I didn't say we shouldn't help them; most assuredly we must not forget them. How can we repay the loss of a leg to a twenty-year-old?

I sketched a hospital corpsman, a patient in one of the Atlantic City hospitals, last Sunday. His two roommates had recently been transferred and he was lonely. That's why they sent me in. He was a youngster with the most wonderful disposition and bright red hair, with a cowlick in back that stood straight up. This kid was in the midst of a series of neuro-surgical operations. He told me how it was to be a medic in the European theatre.

Frank Young

Joseph Rancatore

'You stay behind the lines mostly. Then when the guys get hit, why, you just go help them, and then pull'em out. If things get extra tough, you fight, too. Then there's always one guy who does some fool thing, goes out and gets himself hurt, and you go risk your neck to drag him out. Of course, you swear up and down that you won't do it again – isn't your fault if those guys want to take silly chances! But the very next time you go right after'em and do the same damn thing all over again.'

He told me how he got hit.

'We were taking a machine gun nest and there had been a lot of fire. I crawled out to take care of some of our men. Nearby was a wounded Jerry so I inched myself over to give him first aid. He was pretty bad. The Krauts saw me and ceased firing. They waited until I finished bandaging that guy up and then opened up on me – got me in the leg! Naturally, our guys were mad as hell 'cause they could see the whole thing. They took that whole gang and when the few Jerries that were left marched out with hands up they all waited for the one who got me. He was the last one to come out. Then all together our guys yelled to me, "Hey, look, kid!" and all together they gave it to him. We took the others prisoner.'

When I had finished the sketch and he had approved he told me his name. It was Goldblatt. 'Just call me Goldy.'

This had been another long letter. You asked a question which I feel very strongly.

My wisdom tooth is making its presence known – the one on the upper right side. It hurts when I chew and cramps my eating style. I can't even enjoy a good yawn, but I am sleepy. Bedtime.

Love,
Lila

Shaken by his combat experiences in the Korean War, US Private Al Puntasecca asks his family to 'be patient' with him when he returns home — & — Olwyn Green writes a final love letter to her husband Charlie, who served in both World War II and the Korean War.

Physical injuries do not yield the only scars of war. There can be internal afflictions as well that many – though certainly not all – combat veterans carry with them after their service, from spells of sudden, overwhelming sadness to persistent and life-threatening depression. Upon coming home, they are often confronted with a world that is radically different from the one they have just left. They might experience pronounced mood shifts, sharing feelings of helplessness and vulnerability one moment and becoming distant and uncommunicative the next. Only those who have been under fire can truly understand how searing the experience can be, and how deeply it can wound even the most resilient and mature individuals. After surviving a year of harsh conditions and bitter fighting in Korea from 1952 to 1953, a 19-year-old private from New Jersey named Al Puntasecca learned that he was finally returning to the USA. Puntasecca had served in an artillery outfit with the 25th Infantry Division, 44th Battalion, A Company, and the work was thunderously loud (he permanently lost part of his hearing) and extremely dangerous. Before embarking on the long journey back home, Puntasecca sent a letter to his parents and two siblings, Bud and Emily, forewarning them that he was – and probably would remain – a changed man. (MIA means 'missing in action'.)

Dear Everybody,

I'm coming home! It's official as of this morning. It will be some time before I crash in your door, a few weeks, maybe, but, I'm coming home! Remember I told you how seasick I was on the way over here? Well, I can't wait to do it again.

That little house is going to look like a palace to me and, you people like Kings, and, Queens. People who love you. A clean place to live. A clean place to live <u>life.</u> To sleep in a what do you call it, bed? yeah, that's it, bed. Running water. Hot meals. And, what's this I hear about people having private bathrooms, and, private showers? Really? Is it true some people eat three times a day, or, more? and, they sit on a <u>chair,</u> by a <u>table.</u> What's the matter, can't they dig a hole in the back yard like everybody else? A place where you can close your eyes any time you want to, no more 90 day wonders, no more Sargeants with Patton complexes, 'All right, you bastards! Off, and, on.' No more this! No more that! So, ma, put the spaghetti on right now. Plenty of sauce, and, a ton of sausage. And, Pepsi! A 50 gallon drum! Yeah, and, 10 lbs of cheese.

Bud, remember you beat me up everytime the Yankees lost? or, your horse lost? or, you lost? or, the day after Sunday was Monday? I think we'll get along much better from now on. Emily, you get busy on that brass band, and, ticker tape parade. Nothing fancy. What Ike had is O.K. It is going to be hard being civilized again. What the hell ever civilized means, so, don't be surprised if you think you have a savage in the house for a while.

Yeah. I'm looking forward to seeing you again, but I'm in no hurry to see the expressions on your faces when <u>you</u> see <u>me.</u> I want to see you try to hide the shock on your faces. You might even ask me for proof I'm your son. Don't feel bad. I see it in my own face every day. I have spent 12 months over here. The longest 30 years of my life. A short time ago I was 18, and, all I was worried about was cars, girls, and, how much beer a <u>real man</u> could drink. No more. Don't get me wrong. I still want a hot car, a hot girl, and, a cold beer, but, there were times I could have traded them all for a warm blanket. A wool hat. A pair of gloves, or, ear muffs. another pair of socks. A shoelace. A goddamned <u>shoelace!</u> There were times I would have traded my soul for a drink of cold water, or a cup of hot coffee. But, I am coming home now. Chuck isn't. He's listed M.I.A. If he's on this side of the line I hope he makes it. If he's on their side I hope he's dead. He'd wish the same for me. Leon is dead. His girlfriend killed him. Stabbed him in the back while he was facing the Gooks.

How many guys have been killed in wars? How many not born because they were killed? Did it start with Cain, and, Able? The caveman? Who? Does it matter? And, for <u>what</u>? What? Has anything changed? Will anything change? No, Never. So what do we do? <u>Nothing!</u> If something could have

372

Private Al Puntasecca

been done I'm sure somebody would have done it. All we can do, all anybody can do is try to understand. I can't hear as well out of my left ear anymore. The 105 is no slingshot. Something about the big cells of the ear crushing the small cells of the ear further, and, further in until it makes a blockage. I hear what you're saying all right. It just takes time to get to where I can <u>understand</u> it, so, be a little patient, okay?

You know, it's almost funny, we see a guy in a wheel chair, a guy on crutches, one arm, hooks for hands, and, we break our backs trying to help him. But, what about the wounds you can't see? The phantoms, the nightmares, the ghosts in your head? I am going to tell you now. you'll need a lot of patience with me. Patience, and, understanding. We all will. See you soon. See you soon. See you soon.

Jr.

Regardless of whether their loved one is gone forever or returns home a noticeably different person, the spouses, family members, and friends of servicemen and women often undergo their own postwar healing and adjustment period as well. Born December 26, 1919, in South Grafton, Australia, Charlie Green joined the militia at the age of 16 and went on to fight in World War II, first as an infantry officer and then as the commander of an entire battalion. His young wife, Olwyn, longed for his homecoming with great expectations after years of anxious waiting. Their relationship remained strong and loving, but Charlie, as his wife soon discovered after his return, was not the same. The man who had written passionate love letters during the war was now taciturn and often seemed uncomfortable around other people. The battalion commander who earned the Distinguished Service Order found himself struggling to start a farm. He was restless. He missed the camaraderie of his mates and the life-and-death significance of their missions. In June 1950 the Korean War erupted, and, much to his wife's dismay, Charlie was eager to join the fight. 'Racehorses will gallop,' was his explanation. In September he was appointed the commanding officer of the 3rd Battalion, Royal Australian Regiment. On September 12, while in transit to Korea, Charlie sent his first letter

Charlie Green playing with his daughter Anthea and their dog Sandy.

home: *'The trouble is not as bad as you would believe,'* he wrote to Olwyn, *'in fact it's rather more like civil war and with our unit we will have little to worry about.'* Just over two weeks later he was in Korea, and the tenderness he had so frequently expressed in his World War II letters appeared once again. *'How are you keeping my sweet and Bubby too of course,'* Charlie wrote on October 27, referring to their three-year-old daughter Anthea.

> *I do hope you are well and as happy as can be. We have only about another twenty miles to go to our final objective and after that the thing should be over. . . . God bless you my darling and keep you well. I love you more than ever and hope that we are together again in a little while.*

Before Olwyn received his letter, the local telegram boy came bicycling up to their house in Grafton carrying a pink envelope. She stood frozen on the front step. *'Regret to inform you that your husband, 2/37504 Lieutenant Colonel Charles Hercules Green,'* it began, *'was wounded in Korea Stop Suffering from shrapnel wound . . .'* Although there was reason for hope – he was 'only' injured – Olwyn knew that her worst fears had been realized. At about midnight the next evening, after an agonizing wait, she received the notification that her husband was in fact dead, killed during a Chinese artillery attack. He was 30 years old. Decades later, Olwyn Green sat down and relived their relationship through all of his letters that she had preserved, but, until that time, had not reread. In 1992, and living in Sydney, Olwyn Green penned one last letter to her husband.

Sydney 1992

My dearest Charlie,

It's a long time since I've written you. I didn't think you would get any messages. Now I am not so sure.

You see, I've been going over the past. I went back over your life before you met me. I loved doing that. That picture of you as a lad reminds me so much of what Anthea was like as she grew up. I've been dwelling on the

376

short but rich time we had together. The good times were wonderful, weren't they? It all seemed like yesterday and you were so vividly present. Then I had a dream about you. That's why I felt I should write.

I think I have learned a lot, my darling. There's no point in questioning or regretting the past. It's gone. For years I worried about what happened to us. One thing doesn't frighten me any more. It is Time. Time doesn't exist. We make a big mistake in measuring it out in minutes or years, or in past or future. Our marriage was a lifetime. And the couple of frightening occasions when I saw into the future have made me realize that maybe, once in a while, we are permitted a glimpse of infinity. I think it is fear that prevents us from seeing into the future – or from seeing straight. It is forty odd years since I saw you, but they seem to have disappeared.

Lately, I've stopped having the bad dream that you were so far away and couldn't get in touch with me. I hated that dream I had over and over again. I could never understand it.

As I said, the other night I dreamt about you. It was a very different dream. You came close to me. Then a very strange, bright light shone down on the left side of your face, illuminating it so that I could see your eyes. The light showed me the tears in your eyes. That woke me up. I can't bear to think of you crying. Please don't cry. There must be no more tears – yours or mine. There is no need for us to cry. What we shared was too beautiful to cry about. And though we failed in a way, God knows, we tried.

I am not young any more, Charlie. I have wrinkles and grey hair. That youthful beauty you told me to preserve has gone. I still have a fair bit of energy, though. I've needed it when I have been minding those grandchildren of ours.

I feel a kind of mellowness now. And I don't have that physical ache for you that I used to suffer so strongly. In fact the way I feel keeps bringing a line from Keats to my head: 'Season of mists and mellow fruitfulness.' That is exactly how I feel. Remember how I love poetry. I can't stop it from running through my head. That's how we got Anthea's name.

I worked and saved to fill the years. Now I can enjoy these autumnal days. I feel content, and, yes, I feel rich, even though I've never filled the gap you left. It wasn't an empty gap. I've always had your love to sustain me.

What I look forward to is seeing our two grandsons grow into manhood.

They are beautiful boys. The younger one is the image of Anthea when she was little, in looks and in a determination to carve an individual path in life. Anthea's path took many deviations before she resolved into her true, exceptional self. Your daughter has your strength. The elder one is like me in his ways, some people say. In appearance, he is like you – handsome.

In all those hundreds of letters I wrote to you, I always told you how much I loved you. I probably didn't tell you: You are the finest human being I have ever known.

Please be at peace and remember that I've always loved you.

Your loving wife,
Olwyn

Abdul Hameed Al-Attar, a Kuwaiti whose son was imprisoned during the Iraqi occupation, sends a message through the Red Cross in a final, desperate effort to find his son alive.

During the Iraqi occupation of Kuwait that began in August 1990, thousands of Kuwaitis were imprisoned for 'crimes' as minor as joining a protest march or displaying the national flag. They were interrogated, tortured, and, in many cases, brutally executed, especially if they were believed to be members of Kuwait's armed forces. After the country's liberation in February 1991, the terms of surrender accepted by the Iraqi regime in March demanded the return of all POWs (or their remains). A month later, United Nations Resolution 687 stipulated specifically that

> *in furtherance of its commitment to facilitate the repatriation of all Kuwaiti and third country nationals, Iraq shall extend all necessary cooperation to the International Committee of the Red Cross [ICRC], providing lists of such persons, facilitating the access of the International Committee of the Red Cross to all such persons wherever located or detained and facilitating the search by the International Committee of*

378

the Red Cross for those Kuwaiti and third country nationals still unaccounted for. . .

Approximately 6000 Kuwaitis were repatriated in the weeks following the cease-fire. But in April Iraq claimed there were no remaining prisoners and refused to cooperate with the ICRC's efforts to account for every POW. In February 1993, Kuwait presented documented evidence that 570 of their citizens, including more than 120 students, were still missing. (Thirty-five foreign nationals who had been living and working in Kuwait had also disappeared.) The family members of these prisoners held out hope that, in time, the missing POWs would be found alive in Iraq. One Kuwaiti, Abdul Hameed Al-Attar, had last heard his son Jamal's voice when the boy cried out for him while being held in a Kuwaiti police station, which had been converted by the Iraqis into an 'intelligence center.' Four years later, his father made one last attempt, through the ICRC, to get a letter to his son, wherever he might be.

Dear Son Jamal,

Today is September 13, 1994, and four years have already passed since we lost your trace, exactly four years have gone since I received that telephone call informing me about your arrest by the Iraqi soldiers on that afternoon.

My Dear Son Jamal, four years have passed but your voice is still shaking in my head from when I went to Rumaitheya police station trying to get you out or at least know your condition, but the Iraqis denied that you were there or knowing anything about you. Then moments later you heard my heated argument with the Iraqi soldiers and called me saying, 'Father father I am here!' and then I heard you screaming from the pain when they began lashing and hitting you, and then your voice vanished to this day.

My Dear Son, so far the Iraqis are strongly denying the existence of any Kuwaiti prisoner in Iraq, but they offered the possibility of some missing Kuwaitis still wandering somewhere inside Iraq but afraid to show themselves up, so I and members of the family are still hoping that this story is real, but yet if this is the case, how will this letter reach you?

Even so I must tell you that your mother is still keeping your personal belongings in your room, checking them every morning as if you will be coming soon (probably today or tomorrow) she says with tears pouring from her red eyes, and she always repeats your jokes which you used to tell us from time to time, but instead of laughing she cries and then weeps and wails, and we all share her sadness and sorrow for your long absence.

My Dear Jamal, if you receive this letter from the ICRC read it with full confidence in yourself and trust in mighty God that he is with you and with every person on earth all the time, and be assured that we and all of the Kuwaiti people will never, never forget you or any of your mates. Have confidence in yourself that you are great in all circumstances and even if you die – 'May God forbid that' – you and your other missing or prisoners will forever be our national pride.

You will remain in our minds and hearts forever. May God be with you, dead or alive.

We miss you.

Your sad father on behalf of all the family.

When Coalition forces invaded Iraq in the spring of 2003, many family members of the missing POWs prayed that their loved ones would be discovered still in confinement – but at least alive – in Iraqi prisons. Tragically, not one was found.

Captain Peter Caddick-Adams, serving with the UN peace-keeping forces in Bosnia and Herzegovina, describes Christmas celebrations in 1996 in battle-scarred Sarajevo to a friend back in England.

Although their efforts tend to receive less attention than those of the frontline troops who charge into battle, the role of United Nations, NATO, and other peacekeeping forces is equally critical to the world's security. They, along with civilian aid workers, are responsible for maintaining the often fragile cease-fires in nations plagued by violence, thereby ensuring that the hard-won peace does not unravel in the months and years to follow. In addition to stabilizing the region, by force if necessary, they provide medical assistance and supplies for the sick and wounded, monitor elections, prevent human rights abuses, train native police forces, rid the area of land mines, and assist with countless other duties to bring humanitarian relief and protection to those in desperate need of both. Casualties are rare, but they do occur. Hostile acts represent the second most common cause of death after accidents, which are frequently the result of vehicle-related fatalities on battered and unsafe roads. During the 42 months of warfare in the Balkans, which began in 1991, hundreds of thousands of Bosnian Muslims and Croatians were killed by Serbian troops, and a million more became refugees. The 1995 Dayton peace agreement brought a tenuous cease-fire, and tens of thousands of NATO troops were sent to serve, first as an 'implementation' force – known as IFOR – and later as a 'stabilization' force, SFOR. One of the SFOR soldiers, a captain with the British Army named Peter Caddick-Adams, wrote vivid accounts detailing his experiences in Bosnia and Herzegovina. The following letter, addressed to a friend in London two days after Christmas in 1996, is laced with humorous observations about military life and the inevitable clash of cultures when international forces work together, but it also accentuates the heartbreaking conditions the citizens of Sarajevo had endured for almost four horrific years.

Dear Nigel

Christmas morning dawned with not a flake of snow in sight. We'd had some earlier in December, & plenty of the white stuff was forecast, but so far, our gathering of the world's most qualified military meteorological experts had failed to come up with the goods. I had reasoned that if there was one place on earth that could guarantee a white Christmas, it would be Sarajevo. First call of the day was to our headquarters on the far side of the city for a Festival of Nine Lessons and Carols. Organised by our transatlantic cousins, the service was in fact a competition to cram in as many carols as possible – the final tally was fourteen, at which point my voice gave out. The cousins changed the tunes of several favourites, & introduced a carol new to me, to the tune of Greensleeves (thumbs down). The congregation were the English speakers of SFOR, & included a few brave Germans & Dutch. Americans have a thing about singing holding lighted candles, so we provided a fair rendering of Silent Night to the accompaniment of burning hymn-sheets, treading the hot wax into the carpet. Events like this have to be recorded by US television, & I must admit I got rather irritated by the pop of flash bulbs in my face as I tried to put meaning into See Amidst the Winter's Snow, but a glance outside confirmed that there was still none of the white stuff.

The carol service in Sarajevo Cathedral on Christmas Eve was one to remember. This was organised by the Wehrmacht &, although advertised as an English-German service, only two words of English in fact surfaced – Hape-ey Cvist-mase. They'd have done better to stick to Latin. The Wehrmacht had been ordered to attend 'in a voluntary capacity', & neat rows of them appeared in full kit, as though hot foot from Nuremberg Torchlight Prayer Meeting. These days, they wear a leopard-spot camouflage uniform with matching field cap, looking for all the world like an earlier generation who distinguished themselves so well in Normandy, Arnhem, & in The East. I sat next to Oberfeldwebels Steiner, Kruger & Heinrich. This is, of course, their first operational deployment since 1945; perhaps it is fitting that they should return to a campaign 'where the iron crosses grew'. Some of them are excellent coves, if humourless. I seem to have found a fellow soul in one of their majors, the second in command of a battalion in the 10th Panzer Division, who has just completed a history of his division 'in the old days'. ('The only scrap we missed was Poland, until you captured us in North Africa in '43. You know, von Stauffenberg was one of our staff officers.') Christmas Eve's service was memorable by some excellent Handel and Mozart on the Cathedral organ, & singing Still Nacht, Heilige Nacht, in candlelight. It's one carol that sounds so much better in its original German, and has echoes of communal singing in the trenches, during the 1914 Christmas Truce. German camera crews recorded the service & I gather I made an appearance on Christmas day television in the

Fatherland, alongside the singing Oberfeldwebels. The standard of celebratory fire (point your gun in the air & empty the magazine) is not what it used to be in Sarajevo. Time was, a year or two ago, when you could sit on the rooftops and watch the most spectacular fireworks modern armies could buy. Tracer arching up to the heavens, artillery rounds and signal flares popping all over the place. Last year I gather Christmas Eve was spectacular. This year, I counted fifteen rounds fired from a machine gun nearby, and that was it – bit of a damp squib, if you ask me. Expecting better on New Year's Eve.

Time for Christmas lunch. First, in time honoured tradition, serve the chaps – not many of them, as this HQ is all chiefs and no indians. Then the generals (no shortage of them) served us. Catering for so many nationalities, the menus were rather mixed up, and I ended up a plate of roast beef, turkey, ham, mint sauce, and chips ... Onto pudding, and the (Bosnian) chefs had made an outstanding effort with the British Christmas pud – done to a crisp ... A pneumatic drill required to tackle the outer case, and a drinking straw the interior, which was as molten lava. A glance outside, and yes, the white stuff was tumbling down, and by evening a very respectable four inches had accumulated. Her Majesty's annual broadcast being sadly unavailable, I made do with a showing of Independence Day, & a bucket of pop corn, courtesy of the cousins, in the office next to mine – yes, we carried on working, and in uniform. Being predominantly Muslim, the city carried on too. I spotted just one Christmas tree, and two festively-dressed shop windows in a walk around town on Christmas Eve; rather a refreshing change from an English high street at this time of year. No invitations to challenge the national debt, or over-consume. Unfortunately, the Christmas spirit did not dissuade some fundamentalist Muslims in Sarajevo from deciding that Santa Claus threatened Islam, and that the solution was to mug any Croat Father Christmases they encountered. We at the Residency have all received greetings cards from American primary school children. Delightful creations in crayon and pencil, mine from Amy (six-and-a-half), contained a picture of a man with a gun (me, I presume) & the message 'Hpaay Crsmas Sowder, Com Hoame Safe'. As I write, the snow has accumulated to a very ski-able fourteen inches, with the overnight temperatures plunging to minus seventeen. I'm sure the novelty of so much of the stuff will soon wear off, but for now, Sarajevo is a vignette from a Brothers' Grimm fairy tale – some pretty, winding cobbled streets, a jumble of ancient, half-timbered houses, with steep pitch roofs, all laden with snow, glistening icicles & snow-dusted pine trees on the hills beyond. This is the first Christmas the Sarajevans will enjoy since 1991. Last year, although at peace, they were still suspicious that the fragile Dayton Peace Agreement would fail, and were just recovering form the siege, lifted in October. One of our interpreters told me the story of her sister & the camel hair coat. Sister gave birth to her second child in the winter of 1993. She ran out of fuel to heat her house, and wood was too expensive. Spare furniture & every nearby tree or bush had already been sacrificed to the hungry stove. To provide warmth, she decided to burn her best camel hair coat. It burned slowly, but well enough to provide warmth all one weekend, & long enough to bake a week's supply of bread. The coat meant a lot to her, & her face was wet with tears all weekend whilst it burned – it was her last luxury, the final ink with civilisation. She doesn't want another, because it will remind her of the four-year siege, & of the child who died of hypothermia afterwards. On a lighter note, I discovered that our (four-star) general, commanding SFOR, has only brought two books with him, to last for the whole of the operational tour – & he's already coloured one of them in! We had a major scare the other day. One of our jet pilots reported he had a 'lock-on' from a ground radar. Such events in a pilot's life are rare, for they're usually followed by a ground-to-air missile, & instant death. Our chap took evasive action, and escaped. We shouted at the Serbs, threatened the Muslims & swore at the Croats, but all claimed innocence. Then we found the culprits: two military policemen who'd got bored with zapping speeding Landrovers with their radar gun, and pointed it at a passing jet. I must extend my thanks to those of you who sent me Red Cross parcels. The files in the Christmas cake will be most useful, as would have been the miniature compass in the mince pie, had I not eaten it. I'm looking forward to experimenting with the sewing kit to turn my issue blanket into a guard's dress uniform, but unfortunately, the ink of the escape map printed on the silk handkerchief ran, and I now have obscure parts of Hungary over my nose. Please, are the fake identity papers & bank notes in the Gentleman's Relish, Belgian chocolates or the marmalade?

With the very best wishes for Christmas and the New Years.

Back Feb. 5th.
Hope all is well.

                                                                    Peter

Separated from his mother in South Korea for 50 years, a North Korean man named Kim Sung Ha is given permission to write her a single letter.

What was remarkable about the short, sweet love letter by a husband to his wife was not only its lyricism and beauty, but that it represented their first communication in five decades. 'I wish I could meet you my sweetheart,' 79-year-old Kim Kyong Bin wrote to Song Il Soon. 'If I were a bird, I would fly and sit on a branch of a tree in our garden and pour out my heart.' In one of the most terrible legacies of the Korean War, which destroyed countless lives, an estimated 7–10 million family members were permanently separated from one another during the chaos of the fighting. North Korea's Communist regime prevents its citizens, like Song Il Soon, from traveling where they choose or communicating with whom they want, regardless of whether one is a spouse, child, or parent. They are trapped in their own country. Kim Sung Ha, the second oldest son of a family with 10 children, was a young man studying for his postgraduate degree in Seoul when the North invaded the South in June 1950. One day during the war, he simply vanished. His family later learned that Communist troops had taken him by force. Two other siblings, Chang Ha and Ok Hee, disappeared as well. As time passed – months, years, then decades – the family feared the worst. And then, in January 2001, the Kims were notified that Sung Ha and his brother and sister were, in fact, still alive and had been living in North Korea all these years. In March, the two Koreas negotiated an agreement allowing several hundred people to exchange letters with a loved one on the other side. (The

South Korean participants were chosen by a computer lottery; the North would not reveal its process.) Sung Ha had been granted permission to write to his mother, who lived in South Korea and was 101 years old. North Koreans fortunate enough to be selected for this mail exchange had to include enthusiastic praise for the 'love and generosity' that their Dear Leader, Kim Il Sung (who ruled from 1948 to 1994) and his son and successor, Kim Jong Il, had bestowed on them. (The fact that Kim Sung Ha, whose underlying anguish is evident throughout his letter, has not been able to communicate with his own mother for half a century speaks to how loving and generous the Dear Leader was toward his citizens. Kim also did not know he had three other siblings, born after he was taken to the North.) On March 5, 2001, Kim, now in his 70s, wrote the following.

Dearest Mother,

The much-awaited, but unbelievably surprising news came today that you are still alive. Until now, I have worried day and night. Last night I couldn't sleep because I was thinking of you. For the first time in 50 years, my heart is beating so hard as I write this letter to you.

We have been apart for 50 years! I can't even describe how much I have missed you. I can only imagine your pain of not knowing the whereabout of your children.

Among seven children, you loved me dearly. I vividly remember as a kid following you everywhere from one room to another, wanting to be with you all the time.

I have been living comfortably under the warm care by our leader Kim Il Sung. Words cannot describe the love and generosity I have received from him.

I always thought of you when I had a joyous occasion in my life, such as meeting our great leader Kim Il Sung in college, receiving a watch engraved with the name of the great leader, and receiving a Ph.D. I wish I could make you proud of me in those moments. The nation took good care of me.

Mother, please forgive this son who couldn't even send you a letter for such a long time or buy you nice clothes and warm meals on your birthday

I miss you Mother.

Kim Min Ha

My two siblings in North Korea are living comfortable lives under much love and care of our great leader Kim Il Sung and Marshall Kim Jong Il. Do not worry about us.

Ok Hee, Chang Ha, and I each have several children who all went to college and have decent jobs. We all get together in one house and spend time together during national holidays and vacations. I always feel great sorrow because of you and my other brothers and sisters in the South.

I am already over seventy years old and have grey hair, but I am healthy and currently working as a professor. I have the great leader Marshall Kim to thank for that.

How are Min Ha, Ok Nae, Ok Leo, Ok Hwa, and Shin Ja doing in South Korea? No matter how much time goes by or how things change over the years, I can never forget the days in your arm with my siblings. Thanks to the great leader Kim Jong Il, I received the opportunity to write you this letter. Now I firmly believe that I will be able to meet you in person in the very near future.

As your son, I will continue to live honestly in the North. I promise you won't be disappointed in me when I finally see you in person, as our two nations become one.

I don't know where to begin and what to start with. There are so many things to tell you and fill you in on.

Today, I will end here. Please take care of yourself and be healthy. I also wish health and happiness for my younger siblings in the South. I enclose two photos.

From your son,
Kim Sung Ha

Kim Min Ha, one of Sung Ha's younger brothers, received the letter and read it to their mother. She died the following month. Kim Sung Ha never had the opportunity to see her again.

A refugee from Afghanistan, Masuda Anna Mohamadi, returns to her homeland in 2002, and describes her impressions of the war-torn country in an email to her friends.

When tens of thousands of Soviet troops invaded Afghanistan in December 1979, the Soviets claimed they were 'invited' by the existing Communist government to crush a growing insurgency of Muslim fundamentalism. The Soviet's ferocious bombardment of Afghan towns and villages sparked a refugee crisis of astonishing proportions. Millions of Afghan men, women and children fled to neighboring Pakistan and Iran. A six-year-old girl named Masuda Anna Mohamadi escaped from Afghanistan with her family and made it to the USA, ultimately settling in Virginia. In 2002, after the US-led Operation Enduring Freedom (OEF) toppled the Taliban regime, which had been ruling Afghanistan since 1996 (the Soviets having left in 1989), her father Mohamadi decided to return to Afghanistan and become a teacher. The rest of the family joined Mohamadi in October 2003. Twenty years of ceaseless violence had devastated the country, and Mohamadi, in emails to friends back in the USA, chronicled the range of emotions she experienced after returning to the country of her birth. The following is dated November 14, 2002.

Dear friends,

Satar is one of the men who guided us through the mountains 23 years ago. He is handsome with dark eyes, a thin tan face, and a peaceful and gentle disposition. He ate dinner with us at my uncle's house. After he left us at the border of Pakistan in 1979 he began fighting with the mujahedin. I asked him to tell me stories about his life and he leaned back and began speaking.

He told me about the night the soviets were bombing Jaji daily and the villagers fled to the mountains. They set up camp in crevices along the rocks and used logs and leaves for shelter. It began to rain one night and the mountain streams flooded their hideouts. Satar had been shot in the arm and his elbow was shattered. He held onto his children with one hand while his broken elbow rested against his chest. By morning dozens of people were missing swept away by the water but the villagers couldn't go down to the fields in the daylight because of the bombings. They waited until the next night to search for their relatives and bury them in the dark.

Satar's elbow ached and he went to find the village doctor. The doctor told him to find some fish and hold the meat against the wound until the bones softened a bit and then the doctor would set the arm in place. Satar replied, 'How am I going to catch a fish when bombs are falling from the sky?' Satar walked to Pakistan where a doctor took an x-ray and fixed his arm.

During another battle Satar was with my uncle Abdul, who had been shot in the thigh. Satar tried to carry Abdul but he was too heavy. He hid my uncle in the mountains and he went to look for a donkey to carry Abdul out. As he was walking past a field he saw hundreds of dead bodies. He had to be careful not to step on them. They were Afghan soldiers employed by the Soviets. He said the dogs were eating the bodies because they lay rotting for so long.

I asked him if he had nightmares from the war. He said, 'When I first started fighting all the spit in my mouth went dry from fear but after a few years it was just a part of life. Nothing scared me. I fought the soviets but after they left I stopped. I am at peace with what I have done.'

My uncle Abdul (Zahir's younger brother) had been sitting in the room as we talked along with four women and six children. We had all eaten dinner together on the floor, digging into the same bowls and plates of rice, spinach, kidney beans, and salad with our hands. After dinner we drank tea and ate baked chickpeas sprinkled with red pepper and I listened to more stories. The men, women, and children sit with each other and they listen to each other, make fun of one another, yell at the children, eat, tell stories, hug and pinch, and so much cursing. They share a love that is real and raw. In the house they don't have a television, furniture, beds, electricity, or toys or books for the children but they laugh so much and with so much life. I am so fortunate to sit with them.

Abdul always ends the night with a few sarcastic remarks. This one is his favorite, 'I almost lost my life trying to save Afghanistan and all anybody wants to know now is if I can speak English and work a computer. God damn all of you.'

much love,

maso

Ten days later, Mohamadi described her visit to the prison where he father, who had worked in the Afghan government, had been confined during the Soviet invasion in 1979.

Dear friends,

We started our English classes today but mine won't start until Saturday because there isn't any heat in the room. We sent out notices to the students this morning at 8 to show up at 8:45 so you may guess that not too many showed up today but tomorrow is another day. The bathroom in the hallway doesn't work, the toilets are dry and dirty with missing seats, faucets caked with mud, trash on the floor, no running water but there is a beautiful sign on the front door that says toilet.

I'm hungry and I still have ten more days to go until the end of Ramadan. When I get hungry I get cranky and irritable and when I go home at 2 I sit in front of the oven and eat until I feel like passing out.

On Friday I went for a drive with my mom and sister. Our driver is a sturdy man named Abdullah who carries an automatic rifle at all times. We headed to pul-i-charki, the place where my father was imprisoned for 8 months 23 years ago. We followed a paved road that led us out of the city for a long time and then turned right into a narrow dirt road lined with market stalls filled with radishes, long spring onions, and fat cauliflowers. It's the end of November but the days are still warm, the sky blue and sunny. As we neared the prison it looked as I had imagined it. It's strange to visit places that I have written about but never seen. The walls were lower than I thought, all stones, with the watchtowers crumbling.

At the front gate five soldiers stopped us. My mother rolled down her window and said that her husband was imprisoned here and that her daughter wanted to see the place. They looked at each other with strange glances and one of them even smirked. They said usually we don't let anyone in but since you are women and you have traveled from so far we'll give you a tour. The driver was hesitant because they wouldn't let him drive in and he didn't want to leave the car alone. My mother and sister stayed in the car and the driver, his rifle, and I walked in with four soldiers.

The prison was emptied out after the fall of the Taliban. My father had been kept in block 2, which was at the far right end, and the driver didn't want to go that far so we went into the first building on our path. There was a mile long heap of rusted buses, cars, and metal. Once inside the building, we went up three flights to a hallway with tiny individual cells which had metal bars for doors. There was also a large room with huge metal bins that were used for washing clothes. Water dripped in through the walls and the floors were wet, the ceilings low. We went into another hallway lined with cells and I stared out the thin, triangular window. On the cell window I saw a rusty lock. I grabbed it and held onto it. I asked them where the torture room was. They said those rooms were hidden in places they couldn't even find and once they found them they couldn't get out.

We walked outside again and the entire place was eerie. During my father's time close to 60,000 men were imprisoned here and many of them killed. The prison is in the middle of a dusty field and if you look out you see huge dents in the ground possibly from the massive graves.

A heavy energy rested inside of me as soon as I arrived there and it hasn't quite left. I think there are thousands of ghosts in and around pul-i-charki seeking justice or peace.

I was disappointed I didn't see the exact room my father was held in but I was nervous about my mom and sister being alone in the car. At first I was nervous about the soldiers but they spoke in pashtu with us and they seemed harmless. It's so hard to imagine my father surviving in that prison because he's such a gentle man. He'll chase an ant around the room and take it outside rather than kill it. He was never tortured but many of his friends were. Two of his friends were beaten so badly that they couldn't walk and he had to watch them drag their bodies from place to place.

They are slowly rebuilding the prison but I wish they'd make a memorial instead for the lost lives. I'm not usually one for memorials but this time I think it would be healing, not only for the land, but also for those people whose family members disappeared in the surrounding fields.

much love,
maso

Amidst the widespread poverty, lingering oppression of women, virtually non-existent health care, hostilities between tribal factions, daily fears of terrorist attacks by those loyal to Osama bin Laden and al-Qaeda, and a vast array of other problems and threats, Mohamadi was reminded of the richness and beauty of her native country during

her frequent trips to smaller towns and villages outside her home in
Kabul. The following was written on January 26, 2003. ('Mazar' is
Maza-r-e Sharif, located in northern Afghanistan.)

dear friends,

I returned from mazar on Friday after an eleven hour drive, through the
solang pass, a one mile tunnel that took us half an hour to get through
because two looray's (big colorful trucks) moving in the opposite direction
were stuck to each other. We sat in our 4x4 white UN car inhaling fumes.
Then one of our cars got stuck driving across a metal bridge and it took three
hours to pull it out, bang the rim back into shape, and drive slowly to a
mechanic. Some men from the village crowded around the bridge. When I
got out of the car to assess the situation and a group of young boys circled
around me staring so hard that I quickly climbed back into the car.

One boy came by my window and peered in, his cheeks red from the
cold. He had beautiful brown eyes and I smiled at him and he smiled back. I
felt like we had been friends for a long time and he became my protector
keeping the others away.

I didn't know what to expect in mazar except that it was dangerous with
frequent kidnappings so I took my mace just in case. We had traveled to
Mazar to choose about twenty government employees to take part in our
capacity building program, a three-year program geared to teach them
English, computers, management skills, procurement, and everything else
needed to run a government. When our work was done we were ready for
some sight seeing and we were taken to the ziarath, the supposed burial place
of the fourth caliph Ali whose tomb rests inside.

The Ziarath is a blue gem in an otherwise muddy, drab city of crumbling
buildings littered with the remains of old, rusted cars and tanks. White
pigeons have made the place their home resting along the ledges and flying
from one minaret to the other. As soon as I walked past the front gate I was
filled with a warm energy. A group of children ran up to me begging for
money which I was told not to give them or else I'd be mobbed so I took
their picture instead.

I was a bit nervous as I walked in because I wasn't sure what to do inside.
I followed my traveling companion who walked up to a wooden box in front

of the room, which was the tomb. A woman in a white burqa was kissing it. I sat down on the burgundy rug and lifted my hands to my chest and cupped them open and I prayed for peace in Afghanistan. Behind and around us sat more old men with copies of the Quran in front of them accepting money. When I walked back outside the swarm of kids ran up to me so I quickened my pace to the car but they kept up, begging for money, telling me they were orphans. They were professionals.

From the car I stared out at the structure, so startlingly blue and beautiful, amazed that it had survived, and I could see and feel how such a place could sustain the hopes and prayers of the people.

I had left Kabul with two images swirling around inside me. One was of a man who was missing the bottom half of his body. He had wrapped a rice sack around his waist and he was lifting himself up and forward with his fists rhythmically moving down the street, the top half of his body strong and sturdy. On the same day I saw a little girl sleeping on the side of the road with a stone under her head for a pillow and a lime green scarf covering her face. I desperately wanted to replace these images or balance them out with something beautiful and I found that something in Mazar.

much love,
maso

Three months later, after suffering a sudden, horrible loss, Mohamadi wrote to her friends: 'In the Afghan people, I found love and beauty and hope, and I couldn't imagine being anywhere but with them. But it was always by my father's side, doing all these things as his daughter, taking pride in his name and his work. And now he is lost and I'm crippled without him.' Mohamadi's father was President Hamid Karzai's Minister of Mines and Industry. In late April 2003, his plane mysteriously vanished over the Arabian Sea. No one knows if the plane experienced mechanical failure or if sabotage was involved. On March 31, Mohamadi wrote:

Nothing hurts more than looking at my mother, her face long and sad, white streaks grown in over her auburn hair, pools of tears welling up in her eyes everytime she looks at me, knowing I remind her of my father, of the past four months we spent together. She doesn't know if we are the fortunate or unfortunate family. Would it be better to be grieving over a gravestone right now or trapped in the not knowing, stuck somewhere between madness and hope. I imagine this is how my people have felt most of their lives and now I am no different.

As heartbreaking as the loss remains, Mohamadi continues to create positive and lasting change in Afghanistan; in 2003 she founded a nonprofit organization called Support Education in Afghanistan, which is working to build primary schools in rural areas of the country.

After losing her son in Afghanistan in 2004, Terry Ward appeals for help from Gloria Caldas, a mother whom she believes will understand her pain — & — Gloria Caldas replies to Terry Ward.

As in Iraq, in Afghanistan the majority of US casualties occurred after it seemed that major combat operations were over – by December 2001, when the Taliban authority had all but collapsed. But, on September 20, 2004, as Terry Ward was unloading groceries outside her home in South Carolina, a family friend rushed over and told her to go inside and wait for an urgent phone call. When Ward asked if something was wrong, the friend repeated, 'Just get to the phone, get to the phone.' Soon after she walked in the door the telephone rang and her daughter-in-law, Tammy, told her the terrible news: Ward's 30-year-old son, Staff Sergeant Tony B. Olaes, had been killed in Afghanistan. A few minutes later several US Army vehicles pulled into the driveway, and a military chaplain and casualty officer confirmed that Ward's son was dead. Olaes was a Green Beret combat medic, and he and another soldier, Robert S. Goodwin, were shot during an ambush in Shkin, Afghanistan. Unbeknownst to Ward, a website honoring fallen troops created a memorial page that paid tribute to her son. Ward learned of the site about a month after her son had died, and she came across a message posted by a total stranger:

To Tony's Family and Friends:
On behalf of the Blanco-Caldas family, we send our sincerest condolences. We share the same loss . . . the same pain. Our prayers are with you in this most difficult time and we thank you for your soldier's bravery and sacrifice.
*   Sincerely,*
*   The Family of Capt. Ernesto M. Blanco-Caldas, 82nd Airborne*
*   KIA Iraq 12/28/2003.*
*   Gloria Caldas (The Big Ern's Mom) of San Antonio, TX*

Ward was deeply moved by what Gloria Caldas had written and felt an immediate connection with a mother who was experiencing the same sense of despair. Ward sent Caldas the following email:

DEAR GLORIA,
THANK YOU SO MUCH FOR THE CONDOLENCES ON THE FALLEN HEROES SITE FOR MY SON. MAY I ALSO EXPRESS MY CONDOLENCES ON THE LOSS OF YOUR OWN SON. I AM SO DEVASTATED AND I CANNOT FIGURE OUT HOW TO GO ON. HOW DO YOU MANAGE EVERY DAY?
   MY SON HAD 3 YOUNG SONS, 11, 10 AND 7. HOW DO I HELP THEM? AND HIS WIFE, WHO LOVED HIM SO MUCH. I KNOW I NEED TO BE STRONG FOR THEM ALSO, BUT I AM SO SAD MYSELF.
   SO SORRY TO ASK YOU THESE QUESTIONS, BUT YOU HAVE BEEN THERE ALSO, SO I KNOW YOU UNDERSTAND.
   PLEASE FORGIVE THE CAPITALS, BUT I AM LEGALLY BLIND AND HAVE A HARD TIME ON THE COMPUTER, IF THE LETTERS ARE NOT BIG.
   I HOPE YOU DON'T MIND ME WRITING YOU, BUT I

396

FIGURED THAT IS WHY YOU GAVE YOUR EMAIL ADDRESS.
HOPE I AM NOT RAMBLING.

I LOOK FORWARD TO HEARING FROM YOU, AND HOPE
MAYBE YOU CAN GIVE ME SOME INSIGHT.

YOURS TRULY,

TERRY A. WARD

MOTHER OF SSG. TONY BRUCE OLAES

KIA SEPTEMBER 20, 2004

Caldas responded right away.

Oh Terry! I know so well the pain you are going through. I wish no one
else would have to go through what our families have experienced.
During the first several weeks after Ernie's 'Homegoing,' I fell into a black
hole.

I guess this was the Lord's way of protecting me from the horror of the
unthinkable. Losing a child is a bad thing. In my anger, the Lord and I had
quite a few very lively discussions! But little by little, I began to climb out of
the despair with the loving support of family, friends and my faith. Ernie was
not married yet, but he did leave a grieving fiancee who has not yet
recovered. They were scheduled to marry on June 12th. It's now been 9
months since he was killed, I am finally able to provide support and comfort
to those around me . . . his sister, grandparents, aunts, uncles, cousins and all
those who have also been deeply affected by his loss.

Normal will never be what it was before . . . we've all had to redefine
'normal.' Nothing will ever be the same, but you learn to just take one day at
a time. Sometimes there are bad days, sometimes worse days. But I know
that as long as I have a breath in my body, my son will live in my heart. I'm
sure you feel the same. My faith sustains me and I know that I will be
reunited with him when I too go Home. I know I'm rambling, Terry.

My heart aches for you. Please get back to me. Tell me more about Tony.
I'm sure your extremely proud of him, as I am of Ernie.

By His Grace,
Gloria

Gloria Caldas and Terry Ward continued to email one another words of support and encouragement after their initial exchange. 'JUST WANTED TO LET YOU KNOW THAT I AM THINKING OF YOU AT THIS DIFFICULT TIME,' Ward wrote to Caldas after Christmas 2004. 'I AM ALSO KEEPING YOU IN MY THOUGHTS AND PRAYERS AS THE ANNIVERSARY DATE OF ERNIE'S DEATH APPROACHES. JUST KNOW THAT YOU ARE NOT ALONE.'

—— FEATURED SERIES ——

'Reconciliation, Confrontation and Dialogue'

Lois Hoffman, the widow of an American World War II veteran, receives a stunning letter from a man who had known her husband in the war — & — A Japanese woman, Takako Yamakawa, writes to an American World War II veteran, Jerry Yellin, about her feelings for his son — & — Yellin and Takako's father, Taro Yamakawa, a Japanese World War II veteran, correspond about their children's desire to marry one another — & — Khaled Al-Maeena, a Saudi-Arabian editor, initiates a written dialogue with a reader who had sent him a hate mail in the aftermath of 9–11.

Dated January 2, 1992, the letter began like so many of the other messages of condolence that Lois Hoffman had received from veterans who had known her husband, George, before he died at the age of 80. 'The new year 1992 was not yet one and a half hours old when William Dutton called to inform us that George had died,' wrote Gunter Leopold, a longtime friend of Hoffman whom he first encountered when both men were navy commanders in World War II. 'Although I was aware of the fact that

George had been a very sick man owing to his lung problems, I was shattered by the news of his demise. With him a very short, but intensively experienced period of our mutual past was borne to his grave.' Unlike Hoffman's fellow veterans, however, this old friend, Gunter Leopold, was Hoffman's enemy in 1944. Leopold was the Austrian commander of a submarine in the German Navy that Hoffman's destroyer, the USS Corry, *had sunk. As the letter continues, Leopold expresses the grief that he and his wife are feeling because of Hoffman's death, and he recalls Hoffman's extraordinary decency and the unique relationship the two men began during the war. (The minor mistakes are the result of Leopold's attempt to write in English, which he understood very well but did not speak fluently.)*

I am mourning for a very good friend. Indeed, true friendship it was, although we found ourselves in a war against each other – he, the American destroyer commander, and I, the German submarine commander. But this war was only the dreadfully loathsome setup which compelled us to fight against each other, but in our hearts we naval men never felt hatred against each other. As soon as one of us was no longer able to fight, all so-called enmity ceased and was replaced by the awareness of the always existing solidarity among Atlantic navies. Therefore it had seemed to be just a matter of course that the American pilot of the plane that we shot down while it dropped the fatal bomb on our submarine, who had not been scratched, helped me, the seriously wounded 'enemy', into his liferaft and rendered first aid. And when after two or three hours George's destroyer 'Corry' came up, an American sailor climbed down into the water up to his chest, in order to bundle me up within the liferaft, so I could be pulled up aboard for owing to the loss of blood I had been to weak to climb aboard by myself. Although it was midday-time on a Sunday, and in the officers' mess the table had been set for lunch, George ordered all dishes to be removed, and though I was smeared with diesel oil from top to toe I was put on the table in order to be operated. I was cleaned off oil, and before the young doctor Anderson of Swedish descent started surgery, George welcomed me as his guest aboard his ship, addressing me as 'captain', and offered me for the duration of my stay his bunk in the captain's room. When the doctor was about to take off my right leg just above the knee, warning of the danger of gangrene, I protested, and the admirable physician willingly took great pains to save my leg, by removing dozens of fragments, by taking care of severed tendons, muscles and nerves and by heaping lots of penicillin onto the wound, before he devoted himself to the other injuries. When George was informed that I had to come round, he came to 'my' bunk and advised me to pray that there would be no gangrene.

I have the most pleasant memories of my stay aboard the destroyer 'Corry', because it was marked by the chivalrous way of thinking by George, the American commander, who looked after me day by day, sitting at my bedside and devoting many hours to tell me about America, his family and his service in the navy. He never made me conscious of the fact, that meanwhile I had the status of a prisoner of war. I was, as he time and again emphasized, his guest. (Secretely I was not at all sad about my fate, since I was fed up to the brim with this kind of war, when German submarines were hunted like hares on account of the American superiority in radar and sonar, and I would have been even happy about the change in my fortune, if not so many of my crew had died.) With his great tactfulness George never asked me a military or political question. When after a few days I was able to hobble about with my leg in thick plaster (and with a turban-like head bandage), George dragged me to sunny places on the upper deck and he insisted that I put my arm round his shoulder, not allowing anybody else to heave me about. Twice I was invited to have the evening meal in the officers' mess, where I was assigned the seat of honour next to him. When subsequently a motion picture was shown, George bent underneath the table to push a cushion under my foot and kept inquiring about how I feel. In my lifetime I have respected and admired George in view of his personality and his humanity. During manoeuvres I also got to know him as an extremely proficient mariner and as a man of courage to stand up for his humanitarian beliefs. When the admiral aboard the aircraft carrier 'Block Island' ordered my transfer to his ship, George declined to execute this order with reference to my 'critical condition'. When the 'Corry' entered the harbour of Boston in the afternoon of March 29th, 1944, I, the German prisoner of war, stood next to the captain on the bridge and was even allowed for a short while to act as his helmsman. Saying goodbye to George I was on the verge of tears since we had become pretty close. I had forebodings that in the forthcoming custody of the army I would in all probability have to go without this unique quality of George's warmheartedness. (My premonitions proved true: at the Fort Devens army hospital I was referred to as the 'Nazi subcommander', ended up in a padded cell of 'Section eight' for loonies and had to eat chops with a spoon, until I was 'rescued' by naval intelligence officers.) On parting George gave me one of his khaki-uniforms, in which I looked very much American. When, lying on a stretcher, I left the 'Corry' and his captain, the sailors showered masses of chocolate, cigarettes, chewing gum and other goodies upon me. While being carried over the gangway, all men on deck saluted to me, the German PoW. This generosity symbolizing a spirit of decency of mind was doubtlessly the result of George's splendid example as a commander. To the best of my recollection I have told the story of George Hoffman a thousand times as that of a knight in shining armour in a heroic epic.

Dear Lois, at our age we are especially affected by the death of someone whom we love, becoming conscious of how quickly human life may come to an end. From my own sorrowful experience I know that the confrontation with the finality of death produces deep emotions which tend to brighten up the memories of the deceased in our heart. In my view the image of George cannot grow brighter than it has been up to now. He will always rank foremost among those few whom I consider an exceptionally good friend.

Very affectionately yours
Gunter and Katinka

Just months after Hoffman had rescued Leopold, the USS Corry *was destroyed when it struck a German mine off the coast of Normandy during the Allied invasion of France on June 6, 1944. More than two dozen of Hoffman's men were killed, and he himself barely survived; Hoffman was the last to leave the ship, which sank in only eight minutes, and he was pulled out of the water unconscious. After being sent to England, Hoffman returned to the USA on the* Queen Mary *in July 1944. Leopold, who was being treated in a US military hospital, was able to find Hoffman's address and the two began a regular exchange of letters for almost 50 years. (They were not, however, ever able to meet again after the war.)*

Friendships between veterans who were once adversaries are not uncommon – and the connection can become a strong one, as they have shared, albeit from opposing sides, traumatic experiences that even their closest friends and family members might not be able to understand. But these relationships are not always initiated voluntarily. For an American veteran named Jerry Yellin, recollections of his World War II service in the

Pacific, where he flew bombing missions against the Japanese, provoked intense emotions and lingering anger. Forty-two years after he returned to the USA, Yellin unexpectedly found himself back in Japan – sitting in the house of his youngest son Robert (who had gone to Japan to teach English), and meeting Robert's girlfriend, Takako Yamakawa, for the first time. Yellin and his wife, Helene, knew that their son was in love, and Yellin suspected that Robert intended to stay in Mishima with Takako. 'We're really pleased to be here, and to meet you,' Yellin said to Takako, trying to be polite. 'I don't know what Robert's plans are, but I want you to know that whatever Robert decides to do, including living in Japan, will be all right by me.' But the memories of the war, of close buddies losing their lives during raids over Japan and the stories of atrocities committed against American POWs, could not be erased overnight. Yellin, who later wrote of the conversation in his memoirs, then said to Takako in absolute candor:

> I have many concerns, however, about my ability to accept [Robert's having] a serious relationship with a Japanese woman. I flew over your country several times as a young man. Many of my friends were killed. I have not resolved all of that in my mind yet. As a father, I will not stand in the way of my son's decisions. But as an American, I am not sure I can accept his decision whole heartedly. I also don't know anything about your father and his feelings about Robert, about America, about the war.

Takako's father, Taro, was indeed a veteran with his own very painful memories from the war, and he disapproved of the relationship entirely. Takako had, however, expected sympathy from her mother Hatsue, who, as a young woman, had also suffered the disapproval of her prospective parents-in-law, who regarded her as socially inferior to their son. But when Takako handed her parents a bottle of brandy from the Yellins, offered as a gesture of goodwill, her mother's immediate reaction was severe: 'I know you are interested in [that] gaijin,' she exclaimed, using a derogatory word for outsiders. 'I want you to know you can marry any Japanese man that you choose, but you will not bring a foreigner into our family.' Over time, however, Takako was able to encourage her parents to at least meet with Robert, and in a letter to the Yellins, she described the result of that encounter.

Dear Mr. and Mrs. Yellin,

I was very happy to meet you and Jerry last March. I am sorry to have taken so much time to write to you and thank you for your encouragement. I wish my parents felt as you do. My mother was against my involvement with Robert, but I am set on my plans to marry him. I needed time to find the courage to tell my father. My mother is the type of woman who would agree with any decision my father would make, so he is the one I had to convince. But it has taken me much longer than I ever thought it would to speak to him about Robert. Robert is an American who, I thought, couldn't speak Japanese too well. He wore a full, heavy beard. That alone seemed bad enough, but on top of it, his father had actually attacked Japan from the air during the war, even strafing the very town where I had been born. I couldn't see Robert making a good impression. I cried a great deal and became far too upset and afraid to say anything. Instead of acting to clear the air, I just became more and more depressed.

Finally in August, with my friend Kiyo's encouragement, I did speak to my father. I told him I had someone I wanted him to meet.

'I see,' said my father. 'You must mean that foreigner. Give me some time to think about it.'

Days passed with no conversation about our talk. Then, with no warning, my brothers arrived. One came from Kanazawa, seven hours away, and the other from Yokohama, a three-hour journey. The emergency family council took place. I was asked many questions from all sides. What kind of a person is Robert? Why is he in Japan? Does he intend to return to his country soon? What kind of school did he graduate from? What is his religion? And more. Most of the questions were asked by Tadashi and Kiyotaka, my brothers. My father kept his mouth closed and watched the scene out of the corner of his eyes, and just listened. My brothers finally gave their permission to arrange a meeting with Robert.

When the day of the meeting arrived I was apprehensive and nervous. My father had arranged for us to have lunch in a private room at a Japanese family restaurant with a lovely garden. The meeting went much better than I had expected. In fact, now that I think about it, I wonder how my father was able to hold back all the emotion I knew he felt. He always had dreams for his only daughter, and they did not include marrying a foreigner, especially an American, his old enemy!

That night, I sat down with my father and talked with him about the meeting with Robert. He told me, 'The day you showed me the picture of all of those foreign men and said you wished to marry one of the men in the picture was a difficult day for me. I knew that some day I would have to let my "treasured daughter" go, and I knew you were now reaching a marriageable age, but I was astonished by the suddenness of the proposition.

'In the picture were several foreign men, but of all the choices, the heavily bearded American one was your choice! Again I was shocked. My feelings towards America and the war were frozen deep within me. I was just beginning, after forty-three years, to accept the changing times. For all those years, I was pretending to be flexible and adaptable. But now you, my daughter, wanted to marry an American, out of all the choices available to you among Japanese men. To marry the son of my enemy!

'I had brought up my children without interfering in their lives. I always believed in the child's independence as much as possible. I only forbid actions that would interfere with other's wellbeing. I encouraged my children to strive for whatever they believed in; but this? It seemed that you had thought through your decision very well. I knew that you had talked to your mother and that she had been quite adamant. "No gaijins in our family," your mother said.

'If I said no, it would go against my philosophy. Your mother and I put our heads together and finally decided that the least we could do was to meet your young man.

'I was quite surprised to find that Robert was accustomed to the Japanese language, as well as the Japanese lifestyle. Moreover, I found, he was a likable person with a keen interest in wabi and sabi (the taste for simplicity and tranquility the Japanese consider the ultimate state of being), even beyond the level a Japanese man might show. He also possessed a stillness that has become rather rare in modern-day Japan. I liked him very much. Then, in the ensuing conversation, I learned that his father and I had a lot in common, both in age and in our life experiences. When I heard that Robert's father had been an ace pilot in the war, I had a premonition of the decision that I would make regarding your marriage.

'For myself, even though I sought the path of a pilot in the war, I never realized my dream. But I steadfastly held to the firm belief that there were no enemies in "the ones who flew in the sky." Although in the past we were enemies, there is an affinity between all fellow fliers, just from the experience of flying; regardless of being a friend or foe.

'Robert also mentioned that his father had flown a P-51 Mustang over Japan. My emotion changed from simple admiration to overwhelming wonder. The P-

51 had been the object of adoration of all Japanese student pilots. I imagined that anyone flying that plane would be an extraordinary person, and I was convinced that this young man had, in his blood, much of what I admired. It was all I could handle to keep my composure, suppressing my desire to shout for joy that my only daughter would pick such an excellent counterpart. I did not say anything to you about my thoughts, because I wanted to speak to your mother first. When I told her about my feelings, that I thought your young man was suitable for you to marry, she quickly agreed to my decision. So, Takako, I am very happy for you, and most anxious to meet your new parents.'

I cried with joy at what my father had told me.

That conversation cleared the air between my mother and me so we began to look for a place to have the wedding reception. We already knew that I would have the ceremony at the Mishima shrine, that is where all of our family occasions are held. We hope to get the Skylight Room at the Mishima Plaza Hotel for the dinner reception after the wedding ceremony. Robert will call you as soon as we have set a firm date.

Takako Yamakawa

The Yellins were extremely touched by the letter, and Jerry decided it was time to write to the family that would soon, through Robert and Takako's wedding, become part of his own.

My Dear Yamakawa Family:

It is with great pleasure that I send you greetings from America. We were very pleased when Robert phoned us last night and informed us of his plans to marry Takako in March of next year. We think it is exciting for them. You can be assured that Takako will be welcomed into our family by Robert's brothers and my wife and me, with love and respect.

We were told by Takako in April that you Yamakawa-San, and I share a lot in common. It seems we were born in the same month of the same year, shared similar experiences in our youth, and then devoted the rest of our lives to what we felt was most important of all, raising our families. Both of us have four children, all of whom have good education and futures. You and I have strong marriages, and now, these two families will be joined together by the marriage of our youngest children.

I can fully understand that you might be upset by Takako's decision to marry a man other than a Japanese because of the differences in tradition and culture. We, too, had some doubts as to the wisdom of the decision. However, the more we examined your traditions and culture, we saw that there were many more similarities than differences. Truly what matters to us is the respect that two people have for each other and the fact that they want to be with each other as a family, much as we have led our lives.

We want you to know that we are all happy for Takako and Robert and we wish them a long and happy life together.

We look forward with great enthusiasm to meeting you and your family in February and being part of the wedding on March 5th.

Signed,

Jerry and Helene Yellin

A few weeks later, the Yamakawas replied – both in English and Japanese, in the form of an elegant scroll handwritten on beautiful paper.

Dear Mr. And Mrs. Yellin:

Here the season of autumn is beginning to appear in the trees and in the air. It seems that fate has brought your warm letter to us from so far away. We are grateful that Takako is welcomed into Robert's family with such a warm feeling. We would like to thank your family.

When Takako told us of Robert and their plans it was like a bolt out of the blue. But after we met Robert and saw his quietness and consideration, we found that our daughter's eyes were correct. After Robert told us about his father, it seems we are of the same age and shared similar backgrounds. We feel happy to see your pictures and know that Takako will be accepted into such a good and healthy family.

Although our customs and lifestyles are different, in these modern times, they may be interchangeable. I expect that Robert and Takako will be able to do this. Our family is not so well off, but our hearts and feelings are like the sky. We always want to have that feeling, plentiful, and wide like the blue sky. Our distance is far but we are happy to be family and relatives, distance cannot change these situations. We are very happy.

March 5th is a lucky day for marriage at the Mishima Shrine. It will soon be here. At that time you will be here, we look forward to that day and are glad to think of it now. We answer your letter in happiness and wish you health and happiness in your life and work.

Signed,

Taro and Hatsue Yamakawa

Yellin was so moved by their words that he wrote one more time to the Yamakawas before the wedding.

Dear Yamakawa-San:

I am writing to you today with a wonderful feeling of happiness, respect and gratefulness to you and your family. Your letter expressed, in poetic terms, a beautiful sentiment that could only come from a man of depth and great understanding. Both Helene and I are deeply touched by your words and your thoughts.

Even more, it has given us an insight into Takako's background and upbringing and strengthened our feelings about the coming wedding. Only you and I, Yamakawa-San, can know about the soul-searching we both had to go through to reach this level of complete acceptance. We are soon to be family and share in the joys of that which families experience. This is all the wealth that I believe a man needs. We indeed are both fortunate to have reached this stage of life.

We will be arriving in Japan on Saturday, February 27 and plan to stay two weeks. We look forward to meeting you and your family and spending time getting to know you.

Please give my warmest regards to your wife, your sons, and my future daughter.

Signed, Jerry Yellin

Robert and Takako remain happily married to this day, and the Yellins and the Yamakawas are now the proud grandparents of three children.

In the years preceding and following the Vietnam War, the USA had only one formidable opponent – the Soviet Union. No other power in America's history had the ability to bring about the nation's total annihilation. But that threat was mitigated by the fact that the USA could retaliate with equal, if not greater, force. The collapse of the Soviet Union in 1991 heralded an age of near invulnerability for America. The bombings of the World Trade Center in 1993 (which killed 'only' six people), the Oklahoma City Murrah Federal Building in 1995 (an act of homegrown terrorism), the US embassies in Tanzania and Kenya in 1998, and the Navy destroyer USS Cole in 2000 rattled, but did not destroy, that sense of security and confidence. And then came 9-11. Suddenly the USA was confronted with an agile, almost invisible enemy consumed with the desire to kill as many innocent civilians as possible, decapitate the nation's government, and, in targeting its financial infrastructure, bring about America's economic ruin. President George W. Bush was emphatic, from the very beginning, that even though all the 9-11 terrorists were Muslims, the USA was not at war with Islam. Nevertheless, relations between Americans and Muslims in the USA and abroad deteriorated rapidly. One man caught between these two worlds is Khaled Al-Maeena, a Saudi Arabian journalist, who had been educated as a young man in America, and sent most of his children to college there as well. He still travels to the USA frequently to visit close friends and participate in educational events created to foster mutual understanding and dialogue between Muslims and people of other faiths. In his role as Editor-in-Chief of the English-language daily Arab News, *he personally receives letters and emails voicing a wide range of reactions to current affairs covered in either the paper's news section or editorials. Many are carefully reasoned, well-articulated criticisms of opinions expressed in the paper. But some are pure venom. 'F - - - you, Towel headed camel jockey ... son of a pig and monkey,' read one. 'There are NO civilized countries in the muslim world,' began another. It went on to call for the incineration of the Middle East. (The typos are in the original.)*

> *If you people want to turn back the clock to 800 years ago, then I think we should help to turn back the clock even more ... ALL THE WAY BACK TO THE STONE AGE. I think that my country should just NUCK you bastards and get it over with!!!*

Arab-Israeli relations were fodder for countless messages:

> *You Arabs are the biggest losers. Israel with a population of 5 Million kickes your ass. you have like what?? 300 Million Arabs and 3000 times bigger countries?? haha you are the joke of the hole world : -)*

408

Another reader offered the following menacing email with a gleeful tone:
'Congrats to U, my little buddy and to your fabulous country, your #3 on
the list, hehehe: 1) Iraq . . . . 2. Iran . . . . 3. Saudi Arabia . . .' And along
a similar theme:

> *God, I really hope we go to war with your country – I look forward to the*
> *day we destroy your country and those of Syria, Iran, and Iraq. Your*
> *playing with fire you jerkoffs, in continuing to taunt and embarrass the*
> *United States – my sincerest wish is that we takeover your country, open up*
> *a Club Med in Mecca, complete with Strip Joints . . . and 24-Hour bars and*
> *taverns for our military, and let the Israelis govern the rest of your country*
> *as military dictatorship – now that would be poetic justice.*

Al-Maeena tries to respond to every message, no matter how vituperative.
Many of the readers do not care or are unwilling to engage in a rational
discussion about whatever issue had inspired them to write, but some do,
prompting candid exchanges between Al-Maeena and his readers. Soon
after the 9-11 attacks, a Montana resident named Ray, who had come
across Arab News on the Internet, sent the following combative message.
(Ray included his full name with the email, but his last name and other
information has been deleted here in the interests of privacy.)

This American thinks that ALL Arabs, Muslims, and Islam in total should be sent
to dwell in hell at the hands of Christian warriors. And God would view this as a
good fight to rid the world of evil and send them to hell where they belong. You
people are nothing but filthy, hateful, cowardly, pigs. You are lower than swine.

Where is the sanity in some stupid, jack ass Imam accusing 'Zionists' of state
terrorism – Why does he not talk about the thousands of innocent people that
bin Laden the ARAB Muslim has killed, the children he has orphaned, and the
widows he has created!? I have never felt such true hatred until recently – when
I saw all the swine Muslims dancing in the street rejoicing the death of thousands
of people. My hatred continues to run deep and extends to Saudi Arabia. The
Islam religion is built on a foundation of hatred, intolerance, and violence –
which will beget the same from Christians – one hundred-fold, and lead to it's
downfall – the end of Islam. I hate you people so much. You filthy, murderous,

409

satanic pigs. I HATE YOU ALL – THE Q'URAN IS THE BOOK OF SATAN THE DEVIL, THE TEACHINGS OF EVIL, THE BOOK THAT IS USED TO JUSTIFY MURDER. ANYONE WHO WORSHIPS ISLAM IS THE DEVIL'S CHILD. THERE WILL BE A GREAT CONFLICT IN THE FUTURE, A CONFLAGRATION BETWEEN ISLAM AND CHRISTIANITY AND THE CRUSADERS OF CHRISTIANITY WILL RID THE WORLD OF THE SATANIC HELL THAT IS ISLAM – YOU SHALL PERISH FROM THE EARTH!!!! GOD WILL SEE TO IT FOR THE DEEDS THAT YOU HAVE DONE!! I ABSOLUTELY HATE ALL OF YOU IN THE MOST PURE FORM OF HATRED.

Ray

Recognizing there was probably little he could do to change the mind of someone so beset with rage, Al-Maeena sent back a simple message, emphasizing that, 'Instead of such vitriol, I would request you to join us in a prayer for world peace. Sincerely, Khaled A. Al-Maeena.' Perhaps taken aback that he had received a reply offering even a semblance of cordiality, or possibly already feeling remorseful for his outburst, Ray sent the following, remarkably conciliatory email:

Sometimes, during the course of human events, when tragedies occur, our minds and souls can be so stirred as to evoke great emotions. These emotions are not always pleasant. Indeed, emotions can become quite strong enough as to cause people to do things that come from the emotional mind rather than the heart. This is what happened to me.

Recent events caused me to write the very nasty email that you received, with the intent to provoke you into an argument so I could 'vent' my feelings, and make myself feel better at your expense. This was wrong, very wrong. I believe that God let me do this to teach me a lesson. The lesson I have learned is that making others mad does not, in the end, make one feel better about themselves. Rather, it makes one feel bad about themselves. I have learned a good lesson, but I must express my most sincere apologies for directing my anger at all of you. I am not the kind of person that my messages would indicate. And I already knew that people can't carry around hatred, but I needed to learn again. I have found that I can not hate people, I was not raised that way, and it is much too heavy a burden to carry. If my father read what I wrote, I would not be able to type any letters as he would have broken my fingers. I will not offer any excuses for my actions, because the way I have been effected by recent events is not at all your problem.

I have never seen nor have I read the Q'uran – where I live, it would be hard to find such a book. Anyway, I'm sure the Holy Q'uran is a good book full of words of goodness, love, and peace. I hope you will find it in your hearts to forgive me for my outburst of false emotions, and except these words from my heart: please forgive me, and may we all be blessed so that we may one day live in peace – if not for us, then for our children.

If any of you ever come to Montana, I would welcome you in my home so that I may gain a greater understanding of Islam.

God Bless You Everyone,

Ray

Al-Maeena responded almost immediately:

Greetings and peace from Saudi Arabia.

I was overwhelmed by your letter. God Bless you and all Americans. I would like to welcome you as my personal guest any time you wish to come.

As for the Qur'an or other books you need please let me know and I shall send it to you.

Hopefully you and I will be part of the 'dialogue of civilizations'.

As the father of five children, four of whom studied in America, I am determined that the evil acts of some depraved people, be they of any race, not spoil the strong relation between America and us.

If there is anything else you need to know please feel free to ask.

Respectfully,

Khaled A. Al-Maeena

On December 24, just a few weeks after they had begun their correspondence, Al-Maeena sent Ray a special gift – a transcription from the Qur'an of the story of Mary and the birth of Jesus Christ. Al-Maeena's new pen pal was moved by the gesture.

Dear Mr. Al-Maeena:

On the eve of Christmas, I have received a wonderful gift. Tonight when I retire, in that time when thoughts pass through one's mind before sleep comes; I shall pray to the Lord and thank him for the understanding and forgiveness you have shown to me. And, I will thank him and ask that his blessings be bestowed upon you for the wonderful gift you sent me. The story of the birth of Christ from the Qur'an was beautiful.

Merry Christmas to you and your family, and a wish that the coming New Year, be full of goodness, health, and prosperity.

Maybe we will be one year closer to world peace.

Season's Greetings,

Ray

Several months later, Ray, a World War II veteran in his 70s, passed away. Al-Maeena heard the news from Ray's son, Jeff.

I am sending you this message at my father's behest. Last Friday he had a heart-attack and he seemed to know that he was not long for this world. He would have been 76 in July. He told me of the first e-mail he sent to all of you and how he regretted that his anger had gotten the better of him. He also told me of the respect he had for all of you for your forgiveness and continued messages.

My father was a warrior. I suspect his brief encounter with all of you helped give him some peace of mind. My father had obtained a copy of the Holy Qur'an and had been reading it. In one of my last conversations with him, he told me that he believed no matter a man's faith, we are all children of God and therefore we are all brethren. With that in mind, I shall end this letter to you by saying based upon his beliefs, he will be looking forward to meeting you.

Go in Peace,

Jeff

EDITOR'S NOTE

'What, specifically, are you looking for?' This is often the first and most understandable question people ask me when I appeal to them for extraordinary war letters, and to this day I am unable to formulate a succinct response. The problem is that whenever I try to come up with a definitive list of themes and topics, someone surprises me with a letter that is unlike anything I have read before.

A quick example: In Belgrade I visited the Archives of Serbia and Montenegro to search for letters written by Serbian soldiers during World War II, a time when our two nations were united in fighting the Nazis. A very gracious curator, Predrag Krejik, showed me a letter by a Serbian prisoner of war (POW) named Branislav Popovic and began translating it aloud in English. Addressed to Popovic's son, it offered little more than a perfunctory update on his situation and a brief mention of family friends (or possibly old neighbors) – the Zmijovics, the Stakorics and the Gladovics – held in the same camp. I thanked Predrag for letting me see the letter and asked if Popovic had possibly written something a little more candid. Predrag smiled, recognizing that I didn't understand the significance of the message. Zmijovics, Stakorics and Gladovics, he explained, were the words 'snakes,' 'rats,' and 'hunger' manipulated to look like Serbian last names. This was Popovic's way of evading the censors to inform others that, despite German assertions to the contrary, the prisoners were starving and confined in wretched circumstances. It was the first coded POW letter I had ever seen. (Due to space limitations I was unable to include the letter itself in this book, but the story is what is relevant here.)

Determining what makes a letter 'extraordinary' is of course subjective, but overall I'm partial to correspondences that accentuate the individual human drama within the vast sweep of history. They are less about the size and scope of warfare – casualty estimates, troop movements, military strategy – than the singular, dirt-under-the-fingernails experience of what it feels like to plunge headfirst into battle. These letters pack an immediate visceral punch and reveal the distinct voices and personalities that make the larger stories more accessible and real.

Although I was initially only interested in combat-related material, I discovered that some of the most emotionally intense war letters ever written make no references to battle. They are heartfelt messages by parents and spouses writing home about missing the birth of a child or a wedding anniversary or a family reunion. Some are letters by teenaged soldiers who have matured considerably since they left for the front lines and are now apologizing to their parents for their past rebelliousness. Or they are letters full of wry humor, emphasizing to those back home that there is nothing to be anxious about. And in so many cases, their words represented the last ones they would ever write. These letters are not as dramatic as brief messages hurriedly penned in foxholes as bullets kicked up dirt just inches away. But written in the life-and-death context of war, their quiet, reflective sentiments are as potent as any description of hard fighting.

Before embarking on my trip around the globe, I made up an extensive inventory of 'must find' letters that related to topics and historical events significant to each country. (From the outset I had decided to concentrate only on major wars in which troops from many different nations had put a substantial number of 'boots on the ground.' To expand the focus beyond this would have been too unwieldy, although it did mean having to forgo pursuing stories from some of the world's most fascinating confrontations. One of the most intriguing, to me, is the 1896 clash between Great Britain and Zanzibar, considered the shortest war in history. The whole affair clocked in at about 45 minutes.) In England I wanted letters about the Christmas Truce in 1914 and the Luftwaffe air raids during World War II, among many others. In Seoul I sought out letters by South Korean troops who had served with the Americans in Vietnam. In Amsterdam I hoped to find letters by Dutch soldiers who had been at Srebrenica. In Baghdad I asked the few Iraqis I had the chance to meet where I could find any letters or emails written since the March 2003 Coalition invasion. The final 'must find' list I compiled was more than a dozen pages long, single-spaced. The purpose of this was not to try and represent every major battle or historically significant moment, but to create a more impressionistic depiction of warfare, and these events – along with many others – were the ones that I felt promised to capture the emotions and perspectives I thought would be the most vivid and memorable.

With the indispensable assistance of first-rate guides, I pored over thousands of letters, many of which I copied and mailed back to the USA where I later cataloged them by country and by topic (love, combat, humor, etc.). If they required translating and seemed destined to be included in the book, I often had them checked by a second and even third party to ensure I was being faithful not only to the words, but the tone and spirit of the text. Combining these foreign letters with the American ones I had already collected (after having traveled throughout the USA for almost two years) was the next challenge.

The main question was whether to arrange the letters by war or by theme. I settled on the latter; what I had found so intriguing about these correspondences was how people from vastly different back-grounds over hundreds of years articulated strikingly similar emotions – yet each from their own unique cultural perspective.

415

Within the chapters, and to impose some semblance of order on the book, I decided to arrange the letters chronologically. I made some exceptions for the 'Featured Series' sections, which focus on a particular subject as expressed in related letters from many conflicts. And these letters, although designated as 'featured,' are not necessarily any better or more interesting than others in the collection. They simply worked well as a self-contained group. Some of the letters in the book could certainly have been placed in one of several chapters, but this is understandable considering that war elicits so many profound and intermingled emotions. Each letter was placed in its respective chapter not only for its content, but how it contributes to the overall arc of each section.

The vast majority of the book's approximately 200 primary letters and emails (i.e., the correspondences set in roman font and introduced with headnotes, which are in italics) are unedited and transcribed exactly as they were initially written. Misspellings, typos, grammatical and syntactical mistakes, curious asides in the middle of otherwise gripping stories, and everything else have been left intact so that each letter reads as true to the original as possible. There are a few exceptions to this, and in most cases they relate to deleting personal information or changing a name to protect an individual's privacy. Any such alterations are indicated in the headnotes. In several instances regarding letters with minimal or no punctuation, I have added a space or two in appropriate places to indicate the end of a sentence. Due to the shortage of available paper, some writers covered every inch of their letters, front and back, with writing and made no indentations to mark the beginning of new paragraphs. This can make for arduous reading, so when it appeared to me that a writer was beginning a new thought, I took the liberty of starting a new paragraph.

Throughout the headnotes I have interwoven excerpts from letters I could not use in their entirety but that nevertheless offer insights and observations that reinforce the primary letters immediately before or after them. (Unlike the primary letters that represent the core of the book and are extremely rare or previously unpublished, a handful of the excerpts in the headnotes come from other well known anthologies and sources.) Similarly, at the beginning of each chapter there are several epigraphs that relate to the larger theme of the section that follows. Some of these epigraphs have been edited for length, and they have been done so without adding ellipses to maintain an aesthetic simplicity. Needless to say, no words have been added to these texts, nor has the essence of the correspondence been changed.

A final note about the editing process: while fact-checking the headnotes, I was struck by the degree to which there are wide discrepancies in the casualty estimates used even by respected historians regarding certain battles and attacks on civilians. I made every effort to obtain the most accurate data, and I have tried to indicate where the largest differences among scholars exist. Inevitably people will disagree about these statistics, and I welcome feedback from those who have reliable and updated information.

Although I believe I was successful in tracking down the letters I most wanted to find, some ultimately proved elusive. I regret, for example, not being able to locate letters by African soldiers who fought side by side with Allied troops during the world wars and in other major conflicts. Also, although I had uncovered some remarkable correspondences pertaining to the Cold War for my last book, *War Letters*, this time I came up empty-handed. I am enormously grateful to the American troops who shared with me their letters and emails from Iraq, but my single greatest frustration was my inability to obtain anything by other coalition forces who were deployed to the region. Along those lines, I was disappointed that I could not find more correspondences by men and women who serve in the US military but who are not originally from America. (Approximately one out of every 40 people in our armed forces is foreign-born.)

In Mexico my wonderful guides, Angelica Morales Carballo and

Pablo Mondragon Silva, and I had a lead on a fascinating story about Irish soldiers who served with US troops during the Mexican-American War but eventually began to sympathize with the Mexicans and switched sides. But letters by these Irish soldiers did not seem to be archived anywhere in Mexico or in Ireland, which I visited as well. I also was unable to unearth any letters written by Mexican troops during the war with the USA.

While in France I had hoped to locate previously unpublished letters by several of its most famous citizens: the pilot and children's author Antoine de Saint-Exupery, Marguerite Duras (who I was told had interrogated Nazi collaborators during World War II), and famed sea explorer Jacques Cousteau, who also served in the Resistance. In each case, nothing. In Berlin and Munich I hunted for World War II pen-pal letters by German children writing to English boys and girls to promote friendship in a time of conflict. Except, as the story was told to me, the whole effort was part of a German intelligence operation to determine British morale during the war. In Australia I held in my hands a sensational World War I letter by an aboriginal soldier, but much to my dismay one of his descendants did not want the letter published under any conditions, even anonymously. It was heartbreaking to have to relinquish such a find, but respecting the wishes of those who own the letters is paramount, so that was the end of that.

There were some misses in the USA as well. The grandniece of a World War I serviceman told me that when her great-uncle died in the war, the family feared that his mother – who was terribly sick – would lose the will to live if she learned her son had been killed. One of the man's siblings decided to write letters as if they were from the soldier himself, forwarding them first to a friend in Paris who then mailed them (so they would be properly postmarked) back to the USA. The mother died peacefully some time later, but was comforted by the thought that her son was alive and well in France participating in the country's reconstruction. All of these letters have since been lost. In a somewhat similar vein, during his service in the Coast Guard, a gifted young wordsmith ghostwrote love letters for his buddies to send to their spouses or girlfriends. What makes the story especially appealing is that the sailor was Alex Haley, who would go on to write *Roots* and become one of our nation's most influential authors before his death in 1992. I pursued every possible lead I could think of to locate 'Haley's' letters, but with no luck.

The publication of *Behind the Lines* does not, however, represent the end of my search for these and other letters. This book is part of a larger mission to ensure that wartime correspondences are preserved for future generations. Hopefully it will inspire others to recognize the value of their wartime letters, show them to their families, and, ideally, share them with the rest of the world.

ACKNOWLEDGEMENTS, PERMISSIONS AND SOURCES

From the time *Behind the Lines* was little more than a faint glimmer of an idea to the moment it became a completed, tangible creation, this book has benefited from one small miracle after another. Whenever help was most needed, someone stepped forward to lend a hand, track down specific letters, or extend their hospitality as I traveled throughout the USA and abroad. I doubt I will ever be able to express to them all the depth of my gratitude for their kindness and generosity.

My good fortune began on November 11, 1998, when Abigail Van Buren ('Dear Abby') and her daughter Jeanne Phillips profiled the Legacy Project in their column. Everything that has happened since is thanks to them (we are now up to an estimated 75,000 war letters from every conflict in the nation's history), and I will be forever indebted to Jeanne and her mother for bringing attention to this little effort from the start. I also want to thank Olivia 'Newt' Vis, who works in their office, for all of the consideration she has shown me over the years.

I am grateful beyond words to Miriam Altshuler, who is everything an author could ask for in an agent and everything a person could want in a friend. Miriam is one of the most genuinely caring individuals I have ever met, and I would be lost without her. No matter what crisis or problem emerges, Miriam is there with a shoulder to lean on, words of support, and indispensable guidance and advice. I also want to thank her assistant, Sara McGhee, who is incredibly gracious regardless of how many times I pester her with questions or concerns about some matter.

I am also indebted to Miriam for helping me find first-rate editors for both this book and my earlier ones, each of which was a labor of love. It was a joy to work with Deborah Baker on *Letters of a Nation*, and then with Gillian Blake on *War Letters*, and I adore them both.

I am now extremely lucky to be working with Colin Harrison, the editor of the American edition of this book (published by Scribner) and a brilliant author in his own right. Colin understood my vision of *Behind the Lines* from the outset, and he has provided impeccable editorial insight throughout this process. He is truly one of the best in the business. Due to the staggering amount of work required and the nature of the material, which can be emotionally overwhelming, there were some very hard days while writing this book. But despite my nerve-wracking delays and failure to complete chapters on time, Colin responded with empathy and understanding (and the occasional gentle nudge), and it has been a pleasure and a privilege to work with him at every step of the way. Colin's assistant, Sarah Knight, deserves recognition for everything she has contributed to this book as well. Sarah is one of the hardest-working and most all-around stellar people I have encountered in publishing, and she has my deepest appreciation.

Along with Colin and Sarah, there is a team of people at Scribner who invested a tremendous amount of their time and energy in this project. First and foremost is Susan Moldow, the publisher, whose support from the beginning has been truly phenomenal. Susan, along with Nan Graham and Roz Lippel, sees *Behind the Lines* as something more than just an anthology of wartime letters, and I cannot express how grateful I am for all that they have done for me and this book. Every author should be so fortunate as to have such a publisher, and it is a true honor to be part of the Scribner family. I also want to extend my thanks to Suzanne Balaban, Lucy Kenyon, Kate Bittman, and Sue Fleming who, along with many other extremely talented and creative people, are responsible for publicizing and marketing the book. John Fulbrook, Mia Crowley-Hald, Erich Hobbing and Aja Shevelew have all worked countless hours to see this book through a very intense production schedule, and I know I've caused them all many headaches.

For the British edition of *Behind the Lines*, I am eternally indebted to Claire Kingston, Rachel Rayner and Jake Lingwood, in particular, who had faith in the idea for this book from the very beginning and could not have been more supportive. Everyone at Ebury has been phenomenal to work with, and I am grateful to them all.

Because I was away traveling for so long to research this book and then deeply immersed in the writing process after I came home, I have been appallingly delinquent in spending time with family and friends. They, in return, have been nothing but loving and supportive. I am truly sorry to them for being absent for so long, and more grateful to them than they can know for putting up with me throughout all of this. I am particularly indebted to my parents (especially considering that I fibbed to them when I said I was not going to Iraq and Afghanistan, although it was only because I didn't want them to worry), who took in all the packages of research material I sent home, and simply kept me going through it all with their prayers, inspiring messages, and phone calls along the way.

Perhaps the greatest of the 'small miracles' came after a phone call I received from Nate Mick in Senator Chuck Hagel's office the summer before I left on my journey. Nate and I had worked briefly together on a project that distributes free books to our troops overseas, and Nate asked if I was in need of an intern. 'His name is Jared Wells, he's just out of college, and he's a first-rate guy,' Nate assured me, and indeed he was – and still is. Jared worked with me for more than six weeks on a volunteer basis before I headed overseas, and I was so impressed with his intelligence, integrity, humanity, maturity and sense of humor that I asked him if he would be interested in working with me on a full-time basis when I returned. He agreed, and there is no more direct way for me to say this: without Jared, this book could not have been written. Jared is responsible for finding some of the best letters in the book, including those by the Iraqi civilians and the Guernica exchange at the beginning of the 'Aftermath' chapter. He spent weeks poring through previously unpublished letters at the Library of Congress and National Archives, he helped edit every draft of the manuscript I wrote (and he did so with a deft touch), and he has simply been there – no matter how grueling the hours or challenging the assignment – whenever the need was most critical. He and his girlfriend, Deanna Durrett, who is equally amazing, helped me maintain my sanity through some of the most stressful periods as deadlines loomed. Jared also happens to speak three languages, which, considering the nature of this project, came in handy on numerous occasions. Jared is going to go far in life, and I will be proud to say 'I knew him when . . .' after the rest of the world sees how much he has to offer as well.

Most importantly, there would be no Legacy Project if it were not for the tens of thousands of people who have sent us letters (and now emails) of great personal significance. For those of us who are civilians, it is difficult to understand fully how much military life demands of the men and women who serve in the armed forces, and I hope these correspondences will give us a glimpse into what they and their loved ones sacrifice both on and off the battlefield. The names of those who have contributed the letters and emails featured in this book, as well as those who have helped me regarding the trip around the world in other essential ways, are acknowledged below. Again, I cannot express how grateful I am to them for everything they have done to help make this book a reality. I am mortified at the prospect that I have forgotten to mention people integral to the trip, this book, or the Legacy Project in general, and, if I have, I truly apologize. (Not all of the countries I traveled to are listed here, as in some cities, especially those I stayed in only briefly, I was able to get around on my own and made the visit more to see a war memorial or military cemetery than to find letters. Conversely, I discovered letters along the way written by soldiers from countries that I did not visit. These are mostly correspondences that were picked up after a battle by either comrades or enemy troops and eventually made their way to archives and museums in nations other than the fallen soldier's homeland.) Here we go:

United States of America: Christine Albert and Richard D'Abate, at the Maine Historical Society; Ted Alexander with the National Park Service; JoAnn Ballard, Joe Carbo, and Michele Mendez, at our building, who kept the office safe and secure while I was away; Rick Baillergeon, who has been a great friend and supporter of the Legacy Project from its earliest days; Scott Baron, one of my heroes, who is responsible for finding the Demetria Barber letter, and is the author of several terrific books, including *They Also Served: Military Biographies of Uncommon Americans* (MIE Publishing, 1998) and *International Stars at War* (Naval Institute Press, 2002); Terry Baxter, who sent me a copy of the Tetsuko Tanaka letter; Judy Bellafaire and Britta Granrod, at the Women in Military Service for America Memorial at Arlington National Cemetery; John Bernard, who got me onto the *USS Kitty Hawk*, which was, without question, one of the greatest experiences of my life; Stephen Brengle; Paul Brockman, at the Indiana Historical Society, who kindly sent me a photocopy of the Kurt Vonnegut letter from their archives; my revered mentor/guru/sensei, Chris Buckley; Bruce E. Burgoyne, who is America's foremost expert on Revolution-era Hessian soldiers and the author of many books on the subject, and who provided me with the Christian von Molitor letter; Dorothy Butchko; Dr. Nic Butler, Dr. Eric Emerson, and Karen Stokes at the South Carolina Historical Society; Parker Calvert, for introducing me to Lois Hoffman, who shared with me the Gunter Leopold letter (coincidentally, Lois's daughter, Constance Phelps, had sent me the same letter years before, but I was only focusing on American letters at the time); G. Wade Carmichael Jr., who first told me about the Kurt Vonnegut letter; Marjorie H. Carne, for sending me the Angela Petesch letter (and I am also grateful to Kristin Gilpatrick, who wrote *The Hero Next Door* [Badger Books, 2000], and Todd Hunter of Hunter Halverson Press, LLC, who will be publishing a book of Angela

Petesch's letters, *War Through the Hole of a Doughnut*); Mary Carter, who is constantly keeping an eye out for great war letters for me; Emily Catherman, who is one of the people most responsible for making the trip possible at all. Just days after Scribner accepted the idea for this book, I was suddenly seized with panic at the enormity of the task ahead of me. Emily, whom I had met in North Carolina while I was traveling throughout the USA looking for American letters, called me out of the blue and asked if I needed assistance with anything in particular. I told her I appreciated the offer, but the main chore ahead of me – finding contact information for hundreds of military-related institutions around the world that might have war letters in their archives – was not something I presumed she or anyone else would be terribly interested in doing on a volunteer basis. Not only did she do it enthusiastically, but she was absolutely meticulous in her work, and I simply cannot thank her enough; Chan Chrisman, who found the Samuel Bard letter; Charlotte Cole, who has always gone out of her way to help with the Legacy Project's mission; Dave Cooke, who has also been extremely supportive over the years; Dr. Kazimiera J. Cottam (one of the foremost experts on Russian women who fought in World War II), who very considerately shared with me dozens of letters from her own files that she took not only the time to select, but to translate for me as well; Sharon Curry, who generously forwarded me emails by her son Scott, who served in Iraq; Richard Danzig, who provided me with numerous first-rate contacts around the world; the entire Davidson family, and especially Tommy, who is single-handedly responsible for the fact that the manuscript for this book was late; Frank Davies, who has gone beyond the call of duty to help the Legacy Project bring in letters; Alvin Deutsch, who is my lawyer and a wise and gracious friend; John F. Di Virgilio, in Hawaii, who went out of his way to help me find Pearl Harbor veterans – both American and Japanese; Isabel and Ovidio Diaz, who forwarded me a copy of Denis Silva Torres's incredible letter about Iraqi children; Terry Dorman with the National Park Service; Jono Drysdale, a close friend and my resident Canadian expert (and I am also grateful to his girlfriend, Meredith Margaret Henne, for putting me in touch with Margaret Tilley, who reviewed the American Revolution letters); everyone at the Eisenhower Center, particularly Doug Brinkley, Kevin Willey, and Michael Edwards; John Elko, who put me in touch with Max Young and has been a steady and supportive friend throughout this process; Clay Feeter, who contributed great Civil War letters to the Legacy Project; Duery Felton Jr., curator of the Vietnam Veterans Memorial Collection, who has always been generous with his time and assistance; Nate

Fick, a US Marine who was one of the first combatants to share with me his letters from Iraq (and I am also indebted to Denise Gitsham for introducing me to Nate); Pearl Harbor survivor Dick Fiske; Merrilee A. Foley, for sending in David A. Thompson's letter; Nessa Forman, who initiated an effort similar to the Legacy Project's in Pennsylvania and shared with us some of their best letters; Christopher J. Fox, at Fort Ticonderoga, who provided me with letters from numerous 18th- and 19th-century conflicts, particularly the French and Indian War; Roger France, who provided the BJ Armstrong letter; Brad Fultz, a US Marine who helped me catalog some of the German letters; James Gaines, who delivers the mail at my building and always looks out for me; Shawna Gandy and Lucy Kopp, at the Oregon Historical Society, for all of their help with the George P. Telfer letters and photographs from the Philippines; everyone at the Gilder Lehrman Institute of American History, especially Jim Basker, Karina Gaige, Richard Gilder, Lesley Herrmann, Lew Lehrman, Susan Saidenberg and Sandy Trenholm; Dan Gillcrist; Caroline Gluck with the BBC, who put me in touch with Kevin Kim (who led me to the Kim Min Ha letter); Chris Goddard, who wrote about Roff, the German messenger dog, and provided me with all of the information used in the profile of Roff; Bill Groniger, who is one of the most patriotic Americans I know; Ilana Greenstein, who has assisted the Legacy Project over the years in numerous ways; Emily Grosvenor, who translated many of the German letters and has simply been a joy to work with; Erin Gruwell, who is one of the most amazing and inspiring individuals I met on the entire journey and is now a dear friend; Sylvia Helene Hairston, who kindly provided me with the Oscar Mitchell letter; Joyce A. Hallenbeck, whose constant love and support is always appreciated; Shane T. Hamilton and Megan McLaughlin at Miller & Chevalier, who have offered indispensable legal assistance over the years; Greg Henry, who provided me with much-needed travel information before I embarked; Linda Howell, who helped track down letters from several wars; Paula Huntley, author of *The Hemingway Book Club* of Kosovo (Jeremy P. Tarcher/Putnam, 2003); Karen Hurd, who put me in touch with her son, Chris, who wrote a profoundly moving letter about the death of a friend; Pearl Harbor survivor Everett Hyland, who gave me the best tour a visitor could hope for at the *USS Arizona*; Sunil Iyengar; Jake Jeppson, who researched embassies around the world for me and had been my assistant on *War Letters* before he went off to college; Alan and Sue Johnson-Hill, for taking so much time to help me include Kenelm Clifton Johnson-Hill's letters/journals to his wife; Terry A. Johnston Jr.; David Jones, who advised me on where to go in Vietnam; Mary Karcher at Leatherneck, who has done more to help me find letters and emails by marines than anyone; Garrett Kasper, who was my excellent host and guide in Bahrain; David Kennedy with Dan Curtis Productions; Courtney King, who has assisted me in many ways, particularly with my trip to the Middle East; Brian Knowlton, at the *International Herald Tribune*, who wrote about my (at the time) planned trip to find war letters around the world; Yumi Kobayashi, who read through stacks of barely legible war letters found at a flea market in Japan on my behalf and earned my undying gratitude; Yvonne Latty, who wrote the sensational *We Were There: Voices of African American Veterans, from World War II to the War in Iraq* (Amistad, 2004), and who found the Waverly Woodson letter; Chris Lillie, at the Pentagon, who helped me with the book distribution project for the troops; Brian Lipson, my fellow history buff and agent extraordinaire in Los Angeles; Jan Lorys and his staff at the Polish Museum of America, who provided me with a copy of a book they self-published, Metchie J.E. Budka's *Autograph Letters of Thaddeus Kosciuszko in the American Revolution* (The Polish Museum of America, 1977, Chicago), which contains a facsimile of the Kosciuszko letter in this book; Pam McDonough, my technical adviser extraordinaire who advised me to film and photograph the trip (and Brad Smith at Penn Camera who set me up with the equipment); Pat McGhee at Fort Hood; Flo and Harold McKenzie; Ross McMullin, who is the world expert on Harold 'Pompey' Elliott and essentially ghostwrote the introduction to Elliott's Gallipoli letter; Kathy McNeeley and Christopher Purdell, who found the James Williams letter; my pre-trip medical team, Drs. Alex Chester, Marc Doctors, and Arnold Miller, as well as Jennifer Dunphy, who advised me on health issues before I traveled around the world; Douglas Osama Meehan, for assistance with my trip to Vietnam, and his amazing wife, Caroline Suh, for her advice on camera equipment; Richard Mei Jr., who set up the small gathering in Belgrade that led to my meeting Patricia A. Andjelkovic (Richard also put me in touch with the staff at the US Embassy in Tokyo, where he worked, and he has since become a dear friend whom I admire greatly); Mike Meyer, at the VFW, to whom I am eternally indebted for everything he has done for me and the Legacy Project over the years (and I am also grateful to Becky Curtis, who works with Mike); Allen Mikaelian, who assisted me early on with finding war museums and archives around the world; Harry Miller, at the Wisconsin Historical Society, who once again saved me by sharing first-rate letters from their collection; Marja Mills, a dear friend who has also been instrumental in helping us spread the word about the Legacy Project; Lynn Mooney, who helped shape the focus of this book; Conrad J. Netting IV, who kindly shared with me his mother's incredible World War II letters and is writing his own book, *Delayed Legacy* (Maverick Publishing Co., 2005), about the courage and heroism of both his parents; Larry Ng; Zabih U. Noori at Print Time; Tom O'Sullivan; Florence Ochi at the Japanese American National Museum; David Pelizzari, who not only seems to be fluent in every language spoken on this earth but is also one of the most generous souls I've ever met; Nancy Pope, my epistolary comrade-in-arms at the National Postal Museum; Alice Leccese Powers; Pam Putney, for her love and travel advice; Nadia Rawls; John Rees, who generously shared with me numerous letters from the American Revolution, including the letters by Henry Johnson; Bonnie Reich, who found a copy of the stunning Pearl Harbor letter by William Czako in her house, left behind by the previous tenants; Danielle and Jason Ritter, for sending in the great photo of Jason with 'Turbo'; Ken Robinson and his brother Steve, both of whom I admire enormously; Joe 'Buck' Rogers, a true American patriot; Nikki Roth-Stiles, who assisted me in finding the Jonathan S. Mosby letter; Lorraine Sais and Elana Samuels at the Museum of Tolerance in Los Angeles; Susan Salm, who is one of my favorite Texans and put me in touch with Alisa Johnson at the Daughters of the American Revolution National Society, who helped me find great War of Independence letters; Barbara Schneider, who generously shared with me letters by her son Stephen Webber; Rye Schwartz-Barcott, a US marine whose friendship and advice throughout the years I value enormously; Jan Scruggs and everyone else at the Vietnam Veterans Memorial Fund (especially Holly Rotundi and Alan Greilsamer), for their support and for making my trip to Vietnam so memorable; Lottchen Shivers; Alex and Pat Shakow, who first shared with me their son Tom's letters from Sarajevo; Jane Singer, who very generously shared the Civil War terrorism information and correspondence with me and is doing her own book on the subject, *The Confederate Dirty War: Arson, Bombings Assassination and Plots for Chemical and Germ Attacks on the Union* (McFarland & Company, 2005); Ilene and Sid Slagter, who have been helpful in numerous ways and edited *Chicken Soup for the Veteran's Soul* (HCI, 2001); Martha Smalley at the Yale University Divinity School, for sharing the James H. McCallum letter; Corey Smathers and everyone else at Lincoln Action Program who assisted us with finding letters and email from the current war; Megan Smolenyak, editor of *Honoring Our Ancestors* (Ancestry Publishing, 2002), who helped the Legacy Project get its message out to the genealogical community; Mark von Sponeck, executive director of the extraordinary Global Nomads Group, who helped me locate email by Iraqi civilians; Joel Swerdlow, for providing invaluable help with this book and so many other projects; Alex Thomas at Travel Documents; Margaret Tilley, who helped review the American Revolution letters; Liza Tobin, whose support through this whole period of travel and writing was more appreciated than she will ever know; Tim Todish, author of *America's First First World War: The French and Indian War*, 1754–1763 (Purple Mountain Press, 2002), who, along with Chris Fox, helped me find French and Indian War correspondences; Sheri Travillian, who shared with me the incredible email by her nephew Gary Chandler who is serving in Iraq; Martin Vigderhouse; Pearl Harbor survivor Herb Weatherwax; Don Wilson, who put me in touch with Masuda Anna Mohamadi; Greg Wessel, a stamp and letter collector who was one of the first to suggest that I search for foreign war letters; Rob Wilson, whose selfless work with the Veterans Education Project is an inspiration to me and so many others; Ellen Wingard, for her love and support; Jerry Yellin, who graciously allowed me to publish his postwar letters, and is the author of a powerful memoir titled *Of War and Weddings: A Legacy of Two Fathers* (Sun Star Publishing, 1995); Ann Sherman York, former president of the American Gold Star Mothers; Massimo Young, about whom I cannot rave enough – Max is one of the smartest and most remarkable young individuals I have met, and he assisted Jared Wells and me with research, translating letters, organizing the Legacy Project collection, and in countless other ways; James W. Zobel at the MacArthur Memorial Archives, who, once again, provided me with an extraordinary, never-before-published letter by Douglas MacArthur; I'd also like to extend a word of thanks to the good people at Expedia.com. Seriously. I planned almost the entire trip on the Internet, primarily using Expedia, and in seven months of travel to more than 30 countries, not one thing went wrong. That, in itself, is a miracle. Afghanistan: Masuda Anna Mohamadi, who very generously shared with me her extraordinary emails; Khatera Atayee; Haroon Gharzai; Mustafa Merzazada; and the staff of the Intercontinental in Kabul. Despite the bombing, the hotel remains one of my favorites from the entire trip. Australia: Lynette Aitchison, David Jolliffe, Margaret Lewis, and Ian Smith at the Australian War Memorial, and I am particularly indebted to Emma Jones, who helped me locate many terrific letters while I was in Canberra and has endured a barrage of email since I returned to the USA. Austria: Dr. Christoph Tepperberg, at the Austrian State Archives/War Archives in Vienna. Belgium: In Ypres – my guide Kristof Demey; Dominiek Dendooven at the In Flanders Fields Museum

Documentation Center, who provided me with numerous first-rate World War I letters; and General James Jones, Supreme Allied Commander, Europe, to whom I am especially grateful for taking the time to meet with me during my visit to NATO Headquarters in Mons. (Paul Whitfield and Shirley Richardson were also very kind in helping to set up the meeting.) Bosnia and Herzegovina: Dalila Sinanovic and Nidzara Beganovic, in particular, at Veterans and Invalids of the Patriotic War, for providing me with letters by residents of Sarajevo written during the siege; Fatima Sirucic, who put me in touch with Amir Telebecirovic. As I mention in the introduction to this book, Amir was not only one of the best guides I had on the trip, he has become a dear friend whose compassion and love for his country, along with his desire for reconciliation with those who viciously attacked it, affected me deeply. Canada: Wayne Abbott, whose Northern Sky Entertainment did a fantastic documentary based on World War II letters (*From a Place Called War: 1939–1945*), several of which he and his very gracious sister Laura Abbott shared with me; Timothy Dubé and Andrew Horrall at the Library and Archives, Canada, who were extremely generous with their time and expertise (and Andrew is responsible for helping me find the Canadian censored letters in my chapter on humor 'Laughing through the Tears'.) I am also grateful to Tim for putting me in touch with Stephen Fochuk, a freelance researcher who tracked down letters after I left Canada. Despite the fact that they were closing their archives in a matter of days (in preparation for a move to a new building), Carol Reid, Patricia Grimshaw, Dean Oliver, Maggie Arbour-Doucette and their colleagues at the Canadian War Museum were incredibly helpful in directing me to promising collections in their archives. Most of all, I am indebted to my good friend Dr. Stephen Davies at Malaspina University-College. Stephen started an effort similar to the Legacy Project, called The Canadian Letters and Images Project, and he has preserved thousands of Canadian war correspondences and photographs. The Hart Leech and William Mayse letters are both from Stephen's collection. China: Charlie Chi in Beijing, who assisted with some of the initial research; Malia DuMont; Lucia Buchanan Pierce; Benjamin Kostrzewa, who was living in Beijing at the time and, being fluent in Chinese, offered to serve as one of my guides (and who also enlisted the support of three exceptional translators to go through the letters he found, Tang Hanjie, Zhang Huyue and Yi Xiaojie); Vivian Lee, who, along with Ben, was indispensable and a joy to work with, served as my main translator and is responsible for finding the Zhao Yi Man letter, for which I am extremely grateful; Wang Yi at the National Museum of China;

Sandy Zhang, who volunteered to serve as my guide and translator in Nanjing (and I am also grateful to Ying Shen and Shen Tao for putting us in touch); and Zhu Cheng Shan, director of the Nanjing Massacre Museum. My trip to Nanjing was an especially profound one, primarily thanks to Iris Chang. Iris wrote the international bestseller *The Rape of Nanking* (Basic Books, 1997), and despite the fact that we had had no previous connection, she promptly answered a rather lengthy email from me asking all sorts of questions about where I should go and whom I should visit on my trip to China. She could not have been more supportive and thoughtful. This began an all-too-brief friendship, and Iris, who took her own life in November 2004, will be missed dearly by everyone who knew her personally or indirectly through her work. Czech Republic: Milada Hladikova, who went out of her way to help me plan my trip to Prague, and Major Eduard Stehlik at the Historical Institute of the Army of the Czech Republic, who was responsible for finding the Jan Kubic letter. Major Stehlik is, himself, the author of an incredible book titled *LIDICE: The Story of a Czech Village* (available in English through the Lidice Memorial), which focuses on the massacre of innocent Czech citizens that took place after the assassination of Heydrich Reinhart. Egypt: Marwah Afifi, who essentially (and flawlessly) organized my entire trip to Alexandria, El Alamein, and Cairo. England: Vicky Britton, who helped with research after I left England; Justin Clegg and Tim Thomas, at the British Library; Richard Davis and other staff members at the Leeds University Library; the brilliant literary agent Sara Fisher; at The Second World War Experience Centre in Leeds, I am indebted to Claire Harder and especially Dr. Peter Liddle, the director of the Centre, for allowing me to go through their archives and use some of their best letters (Dr. Liddle has probably done more to preserve British wartime letters than anyone alive); Alison Miles and Emily White, at the Tate Library and Archive in London; Christopher Miller, who did an enormous amount of research for me at the Imperial War Museum; journalist Chris Redman, who helped me try to get in touch with British troops in Iraq; Anthony Richards and Roderick Suddaby at the Imperial War Museum, which is quite simply one of the best war museums in the world, went out of their way to help me find stellar letters in their extraordinary archives. I truly cannot emphasize enough how hospitable and generous Anthony and Roderick were, and I am enormously grateful. France: In Normandy – my guide Catherine Mennesson; Françoise Passera, who shared with me letters from the Memorial of Caen, one of my favorite museums; Lucien Tisserand at the German Military Cemetery; and Thomas Schlich, who is passionate about preserving wartime correspondence as well. In Paris – Marie-Jeanne Badault, an incredible teacher who gave me the opportunity to come and speak at her school; Jean-Pierre Gueno, who has brought enormous attention to the importance of saving wartime letters in France, and who has edited several first-rate books, including the sensational *Paroles de Poilus 1914–1918*, published by Librio in cooperation with Radio France; Nicole Guillou at the US Embassy in Paris; Chaibong Hahm and Gillian Whitcomb at UNESCO; Patrick Jarreau with *Le Monde*, who put me in touch with Annick Cojean, who did an incredible article for the newspaper on the Legacy Project. In Lyon – Caroline Gurret and Chantal Lorro at the Museum of the Resistance. In Verdun – my guide Ingrid Ferrand; Catherine Jung at The World Center for Peace; Isabelle Remy at the Verdun Memorial; Corentin Seznec at the Alliance Française de Washington, DC; Major General Pascal Vinchon at the French Embassy; Drew Tarlow; and Ann Kordahl, who introduced me to Gail Noyer, Lisa Aidan, Tama Carroll and Janet Lizop in Paris to help me in my efforts. Janet, in particular, has been my lifeline to France since I returned to the USA, and she has gone out of her way to help me track down essential contacts and is single-handedly responsible for finding the Jacques Aulong letter. I also wish to thank Pierre Lescault for assistance with finding the Vietnam letter written by the French soldier in 1949. Germany: Dr. Peter Jahn, at the German-Russian Museum Berlin-Karlshorst, for providing me with extraordinary letters by German and Russian veterans; and Dr. Klaus A. Lankheit, at the Institut für Zeitgeschichte, one of my earliest and most helpful German contacts. Dr. Gerhard Bauer, Jan Hoffman and Harald Schindler at the Militärhistorisches Museum der Bundeswehr in Dresden; Ewald Behrschmidt; Friedrich Richter at the Dresden Stadtmuseum; Dr. Irmtraud von Andrian-Werburg at the Germanisches National Museum; my exceptional guide and translator Sally Slenczka, who put me in touch with Michael Kaiser; and Von Hartmut Voight at the Nürnberger newspaper, who helped us spread the word about the project; I am especially grateful to Dr. Katrin Kilian and Dr. Clemens Schwender at the Feldpost-Archiv Berlin, who provided me with several of the best German letters in this book. Their efforts with the Feldpost-Archiv have helped preserve countless German wartime letters, and they are providing an invaluable service to history. They could not have been nicer or more cooperative. The person most responsible for making my visit to Germany, and especially to Berlin, a success is Christian Scharnefsky. When we met, he presented me with a meticulous schedule for my week in Berlin that, he assured me, was planned so that all outdoor tourist activities would take place on sunny days and all indoor research would be conducted on gloomy ones. Considering he had confirmed the schedule weeks before I arrived, I assumed he was joking. As it turned out, he was not. In spirit (and somewhat in looks), Christian reminds me of a younger version of the great theologian Dietrich Bonhoeffer; Christian is a man of integrity, humor, and conviction, and spending time with him and his wife, Katrin, was a highlight of the entire trip. India: David Omissi, who edited *Indian Voices of the Great War: Soldiers' Letters, 1914–18* (MacMillan Press, 1999). We have never met or communicated, but it is his incredible work that inspired me to go to the British Library to find more of these letters in their collection. Information I quoted about the Indian troops came primarily from Omissi's book; and Shyam Singh Saklani, Kirit Singh Rathore, and Amit Majumdar, my guides in New Delhi. Iraq: Eric Clark, Dave Farlow, David Gercken, Andy Meissner, Mark Rickert, and Chris Stannis, who hosted me in Iraq, and Muammal Jaafar, who helped me find letters and email by Iraqi civilians. Ireland: Ciara McDonnell, at the National Library of Ireland, who could not have been more helpful both during my stay in Dublin and after I returned to the USA. Italy: Maria Teresa Tringali, who I found serendipitously through a friend of a friend of a friend, was one of the best organizers and guides I encountered on my trip. (And I am indebted to Alice Power and Mike Dolan for helping me find Maria Teresa.) When it seemed like we were going to have trouble finding war letters in any Italian museum, Maria Teresa located the Fondazione Archivio Diaristico Nazionale, which has been collecting letters and diaries for years. I am extremely grateful to Loretta Veri and Andrea Franceschetti for sharing with us material from their collection. Maria Teresa and I also traveled to Anzio, and Silvano Casaldi, curator of the Museum of the Allied Landing, was very generous in providing me with letters from his archives as well. Japan: In Hiroshima – Kahori Wada and Minoru Hataguchi at the Hiroshima Peace Memorial Museum. In Nagasaki – Nobuko Kamata, with the Nagasaki A-Bomb Testimonial Society, who shared with me the extraordinary letter by Masao Sakai; my guide, Joji Nakamura, and Takashi Morita at the Nagasaki Atomic Bomb Museum. In Okinawa – Dave Davenport, who runs the Battle of Okinawa Museum; Futenma Choukey at the Himeyuri Peace Museum, Takayasu Fuji and Hirokatsu Tamatsu at the Okinawa Prefectural Peace Memorial Museum; Professor Hiroshia Hosaka at the University of the Ryukyus; and my trusty guide, Ueda Shoji. In Tokyo – Kitano Ryuichi at the Asahi Shimbun newspaper; Lee Hyon Suk at the Foreign Correspondents Club of Japan; Naomi Shin, her father Zenji Abe, and the rest of their family for taking the time to come and meet me during my all-too-brief stay in Tokyo; Chikara Ishii, Fusako Watanabe, Okada Hiroyuki, Sakae Tani, and Shigeru Ishii at the Japan Memorial Society of the Students Killed in the War (Wadatsumi Society), who share a passion for preserving wartime letters and whose letters were used to create a phenomenal book titled *Listen to the Voices from the Sea*, translated by Midori Yamanouchi and Joseph L. Quinn (University of Scranton Press, 2000); Iki Hiroshi and Takahashi Daisuke, as well as the Yushukan and Public Relations Office of the Yasukuni Jinja, who provided many of the Japanese letters in this book; and my incredible guide and translator Amiko Nobori, who also continued to serve as my link to Japan once I left. The US Embassy was extremely helpful, and I am especially indebted to Mark Davidson, Margot Carrington, and Erika Wada. They are three of the most amazing people I met on my journey. Kuwait: Dr. Youssef Abdul-Moati, who generously shared letters from the Center for Research and Studies on Kuwait; Yacoub Abdulla, who was the perfect host and is responsible for helping me find all of the Kuwait-related letters in the book; Dr. Fatma Al-Khalifa; and Tahani Al-Terkate, Sarah Deyyain, and Tory Randall at the Kuwait Information Office, who helped me plan my trip. I also wish to thank Anna Maria Slemp, my military contact in Kuwait, who helped me get in to (and, most importantly, out of) Iraq. Malta: John Galea, a taxi driver who, in one day, rushed me around the island at a breakneck pace to show me one extraordinary war-related site after another. Mexico: Although we had difficulty finding Mexican war letters, primarily because very few seem to exist, my guides Angelica Morales Carballo and Pablo Mondragon Silva made my trip to Mexico City one of the most enjoyable of the entire around-the-world journey. I am indebted to my friend Abigail Seymour for helping me find Angelica and Pablo. I also want to thank Aida Flores at the US Embassy for her assistance as I was planning my visit, and Maria Eugenia Sevilla for profiling the search for Mexican war letters in Reforma. Netherlands: In Amsterdam – Hubert Berkhout, René Pottkamp, and Erik Somers at the Netherlands Institute for War Documentation, where I found the letters by Dutch resisters; Frits van Suchtelen at the Dutch Resistance Museum; Hans Masselink at the Trouw; and Alissa Ede. At the Veterans Institute's Centre for Research and Expertise, I cannot thank Gielt Algra enough for all of his assistance and hospitality during my stay in Holland. (Joanne Mothaan and Martin Elands, also at the Institute, were very helpful.) I am especially grateful to Gielt for putting me in touch with André Dekker, who shared with me his letters regarding Srebrenica. New Zealand: Dr. Alistair Carlile, Diane Gordon, and,

433

in particular, Bruce Ralston, at the Auckland War Memorial Museum, who helped me find letters in their collection. I was extremely fortunate to meet Rob Bailey at the Museum; he was researching a similar topic and told me about letters he had already located, copies of which he very kindly shared with me. Due to time constraints I did not have a chance to visit one of New Zealand's best resources, the Kippenberger Military Archive at the Army Museum Waiouru, but the archivist there, Dolores Ho, went out of her way to send me material from their collection. I am also grateful to Scott MacLeod at *The New Zealand Herald* for profiling the search for Kiwi war letters. Northern Ireland: Amanda Moreno, at the Royal Irish Fusiliers Museum in Armagh, who shared letters from their collection and also put me in touch with Jaki Knox at the Royal Ulster Rifles Museum in Belfast. Jaki, too, was immensely helpful, especially in suggesting the Charles Sweeney correspondence. Philippines: Gerard Alolad, who lives in the USA but has family in the Philippines and did initial research for me during one of his college breaks; Ramon Alonso Jr., who served as the tour guide during my visit to Corregidor; Elissa and Lysander Canlas for their advice as I prepared for my trip to Manila; Waldette M. Cueto, the librarian at the American Historical Collection, Ateneo de Manila University; Maita Oebanda at the University of Santo Tomas Museum of Arts and Sciences, who helped me find other archives and collections. Maita pointed me in the direction of the Filipinas Heritage Library, where I found the Marcial Lichauco letters. Through a wonderful bit of good luck, my contact at the US Embassy, Joe Mussomeli, was – only weeks before my arrival – vaulted into the position of, essentially, the acting US Ambassador to the Philippines. (My profound thanks go out to my old friend John Meyers for putting me in touch with Joe.) Joe and his wife could not have been more welcoming, and it made the whole trip to the Philippines that much more special. Poland: Aleksandra Bukowska and Zdistaw Zajdler, at the the Muzeum Wojska Polskiego; Eva Gryk and her father Jan Niebrzydowski, who so generously went through his personal archives and offered many remarkable letters; Andrew Koss at the US Embassy; Anna Kowalczyk, who helped me try to find letters and email by Polish troops in Iraq; Magdalena Kowalska, my initial contact and now dear friend in Warsaw, who helped me plan my trip to Poland, and Joanna Kowalska, who helped us spread the word about the project through *Newsweek Poland*; Edyta Kurek at the Jewish Historical Institute in Warsaw, and the Institute's director, Dr. Feliks Tych, who could not have been more gracious or generous with their time; Krzystof Molenda, who put me in touch with Rafal Nowakowski at the

ACKNOWLEDGEMENTS, PERMISSIONS AND SOURCES

Muzeum Literatury; Lynne Olson and Stanley Cloud, who wrote a phenomenal book called *A Question of Honor: The Kosciuszko Squadron* (Knopf, 2003) about the Polish pilots who flew with the RAF during World War II. Lynne and Stanley were extremely helpful, and I am especially grateful to them for putting me in touch with Ewa Sobotowski, who has gone to heroic lengths to help me find letters from Poland and is a joy to work with; Beata Czekaj-Wisniewska, Malgorzata Gwara, and Andrzej Wesolowski at the Centralna Biblioteka Wojskowa, who provided Zbigniew Janicki's letter; Krzysztof Piotr Starzecki, my guide in Warsaw; and Marzena Weidrzyk-Kaszuba, my guide at Auschwitz-Birkenau. Russia: Elizabeth Adams, who has, without question, contributed more to helping me find Russian war letters than any other person, and she has my eternal thanks for her seemingly boundless generosity. After hearing about the Legacy Project, Elizabeth contacted me before I left for Russia and was instrumental in setting up my trip, finding guides and translators, tracking down archives with letters, translating letters with impeccable skill, and simply being of assistance whenever a problem or crisis came up. I want to say a special word of thanks to Alexey Rumyantsev, who first communicated with me after I left Russia and, along with Elizabeth Adams, is one of those essential contacts without whom I would not have found the Russian letters that ended up in this book. I am also grateful to Leonid Frolov, one of my neighbors here in the USA, who kindly did some last-minute translations for me. In Moscow – Boris Semyonovich Ilizarov, a kindred spirit who has been collecting letters by 'common' Russian soldiers; Diana Kondratenko at the State Historical Museum; Dr. Andrey A. Lebedev, Deputy Chief of Izvestia; Colonel Alexander Konstantinovich Nikonov at the Central Armed Forces Museum, which provided the majority of the Russian letters in this book; Jeremy Weinberg, my old high school classmate, who put me in touch with reporters at the *Moscow Times* (*Oksana Yablokova*) and *St. Petersburg Times* (*Irina Titova*); and Dr. Nikolai Yakuba at the Central Museum of the Great Patriotic War. The US Embassy was extremely helpful while I was in Moscow, and I especially appreciated the advice and assistance offered by James P. Sonborn, Michael Allen, Yrui Boguslavsky, David Hasenauer, Thomas Shipp, and Ralph T. McCall. In St. Petersburg – Dr. Sergei Efimov and Colonel Alexander Sergeevich Monaenkov at the Military-Historical Museum of Artillery, Engineer, and Signal Corps; and at the State Memorial Museum of the Defense and Blockade of Leningrad, director Anatoliy Alexandrovich Shishkin and senior research assistant Nikolay Petrovich Dobrotvorskiy provided me with the exceptional letters by the young Russian children writing during the siege. In Volgograd – I am grateful to my guide Tamara V. Fyodorova. Scotland: Dr. Iain Gordon Brown and Colm McLaughlin, at the National Library of Scotland; Edith A. Phillip, at the National War Museum of Scotland, who went out of her way to help me find Scottish letters in their collection; and although I was not able to find letters or emails by Scottish troops in Iraq, Gethin Chamberlain and Lieutenant Colonel Hugh Blackman both very kindly assisted me in my search. Serbia and Montenegro: Zermen Filipovic, for helping with translations; Vesna Injac-Malbasa, at the National Library of Serbia; Milica Jovanovic, at Danas, for helping to spread the word about the Legacy Project; and Predrag Krejic and Dragos Petrovic, at the Archives of Serbia and Montenegro, for sharing letters with me. At the US Embassy in Belgrade I am indebted to Jasna Kunic, Allen Docal, and Richard Mei Jr. for their kindness, hospitality, and support before, during, and after my trip to the Balkans. South Korea: Michele M. Cenzer and Kim Su Nam at the US Embassy, who helped me plan my trip to Seoul and put me in touch with Kim Hoo-ran at *The Korea Herald*; Kevin Kim at the BBC in Seoul, who, despite the fact that the South Korean government was in the midst of a major presidential crisis, took the time to help me find Kim Min Ha. Most importantly, I am indebted to Lee Kyu Young (a.k.a. 'Shawn') for being my primary guide, translator, and researcher before, during, and after my stay in South Korea. His persistence and humor made the trip a resounding success. Spain: Iratxe Momoitio Astorkia, director of the Gernika Peace Museum, and Ana Teresa Nuñez Monasterio, who works in the Museum's documentation center; Tom Hare, who found and translated the Guernica letters; and Amanda Olivia Guglieri Lillo, who helped me with my search for letters and email describing the March 11, 2004, bombings in Madrid. Thailand: I am grateful to my guide Pramai 'Mike' T. West, who took me out to Kanchanaburi. I am especially grateful to Rod Beattie at the Thailand-Burma Railway Centre, for telling me about the Kenelm Clifton Johnson-Hill letters/journals. Vietnam: Huynh Ngoc Van at the War Remnants Museum; Nguyen Quang Hoa, my guide in Hanoi; My Hang, who assisted me with spreading the word about our efforts through the media; Nguyen Van Thanh, my temporary guide in Ho Chi Minh City, who had the terrific idea of visiting antiques shops that sold old envelopes to see if there were wartime letters inside (there were); Nguyen Huu Viet, my primary guide in HCMC, who was tireless in contacting museums and archives throughout Hanoi and HCMC and is responsible for finding the 'Dear Tan' letter; Robert Kulp and Dr. Phan

ACKNOWLEDGEMENTS, PERMISSIONS AND SOURCES

Minh Hien, both of whom assisted me with my search for Diên Biên Phu letters; Chuck Searcy, who helped me find so many of the contacts I depended on during my trip; and Tran Dinh Song, who put me in touch with Hoa and Viet.

The homefront translators: Many of the individuals who assisted me with translations live in the countries listed above, and others, like David Pelizzari and Ewa Sobotowski, were previously mentioned because they helped in numerous other ways. The following translators, who all live in the USA, went above and beyond the call of duty (most either volunteered to work for free or reduced their fees substantially), and needless to say, without them, there could not have been a book: Chie Berkeley, Megumi Furukawa, Radwan Hakim, Sammy Kim, Daniel Lautenslager, Julia Leikin, Luu Pham, Tamar van Raalten, Armend Reka and Ivana Ticha. Listed below are the individuals and institutions that either granted me permission to use their respective letters (or emails) or, particularly in the case of museums, libraries, and archives, granted me access to their collections.

Considerable efforts have been made to trace and acknowledge the ownership of letters under copyright listed below. If, however, there are any mistakes or omissions, please contact the publisher so that these errors can be corrected in future editions. (Several of the letters are, in fact, emails, but all correspondences are referred to as letters.) In some cases, a copyright holder's identity is withheld below due to privacy concerns. The designation 'courtesy of' – used primarily to indicate letters archived in a museum, historical society, or library or privately held by someone with no connection to the letter-writer or his/her family – indicates only that these institutions or individuals have provided physical access to the respective letter. Once again, many thanks to everyone who shared or submitted a letter.

John Abrams letter © Ellen Abrams Blankenship, reprinted by permission of Ellen Abrams Blankenship; Khaled Al-Maeena exchange with Roy and Jeff reprinted with permission of Khaled Al-Maeena and *Arab News*; Abdul Hameed Al-Attar letter © Abdul Hameed Al-Attar, reprinted by permission of Abdul Hameed Al-Attar; Khadum Al-Hilli letter courtesy of Muammal Jaafar; Patricia A. Andjelkovic letters © Patricia A. Andjelkovic, reprinted by permission of Patricia A. Andjelkovic; P.A. Angier letter © E. Diane Feildan, reprinted by permssion of E. Diane Feildan; 'Mme. J. Armand' letter courtesy of Paul A. Saunders; BJ Armstrong letter © BJ Armstrong, reprinted by permission of BJ Armstrong; James Arnold letter © Dovie Stewart, reprinted by permission of Dovie Stewart; Heather Ashline letter ©

Heather Ashline, reprinted by permission of Heather Ashline; Jacques Aulong letter © Jacques Aulong, reprinted by permission of Jacques Aulong; Demetria Barber letter © Demetria Barber, reprinted by permission of Demetria Barber; Samuel Bard letter reprinted by permission of the American Antiquarian Society; Maurice Barnett letter © Rande & Cynthia McCabe, reprinted by permission of Rande & Cynthia McCabe; Elizabeth Barton letter © Karen Duncan, reprinted by permission of Karen Duncan; John 'Jack' Bateman Beer letter courtesy of the Imperial War Museum (London), Department of Documents (86/19/1), reprinted with permission of JE Overall; David Bellon letter © David Bellon, reprinted by permission David Bellon; Roy F. Bergengren letter courtesy of Wisconsin Historical Society (Don Anderson Papers, Box 12); Gaston Biron excerpt courtesy of Jean-Pierre Gueno at Radio France; Denis W. Boyd letter © Anne Lytle, reprinted by permission of Anne Lytle and in memory of all who served on the HMS Illustrious 1940-1941; Christian Brodeching excerpt courtesy of Jean-Pierre Gueno at Radio France; Ted Brush letter © Cheryl Brush, reprinted by permission of Cheryl Brush; Peter Caddick-Addams letter courtesy of the Imperial War Museum (London), Department of Documents (03/20/1); Gloria Caldas letter © Gloria Caldas, reprinted by permission of Gloria Caldas; Robert Stewart Campbell letter © Miss Ruth Mary Campbell, reprinted by permission of the executors of Miss Ruth Mary Campbell (deceased); Guy Carleton letter, from the manuscript collection (IR 7106–1), courtesy of the National Army Museum (London); Gary Chandler letter © Gary Chandler, reprinted by permission Gary Chandler; Alfred Dougan Chater letter © Simon D. Chater, reprinted by permission of Simon D. Chater; Fiorgio A. Contro letter reprinted by permission of Fondazione Archivio Diaristico Nazionale (Santo Stefano AR), 'Caro Marco'/Luca Rossi, E/T2 ADN; Joseph Ball Cralle' letter © David Cralle', reprinted by permission of David Cralle'; H.W. Crowle letter courtesy of Australian War Museum; JJ Cummings letter © JJ Cummings, reprinted by permission of JJ Cummings; Scott Curry letter © Scott Curry, reprinted by permission of Scott Curry; William Czako letter © Sandra Cook, reprinted by permission of Sandra Cook; Shed Karn Das letter courtesy of the British Library, from the 'Reports of the Censors. Indian Mails in France' (L/M/5–825 through 828) in the Oriental and India Office Collections; Benjamin O. Davis letter courtesy of the US Army Heritage and Education Center, US Army Military History Institute (Carlisle, PA), reprinted by permission of Elnora David McLendon; Corbin Davis letter courtesy of Carolyn Curtiss; André Dekker letters © André Dekker

reprinted by permission of André Dekker; Malcolm Leon Downs letter ©
Dot Essex, reprinted by permission of Dot Essex; Thomas A. Edwards letter
© Thomas A. Edwards, reprinted by permission of Thomas A. Edwards;
John Eggleston letter reprinted by permission of the Daughters of the
American Revolution National Society, Americana Collection; Yanagida
Eiichi letter reprinted by permission of the Yasukuni Jinja (Tokyo); Harold
'Pompey' Elliott letter courtesy of the Australian War Museum; E. John
Ellis letter © Steve Ellis, reprinted by permission of Steve Ellis; J.N. Falcon
and Crispina de Garcia letters courtesy of Mary O'Neal; Bill Fant letter ©
Mrs. Joel Fant Trout, reprinted by permission of Mrs. Joel Fant Trout; J. W.
Foster letter © J. W. Foster, reprinted by permission of J.W. Foster;
L.Vincent Francese letter © L. Vincent Francese, reprinted by L. Vincent
Francese; Karl Fuchs letter excerpts from Sieg Heil!: *War Letters of Tank
Gunner Karl Fuchs, 1937–1941* by Karl Fuchs (Archon Books, 1987); Sergei
Galkin letter reprinted by permission of the Central Armed Forces Museum
(Moscow); Joseph Goebbels diary excerpt from *The Goebbels Diaries
1942–1943* (Doubleday & Company, 1948) edited, translated, and with an
introduction by Louis P. Lochner; Kotka Gofman letter reprinted by
permission of the Central Armed Forces Museum (Moscow); Horace
Greeley letter © Jeanne C. Thayer, reprinted by permission of Jeanne C.
Thayer; Alice S. Green letter, from the AS Green Papers (MS 15, 120),
reprinted by permission of the National Library of Ireland (Dublin);
Yvonne Green letter © Penelope E. Nichol, reprinted by permission of
Penelope E. Nichol; Moses Hall letter from the Microfilm Room (RG 15),
courtesy of the National Archives (Washington, DC); Johanne Haas letter
excerpt from Kriegsbriefe gefallener Studenten edited by Dr. Philipp
Witkop (Georg Müller Verlag, 1928); Josh Harapko letter © Pat Moran,
reprinted by permission of Pat Moran; Edward Hassall letters courtesy of
the Imperial War Museum (London), Department of Documents; Ichizo
Hayashi letter reprinted by permission of Japan Memorial Society of the
Students Killed in the War (Wadatsumi Society); Albert Heath letter ©
Arthur and Barbara Munzig, reprinted by permission of Arthur and Barbara
Munzig; David Henry letter © Pat Pehrson, reprinted by permission of Pat
Pehrson; Dr. Roman Herzog letter courtesy of Del archivo del centro de
documentación de Gernika GoGoratuz, Centro de Investigación por la Paz,
Fundación Gernika GoGoratuz; Jerry Hill letter © Jerry Hill, reprinted by
permission of Jerry Hill; Benny Hobson letter © Mary and Norah Craig
(deceased), Bolton, reprinted by permission of their niece, Irene Bell; August
Hopp excerpt from *German Students' War Letters* (Pine St. Books, 2002),

permission of Ernie Kyzer; Lee Jung Ho letter reprinted by permission of The War Memorial of Korea; Hart Leech letter courtesy of the Canadian Letters & Images Project; Gunter and Katinka Leopold letter courtesy of Connie Phelps and Lois Hoffman; Marcial Lichauco letters © Jessie Coe Lichauco, reprinted by permission of Jessie Coe Lichauco; Ronald 'Butch' Livergood letter © Ronald 'Butch' Livergood, reprinted by permission of Ronald 'Butch' Livergood; Maitland Livsey letter © Maitland Livsey, reprinted by permission of Maitland Livsey; Warren C. Lothrop letter courtesy of the National Archives and Records Administration ('Office of Scientific Research and Development,' RG 227, Division 19 Records, SAC-6, T, BAT-X-RAY); Bernard Paul Lyons letter © Mary Jo Meloy, reprinted by permission of Mary Jo Deloy; Douglas MacArthur letter courtesy of the MacArthur Memorial Archives (Norfolk, Virginia); Ian H. Macdonnell letter from the Brotherton Library Special Collections (Liddle Collection) courtesy of the University of Leeds, Leeds, United Kingdom; John Madden letters © John Madden, reprinted by permission of John Madden; Maurius Maillet letter courtesy of Jean-Pierre Gueno at Radio France; William Mayse letter © Susan Mayse, reprinted by permission of Susan Mayse; James H. McCallum letter courtesy of the Yale University Divinity School Library and Professor Herold J. Wiens; Kathy McConkey letter © Kathy McConkey, reprinted by permission of Kathy McConkey; Frederick McIntyre letter © Frederick McIntyre Jr., reprinted by permission of Frederick McIntyre Jr.; Christine McNeff letter © Christine McNeff, reprinted by permission of Christine McNeff; Russ Merrell letter © Pam Merrell, reprinted by permission of Pam Merrell; Justin Merhoff letter © Justin Merhoff, reprinted by permission of Justin Merhoff; Roger Micault letter courtesy of Pierre Lescault; Walter C. Michels letter © Leslyn Michels Goodrich, reprinted by permission of Leslyn Michels Goodrich; Anna Miller letter © Anna Miller, reprinted by permission of Anna Miller; Frank Charles Miller letter courtesy of the Canadian War Museum; June Clevenger Miller letter © Gaylo Conner, reprinted by permission of Gaylo Conner; Richard Millin letter © Peggy Millin, reprinted by permission of Peggy Millin; Masuda A. Mohamadi letters © Masuda A. Mohamadi, reprinted by permission of Masuda A. Mohamadi; Christian von Molitor letter reprinted by permission of the New York Public Library; General John Monash letter courtesy of the Australian War Memorial; Melville Montgomery letter © Elizabeth Dowey, reprinted by permission of Elizabeth Dowey; Edward J. Moore letter © Edward J. Moore, reprinted by permission of Edward J. Moore; Nathan B. Moore letter © Linda Manion, reprinted by permission of

© R. Ali, reprinted by permission of R. Ali; Neil Schmelz letter © Tom Schmelz, reprinted by permission of Tom Schmelz; Hubert A. Schneider letter © Pete Schneider, reprinted by permission of Pete Schneider; Hans Schröter letter courtesy of Stadtmuseum Dresden (from 'Verbrannt bis zur Unkenntlichkeit'), reprinted by permission of the Stadtmuseum Dresden; Shawai Helu Shamkhi letter courtesy of the Center for Research and Studies on Kuwait; Shayma letter courtesy of Muammal Jaafar; Philip H. Sheridan letter excerpt from *The War of the Rebellion: A Compilation of the Official Records of the Union and Confederate Armies, Series 1, Vol. 43, Part II*, p. 671. (Government Printing Office: Washington, 1880); Michael Shiner diary excerpt from the Library of Congress (Manuscripts Room); Denis Silva Torres letter © Denis Silva Torres, reprinted by permission of Denis Silva Torres; Thakur Singh letter courtesy of the British Library, from the 'Reports of the Censors. Indian Mails in France' (L/M/5–825 through 828) in the Oriental and India Office Collections; Christopher H. Smith letter © Eileen M. Barritt, reprinted by permission of Eileen M. Barritt; Ty Smith letters © Ty Smith, reprinted by permission of Ty Smith; William H. Smith letter © Mary Jewel Hester, reprinted by permission of Mary Jewel Hester; Sebron Sneed letter courtesy of A. Jack Jernigan; Earl P. Stevenson letter courtesy of the National Archives and Records Administration ('Office of Scientific Research and Development,' RG 227, Division 19 Records, SAC-6, T, BAT-X-RAY); Noel Streatfeild letter © W. H. C. Streatfeild, reprinted by permission of W. H. C. Streatfeild and the Noel Streatfeild Estate; Charles Sweeny letter reprinted by permission of the Royal Ulster Rifles Museum (Belfast); William Taylor letter © Edith Lenart, reprinted by permission of Edith Lenart; Tetsuko Tanaka letter courtesy of Professor Yuzuru J. Takeshita; William D. Taylor letter © Edith Lenart, reprinted by permission of Edith Lenart; Chuck Theusch letter © Chuck Theusch, reprinted by permission of Chuck Theusch; Tran Thi Anh Thu letter © Tran Thi Anh Thu, reprinted by permission of Tran Thi Anh Thu; Jean Thuiller letter courtesy of the Canadian War Museum; Frederick C. Trenne letter courtesy of the Auckland War Memorial Museum; Thomas Tuckhorn letter © Thomas Tuckhorn, reprinted by permission of Thomas Tuckhorn; Danae Vagliano letter © The Second World War Experience Centre, reprinted by permission of Dr. Peter Liddle, Director of The Second World War Experience Centre; James Van Veen letter courtesy of Elise Kerlin; Robert M. Wada letter © Robert M. Wada, reprinted by permission of Robert M. Wada; Arthur I. Wallace letter © Mary Wallace, reprinted by permission of Mary Wallace; 'Werner Walti' letter courtesy of the National War Museum of Scotland; Ralph Walsh letter (1995.A.1138) courtesy of the United States Holocaust Memorial Museum Collections Division, Archives Branch (Washington, DC); Terry Ward letter © Terry Ward, reprinted by permission of Terry Ward; of Stephen Webber letter © Stephen Webber, reprinted by permission Stephen Webber; Josef Wenzel excerpt from *German War Students' War Letters* (Pine St. Books, 2002), edited by Philipp Witkop and translated by A. F. Wedd; Donald West letter © Elizabeth West, reprinted by permission of Elizabeth West; Jack Wilkes letter © Jackie Hinkston, reprinted by permission of Jackie Hinkston; James Williams letter reprinted by permission of the South Carolina Historical Society; Jimmie Wilson letter © Marjorie N. Wilson, reprinted by permission of Marjorie N. Wilson; Masao Yamaguchi letter courtesy of Nobuko Kamata, reprinted by permission of Nobuko Kamata and the Nagasaki A-Bomb Testimonial Society; Takako Yamakawa letter © Takako Yamakawa, Jerry Yellin letters © Jerry Yellin, and Taro and Hatsue Yamakawa letters © Taro and Hatsue Yamakawa. All letters reprinted by permission of Jerry Yellin; Harry Zaslow letter © Harry Zaslow, reprinted by permission of Harry Zaslow; David Zehden letter © Margery Galluzzi, reprinted by permission of Margery Galluzzi; K. Zehmisch letter courtesy of the In Flanders Fields Museum; Davydovych Zemchenkov letter reprinted by permission of the Central Armed Forces Museum (Moscow); Zhao Yi Man letter courtesy of the National Museum of China.

Anonymous letters (and, again, please note that there are other anonymous letters in the book for which a donor cannot be cited for reasons of privacy or security and are not listed here, but the letters are still under copyright): 'Forever Yours' (Chapter 1): 'French mother from St. Pierre' epigraph is from *Letters from Armageddon: A Collection Made During the World War* (Houghton Mifflin Company, 1930) by Amy Gordon Grant; letters by the father of Mohemad Feroz Khan and by 'Hindu soldier' heading 'off to Paris,' both courtesy of the British Library, from the 'Reports of the Censors. Indian Mails in France' (L/M/5–825 through 828) in the Oriental and India Office Collections; excerpt of letter by 'Pam' to 'Major Martin' from *The Man Who Never Was: World War II's Boldest Counterintelligence Operation* (Bluejacket Books, Naval Institute Press, 2001), by Ewan Montagu; 'Ivy' letter to John 'Jack' Bateman Beer letter courtesy of the Imperial War Museum (London), Department of Documents (86/19/1); letter by Iraqi soldier to his mother courtesy of the Center for Research and Studies on Kuwait; 'Lines of Fire' (Chapter 2): British officer letter from the Periodical Room (Microfilm 3284), courtesy of the Library of Congress; Indian soldier 'Maganlal' letter courtesy of the British Library, from the 'Reports of the Censors. Indian Mails in France' (L/M/5–825 through 828) in the Oriental and India Office Collections; Turkish soldier letter courtesy of the Australian War Museum; 'French officer' letter excerpt about Verdun from *Letters from Armageddon: A Collection Made During the World War* (Houghton Mifflin Company, 1930) by Amy Gordon Grant; 'Dear Tam' letter by 'Kien' reprinted by permission of the South Vietnam Women's Museum; 'Laughing Through the Tears' (Chapter 3): Russian soldier to his 'Dear and beloved wife!' letter courtesy of the State Historical Museum, Moscow, reprinted by permission of the State Historical Museum; 'My dear, dearest, darling,' letter courtesy of the Imperial War Museum (London), Department of Documents [Misc 4 (46)]; 'Dear leader of the company!' letter dated January 2, 1917, courtesy of the In Flanders Fields Museum; 'Willi' letter dated July 10, 1943, reprinted by permission of the Feldpost-Archiv Berlin; Letters intercepted by the Canadian field censors courtesy of the National Archives of Canada; 'Notes for those going on leave' letter is excerpted from page 46 of Antony Beevor's *Stalingrad* (Penguin Books, 1999) and, according to Beevor's endnotes, comes from Tsentralnyy Arkhiv Ministerstva Oborony (Central Archive of the Ministry of Defence, Podolsk (206/294/48, p. 346); and 'Instructions for a smooth homecoming' courtesy of Dayna Kennison. 'Caught in the Crossfire'(Chapter 4): 'A citizen of Falmouth' letter reprinted by permission of the Maine Historical Society; the material relating to the August 25, 1914, letter by 'the brother of a German soldier fighting in Belgium' is from *Belgium and Germany* (T. Nelson & Sons, 1915) by Henri Davignon, in which a facsimile of the letter also appears; the excerpt from the letter by the 'German mother of a soldier (Franz)' to her 'English friend' is from *Letters from Armageddon: A Collection Made During the World War* (Houghton Mifflin Company, 1930) by Amy Gordon Grant; Dutch resistance letters courtesy of the Netherlands Institute for War Documentation (Amsterdam); letters written by the Russian children 'Slavik' and 'Galia' during the siege of Leningrad courtesy of the State Memorial Museum of the Defense and Blockade of Leningrad, reprinted by permission of the Museum; 'Chaim' letter courtesy of the Jewish Historical Institute (Warsaw); the letter by a 'US soldier' writing to 'a buddy back in the States' from Vietnam is courtesy of David M. Rosenthal; 'US Army staff sergeant' letter to Laurie Frost courtesy of Laurie Frost; Iraqi student letter to Mark von Sponeck courtesy of Mark von Sponeck.

The Mission Continues . . .

The Legacy Project is a national initiative that works to honor and remember those who have served this nation in wartime by seeking out and preserving their personal letters (and now emails). We are looking for letters from all of our nation's conflicts and on any subject matter, including expressions of love, descriptions of combat, humorous anecdotes, eyewitness accounts of historic events, reflections on faith or the subject of war itself, and, above all, any well-written letter that describes an incredible story or offers insight into the nature of war and its effect on those involved. We are also interested in letters written by the family members and loved ones of those who serve.

Although we appreciate the generosity of those who have offered, the Legacy Project does not accept monetary donations. Nor do we solicit or accept grants, government funds, or any other form of financial assistance. If you would like to contribute war letters to the Legacy Project, please send a legible photocopy or typed transcript of the material to:

The Legacy Project
Attn: Andrew Carroll
PO Box 53250
Washington, D.C. 20009
USA

Emails can be forwarded to: WarLetters2004@yahoo.com.

We prefer that you do not send us original letters, unless you are planning on disposing of the material otherwise and/or do not want the originals returned. We are a very small organization, and due to the overwhelming volume of mail we receive, it can take us several months and possibly longer to respond. We would be grateful if you would include your address and phone number so we can reach you.

For additional information about the Legacy Project, as well as free information on how to preserve your family's letters, links to additional organizations preserving historic materials, and many other military-related resources, please visit our web site: www.WarLetters.com.

INDEX

Page numbers in *italic* indicate photographs or illustrations.

447

CHRONOLOGY